Japonisme

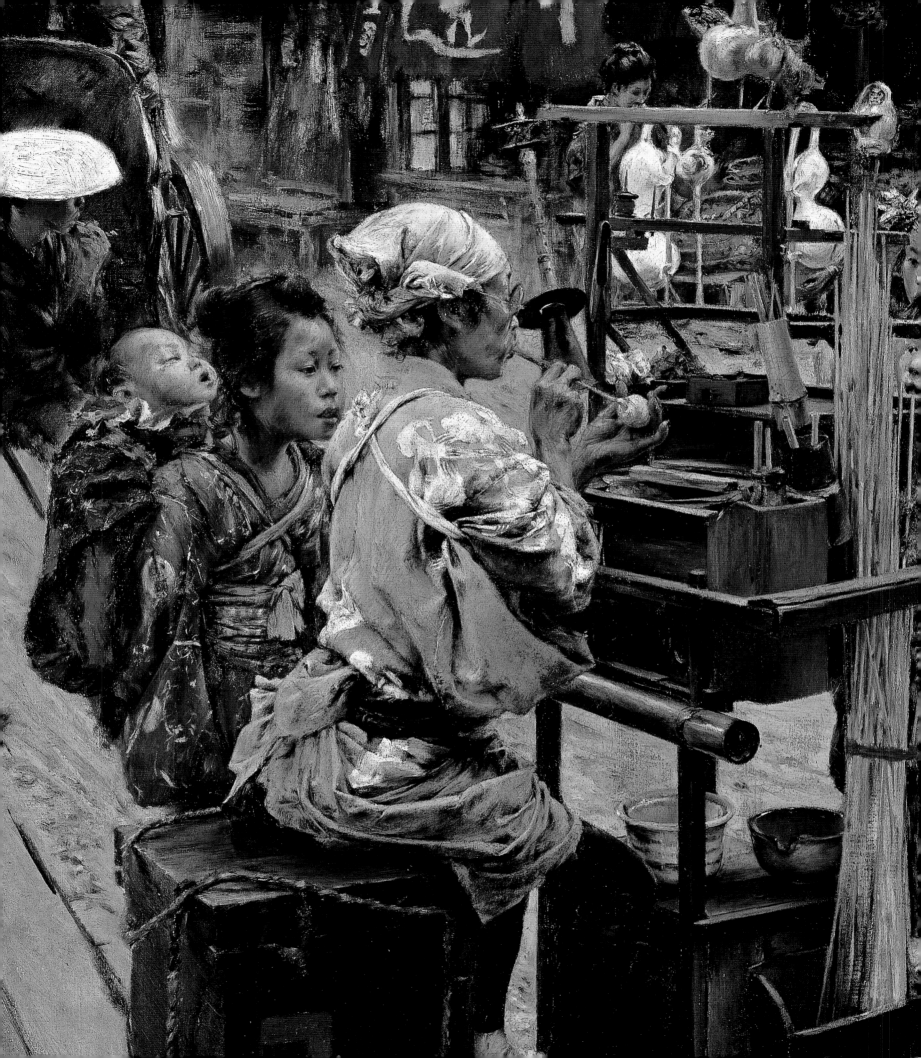

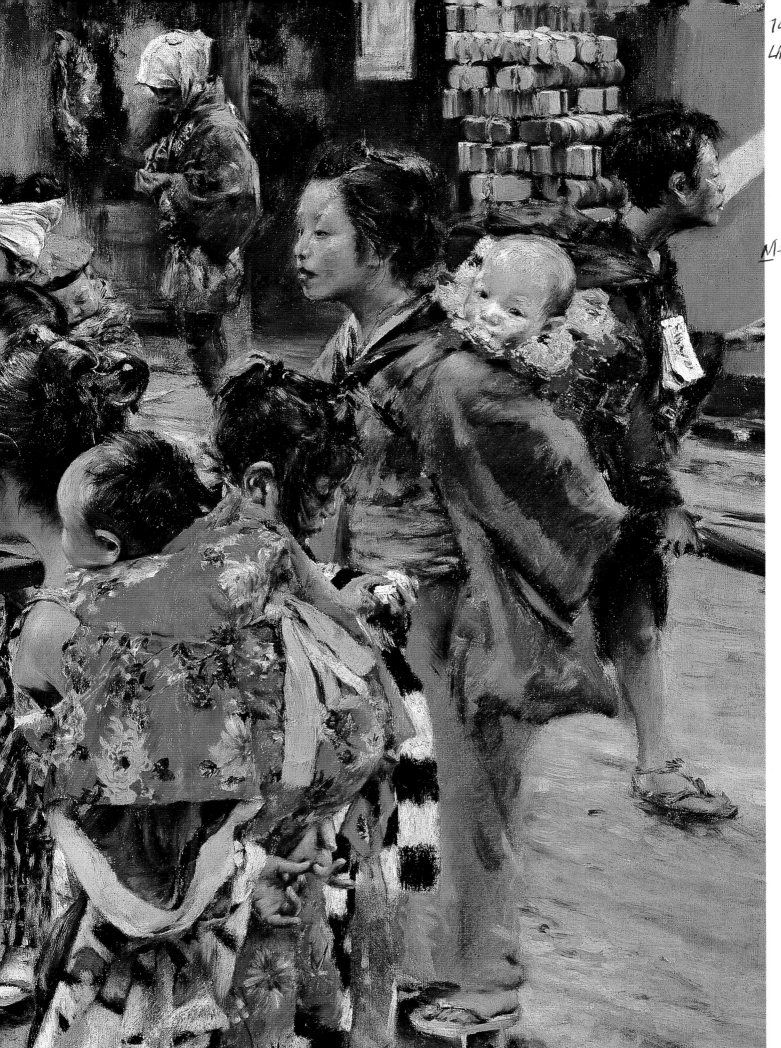

Japonisme

Cultural Crossings between Japan and the West

Lionel Lambourne

Adriaan Reland,
Map of Japan (detail),
1715,
reissued in *Atlas Minor,*
Reiner and Joshua
Ottens, *c.*1740

Phaidon Press Limited
Regent's Wharf,
All Saints Street,
London N1 9PA

Phaidon Press Inc.
180 Varick Street,
New York, NY 10014

www.phaidon.com

First published 2005
Reprinted in paperback 2007, 2008
© 2005 Phaidon Press Limited

ISBN 978 0 7148 4797 9

A CIP catalogue record for this book is
available from the British Library.

Design: Phil Cleaver and James Cartledge
of etal-design
Printed in Hong Kong

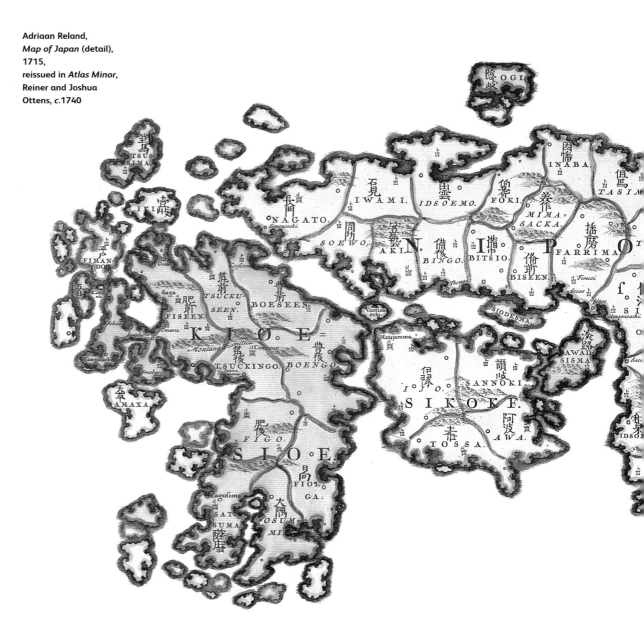

Endpaper: **Vincent van Gogh, *Branches
of Almond Tree in Bloom. Saint-Rémy**
(detail), 1880. Oil on canvas, 73·5 x 92 cm
(29 x 36¼ in). Rijksmuseum, Amsterdam**

Frontispiece: **Edmund Evans, after Walter
Crane, *Aladdin; or The Wonderful Lamp,**
from the 'Shilling Series', 1875
(detail of 137)**

Previous page: **Robert Blum, *L'Ameya:
The Sweet Stall**, 1892 (detail of 159)**

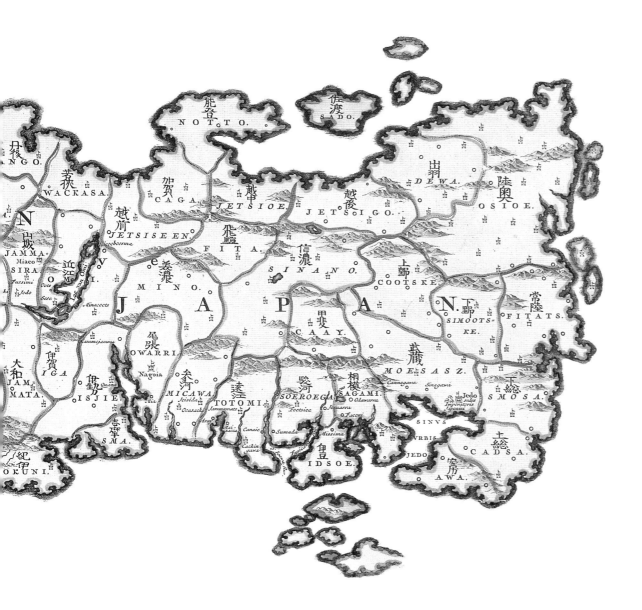

Contents

Introduction

Japonisme is not just a style; it does not lend itself to being used as a concept in place of a style, and it cannot be pinned down to a specific period.
Siegfried Wichmann, 1981

The European taste for things Japanese was at its height in the 1880s. However, the story of Japonisme begins much earlier as indicated by the comments of the influential French writer Charles Baudelaire in 1861:

Quite a while ago I received a packet of Japoneries. *I've split them up among my friends.*

The word 'Japonisme' was coined in 1872 by the French author and collector, Philippe Burty, 'to designate a new field of study of artistic, historic and ethnographic borrowings from the arts of Japan'. To eyes sated with Neoclassicism and the Gothic revival, then in full spate, Japanese art was far more than just a refreshing visual novelty. It is, however, misleading to use the word 'Japonisme' as it infers that it was solely a French phenomenon. While in France it gained its widest acceptance by intellectuals, artists and writers, and became a fashionable craze, it also flourished outside of France in the Netherlands, Great Britain, America, Germany (as *Japanismus*) and many other countries. Indeed, Japanese works of art became potent catalysts for new designs in many disciplines, particularly affecting the ceramic industry, furniture making and textile design.

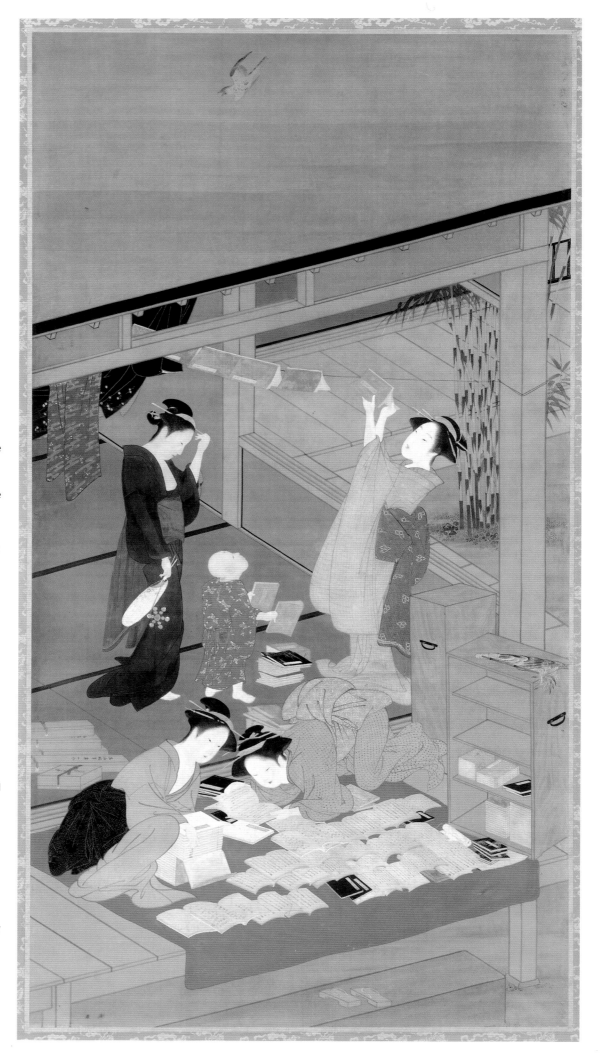

1

Katsukawa Shunsho,
*Girls Airing Out Books
and Scrolls by Drying
Them on a Line,*
**Edo period, 18th century.
Painting on silk,
157·1 x 82·6 cm
(61³₄ x 32¹₂ in).
Freer Gallery of Art,
Smithsonian Institution,
Washington, DC**

The catalyst for the phenomenon of Japonisme was the opening up of Japan to international trade in 1858. For over 200 years previously – from 1639 to 1858 – the great maritime nations of Europe (Portugal, Spain, the Netherlands and Great Britain) had been unable to breach the defences of the enclosed world of Japan, which embraced a policy known as *sakoku* – 'the secluded country'. However, the isolation was never total. From behind this barrier there emerged an extraordinarily exotic mixture of goods ranging from the amazing imagery of Japanese prints and screens to delicate porcelain, powerful pottery and the ornate elaboration of wares. Moreover, in recent years we have come to realize more and more that Japan's relations with the outside world were the result of a gradual, complex process. The fall of an imaginary 'bamboo curtain' in 1858 has analogies with the breakdown of the Iron Curtain and the fall of the Berlin Wall in our own time. In each case curiosity concerning events in the outside world provided the motivation that eventually led to the fall of restrictions and prohibitions. The West's love affair with Japan had been slowly growing for two centuries before it finally blossomed after 1858.

Within a few years of 1858, European technology and American brashness transformed the troubled waters of internal Japanese political manoeuvring.

As early as 1867, the young Meiji emperor (r.1867–1912), although only fifteen years of age, had clear ideas concerning the future direction of Japan. The new era, described as 'the Enlightened Government of Brilliant Rule', was firmly established in April 1868 at an imperial palace in Kyoto, when the emperor signed Article 5 of the Imperial Oath stating, 'Knowledge shall be sought for throughout the world, so that the foundations of the empire may be strengthened', or, loosely translated, 'If you can't beat them, join them, and then perhaps you can beat them later.'

The successful cultivation of this policy would bring Japan into the modern world, although, of course, at a cost. While Japan strove energetically to modernize the country, the process of rapid industrialization took its relentless course. Many people were eager to see the old Japan before it became completely changed by modernization. Foreign visitors and artists were enticed to Japan in quite large numbers from the late 1860s. These early tourists were often initially inspired to make the trip after enjoying the charms of Japanese works in major international industrial and trade exhibitions. These shows created huge interest in the Western world throughout the second half of the nineteenth century.

At these exhibitions and via specialized dealers many Europeans made their first acquisitions of Japanese prints, an experience that for them could possess almost the thrill of a first love affair. In feeling such hedonistic emotions they mirrored the reactions of Edmond and Jules de Goncourt, who in their novel *Manette Salomon* (1867) devoted the whole of one chapter to the fantasies of the hero as he peruses an album of Japanese woodcuts.

The arousal of such emotions owes much to the visions conjured up in the world described by the artists who made *ukiyo-e* prints – 'pictures of the floating world'. This school of popular graphic art recorded the life, fashions and entertainments of the Japanese urban population in the seventeenth, eighteenth and early nineteenth centuries. During this period Japan was virtually isolated under the repressive and censorious regime of the Tokugawa shoguns (1603–1867). Thus *ukiyo-e* paintings, prints and books depicted a society unknown to the rest of the world. It was, according to Edmond de Goncourt in his monograph *Hokusai* (1896), 'life in flux, seen strictly as it presents itself to the eyes of the artist'.

This society was first described in 1665 in the *Tales of the Floating World*, by the Kyoto author Asai Ryoi. A memorable passage reads:

Living only for the moment, turning our full attention to the pleasures of the moon, the snow, the cherry blossoms and the maple, singing songs, drinking wine, and diverting ourselves just in floating, caring not a whit for the poverty staring us in the face, refusing to be disheartened, like a gourd floating along with the river current: this is what we call **ukiyo-e.**

The hedonistic implications of this ephemeral and stylish floating world are mirrored in an attractive work by Katsukawa Shunsho (1726–92), *Girls airing out books and scrolls by drying them on a line* (1). The scene depicted is not a print but a painting on silk. It shows a house in which a vigorous cleaning-up is in progress. The summer rains have ceased and the women of the household dry out books and scrolls while a little boy hands the volumes to a girl drying them on a line. On the verandah two women spread out the volumes, and one becomes involved in reading.

This charming painting, with its homely yet stylized and exotic glimpse of a mysterious world, presents a paradigm of the qualities that proved irresistible to Westerners on their first encounter with Japanese art and artefacts. It can also serve as an allegory for the many books on the fascinating subject of Japanese art, and remind us to try, in our own way, to start out on a historical survey of a rich subject.

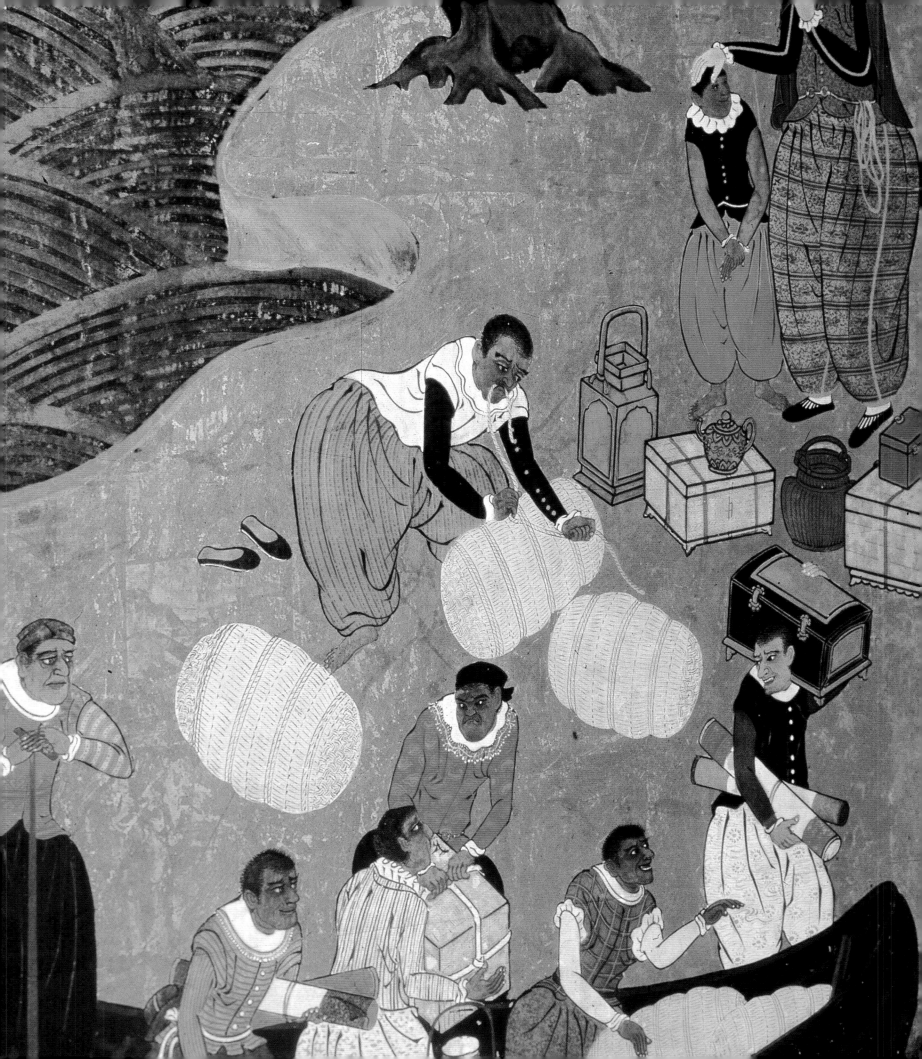

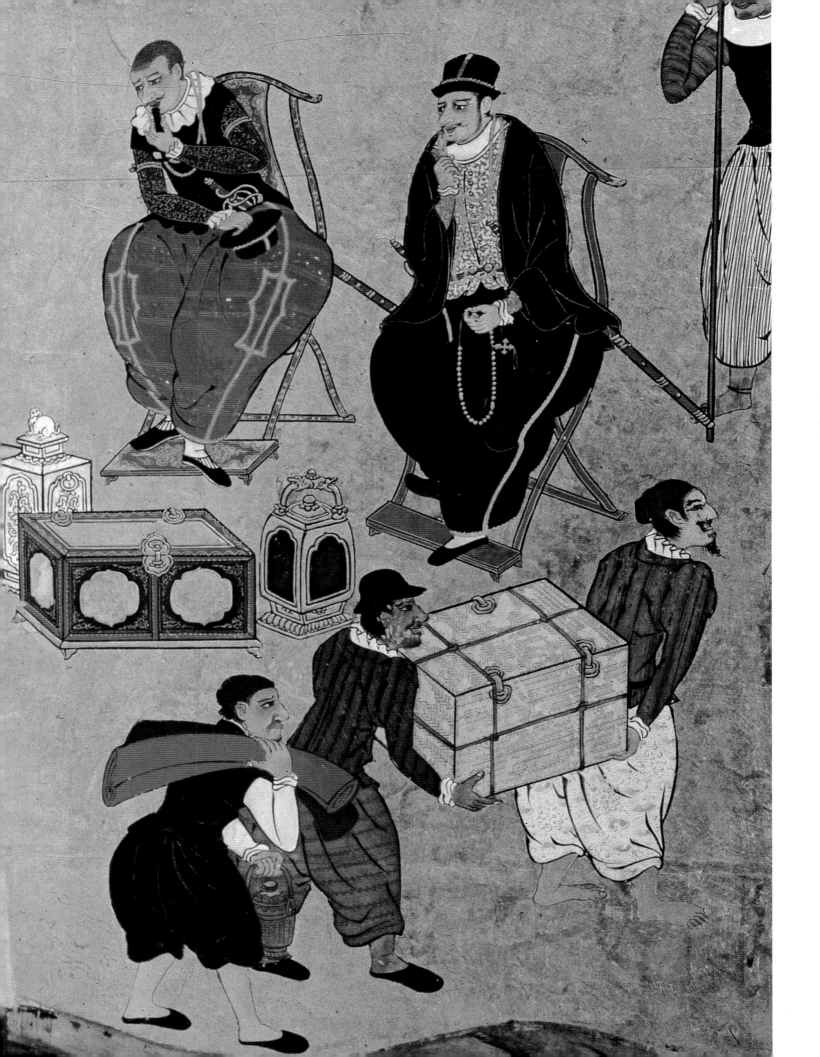

Previous page
**Unloaded merchandise
being counted by a
Portuguese magistrate
appointed by the King,
detail from a** *namban*
**screen depicting the
arrival of the Portuguese
in Japan,**
*c.***1593–1602.
Paint and gold leaf
on wood,
height: 172·8 cm (68 in).
Museu Nacional de Arte
Antiga, Lisbon**

*It is in general the unexplored that
attracts us …*
Lady Murasaki, The Tale of Genji, *turn
of the eleventh century*

*Here, remember, the people really eat
lotuses, they form a common article
of diet …*
Lafcadio Hearn, 1891

The history of Japan really begins
with the accession of the first 'human'
emperor, Jimmu Tenno, in about
660 BC, from whom all the emperors
of Japan descended. Until the year
710 AD the imperial family had no
fixed long-term abode and with each
new emperor the capital of the country
also changed. In 710, however, a
'permanent' capital was established
at Nara, some 40 miles (64 km) from
Kyoto, which, though it lasted for less
than a century as a capital, saw the
creation of some of the most exquisite
buildings in Japan. Nara became a
veritable Buddhist crossroads, steeped
in the religious and artistic influences
of the differing forms of the Buddhist
faith from India, China and Korea.

To escape from this deeply religious
environment and the influence of the
monks, the worldly Emperor Kammu
(r.781–806) decided to build a new
capital, and the court was moved
again at the beginning of the Heian
period (794–1185) to a new location
in Kyoto, otherwise known as Heian-
kyo, the 'Capital of Peace'.

This proved an auspicious title, for the
Heian era and the ensuing centuries
would enjoy years of relative peace,
the population having little contact
with the outside world, and turning to
their own artistic pursuits. For
landscape painters the beetling
mountain tops and precipices of
Chinese art gave way to native
yamato-e ('pure Japanese painting')
landscapes depicting the gentle, rolling
hills of Yamato (the heart of Japan
containing both Nara and Kyoto).
Narrative picture scrolls with calligraphy
of exquisite formality illustrated some
of the masterpieces of Japanese literature, notably the *monogatari*, prose
tales with poetic interludes. These tales
abound with tragic, dewy-eyed lovers,
selfless servants, gossipy diaries and
passionate love letters, all of which are
combined in the thoroughly readable
Genji Monogatari (*The Tale of Genji*).
Written by a court lady, Murasaki
Shikabu, it is claimed to be the world's
first novel, and is full of delightfully
observed incidents of family life which
would for centuries inspire Japanese
artists and print-makers.

The elegant formality of the Heian
court saw the dwindling of Japan's
contacts with the rest of Asia.
Internally, however, the proliferation
of many Buddhist sects, notably Zen
Buddhism, had a strong influence on
art, not only on landscape scrolls, but
on the art of the sword-smith, whose
blades became legendary, synonymous
with honesty and valour, good faith
and the suppression of evil.

Such blades were put to both symbolic
and practical use during the long
period of conflict between the Taira
and Minamoto clans and the
establishment of a separate capital at
Kamakura, where in 1185 after a great
sea battle the Minamoto clan gained
the ascendancy and began the dual
system of emperor and shogun which
lasted for several centuries. One
shogunate was established in
Muromachi, a suburb of Kyoto, leading
to the period from 1339 to 1573 being
known as the Muromachi era. It was
not a happy time, for clan fought
against clan, and bandits took
advantage of the decay of noble
families to seize temporary possession
of land and treasures.

It is against this stormy background
of warring factions that we must place
the arrival in 1543 of a ship from
Macao, the Portuguese trading port in
China. The ship was driven ashore off
the coast of Kyushu in the southeast of
Japan. The Portuguese sailors were well
treated, and soon afterwards other
ships from Macao began to call at
Kyushu, some going on as far as
Honshu or Kyoto. Trading flourished,
the Japanese delighting particularly
in the smooth-bore musket, an
instrument of destruction which they
soon learnt to make for themselves,
decorating them superbly and
elevating the gunsmith's craft, like
the sword-smith's, to an art form.

These firearms hastened the rise of
Oda Nobunaga (1534–82), a warlord
who aspired to unify the country and
seized power in 1568 from the imperial
court in Kyoto. The power of the
musket had arrived at just the right
moment for this ambitious man and by
using this new and lethal weapon, he
was able to bring nearly half of
Japan's sixty-six provinces under his
control. Although Nobunaga was murdered before the complete pacification
of the country took place, his successor,
Toyotomi Hideoyoshi (1536–98),
almost managed to achieve this
elusive goal. Nicknamed 'the Japanese
Napoleon', Hideoyoshi was physically
almost a dwarf, but had immense
charisma. Acutely conscious of his low
birth, he hoped by his valour to achieve
aristocratic distinction on the battlefield, but two unsuccessful campaigns
against China and Korea, in 1592
and 1597, led to dire defeats.

Nobunaga and Hideoyoshi were
renowned patrons of the arts.
Hideoyoshi loved public spectacle, and
on one occasion he held a huge open-
air tea ceremony to which everyone in
the country, from peasant to lord, was
invited. The festivities went on for ten
days. One of Hideoyoshi's palaces,
Momoyama-jo, or Momoyama castle,
was decorated with profuse carvings
of flowers, mythical monsters, visionary
screens glowing with bright colours and
gold leaf, curving eaves and heavy roof
tiles. This style consequently gave its
name to a period in Japanese history:
the Momoyama period (1573–1614).

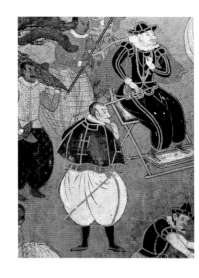

2
School of Kanu,
Portuguese merchants,
detail from a *namban*
screen depicting the
arrival of the Portuguese
in Japan,
*c.*1600–10.
Paint and gold leaf on
wood,
height: 170 cm (67 in).
Museu Nacional de
Soares dos Reis, Oporto

The spread of Christianity also played a large part in the relationships between Japan and European powers. It began with the arrival of several Catholic missionaries from Portugal who are often credited with introducing chiaroscuro prints to Japan, which showed the Western use of light and shade as opposed to the flat unshaded areas of colour used by the Japanese. The most notable of these priests was St Francis Xavier, who came to Kagoshima in 1549 and began to preach with the full permission of the Lord of Satsuma. Xavier stayed for two years and founded a highly successful mission before leaving to find martyrdom in China. Unease grew, however, at the rapid expansion of Christianity (150,000 converts by 1582), a process marred by the dissent between the Jesuit, Franciscan and Dominican missions in converting the Japanese to the new faith. The Japanese were amazed at the unedifying spectacle of Europeans quarrelling over rival brands of a fanatical and merciless creed, which, it was felt, might subvert the social structure of Japanese life. In 1597 there was an outburst of persecution, which led to the martyrdom of twenty-six Christians at Nagasaki, and an edict of 1614 that expelled all missionaries.

The Spaniards were expelled in 1624, and the Portuguese in 1639, which finally ended foreign trade with Japan and severely curtailed all Japanese contact with the outside world.

Before Hideoyoshi died, he came to an arrangement with a rising young member of the Tokugawa family, Tokugawa Ieyasu (1542–1616), who in 1585 established a rigorous military system by posting samurai warriors as police and tax collectors in every district, and beginning a dual system of rule by emperor and shogun military dictators. In 1590, Ieyasu, acting upon Hideoyoshi's advice, settled upon Edo, present-day Tokyo, as his military headquarters, which became the greatest city in Japan. It was Ieyasu who established the lasting dynasty of the Tokugawa shoguns who ruled the country until the restoration of the Meiji emperor in 1868.

On 12 April 1600, the Dutch ship, *Liefde* (*Charity*), from Rotterdam limped into the Japanese port of Bungo in distress. Its pilot, William Adams from Gillingham, Kent, was the first Englishman to enter Japan. As a boy Adams learnt the arts of shipbuilding and navigation, and served against Spain in the rout of the Spanish Armada. Later, with the Dutch fleet he voyaged to the Arctic and Pacific, acting as both buccaneer and pilot, plundering the coasts of Chile and Peru before crossing the Pacific to trade in Indonesia.

Unfortunately, in the Straits of Magellan, the fleet broke up in bad weather and only the *Liefde* reached Japan.

Ieyasu liked Adams and persuaded him to stay in Japan and teach mathematics, navigation, maritime lore and other subjects, while supervising the building of two ships in the European style. Adams, clearly a man of great charisma and individual talents, became a direct retainer of the shogun and a 'naturalized Japanner' who married a Japanese woman by whom he had two children. A bold swash-buckler, Adams loved to dress up as a samurai wearing the two swords of his rank, which upset the Jesuits, jealous of Ieyasu's favour. They denounced Adams as a pirate; but he displayed greater forbearance to them when Ieyasu began to clamp down on the corruption of Japanese officials by European traders, and to issue anti-Christian edicts. Adams became a diplomatic go-between when Dutch and English traders arrived in 1609 and 1613 respectively. Known to the Japanese as Miura Anjin, he lived in Edo in a street named Anjin-cho (Pilot Street), which stood until the great earthquake of 1923. He is still a cult figure today, the hero of novels, films and television to the extent that an area of Tokyo, Anjin-cho, is named after him.

The Dutch trading voyages to the East, which started around 1600, were preceded by almost a century of Portuguese and Spanish expansion to the east and west. In Nagasaki and Kobe the busy activities of both Portuguese and Dutch traders (the Dutch East India Company, or VOC [Verenigde Oostindische Compagnie], was established in 1602) were vividly depicted in the *namban byobu*. These were a type of screen created by Japanese pupils of Portuguese Jesuit teachers to satisfy the deep interest of Japanese society in the strange visitors from abroad, the *namban-jin*, literally meaning 'southern barbarians'. Neither Oriental nor European, the style was a result of the intermingling of the two cultures (see pp.8–9). Typical screens show the arrival of Portuguese ships into the harbour, and the reception of their crews, many of whom are wearing the extraordinary breeches then in fashion, which look as though they have been inflated like balloons (2). Others show the procession of the arriving captain and his retinue greeted by Jesuits in long cassocks. No attempt is made at accurate perspective, but there are myriad anecdotal situations painted in red, green, blue and white on gold paper.

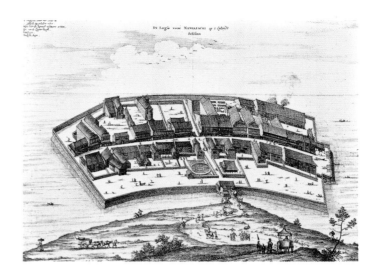

3
World Map Screen, second half of the 18th century. Folding screen, 163·8 x 362·8 cm (64½ x 142¾ in). Kobe City Museum of Namban Art

4
The Deshima Trading Post Before 1699 from A Montanus, *Memorable Embassies*, 1699

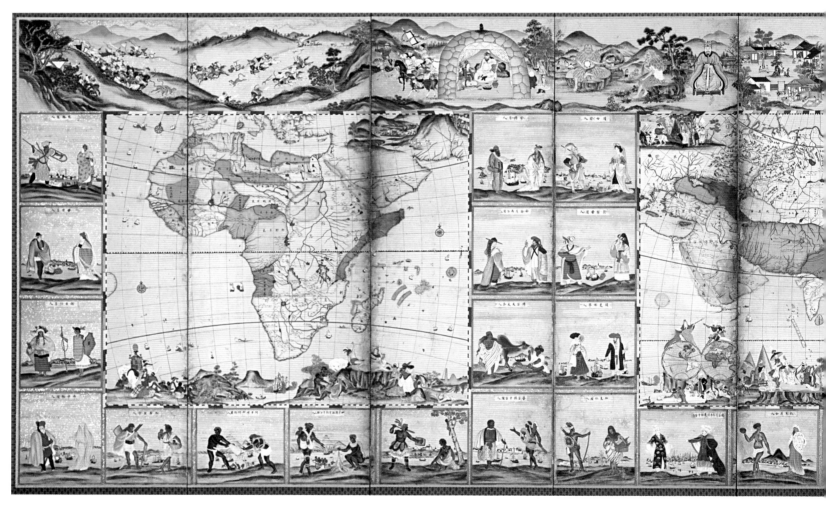

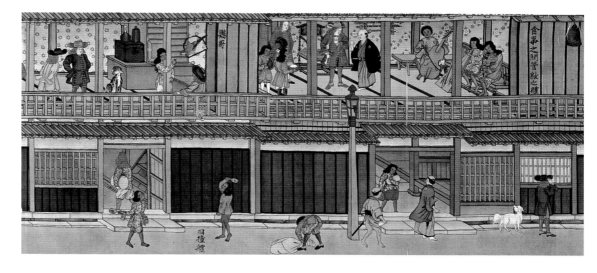

5
Nagasaki School,
The Dutch Factory on the Island of Deshima
detail from a scroll painting, Edo period, 18th century.
Paint on paper, height: 26·7 cm (10½ in).
British Museum, London

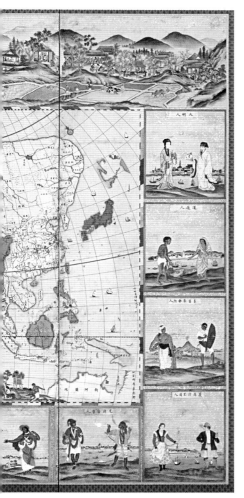
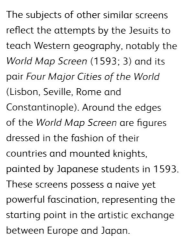

The subjects of other similar screens reflect the attempts by the Jesuits to teach Western geography, notably the *World Map Screen* (1593; 3) and its pair *Four Major Cities of the World* (Lisbon, Seville, Rome and Constantinople). Around the edges of the *World Map Screen* are figures dressed in the fashion of their countries and mounted knights, painted by Japanese students in 1593. These screens possess a naive yet powerful fascination, representing the starting point in the artistic exchange between Europe and Japan.

The exact extent of Japan's isolation after 1639 remains an academic minefield. Throughout the shogunate a small population of Calvinist Dutch traders (with no spiritual designs on the population) were allowed to remain on an artificial island in the bay at Nagasaki. Although he had banished the Jesuits and persecuted the indigenous Christian community, Tokugawa Iemetsu, the shogun who ruled from 1622 to 1651, continued to consider trade desirable. He ordered the flattening of one of the hills in the bay of Nagasaki so that its rocks could be used to construct the artificial island of Deshima, a name derived from the Japanese words *deru* (go out), and *shima* (island). The shape of the island is said to have been settled by a shogun who, when asked what shape the new artificial island, roughly the size of a modern athletics track, should be, threw down his fan and pointed to it without a word (4).

Today it is hard not to draw an ironic analogy between Deshima and Osaka's international airport, which, just over three centuries later, has offshore runways also constructed by the demolition of a mountain. But unlike the vast runways of Osaka, which is designed to attract foreigners by the thousands, the fan-shaped Deshima 'shop window' to the West was relatively tiny – 65-m (71-yds) deep and 175-m (191-yds) wide on the side facing the city, and 215-m (235-yds) wide on the side facing the sea. It was surrounded by a basalt wall.

The pioneering European arrivals in Japan shared one aim – to establish trading posts which could act as stages in bringing various luxury goods back to the West; goods ranging from rolls of silk from China to spices and peppers from the Spice islands and Arita porcelain from Japan. All such goods were kept in compounds comprising living quarters and warehouses, collectively called a 'factory', a term which simply meant a place where factors, or representatives of a merchant company, could live and trade. Where trade flourished, so did hospitality, as we see in one of a series of scenes of Dutch life in the factory on Deshima (5).

The claustrophobic boredom of living on Deshima in such straitened circumstances was alleviated once a year by an annual visit of a delegation to the shogun in Edo. This was the highlight of the year, the only occasion to gain a tantalizing glimpse of the outside world. Otherwise, social contacts with the Japanese were restricted to the prostitutes who were allowed to visit the Dutch on the island, which for 200 years was to play the role not only of a window on the West, but also that of a 'cat-flap' through which some goods could enter or leave, although subject to strict controls. During the more liberal shogunate of Yoshimune (r.1716–45), prohibitions were relaxed, allowing the importation of foreign books (except those relating to Christianity). Slowly and laboriously a Dutch-Japanese dictionary was compiled and translations into Japanese were made of books on anatomy, medicine and astronomy. Eventually Japan became a small but vital link in the trade network of the Dutch in Asia, who sailed under the familiar initials VOC, which for many years was the largest commercial enterprise in the world. In order to maintain good trading relations, the Dutch were expected to present gifts to the shogun every year during their visits to the Japanese court

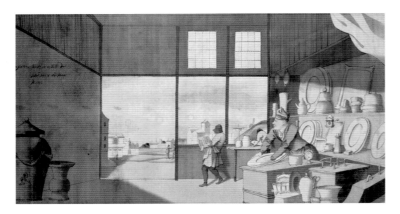

Japonisme

6
Shiba Kokan,
The Pewterer's Shop,
late Edo period,
18th century.
Painting on silk,
63·9 x 129·1 cm
(25 x 50⅞ in).
Kobe City Museum
of Namban Art

7
Shiba Kokan,
The Archery Gallery,
c.1771–4.
Colour woodblock,
25·2 x 19 cm
(10 x 7½ in)

They handed over sumptuous and original gifts, including books, maps and scientific instruments. The Dutch were also obliged to communicate new information, and news of the outside world.

From its headquarters in Batavia (now Indonesia), the Dutch annually sent a fleet of ships to Japan, laden to the gunnels with the exciting secrets of the West, craved for by the intellectual Japanese. So great was the dominance of *rangaku*, or Dutch learning, that it became a term for all Western studies. Among the cargoes were a number of Dutch treatises on landscape painting, and individual prints which were eagerly studied by several Japanese artists, notably Shiba Kokan (1747–1818), who had the most far-ranging interests and made a unique contribution to Japan's contacts with the West. He is credited with producing the first etching made in Japan, a technique learnt from a manual brought to Nagasaki by Dutch traders. He also painted copies on silk, based on a series of etchings showing Dutch crafts and trades (6). In 1799 Kokan published a book, *On Western Painting*, in which he wrote:

Western painting captures the very soul of creation. Japanese and Chinese paintings are like toys and are not of much practical good. Western painters use light and shade to express contrasting effects – smoothness and roughness, distance and proximity, depth and shallowness.

Although attracted by the surface gloss of Dutch and other Western painting, Kokan was even more fascinated by the Western use of perspective, and introduced the novelty of vanishing-point perspective in one of his own prints using *ukiyo-e* techniques learnt from his famous master, Suzuki Harunobu (1725–70). One of Kokan's most interesting prints is *The Archery Gallery* (c.1771–4; 7), which shows a woman giving an arrow to a male archer at a shooting booth, with the caption, 'Ten Arrows for Two Mon'. The illusion of depth is created by the lines focusing on the distant target on the far wall, and is augmented by a landscape glimpsed through the windows of the booth.

On one long-desired journey to Nagasaki, Kokan travelled armed with magnifying glasses, copperplates for etchings, and a camera obscura which he had made based upon a European prototype. Assisted by these 'visual aids', his lectures on world geography and foreign inventions were popular with both peasants and prostitutes. In his entertaining journal he described how much in demand his pictures of Edo were to an audience forbidden to travel.

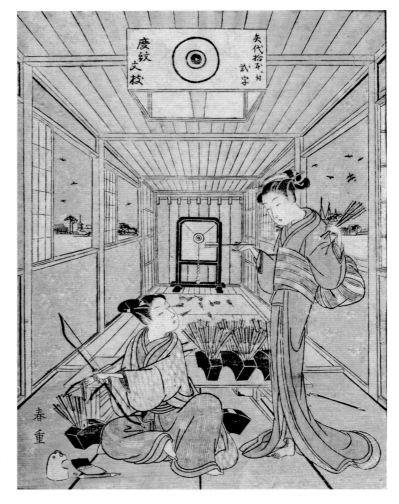

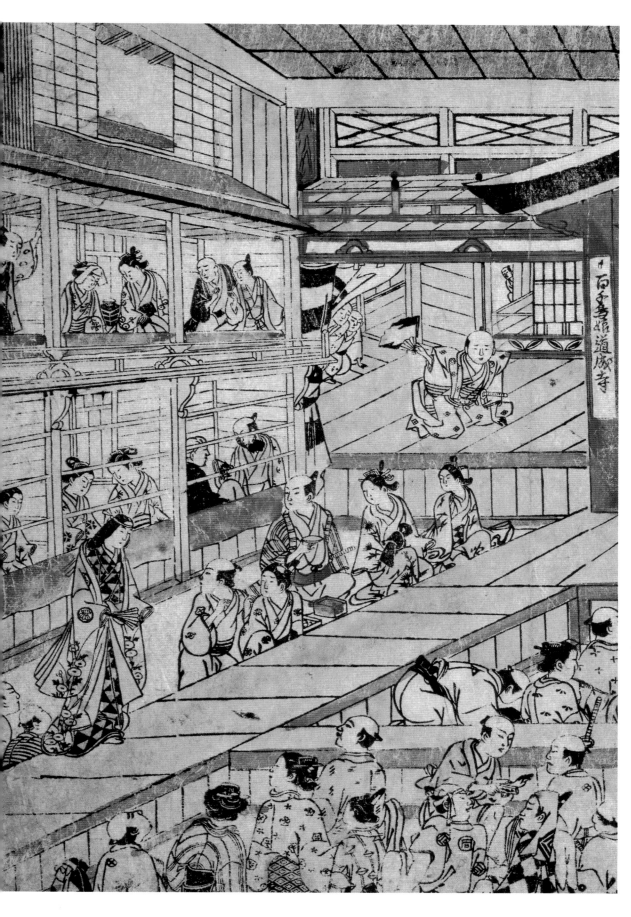

8
Okumura Masanobu,
*A Scene from the Play
Dojoji at the Nakamura-
za Theatre* (detail),
mid-18th century.
Colour woodblock,
full page: 29·3 x 43·2 cm
(11½ x 17 in)

The fame of Kokan's discoveries preceded him, as he described amusingly:

September 4 … To my embarrassment, at least twelve or thirteen women waited on me at the brothel … The women were completely dumbfounded when I showed them my pictures Ryogoku Bridge *and* Enjoying the Evening Cool by the River *through the camera obscura that I brought with me … and from then on we chatted freely. When I left the brothel, the women begged me to return the next day to talk to them again.*

Kokan eventually became interested in Western-style oil painting. Faced with such images Japanese artists began to understand the artistic capital to be made by elaborating a new visual language.

The great importance of Kokan's prints lies in the fact that they influenced early masters of new print-making schools, such as Okumura Masanobu (1686–1764). He was the proprietor of a publishing house that made many experiments and may have originated the tall vertical pillar prints (*hashira-e*). He also enthusiastically adopted the exotic European convention of the vanishing point, and modified it by Japanese practice to produce *uki-e* (perspective prints). His prints vividly capture the gossip and noise of a first night at a *kabuki* theatre (8). In this scene the heroine is entering left on the raised walkway (*hana-michi*) or 'flower way'.

9
Bow factory dish with a Kakiemon pattern,
*c.*1752–8.
Soft paste porcelain,
diameter: 17·2 cm
(6¾ in).
Victoria and Albert
Museum, London

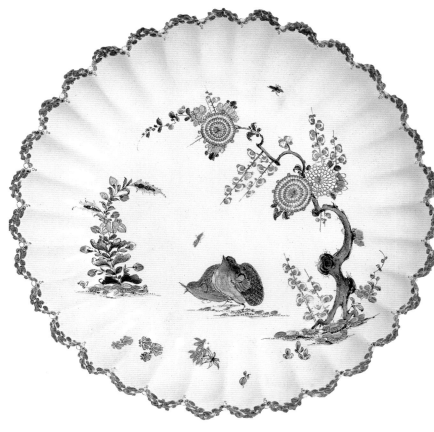

Throughout the closure of Japan, European monarchs continued to vie with each other in forming collections of luxury goods such as Japanese lacquer ware and porcelain. Japanese porcelain manufacture began early in the seventeenth century following the discovery of kaolin clay at Arita, not far from Nagasaki. Some pieces were especially made for the export trade, depicting Dutch merchant ships and brocaded 'Japan' patterns.

One of the most important collectors of porcelain was Augustus II, Elector of Saxony and King of Poland (1670–1733), known as 'the Strong' perhaps because of his large family of over 350 children. He avidly collected Chinese and Japanese porcelain, often paying enormous sums for single specimens. He justified his passion in a letter to a friend:

Are you not aware that the same is true for oranges as for porcelain, that once one has the sickness for one or the other, one can never get enough of the things and wishes to have more and more.

At Dresden, Augustus created one of his most cherished, yet never fully realized projects to celebrate this passion for porcelain, the 'Japanese Pavilion', across the river Elbe from the main palace complex.

The collection was arranged in categories, with Chinese and Japanese porcelain on the ground floor, and Meissen on the first floor. In the panelled rooms furnished with mirrors and chandeliers, the porcelain was shown in cabinets and skilfully arranged on plinths on the walls in formal patterns according to their style and decoration. Today these dazzling displays can still be seen in the Zwinger, the restored Baroque palace. Legends abound about the porcelain collection, a typical story relating to the huge baluster 'Dragoon' vases decorated with Chinese cobalt blue glazes, which were supposedly acquired by Augustus from Frederick William I of Prussia (r.1713–40) in exchange for 600 cavalry soldiers. Other rooms contain some of the finest Japanese Imari porcelain outside Japan, including monumental covered jars and vases. With other less grandiose collectors throughout Europe, Augustus established the immense popularity of export Japanese Kakiemon porcelain, named after the Kakiemon family who worked in Arita from the seventeenth century onwards. Their wares were painted with a restricted palette of turquoise green, light blue, yellow and iron-red, with such themes as the 'Quail', 'Hob-in-the-Well', and 'the Three Friends' (pine, prunus and bamboo). These motifs were depicted in a characteristically asymmetric manner, leaving much of the surface plain and showing the milky-white porcelain to advantage.

10
Japanese black lacquer
cabinet on a William and
Mary giltwood stand,
17th century.
Lacquer and giltwood,
height: 98·5 cm
(38¼ in).
Private collection

The Japanese Kakiemon style of decoration on export wares was copied by many European factories as diverse as Meissen, Chantilly, Chelsea and Bow, often so carefully that the imitations can barely be distinguished (9).

This insatiable European demand for Japanese porcelain was rivalled by a fierce enthusiasm for the lacquer work which poured out through Deshima. One great collector of lacquer ware was the Empress Marie Theresa of Austria (r.1740–80), who bequeathed a collection to her daughter, Marie Antoinette (r.1774–93). When it arrived in France, Marie Antoinette had individual pieces graded as being objects of the highest calibre, a process which led to their preservation during the overthrow of the *ancien régime* in the French Revolution.

At first, in the seventeenth century, screens, cabinets or panels of lacquer were imported, cut up and adapted to form hybrid mirror frames, cabinets, tables and chests. Just as *ormolu* was used to marry Oriental porcelain with European Rococo settings, so Japanese lacquered panels were mounted on elaborate Baroque stands, which formed compositions that still last today in palaces and grand houses all over Europe (10).

There was, however, an easier and cheaper way to meet the demand for lacquered furniture, which was to produce imitation lacquer. The art of 'japanning' quickly became a fashion and a social accomplishment for a young lady. We know this from a letter of 1689 from Sir Ralph Verney, in which he agrees to pay 'a guinay entrance and 40 shillings more' to buy materials for his daughter Molly to be taught japanning at school. To cater for this demand John Stalker and George Parker published in 1688 a useful volume entitled *A Treatise of Japanning and Varnishing*. In a famous passage they proclaimed:

Let not the Europeans any longer flatter themselves with the empty notions of having surpassed all the world beside in stately Palaces, costly Temples and sumptuous Fabricks: Ancient and Modern Rome must now give place. The glory of one country, Japan alone, has exceeded in beauty and magnificence all the pride of the Vatican at this time and the Pantheon heretofore.

The book contains recipes for the preparation of lacquer and instructions on techniques. Standards were, of course, variable and while some pieces of japanning were acceptable, vast quantities of inferior amateur work were also produced.

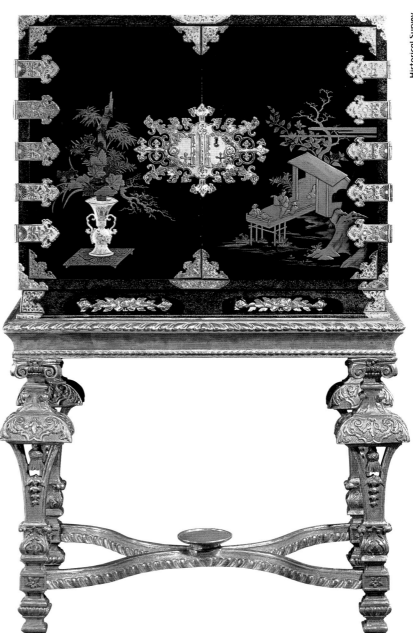

Rivalling the compulsive demand in Europe for the fine and decorative arts of Japan was a thirst to possess specimens and paintings of exotic and unknown flowers, for there was huge European curiosity concerning Japan's flora and fauna. For over a century a number of eager naturalists were employed on short-term contracts by the VOC. They covered their real aims by working as physicians in Deshima and, providing they did not get too involved in internal affairs, they could peer at the flora of Japan through the limited view afforded by specimens brought in via Deshima.

Despite stringent security, smuggling was rife. It was indeed encouraged by the fact that the Dutchman, Isaac Titsingh, who held the post of official overseer (1779–84), was exempt from body searches. He had a special garment made which looked like a diver's suit, and was stuffed full of contraband. Supported by two wild-looking youths, Titsingh staggered out to meet the bowing Japanese. To facilitate other more serious espionage activities he acquired a fluent knowledge of Japanese.

After his return from three tours of duty in Deshima, Titsingh wrote and lectured extensively in England and Europe, keeping an interest in Japan alive for the outside world. He is known to have brought back antiquities and prints, and it was possibly through him that the eighteenth-century botanist, Sir Joseph Banks, acquired his 1788 copy of *Ehon Mushi Erabi* (*Picture-book of Selected Insects*; 11) by Kitagawa Utamaro (1753–1806), which became one of the first Japanese works of art to enter the British Museum collections after Banks' library was left to the museum.

At that time this exquisite example of woodblock printing was regarded solely as a botanical source book. Indeed, plants are far more evident in it than the insects promised by the title. Utamaro also produced entrancing 'Shell' and 'Bird' books. The Swedish botanist and collector, Carl Peter Thunberg, visited Nagasaki en route to Deshima in 1775. He returned with works by the early masters, Harunobu and Isoda Koryusai (*fl.*1765–80s), the most fashionable *ukiyo-e* artists of the day, which can now be seen in the Ethnographical Museum in Stockholm.

The greatest early botanist and collector, however, was Dr Philipp Franz von Siebold (1796–1866), a German working for the VOC, who brought back a comprehensive group of Japanese cultural artefacts and plants. He was perhaps the most important visitor to Japan before it opened its doors to the outside world.

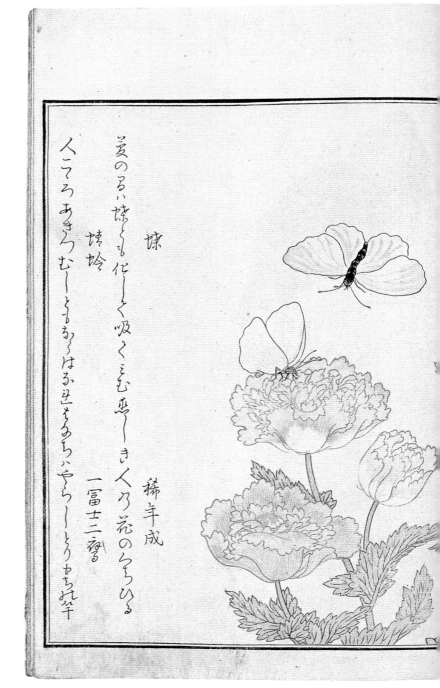

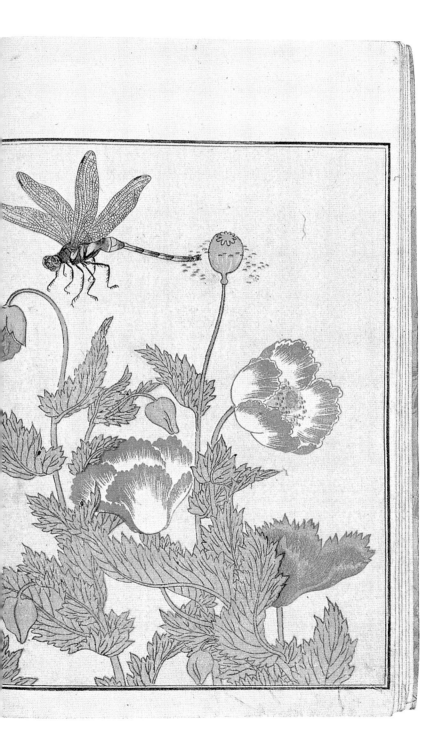

11
Kitagawa Utamaro,
Dragonfly, Butterflies
and Poppies, **from the**
Ehon Mushi Erabi
(*Picture-book of Selected*
***Insects*),**
1788.
Colour woodblock,
each page: 27·1 x 18·5 cm
(10³₄ x 7¹₄ in)

Siebold arrived at Nagasaki on 23 August 1823, to take up his post as surgeon-physician at Deshima. His initial reception was very similar to that which was given twenty years later to Captain Van Assendelft de Coningh, who visited Nagasaki in 1845 and 1851 and had a nasty brush with the Japanese authorities, later recalling how:

I was filled with fear after I had managed to escape from the clutches of the inspectors and entered Deshima through the two solemn gateways where the guards were sitting on mats like silent mummies. The high walls, which enclosed the island, gave me the feeling that we were criminals who had been imprisoned in some sort of institution.

On Siebold's arrival at Deshima he found eleven houses which were at the disposal of Dutch officials, and a number of buildings which were used as warehouses, kitchens, a sick-bay, a cow byre and pigsty. Siebold moved into the doctor's quarters and fitted it out with such Western luxuries as a piano, which he played frequently. We gain a vivid idea of his daily life in the Dutch quarter from an album dating from 1847 showing a jolly lunch party (12) and a group making use of a telescope to look round the harbour.

Despite these excitements it was hard work adjusting to the 'time capsule' inhabited by the long-term resident Dutchmen in Deshima, of whom Siebold wrote:

Initially, we did not have a pleasant impression of the formal court behaviour these men adopted towards each other and to the Japanese officials, nor of the old-fashioned clothing which they wore ... which consisted of quilted velvet coats and black cloaks, hats with feathers, steel swords and Spanish canes with gold handles ... the prevailing atmosphere ... felt as though we were taking part in a seventeenth-century ceremony.

This description sounds almost as though Siebold's colleagues had walked out of a *namban* screen (see 2).

As a doctor Siebold particularly excelled at eye operations such as cataracts, which if successful can produce such amazing results, and which earned him the soubriquet 'Miracle Doctor'. He actually started a school of medicine in Nagasaki for students who were not allowed to visit Deshima. The local fame and admiration that this aroused inevitably caused friction with the Dutchmen in the settlement, who also criticized Siebold's lifestyle when romance entered his life in the form of his 'marriage' to a beautiful and devoted Japanese girl.

In retrospect, the emotional vicissitudes of her life with Siebold form virtually a precursor of the Madame Butterfly story (see Chapter 9). During the winter of 1823–4, the 27-year-old doctor made house calls to sick patients in Nagasaki and met the 16-year-old Kusumoto Otaki, whom he affectionately called by the diminutive name, Sonogi. This may have been her courtesan name for, according to some authorities, she was one of the prostitutes who were allowed to visit the island to satisfy male needs.

Siebold confided in a letter to an uncle:

I have given in to that old Dutch habit and have temporarily become quite attached to a sweet sixteen-year-old Japanese girl, whom I would not willingly exchange for a European one.

Some sources maintain that Sonogi loved Siebold so much that she allowed a red courtesan stamp to be placed in her passport to enable her to visit Deshima, as at that time it was forbidden for a foreigner to marry a Japanese woman. On 10 May 1827 a daughter was born, whom they named Oine.

Following his official duties, Siebold set off on a trip to Edo to pay homage to the shogun and to report on events, a journey that took place only once every four years. The round trip measured approximately 1,750 miles (2,815 km), and was the only opportunity to see more of Japan.

Siebold set out on 15 February 1826 accompanied by the store-house manager J F Van Overmeer Fisscher. Both men were eager to bring back to Europe works which would convey the realities of daily life in the exotic land, and were particularly excited by Japanese woodcuts. Siebold wrote:

panoramas of the large cities and of the famous temple grounds are usual, as well as views of beautiful places and remarkable mountains. Such woodcuts, printed in black or with colours, often produce very naturalistic pictures and they are for sale everywhere.

In another reference to prints he says:

views of landscapes, temples and other buildings, the garments and depictions of notable men and women in the form of coloured woodcut prints are widely spread in Japan, and in Osaka and Edo these prints are worked out very beautifully.

Siebold's companion, Fisscher, was full of admiration for the way in which the Japanese use pigments to:

produce such marvellous colours as are not to be found in Europe … and give reason to believe that the Japanese would make very great progress once they studied the European painting school.

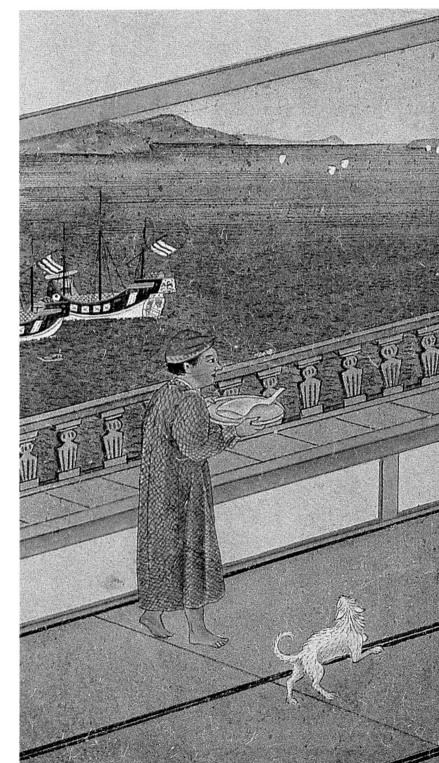

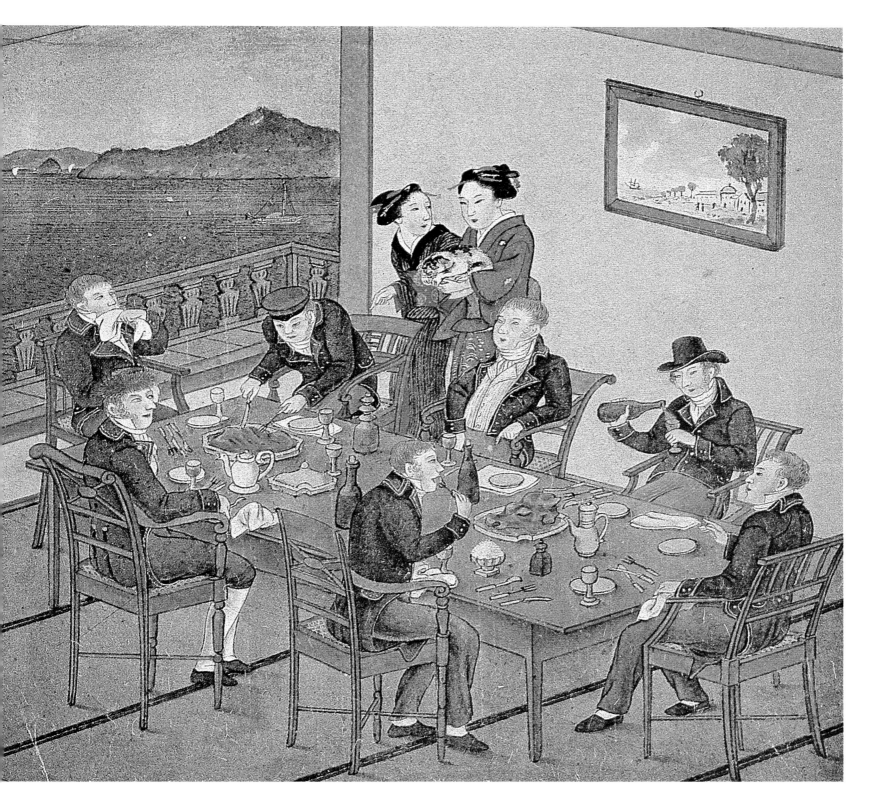

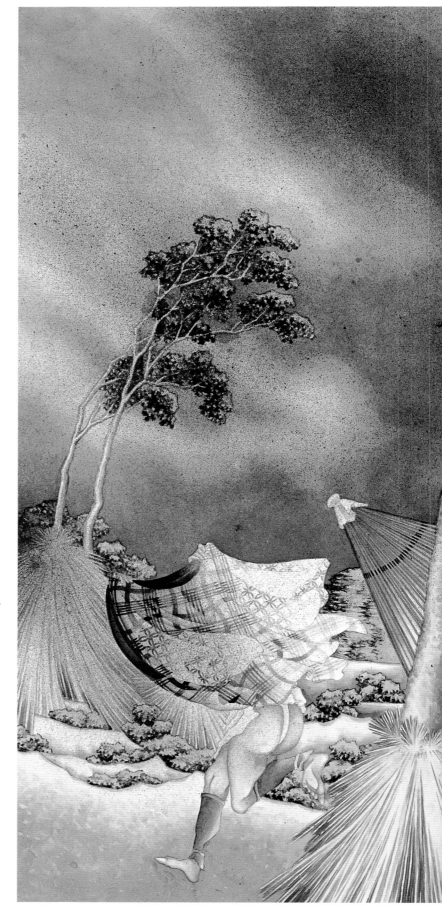

13
Katsushika Hokusai
*Peasants Surprised by
a Sudden Rainstorm,*
*c.*1826.
Watercolour and ink,
27·1 x 40 cm
(10³₄ x 15³₄ in).
National Museum of
Ethnology, Leiden

The journey took two months, for the rules on the itinerary were very strict (although frequently violated by Siebold, who treated many sick people on the way for skin and eye diseases and syphilis). Once in Edo, Siebold became a great attraction for many intellectual individuals eager for knowledge of the outside world. An encounter with Takahashi Sakuzaemon, the court astronomer and supervisor of the Imperial Library, led to an imprudent exchange of maps which was eventually to be Siebold's downfall. If discovered, it made him vulnerable to the accusation of espionage at a time when Russia was threatening Japan's northern borders. Supplying maps to foreigners was punishable by death.

The journey back to Nagasaki passed smoothly, enlivened by such excitements as the illicit act of measuring the height of Mount Fuji with a sextant, and less controversially by visits to a *kabuki* performance in Osaka. Siebold left a vivid description of the theatre:

The gallery, which in Europe opens on a corridor, is left open to let in light, since plays are performed during the day in Japan, not at night, with artificial lighting. Two high, bridge-like passages leading from the back of the theatre to the stage, allow actors to enter, exit and act in the midst of the audience.

Many first-class artists performed … their luxurious costumes were enough to make us forget the poor appearance of the theatre itself … instead of having movable flats, they change scenery very quickly with a revolving stage.

Back in Deshima (reached on 20 June 1826), Siebold was happy for a year cataloguing and enlarging his vast botanical, zoological and ethnographic collections, which had increased dramatically on his court journey. But on 18 September 1828, a typhoon caused the ship *Cornelius Houtman* with eighty-nine crates containing Siebold's collection to run aground on the coast.

Among the cargo were forbidden maps, which when discovered led to the arrest of Siebold, Sakuzaemon, fifty interpreters and forty Japanese who had come in contact with Siebold on his journeys to and from Edo. Sakuzaemon was beaten, and died in prison before sentence of death was passed in March 1829.

After his arrest, Siebold was rigorously interrogated for over a year by the authorities at Deshima, and on 22 October 1829 he was banished from Japan for life. Siebold regarded the sentence as extremely severe for it meant that he could never return to see his wife and two-year-old daughter again.

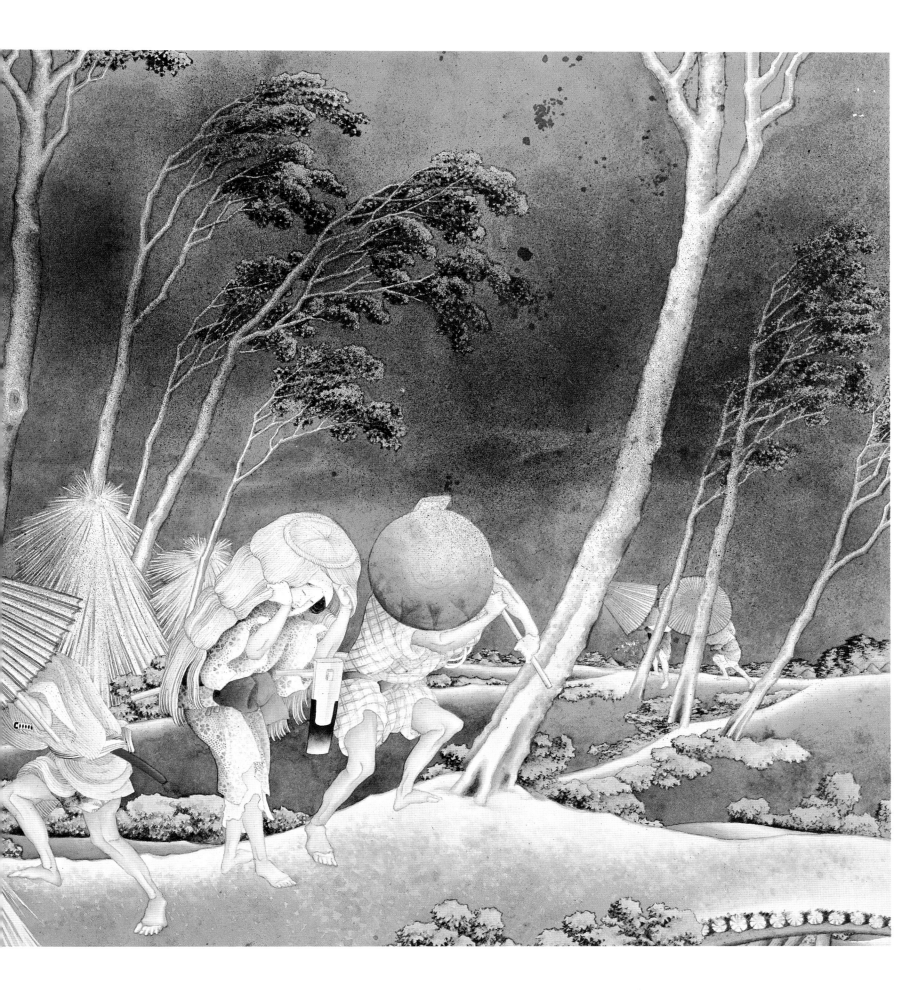

14
Utagawa Yoshitora,
Railway Timetable,
1872–9.
Colour woodblock,
34·4 x 22·4 cm
(13½ x 8¾ in)

He had two miniatures painted of them, which he placed in lacquer boxes together with locks of their hair, and left Japan on 30 December 1829, asking his two best students to share the responsibilities of bringing up his daughter.

As his ship, the same *Cornelius Houtman*, left the next morning a small boat emerged through the mists with his wife, daughter and two students on board to say their final farewells, a moment surely of operatic intensity. Remarkably, Oine and her father would remain in contact through his years of exile from Japan, and he supplied her with Western medicines while Siebold's students gave her Western medical training. She achieved fame by becoming the first woman doctor in Japan and by running a gynaecology clinic in Nagasaki.

Siebold was lucky to escape with his life, and also lucky to return to Holland with over 2,000 illustrated books and prints. Among the more notable artists whose works he brought back were Katsushika Hokusai (1760–1849), Ando Hiroshige (1797–1858), Utagawa Kunisada (1786–1864) and earlier artists such as Utamaro, Suzuki Haranobu, Torii Kiyonaga (1752–1815), together with examples of the rare prints of Sharaku Toshusai (*fl*.1794–5). Siebold was to use copperplate engravings after Hokusai's illustrations in his book, *Nippon* (1832–58).

One work with which Siebold returned is of particular interest, Hokusai's watercolour sketch in the Western style painted in ink and colours on Dutch paper entitled *Peasants Surprised by a Sudden Rainstorm* (*c*.1826; 13), from a series depicting Japanese customs and festivities. It was ordered by Jan Cock Blomhoff, one of Siebold's colleagues at Deshima, and may have been selected and purchased by Siebold from Hokusai himself. The subject of falling rain and snow or high winds fascinated Hokusai, who returned to the theme again and again.

During the next thirty years Siebold's fortunes waxed and waned. On a visit to the health resort of Bad Kissingen in 1840 in his native Germany he met the Baroness Von Garden, twenty-five years his junior. Five years later they were married, and were to have five children, the two oldest sons inheriting his love of Japan. Although appointed adviser on Japanese affairs to the Bavarian court, Siebold was no courtier and was eventually dismissed, only to be re-employed in 1858. The same year he heard, to his delight, that his banishment from Japan had been withdrawn. On 4 August 1859 Siebold returned to Japan with his eldest son, Alexander.

They were met by his Japanese daughter, Oine, now 32, with a daughter of her own. Sonogi had remarried twice in the interim, rather to Siebold's surprise, but we do not know what Sonogi thought of Siebold's marriage and family. One cannot help but consider how the story presents further operatic opportunities, such as memorable solos, duets, trios and quartets. The final solo, however, would surely belong to Siebold's Japanese daughter, whom he met for the last time in Nagasaki on his second and final enforced return to Europe at the end of April 1862. He died in Munich in October 1866.

Denied contact with the outside world, alert Japanese eyes were eager to see more of the exotic figures from the West. This led to the production of the so-called Nagasaki prints, inexpensive souvenirs of foreign ships, visitors and their amazing animals. Like the animals, the Japanese felt that they too were imprisoned, and they stirred uneasily under the dictatorial rule of the shoguns. Russian, British and American ships risked putting in to Japanese ports hoping to do some trading and break the monopoly of the Dutch and Chinese. Some crews were massacred. Others were ordered to leave at once.

After protests the Japanese agreed that ships in distress might put in for water and fuel to their ports. But in 1839, when Congress in Washington sent Commodore Biddle to try to negotiate a trade agreement, the request was contemptuously refused. American pride had been wounded, and even worse, commercial interests were threatened. Enterprising Americans wanted a foothold in Japan, so that they might become the principal traders both there and in China.

A race for a trade treaty with Japan began between America and Russia, just as a century later the two countries would vie with each other to be the first to place a man on the moon. In October 1852 the Russian Admiral Putyatin sailed with four ships for Japan, but he arrived at Nagasaki in August 1853, a few weeks too late, for another fleet of four American ships had reached Japan in July. They were the famous 'black' ships, two steamers and two sailing boats, with nearly 600 men under the command of Commodore Matthew Perry, US Navy. His predecessor, Biddle, had been forbidden to deal firmly with the Japanese but Perry had a free hand. The following year, in February 1854, he returned with seven ships and 2,000 men, and the shogunate realized that no defences would keep out the Americans for long. The first treaties were extremely limited in effect for only Nagasaki, Hakodate and Shimoda were opened to foreign shipping.

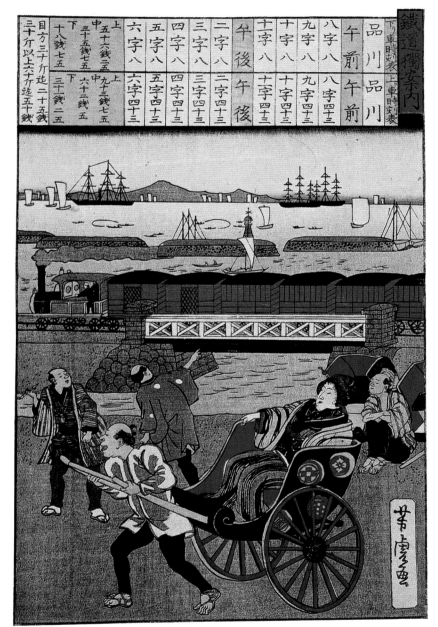

But the commercial process of opening Japan had begun and was not confined to the United States of America; before the end of the 1850s a series of treaties was signed with Great Britain, France, Russia and The Netherlands.

On the second American mission visit to Japan in the *Macedonian* in 1854, Dr Francis Hawks, who kept the official journal, recorded the intense interest in a miniature train given to Japan to introduce the power of steam. It was designed to run on an 46-cm (18-in) gauge track on a 107-m (117-yds) circular railway line at a speed of 20 miles (32 km) an hour.

It was a spectacle not a little ludicrous to behold a dignified mandarin [sic] whirling around a circular road at the rate of twenty miles per hour with his loose robes flying in the wind. As he clung with a desperate hold to the edge of the roof, grinning with intense interest and his huddled up body shaking convulsively with a kind of laughing timidity while the car spun rapidly round the circle, you might have supposed that the movement somehow was dependent rather upon the enormous exertion of the uneasy mandarin than upon the power of the little puffing locomotive which was easily performing its work.

Less than thirty years later, in 1872, a real railway would make its way between Tokyo and Yokohama, and above it would soar the wires of the first telegraph lines (14).

The age of steam would also make its mark in the guise of the company founded in 1840 which would become the Peninsular and Oriental Steam Navigation Company, always known as P & O. For the first three decades of its history passengers and goods had to be transported on camels by land across the narrow isthmus which separated Suez from the Nile. But the opening of the Suez canal in 1869 (celebrated in Cairo with the first production of Verdi's opera *Aida* against a background of the pyramids) gave the opportunity for P & O to use the latest steam ships to destinations in the Pacific and the Far East. Very soon educated Europeans began to visit Japan in surprising numbers.

The first British citizens had arrived in 1859, and while some settled in Nagasaki and Hakodate, most stayed at Yokohama, notably Sir Rutherford Alcock, the first British Minister to Japan. He returned to England in time to organize the Japanese stand at the International Exhibition of 1862, which contained many artefacts that he had collected. His book, *The Capital of the Tycoon* (1863), describes his years in Japan and is still very readable.

Japonisme

15
Utagawa Yoshitora,
*American Drinking
and Carousing*,
1861.
Colour woodblock,
35·4 x 24 cm
(14 x 9³⁄₈ in)

A vivid record of these exciting days, with the ups and downs of daily life of the foreign community, and the rapid adoption of Western ways by the indigenous population, is provided by Nagasaki and Yokohama prints. The first Nagasaki prints had been made at the turn of the century and depicted quaint Chinese and lecherous Dutchmen in a semi-foreign style, but printed according to traditional *ukiyo-e* methods (15). The Yokohama prints (16) are at their most amusing in the naive depictions of 'foreign' capitals, hilarious popular images of London or Rome, which were sold as cheap souvenirs (17). These engaging works were highly successful when depicting foreign ships on the open sea. Although entertaining, they differ greatly from the earlier masterpieces of the *ukiyo-e* school, which when they reached Europe would have a striking effect on the artists and designers of the day.

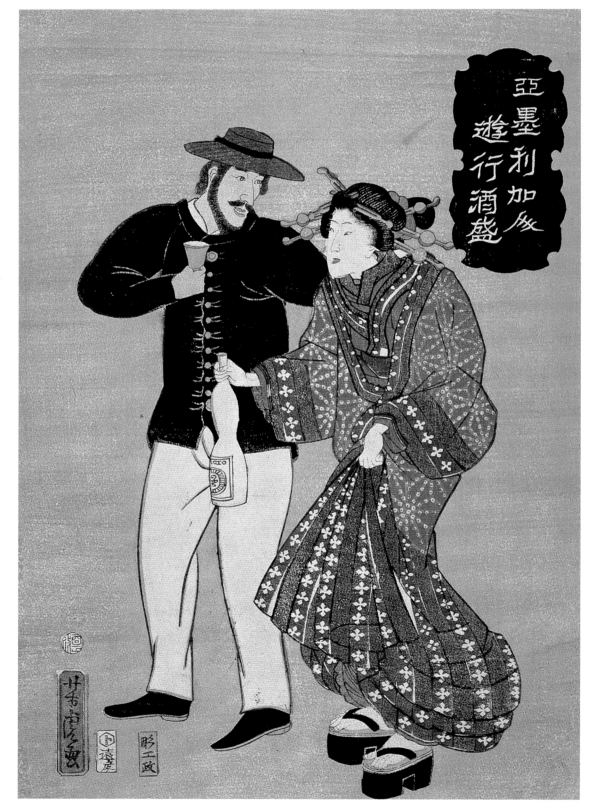

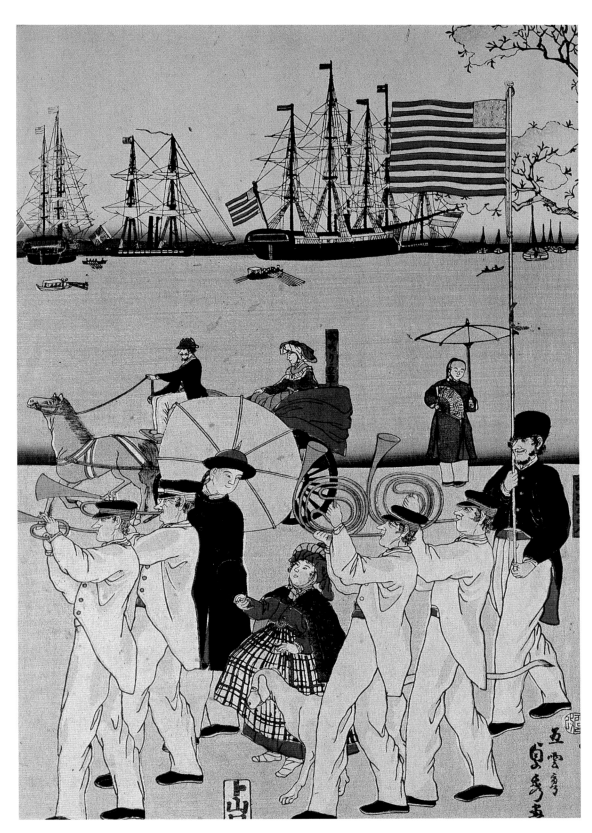

16
Utagawa Sadahide,
A Sunday in Yokohama,
1861–2.
Colour woodblock,
36·4 x 74·2 cm
(14¹⁄₄ x 29¹⁄₈ in)

International exhibitions and world fairs began with the Great Exhibition in the Crystal Palace, London, 1851. Japan was not represented at this first world fair, for there were still a few years to go before the end of seclusion. Once Japan started to be involved with them, however, they became one of the most enthusiastic participants in an endless round of international exhibitions. The London exhibition of 1862 had a Japanese section chosen by the first British Minister in Japan, but it was not until 1867 in Paris that Japan officially participated, and although the shogun government was on the brink of collapse, Japan found much sympathetic support in France. During the more enlightened years of the Meiji era (1868–1912) the empire changed rapidly and enjoyed what has been described as Japan's Victorian age. With the support of the progressive new Meiji emperor, lavish displays were mounted at major and minor exhibition venues in France, thus providing an ideal opportunity for Japanese manufacturers to market their export lines. This competitive stimulus led many European manufacturers to produce reciprocal samples of goods destined for sale in Japan. These 'Japanese' displays also created enduring popular images, visual clichés of Japan that persisted throughout the West well into the twentieth century

Utagawa Yoshitora,
Port of London triptych,
1862.
Colour woodblock,
each section:
36·5 x 73·9 cm
(14³⁄₈ x 29 in).
Kobe City Museum of
Namban Art

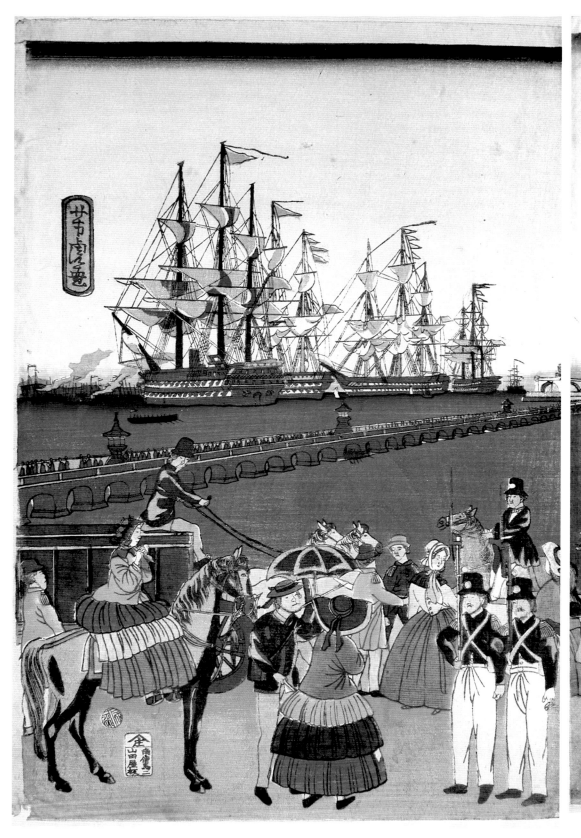

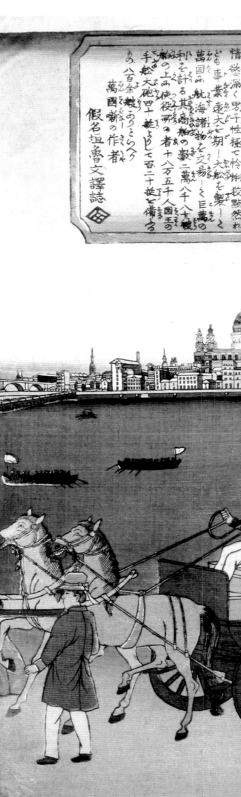

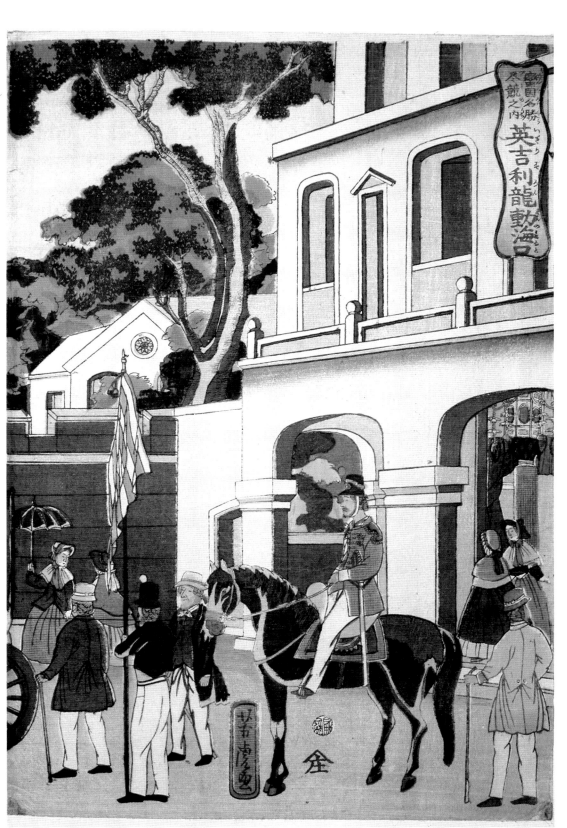

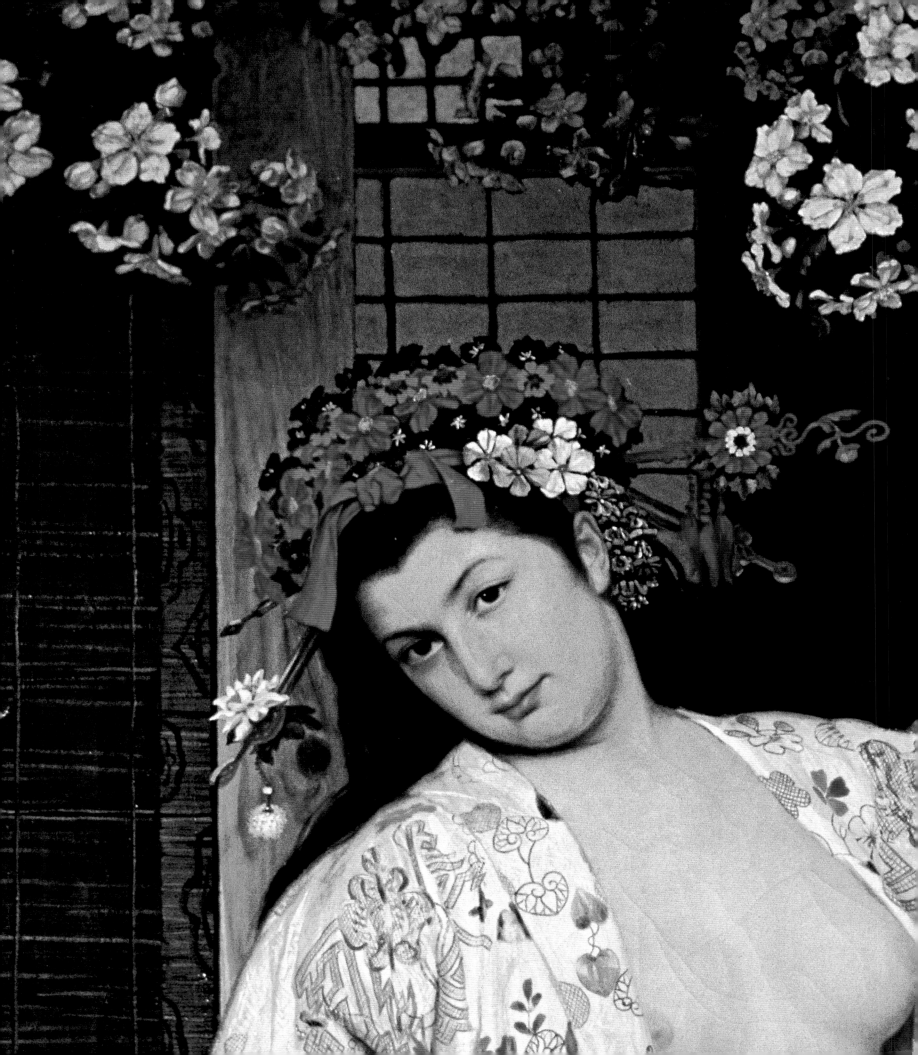

Chapter two:
Japan and the Painters

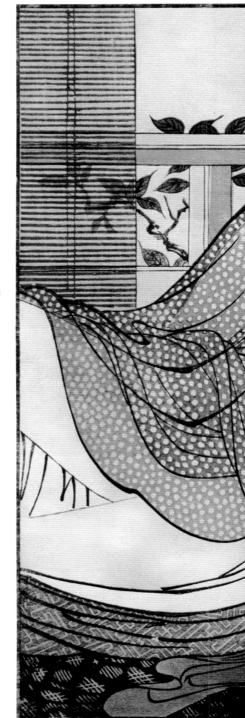

It is strange, this revolution brought by Japanese art in the taste of a people who, in matters of art, are the slaves of Greek symmetry and who, suddenly, are becoming impassioned over a plate on which the flower is not set dead in the middle, over a fabric in which harmony is not achieved by a gradation of tints but by a knowledgeable juxtaposition of raw colours.
Edmond de Goncourt, 1877

Japanese prints ... penny plain and tuppence coloured – illustrations of Yeddo ... excellent no doubt as decorative furnishings but absurd as pictures.
Joseph Péladan, 1884

The influence of Japan upon European art and literature of the nineteenth century was various. From the 1860s to the 1890s the themes of Japonisme provided an exciting new direction for artists such as James Abbott McNeill Whistler (1834–1903), Édouard Manet (1832–83) and Claude Monet (1840–1926), and authors such as the de Goncourt brothers, Guy de Maupassant and Pierre Loti. For thirty years few artists or writers could afford to ignore the obsession with 'things Japanese'. As early as 1867 the de Goncourt brothers published a novel, *Manette Salomon*, in which a chapter is devoted to the hero's Oriental daydreams as he studies albums of Japanese woodcuts, finding:

pages like ivory palettes laden with the colours of the Orient ... sparkling with purple, ultramarine and emerald greens. And from these albums of Japanese drawings, there dawned for him a day in this magical country, a day without shadow, a day that was nothing but light.

This idyllic dream would later haunt many artists, notably Vincent van Gogh (1853–90) and Paul Gauguin (1848–1903), driving them to seek out Japanese themes, either in the form of woodcuts, or by visiting the south of France, a vision of bright sunlight, blue skies, intense starlight and bold colours.

The most important of all advocates for the Japoniste cause were the two brothers, Edmond and Jules de Goncourt. Within the pages of the their intimate *Journal* (1851–70) lie the raw materials for a history of Japonisme, a subject they knew well as collectors, critics and novelists. Their most famous joint art-historical work was *French Eighteenth Century Painters* (1859–75), which reveals not only their passion for accuracy in research, but also their delight in extreme forms of art such as *singerie* (the decorative depiction of monkeys in human roles) and *chinoiserie* (decorative art inspired by the art of China).

Such enthusiasms prepared Edmond for his passionate interest in Japonisme. Jules's early death, aged forty, ended their collaborative work, but Edmond continued to write the journal they had started in 1851. Its nine volumes chart with zest Parisian literary and artistic life, and often make reference to the progress of the cult of Japan, that was a powerful influence on the art of the Impressionists.

In an entry dated January 1862 the brothers express their views concerning the conflict between the two principles of beauty and truth ('*le beau versus le vrai*') which dominated French art throughout the second half of the nineteenth century. They came to be associated in the minds of the artistic establishment of the day with backing the Japanese side in the conflict between Japanese and Greek art, representing beauty and truth respectively. 'Art is not one,' they proclaimed:

or rather there is no single art. Japanese art is as great an art as Greek art. Greek art, frankly what is it? The realism of the beautiful. No fantasy, no dream. The absolute of line.

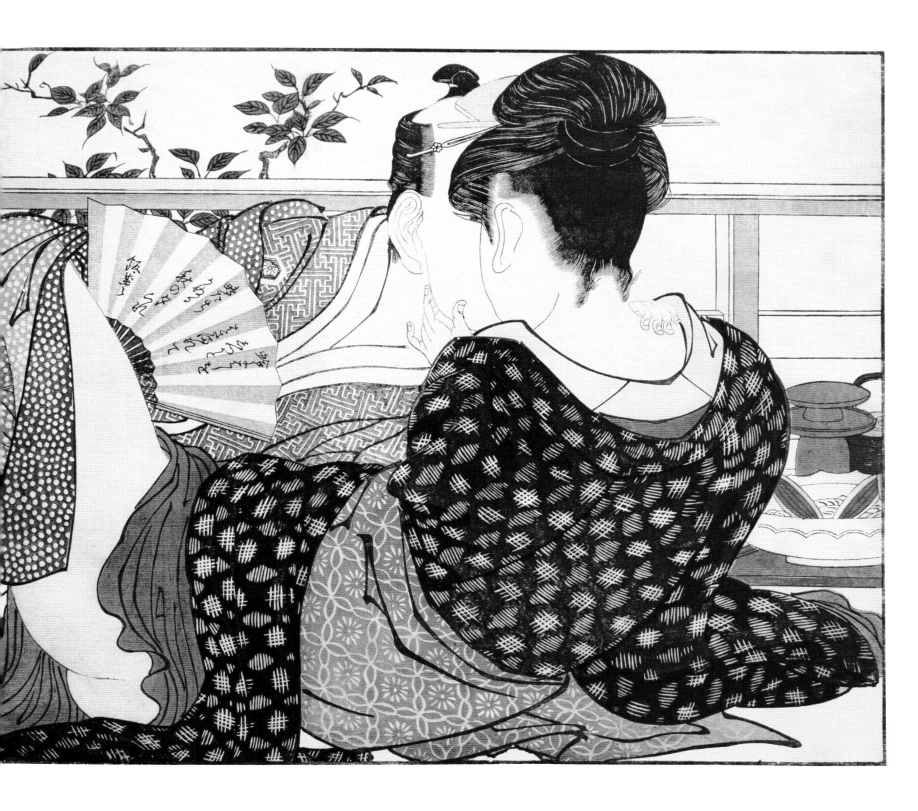

The de Goncourts shared more than their pens and paper, for their sexual lives were said to have been both erotic and economical – it was rumoured that they enjoyed the favours of the same mistress. Their delight in the Rococo sexual frisson possessed by the works of Jean-Antoine Watteau (1684–1721), François Boucher (1703–70) and Jean-Honoré Fragonard (1732–1806) found more explicit satisfaction in Japanese *shunga* or pillow books (18). As early as October 1863 Edmond described how:

The other day I bought some albums of Japanese obscenities. They delight me, amuse me, and charm my eyes. I look on them as being beyond obscenity, which is there, yet seems not to be there, and which I do not see, so completely does it disappear into fantasy.

The violence of the lines, the unexpectedness of the conjunctions, the arrangement of the accessories, the caprice in the poses and the objects, the picturesqueness, and, so to speak, the landscape of the genital parts. Looking at them, I think of Greek art, boredom in perfection, an art that will never free itself from the crime of being academic!

On 19 July 1864 Edmond made a note of the evening sky:

This evening the sun looks like a wafer of cherry-coloured sealing wax, glued onto the sky over a pearl-coloured sea. Only the Japanese have dared, in their colour albums, to give these strange effects of nature.

On 30 September 1864 he praised Japanese artists for their discernment:

Everything that they do is taken from observation. They represent what they see: the incredible effects of the sky, the stripes on a mushroom, the transparency of the jellyfish. Their art copies nature as does Gothic art. Basically there is no paradox in saying that a Japanese album and a painting by Watteau are drawn from an intimate study of nature. Nothing like this in the Greeks: their art, except for sculpture, is false and invented.

An artist who adopted a Japoniste agenda while also keeping a foot in the Hellenic camp was Whistler. His enthusiasm for collecting Japanese art began in the early 1860s when, as a gifted young American painter, he occupied a unique 'mid-channel' role in the artistic world of London and Paris, at a time of great change in the arts in both capital cities.

By the mid-1860s in England, Pre-Raphaelitism had begun to wane and a full-scale Neoclassical revival was underway. Yet for Whistler, like the de Goncourts, the word 'academic' was anathema. While admiring the lightly clad ladies painted by his friend Albert Moore (1841–93), Whistler himself used Japanese art to distance himself from the toga-clad Greeks and Romans of Lawrence Alma-Tadema (1836–1912) and the toiling Israelites goaded by Egyptians by Edward Poynter (1836–1919), which jostled for attention at the Royal Academy in London.

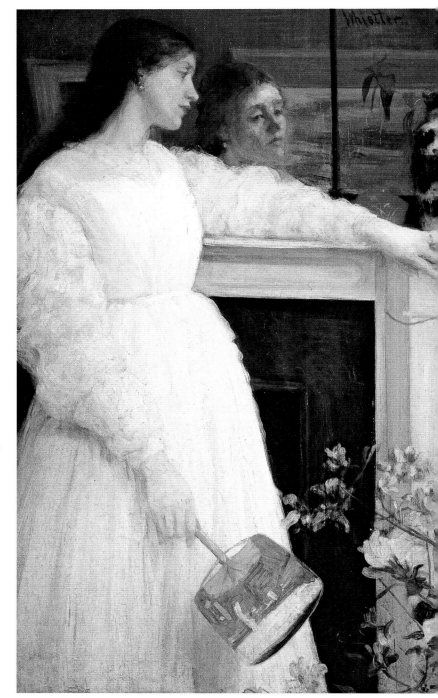

19
James Abbott McNeill Whistler,
Symphony in White,
No. 2: The Little White Girl,
1864.
Oil on canvas,
76·5 x 51·1 cm
(30$\frac{1}{8}$ x 20 in).
Tate Britain, London

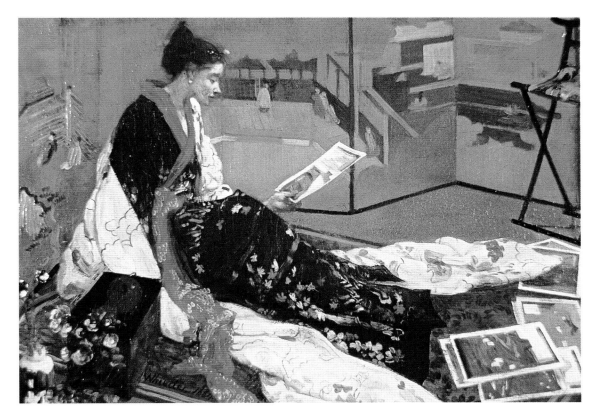

20
**James Abbott McNeill
Whistler,**
*Caprice in Purple and
Gold, No. 2: The Golden
Screen*,
1864.
Oil on wood,
50·2 x 68·7 cm
(19³⁄₄ x 27 in).
Freer Gallery of Art,
Smithsonian Institution,
Washington, DC

Placed against these pseudo-classical subjects Whistler's own paintings are strikingly original. His work would eventually display his profound sympathy for Japanese art, yet at first this expressed itself mainly in the fun of using unusual Japanese artefacts as studio props. In the most hauntingly beautiful of these works, *Symphony in White, No. 2: The Little White Girl* (19), Whistler used his beautiful Irish mistress, Jo Heffernan, as a model. Clad in a voluminous white dress, she leans on a white marble mantelpiece with a pier glass, while her right hand hangs by her side holding a colourful Japanese fan. She gazes at a blue and white jar, a red lacquer bowl and some colourful azaleas, all reflected in the mirror. Whistler would continue to explore the theme of a painting arranged around a single colour and devise unusual colour schemes for several of the apartments he occupied in London in the 1860s, all remarkable for their decor.

In all of them his Oriental porcelain collection played an important role. His mother, who came to live with him in the winter of 1863, wrote to a friend on 10 February 1864 describing her son's 'artistic abode … ornamented by a very rare collection of blue and white china'.

21
James Abbott McNeill
Whistler,
*Variations in Flesh Colour
and Green: The Balcony*,
*c.*1867–8.
Oil on wood,
61·4 x 48·8 cm
(24⅛ x 19¼ in).
Freer Gallery of Art,
Smithsonian Institution,
Washington, DC

Whistler's motives for collecting were
complex, including his delight in the
search for exciting examples, and a
personal enjoyment of the colour
blue, used in Chinese and Japanese
porcelain, subtle variations of which
hue appear in so many of his
paintings. He also delighted in
depicting both his own treasured
pieces and examples borrowed from
the stock of the dealer, Murray Marks.

Whistler took pleasure in rivalling the
freedom of the potter's brush, a theme
developed in his *Purple and Rose: the
Lange Leizen of the Six Marks* (1864),
which shows the model as if intent on
painting the tall figures on the vase.
Whistler also collected prints which can
be seen in another work, *Caprice in
Purple and Gold, No. 2: The Golden
Screen* (1864; 20). In it the model, Jo,
clad not in a white dress but a kimono,
looks at a pile of prints by Hiroshige
from his landscape series *Famous
Views in the Sixty-odd Provinces*.
Jo's head is dramatically silhouetted
against a magnificent *tosa* screen
whose literary theme is taken from
The Tale of Genji.

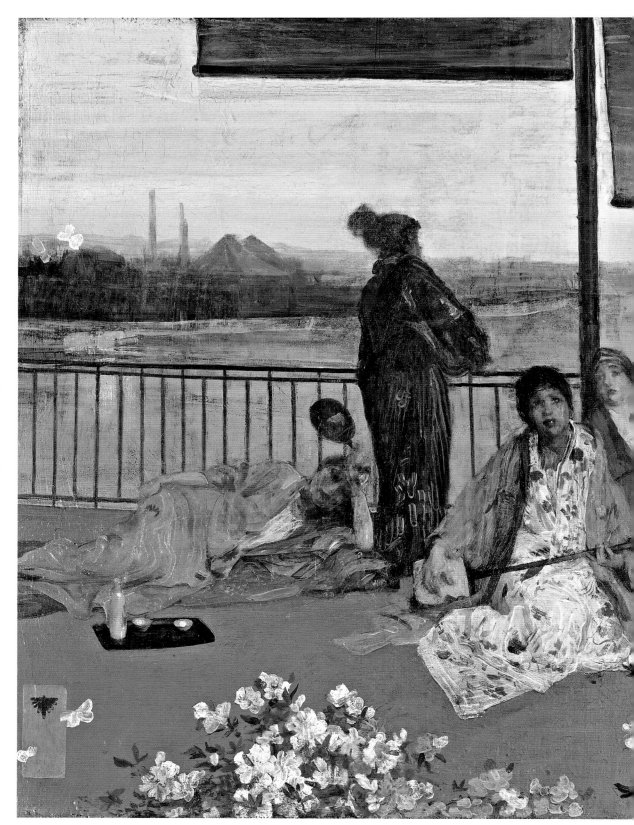

22
Torii Kiyonaga
*The Fourth Month:
Gentleman Entertained
by Courtesans and
Geisha at a Teahouse
in Shihagawa* **from the
series** *Twelve Months
in the South,*
*c.*1783.
**Colour woodblock,
36 x 51 cm
(14⅛ x 20 in)**

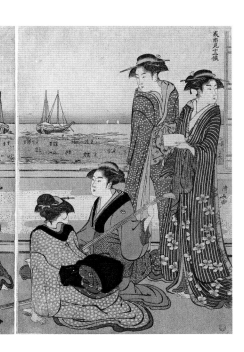

To celebrate his return after his visit to Valparaíso, Chile, at the end of 1866, Whistler gave a memorable housewarming party at his new apartment in Chelsea, London, at 2 Lindsay Row. One guest, W M Rossetti, noted that Whistler 'has got-up the rooms with many delightful Japanisms, etc. Saw for the first time his pagoda cabinet', while Whistler's friend, Alan Cole, focused more critically on 'Jimmy's absurdities with pieces of Liberty silks on the floor' and 'flights of Japanese fans on the ceiling', a decorative innovation anticipating both Manet and Monet's use of the same conceit. These exotic artefacts were set off by the overall simple tonality of the rooms, in subtle and light hues unusual for the high Victorian era.

In possibly the most Japanese of all these early works, *Variations in Flesh Colour and Green: The Balcony* (*c.*1867–8; 21), Whistler posed his models on a Chelsea balcony before the distant factory chimneys of Battersea. The horizontal and verticals formed by the rolled bamboo blinds make this an extremely Japoniste composition. It is clearly related to two woodcuts by Torii Kiyonaga, from a five-sheet composition *Autumn Moon on the Sumida* and the same artist's *The Fourth Month: Gentleman Entertained by Courtesans and Geisha at a Teahouse in Shihagawa* from *Twelve Months in the South* of *c.*1783 (22), both of which Whistler owned.

Whistler's enthusiasm for collecting was infectious and he introduced the poet and painter, Dante Gabriel Rossetti (1828–82), to Madame Desoye's famous shop at 220 Rue de Rivoli in Paris, also known as *La Porte chinoise*. Opened in 1862, it had become the haunt of all those interested in Japanese art. There, as Edmond de Goncourt described (31 March 1875):

enthroned in her jewels like a Japanese idol, sits the fat Madame Desoye; almost a historic figure in our own time, for this shop has been the place, the school as it were, from which this great Japanese movement has evolved which today extends from painting to fashion.

On his first visit to the shop in November 1864, Rossetti bought four Japanese books. He was almost certainly on the hunt for an exotic costume accessory to use in his painting *The Bride* or *The Beloved*, but as he described in a letter:

found that all the costumes were being snapped up by a French artist, Tissot, who it seems is doing three Japanese pictures, which the mistress of the shop described to me as the three wonders of the world, evidently in her opinion quite throwing Whistler into the shade. She told me, with a great deal of laughing, about Whistler's consternation at my collection of china.

23
James Tissot
La Japonaise au bain,
1864.
Oil on canvas,
208 x 124 cm
(82 x 49 in).
Musée des Beaux-Arts,
Dijon

The shop became a legend. The critic and writer, Phillipe Burty, in his novel, *Grave Imprudence* (1880), has his hero Brissot (a mixture of Manet and Monet) take enormous pride in having bought the first album of flowers and birds printed in colours in Madame Desoye's shop after her arrival from Japan. Brissot also admires her 'collection of robes of *guecuhas* and *musmes* which filled her cupboards', using affectionate diminutives for geishas and their pupils, the *mousmés*. It would, however, be wrong to give the impression that Desoye's shop was unique. Ernest Chesneau, in recalling the early 1860s, wrote:

one kept oneself informed about new cargoes. Old Ivories, enamels, faience and porcelain, bronzes, lacquers, wood sculptures, sewn materials, embroidered satins, playthings, simply arrived at a merchant's shop and immediately left for artists' studios or writers' studies.

One of the paintings by James Tissot (1836–1902) described by Madame Desoye was probably *La Japonaise au bain* (1864; 23), perhaps the most sensuous of all his works, although painted from a Western model, and not as sexually explicit as a Japanese treatment of such a theme. Tissot also painted three versions of a picture of *Two Young Women Looking at Japanese Objects*. They were posed in Tissot's house on the Avenue de l'Impératrice, sumptuously furnished with Japanese objects, some of which were presented to Tissot by Prince Akitake.

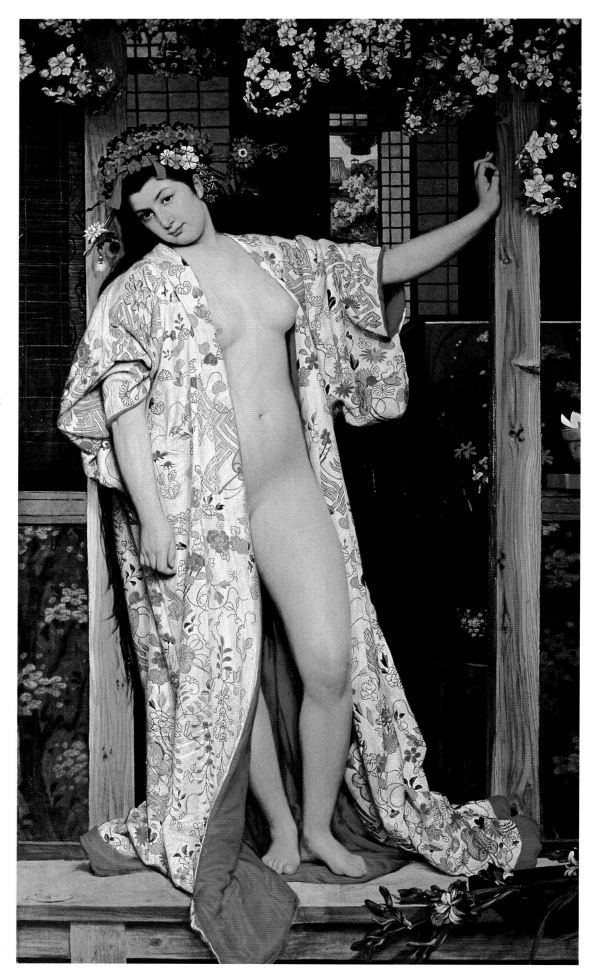

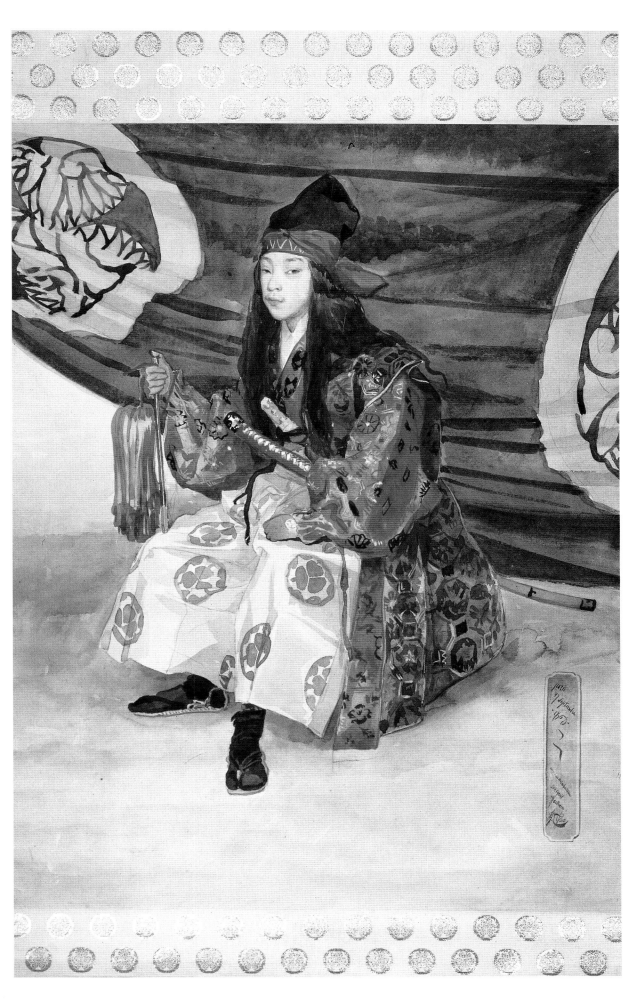

James Tissot,
Portrait of Prince
Tokugawa Akitake,
1868.
Watercolour,
55 x 47 cm
(21⁵⁸ x 18¹₂ in).
Tokugawa Museum,
Mito

The prince was one of the pioneering Japanese visitors to Europe, who came to organize the Japanese display at the Exposition Universelle of 1867. After representing the Tokugawa government at the exhibition, the prince stayed on in Paris, taking drawing lessons from Tissot. A portrait of the prince wearing Japanese dress was painted in 1868 by Tissot with an affectionate dedication to the sitter inscribed on the back. When he returned to Japan, the prince had the watercolour portrait mounted in the Japanese manner in the form of a *kakemono*, a hanging scroll picture (24).

Tissot, like Whistler, was a key figure in bringing knowledge of Japonisme across the Channel to England, exhibiting with Whistler at the Grosvenor Gallery in 1877. In Paris Tissot also kept in touch with Edgar Degas (1834–1917), who, perhaps more than any other European artist, assimilated the lessons of Japanese dramatic composition, viewpoint and perspective, such as cutting off figures with the picture frame. His studies of nude women bathing (25), drying themselves, combing their hair or having their hair combed by someone else, were directly inspired by such prints from the *Manga* vol. 1, *A Noodle Vendor* and *Women at a Public Bath* (26).

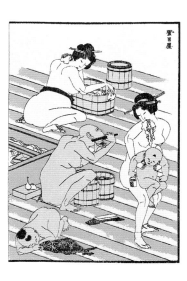

25
Edgar Degas,
The Tub,
1886.
Pastel on paper,
60 x 83 cm
(23$\frac{1}{2}$ x 32$\frac{1}{2}$ in).
Musée d'Orsay, Paris

26
Katsushika Hokusai,
Women at Public Bath,
from the *Manga* vol. I,
c.1820.
Colour woodblock,
17·5 x 11·5 cm
(7 x 4$\frac{1}{2}$ in)

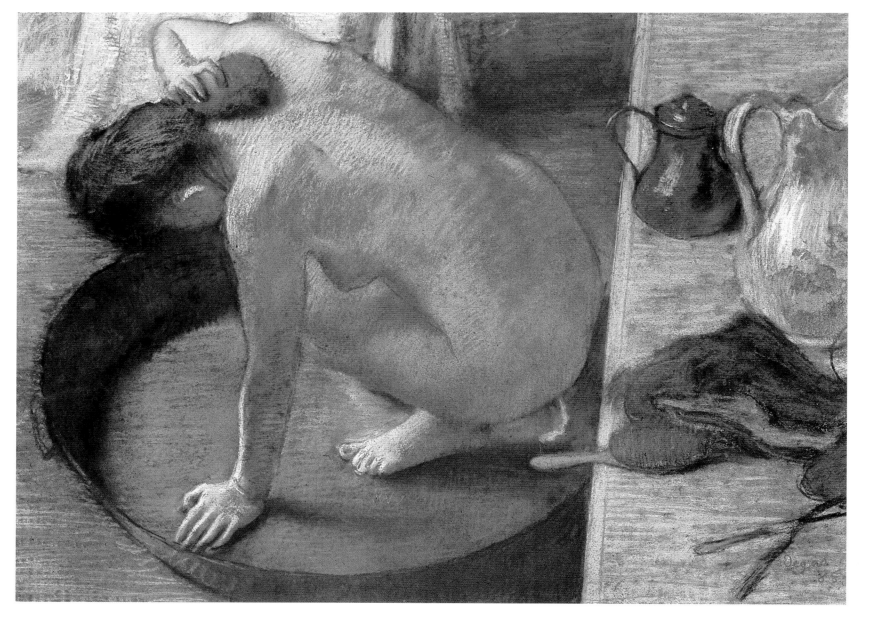

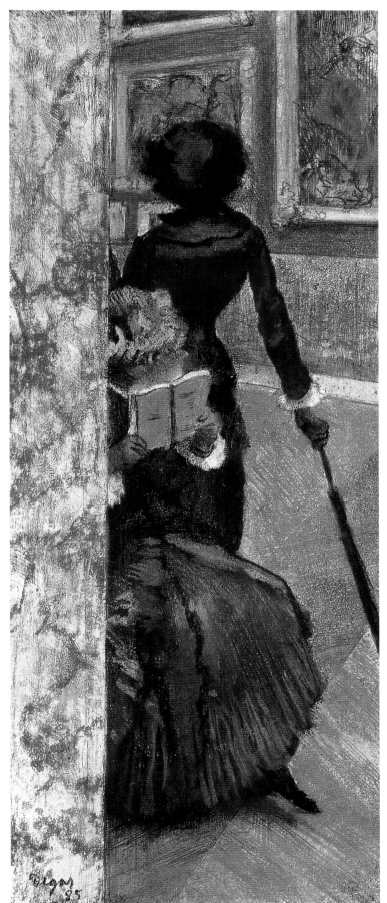

27

Edgar Degas,
Mary Cassatt at the Louvre: The Painting Gallery,
1879–80.
Etching, aquatint, drypoint and crayon électrique heightened with pastel on tan wove paper,
30·5 x 12·6 cm
(12 x 5 in).
The Art Institute of Chicago

The *Manga* were a particularly popular Japanese source from which Europeans continually borrowed motifs. The fifteen volumes that comprise the set created intense interest and were rapidly passed from hand to hand, all over Europe. In France a copy first came into the hands of a printer of etchings, Auguste Delâtré (1822–1907). He showed it to both Whistler and the etcher, Félix Bracquemond (1833–1914), who acquired the books permanently, and introduced them to a wide range of practitioners in the 'fine' and 'decorative' arts.

Degas, after a classical training with an emphasis on purity of form, found welcome relief from Western idealization of 'the female form divine' in Hokusai's vibrant studies of life in the public baths. Such sketches were a bracing alternative to the conventional poses to be seen in the works of the French Salon painters.

Hokusai's vision was echoed in Degas's favoured themes of washerwomen at work in the hot sweaty atmosphere of steamy laundries, nude studies in the brothel, and especially the themes of ballerinas, whether at rehearsals, preparing for their appearances on stage or nursing sprains in the wings of the Opéra.

A great admirer of Degas was the fiercely independent, Mary Cassatt (1844–1926), from Pennsylvania, who from the age of sixteen had studied art in Europe, exhibiting her first painting at the Paris Salon in 1868. She evolved her own special themes – women in boxes at the theatre, the intimate pleasures of maternity and the relationship between mother and baby – subjects she would treat with virtuoso success in every graphic medium. Degas admired her work, tersely perceiving it in 1877 to be 'by someone who thinks as I do', and advised her to exhibit exclusively with the new group of Impressionists, an invitation which, she wrote, 'I accepted with joy. I hated conventional art. I began to live.' She forged a close working relationship with Degas, who portrayed her in *Mary Cassatt at the Louvre: The Painting Gallery* (1879–80; 27), one of the painter's most consciously Japanese works, whose trimmed composition may derive from the tall, narrow *hashira-e* prints designed for hanging on pillars in Japanese houses.

In April 1890 Cassatt wrote to another great woman Impressionist, Berthe Morisot (1841–95), 'you must see the Japanese [prints] – come as soon as you can to the École des Beaux-Arts.' The exhibition had been arranged by Siegfried, also known as Samuel, Bing, the German-born French entrepreneur who was a key figure in influencing a wider understanding of Japanese art and who organized a number of exhibitions, notably the 1890 show which contained a vast display of 700 prints.

28
Mary Cassatt,
The Letter,
*c.*1890–1.
Coloured etching,
drypoint and aquatint,
34·5 x 22·8 cm
(13¹₂ x 9 in)

29
Kitagawa Utamaro,
The Courtesan Hinazuru
at the Keizetsuru, from
the series *Comparing the*
Charms of Beautiful
Women,
*c.*1794–5.
Colour woodcut

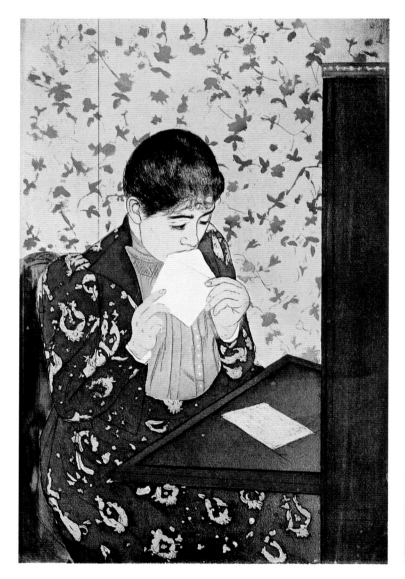

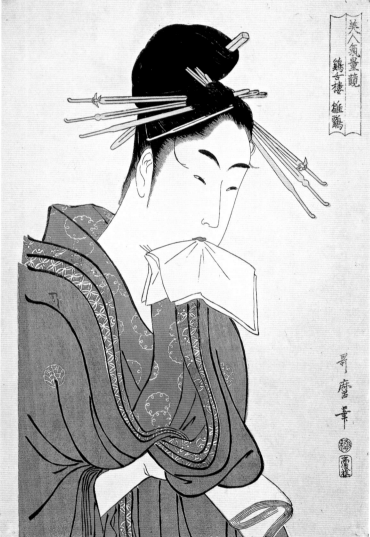

30
Mary Cassatt,
Young Woman Bathing,
1890–1.
Drypoint and aquatint,
36·8 x 26·3 cm
(14³⁄₈ x 10¹⁄₂ in)

There had been large exhibitions
of prints earlier but this was the first
historical retrospective, and, although
Cassatt was already familiar with
Japanese prints, the show had a
profound effect on her, leading her
to produce a series of ten aquatints,
which are among the finest of all
Japoniste works. Among them is
The Letter (1890–1; 28), in which
the sensual lips of the girl licking the
envelope, the curl of her fingers
and the distorted perspective of the
desk top, are surely direct tributes to
Kitagawa Utamaro (29), whom Cassatt
greatly admired.

Cassatt's *Young Woman Bathing*
(1890–1; 30) is one of her rare studies
of the female nude, and one of the
most successful marriages of Eastern
and Western styles. It was inspired
by her delight at the 1890 exhibition
in the prints of Nishikawa Sukenobu
(1671–1750), Toyokuni (1769–1825)
and most of all Utamaro. Degas was
immensely impressed when he saw
this print for the first time, remarking,
'this back, did you draw this?' Another
admirer of Cassatt's technical skills
was the Impressionist painter, Camille
Pissarro (1830–1903), who wrote to
his son Lucien praising Cassatt's
achievement in colour printing
in aquatint: 'the tone, even, subtle,
delicate … the result is admirable,
as beautiful as Japanese work, and
it's done with printer's ink!'

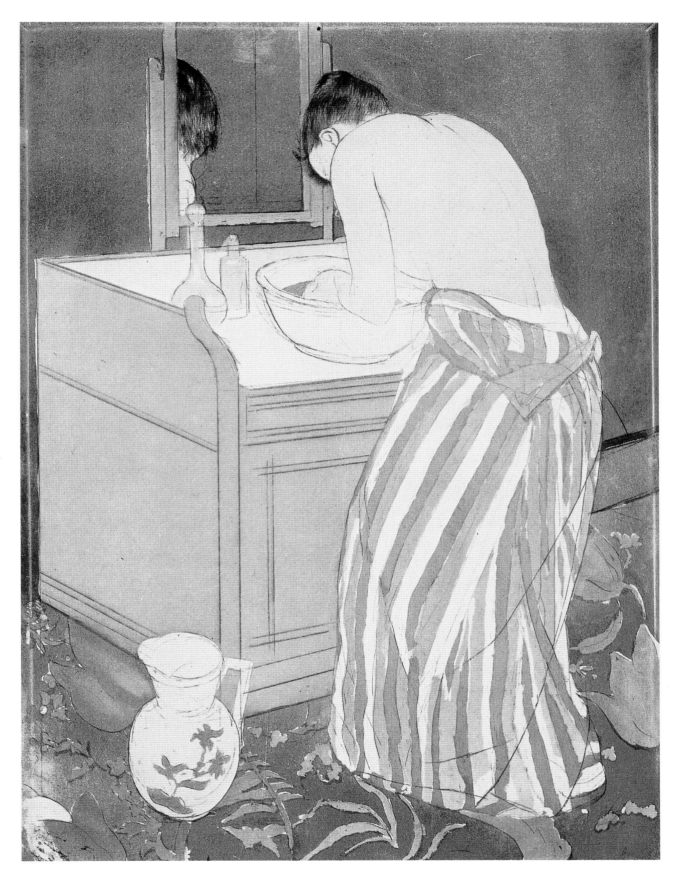

Mary Cassatt,
The Boating Party,
1893–4.
Oil on canvas,
90 x 117 cm
(35¹₂ x 46¹₄ in).
National Gallery of Art,
Washington, DC

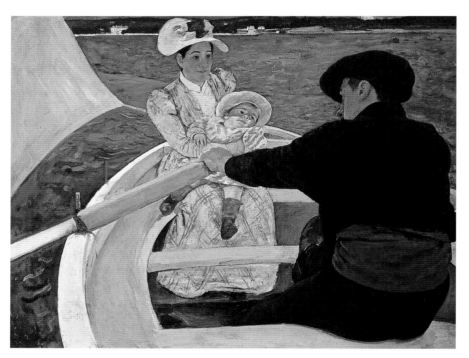

Cassatt also continued to paint in oils, and *The Boating Party* (1893–4; 31), became the centrepiece of her first exhibition in the United States of America. Probably inspired by one of several annual summer visits to Antibes, it is seen by some as a variation of her favoured theme of mother and child by the insertion of the back view of a male figure, the rower. The oar and sail, cut off by the picture's frame and the man's black-clad back, form a composition reminiscent of Hiroshige's *The Benton Ford Across the Oi River* (1856) (see 61).

Vincent van Gogh first discovered Japanese prints in Nuenen, Holland, when reading Edmond de Goncourt's novel *Chérie* (1848), whose hero was the first to voice the famous phrase 'Japonaiserie forever'. Two years later in a letter to his brother Theo from Antwerp, he describes how the Japanese prints he has tacked upon his wall amuse him. This growing interest becomes even more intense in Paris, where in 1887 he organized two exhibitions of prints, one at the café, Le Tambourin, during his stormy relationship with its proprietor, Agostina Segatori, who was probably his mistress when he portrayed her sitting in her café in *Woman at Le Tambourin* (1887). Behind her some Japanese prints can be seen stuck on the walls.

Van Gogh also studied prints at the dealer Bing's premises, purchasing as many prints as he could afford and urging his friends to do the same. He also recommended that they read the de Goncourt novel, *Manette Salomon*, in which the hero, with whom Van Gogh felt a kinship of interests, leafs through a volume of Japanese prints. This experience in his imagination:

gave birth to a day in that enchanting land, a day without shadow, filled with light … a fantasy disturbed by the light of reality, by the wintry sun of Paris, and by the lamp brought into the studio.

Van Gogh's own personal image of Japan began to take palpable form in Paris in 1887 when he painted several careful copies in oils made from tracings and squared-up drawings. These *Japonaiseries* include his painstaking version of Hiroshige's *Sudden Shower over the Shin-Ohashi Bridge* (c.1857) from *One Hundred Views of Edo* (32, 33) painted with a thick, heavy impasto. Years later the great American architect and dealer of Japanese prints, Frank Lloyd Wright (1867–1959), said of this painting:

there's the one that Van Gogh has copied 'after Hiroshige' he called it – but I couldn't see that it was anything but just an oil painting of this print. I don't think he did a very good job of it either, the print was so far superior that it was too bad to look at what he did.

32
Utagawa Hiroshige,
*Sudden Shower over
the Shin-Ohashi Bridge*
from *One Hundred
Views of Edo*,
*c.*1857.
Colour woodcut,
23·7 x 36·2 cm
(9³⁄₈ x 14¹⁄₄ in)

33
Vincent van Gogh,
The Bridge in the Rain
(after Hiroshige),
1887.
Oil on canvas,
73 x 54 cm
(28³⁄₄ x 21¹⁄₄ in).
Van Gogh Museum,
Amsterdam

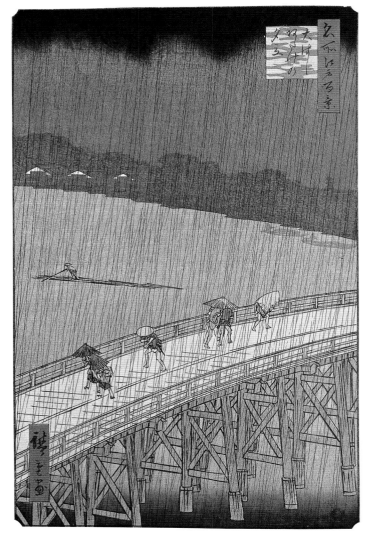

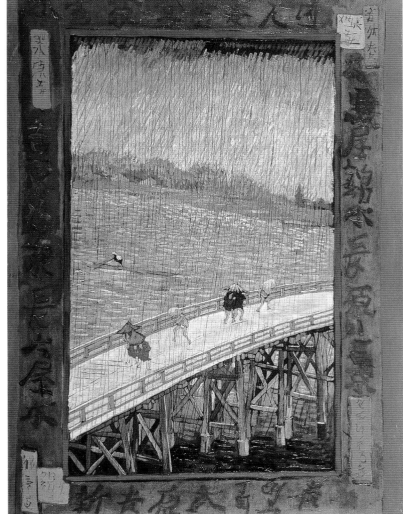

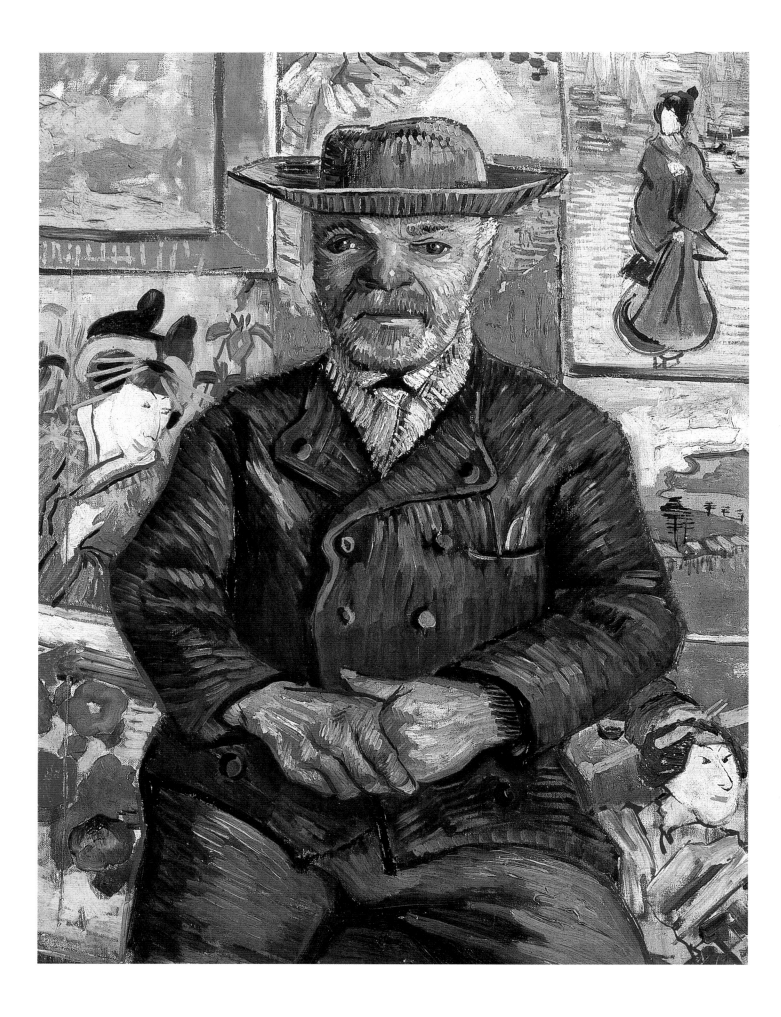

34
Vincent van Gogh,
Portrait of Père Tanguy,
1887–8.
Oil on canvas,
65 x 51 cm
(25¹₂ x 20 in).
Private collection

Around the borders of both this painting and *The Plum Tree Teahouse at Kameido* (c.1887), Vincent copied *kanji* characters which, once doctored by Van Gogh, became little more than gobbledygook, unlike the border of his large copy after the print *Oiran: The Courtesan* by Keisai Eisen (1790–1848). The print had been reproduced on the cover of the journal, *Paris Illustré*, in May 1886. In the borders around the central figure of the Oiran, Van Gogh added a pond with water lilies, reeds and bamboo, two toads and two cranes. Both frogs and cranes were, it should be remembered, slang terms for a prostitute. The 'frogs', actually toads in this print, are copies from Utagawa Yoshimaru's *New Prints of Worms and Insects* dating from 1883, a reminder of how quickly prints were making their way from Japan to Europe.

The most famous of all Van Gogh's works showing Japanese prints, his *Portrait of Père Tanguy* (34), the artist's colour man, was also painted at this time. Colour salesmen, like cobblers, are the subject of legend, for both perform tasks which give them plenty of time to philosophize upon the arts as well as life's ups and downs. Julien (Père) Tanguy started his career as a travelling paint salesman who often met up with Pissarro, Pierre-Auguste Renoir (1891–1919), Monet and other artists in the outer suburbs of Paris. A volunteer soldier for the Commune in 1870, he was captured by the Versailles army and condemned to death, but saved by Degas's friend, Henri Rouart.

After the war Tanguy set up shop in the Rue Clauzel and took a liking to Paul Cézanne (1839–1906), providing him with paints and canvases in return for paintings. Later Van Gogh and Tanguy, politically kindred spirits, also became friends, rather to the dismay of Tanguy's wife, seeing her husband yet again exchange perfectly saleable paints and canvases for unsaleable paintings. He and his shop became something of a legend for the Impressionists.

Van Gogh made three portraits of Tanguy, two oil paintings and one drawing. In all three Tanguy is depicted against a background totally covered with Japanese prints. These were probably from Van Gogh's own collection since Tanguy did not deal in them, but the two men may have shared a private joke of realizing, via the print, a dream visit to Japan composed of such familiar themes as Mount Fuji, geishas, 'morning glory' flowers and typical landscapes of all four seasons.

For Van Gogh Japan became a Utopian dream. In a letter to Gauguin, Vincent recalled the ecstatic feelings he had on his first discovery of the south of France. 'I always remember the emotions which the trip from Paris to Arles evoked. How I kept watching to see if I had already reached Japan! Childish, isn't it?' In the fields around Arles he experimented by using Japanese reed pens with results which, far from being merely Japanese pastiche, can be numbered amongst his most powerful drawings.

In a letter to his sister written shortly after his arrival at Arles in February 1888, Vincent described how his personal vision had changed, that he now saw things 'with an eye more Japanese', and that if she studied Japanese prints she would come to understand modern artists who used bright and pure colours. He added:

as for me here I have no need for Japanese art, for I always tell myself that here I am in Japan, and that consequently I have only to open my eyes and to take in what I have before me.

In late September 1887 Vincent wrote from Arles to his brother, Theo, extolling the benefits of studying Japanese art:

If we study Japanese art, we see a man who is undoubtedly wise, philosophic and intelligent, who spends his time how? In studying the distance between the earth and the moon? No. In studying the policy of Bismarck? No. He studies a single blade of grass … this blade of grass leads him to draw every plant and then the seasons, the wide aspects of the countryside, then animals, then the human figure. So he passes his life, and life is too short to do the whole.

Come now, isn't it almost an actual religion which these simple Japanese teach us, who live in nature as though they themselves were flowers?

In July 1888 Van Gogh read the first edition of Pierre Loti's novel *Madame Chrysanthème*, a cynical precursor of Puccini's *Madame Butterfly* (1904) with illustrations by Luigi Rossi (1853–1923) and Félicien de Myrbach-Rheinfeld (1853–1940) which Van Gogh would transform into his own personal visions of Japan:

Have you read Mme Chrysanthème*? It gave me the impression that the real Japanese have nothing on their walls, that description of the cloister or pagoda where there was nothing (the drawings and curiosities all being hidden in the drawers). That is how you must look at Japanese art, in a very bright room, quite bare and open to the country.*

Van Gogh's continued reading of Loti's novel led to him becoming intrigued by the Japanese word *mousmé* or *musume*, which Loti had defined as follows:

Mousmé is a word for a girl or a very young woman. It is one of the most appealing words in Japanese, for it contains suggestions of moue *(the sweet, funny little moue they have), and above all* frimousse *(that impish little face of theirs).*

Inspired by Rossi's illustration, Van Gogh made his own *Portrait of a Mousmé* (35, 36).

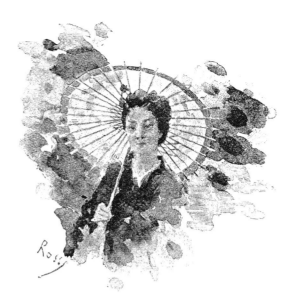

Japonisme

35
Luigi Rossi,
Madame Chrysanthème
from Pierre Loti's
Madame Chrysanthème,
1888

36
Vincent van Gogh,
Portrait of a Mousmé,
1888.
Ink on paper,
32·5 x 24·5 cm
(12³⁄₄ x 9⁵⁄₈ in).
Pushkin Museum,
Moscow

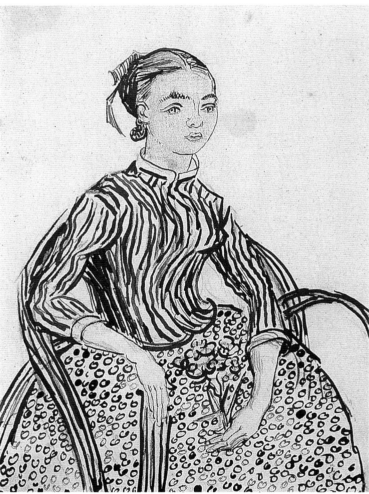

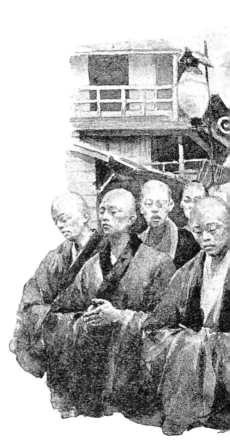

Other illustrations in the novel of funeral processions led by Japanese priests, *bonze* or *bozu* (37), led Vincent to trim his hair, slant his eyes and paint a self-portrait as a *bonze* (38).

Van Gogh was not alone in finding an ideal Japan without actually visiting the 'empire of the rising sun', as Japan was described by the de Goncourt brothers in their novel, *Manette Salomon*. Writing from Norway on 1 March 1895, the painter Claude Monet declared:

I have here a delicious motif, little islands at water level covered by snow, and a mountain in the background. One would say Japan … I did a mountain which is seen everywhere and which makes me think of Fuji-yama.

Monet collected Japanese prints throughout his life (his collection can be seen at his home in Giverny; see Chapter 10). He believed passionately, as he wrote in 1878, that:

We needed the arrival of Japanese albums in our midst, before anyone dared to sit down on a river bank, and juxtapose on canvas a roof which was bright red, a wall which was white, a green poplar, a yellow road and blue water. Before the example given by the Japanese, this was impossible, the painter always lied … all one ever saw on a canvas were subdued colours, drowning in a half-tone.

37
Luigi Rossi,
Funeral Procession from
Pierre Loti's *Madame
Chrysanthème*, 1888

38
Vincent van Gogh,
*Self-Portrait Dedicated
to Paul Gauguin*,
1888.
Oil on canvas,
60·5 x 49·4 cm
(23³₄ x 19¹₂ in).
The Fogg Art Museum,
Harvard University,
Cambridge, MA

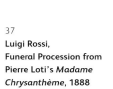

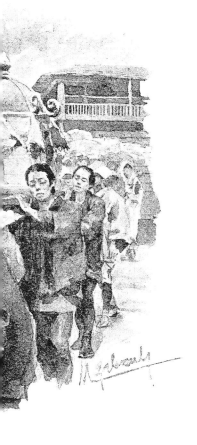

39
Katsushika Hokusai,
South Wind, Clear Dawn,
from *Thirty-Six Views of
Mount Fuji,*
*c.*1830–2.
Colour woodblock,
26 x 38·1 cm
(10¼ x 15 in)

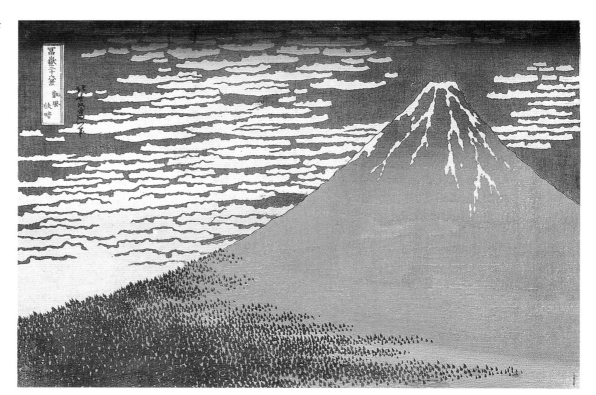

It may well be that Hokusai's *Thirty-Six Views of Mount Fuji*, showing the great volcano in different weather conditions and at different times of day, inspired the sequence paintings such as those by Monet – of haystacks, poplars, the façade of Rouen Cathedral, Westminster Bridge and even the water lilies which occupied the last twenty-five years of his life.

This view is substantiated by the de Goncourt journal in which on 17 February 1892 Edmond noted:

As we were leafing through the big plates of Fujiyama by Hokusai, Manzi [Michel Manzi (1849–1915), Italian painter, publisher, and friend of Degas] said to me: 'Look, here are Monet's great yellow areas.' And he was right. People are not sufficiently aware of how much our contemporary landscape artists have borrowed from these pictures, especially Monet, whom I often encounter at Bing's in the little attic where Lévy is in charge of the Japanese prints.

This encounter took place only a year after Monet had first exhibited fifteen of his *Haystack* series of paintings, whose profound interrelationship with Hokusai's *Thirty-Six Views of Mount Fuji* can be seen particularly clearly between Hokusai's *South Wind, Clear Dawn* (*c.*1830–2), the so-called *Red Fuji* (a copy of which Monet owned; 39), and his own *Haystack, Sunset* (1891; 40).

This is one of twenty-three pictures of haystacks which Monet painted between 1891 and 1892 at different times of day and in different weather conditions. Monet could have seen the full Fuji series either in Bing's shop or at the famous exhibition of Japanese prints held in 1890 at the École des Beaux-Arts in Paris.

It is generally held that Paul Cézanne, of all his contemporaries, the Impressionists, is said to have had the least interest in Japanese art. However, his own long fascination with the depiction of the landscape of Provence led him to paint Mont Ste-Victoire more than sixty times from different view-points during two periods 1882–90 and 1901–6. Remarkably Hokusai did not begin his own endless variations on the theme of Fuji until he was seventy and pursued the subject until his death at ninety. All we shall ever know for certain is that both artists in their later years produced some of the most memorable works of their time, in homage to a specific mountain.

To conclude let us return to Van Gogh's explanation of what he conceived as being the essence of Japan, by turning to another of his letters:

I saw a magnificent and strange effect this evening. A very big boat loaded with coal on the Rhône, moored to the quay. Seen from above, it was all shining and still wet with rain; the water was yellowish white and the clouds pearl grey, the sky violet with an orange streak in the west: the town violet. On the boat some poor boatmen in dirty blue and white came and went carrying the cargo onto the shore. It was pure Hokusai.

Van Gogh might have added, that it was highly reminiscent of the effects of dawn so vividly described in the de Goncourt novel, *Manette Salomon*, which he, a keen reader of novels, had just enjoyed.

For thirty years the Japoniste option would spread from France across Europe and to America. The list of artists affected could be extended to include names as varied as Georges Seurat (1859–91), Paul Signac (1863–1935), Gustav Klimt (1862–1918) and Egon Schiele (1890–1918). The final years of the nineteenth century would see one of the most lasting of all the effects of the Japanese print in the graphic discipline of lithography and its use in the new art form of the coloured poster.

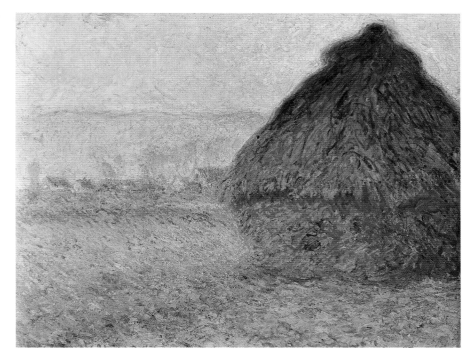

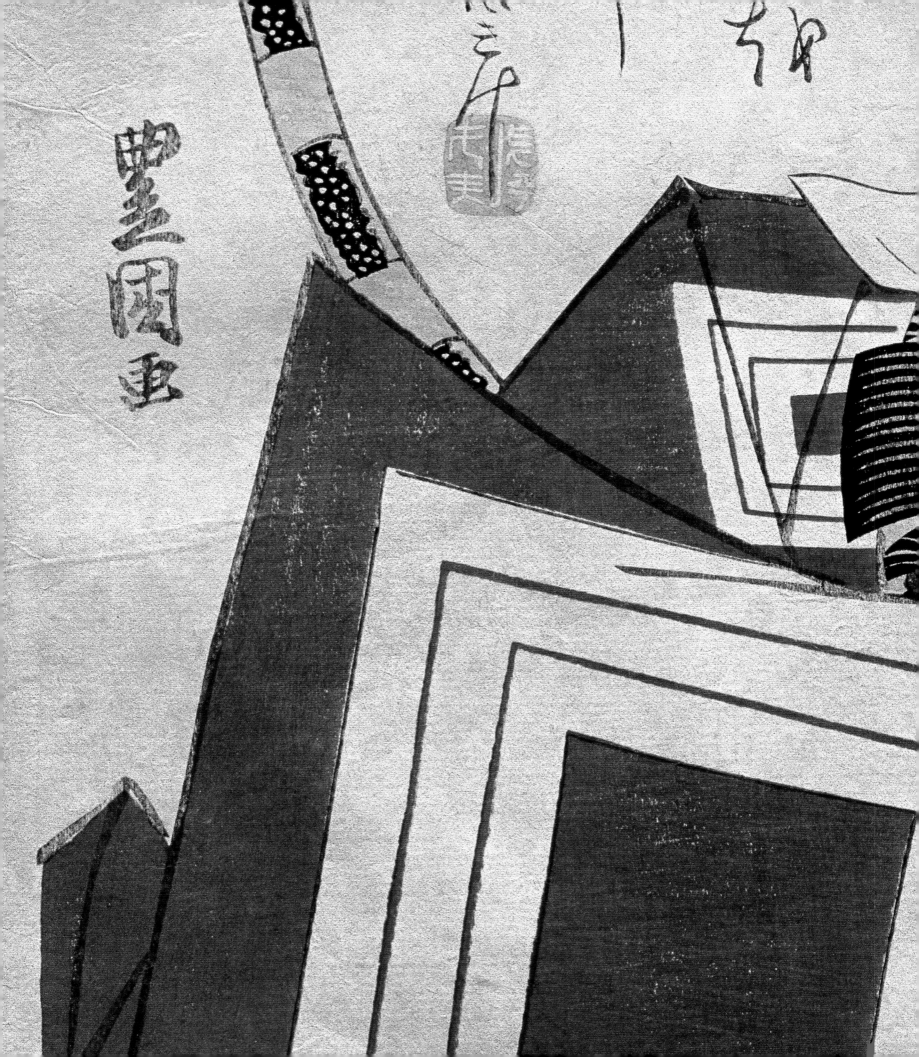

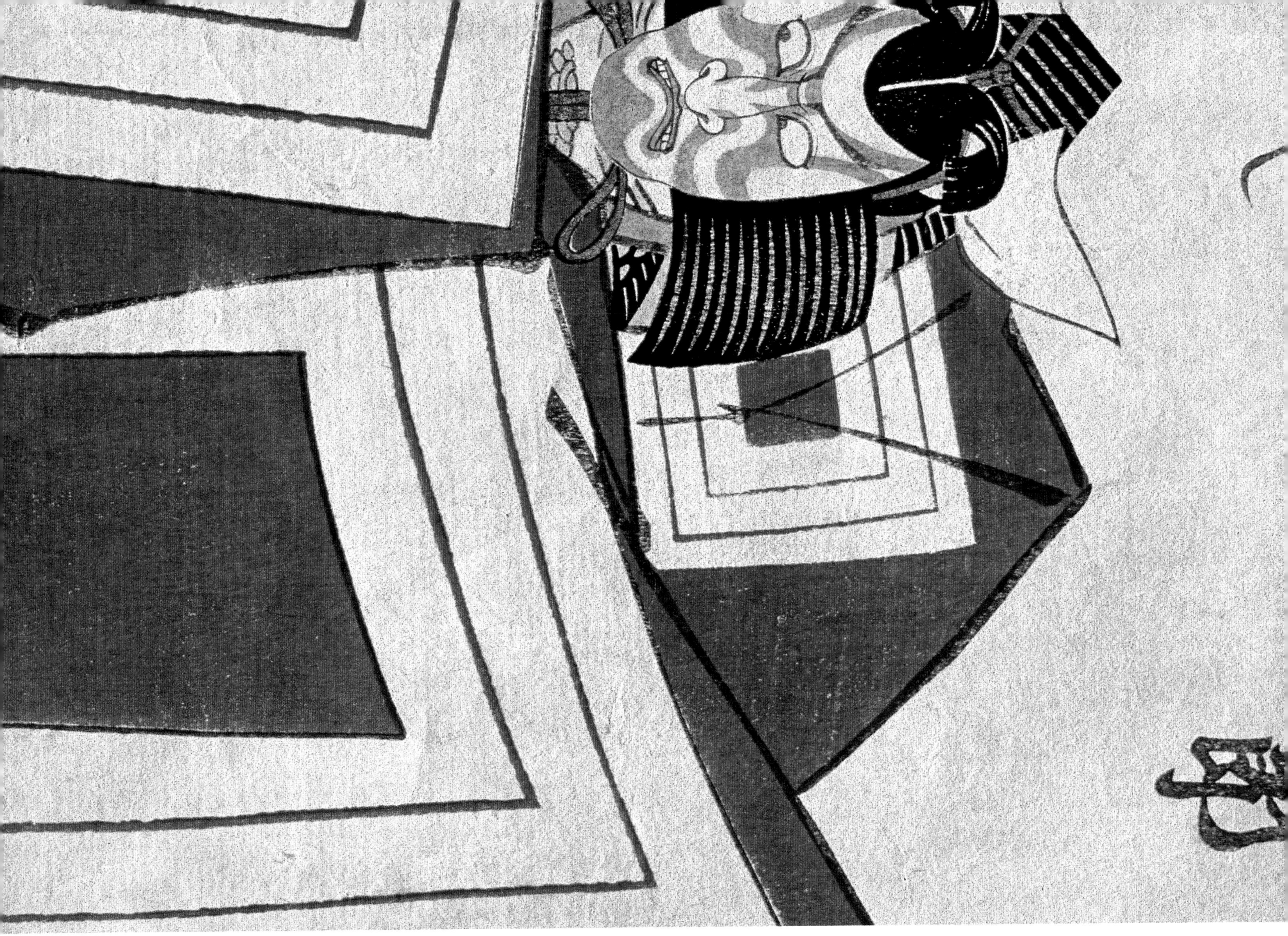

Chapter three:

The Poster and the Japanese Print

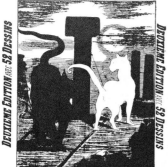

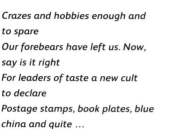

CHAMPFLEURY - LES CHATS

DEUXIEME EDITION AVEC 52 DESSINS

Un volume illustré , Prix 5 Francs
En Vente ici.

Previous page
Utagawa Toyokuni,
Ichikawa Danjuro VII
in the Shibaraku Role
of Kumai Taro
(detail of 44)

41
Édouard Manet,
The Cats' Rendezvous,
from the cover of *Les*
Chats by Champfleury,
1868.
Lithograph

42
Toshusai Sharaku,
The Actor, Sanogawa
Ichimatsu,
1794–5.
Colour woodblock,
38 x 25·7 cm
(15 x 10⅛)

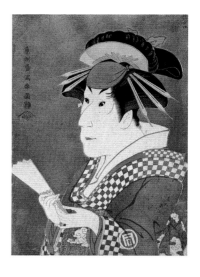

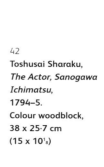

Crazes and hobbies enough and
to spare
Our forebears have left us. Now,
say is it right
For leaders of taste a new cult
to declare
Postage stamps, book plates, blue
china and quite …
Dozens of things most aesthetic
and mystic
Pass for the moment away out of sight
Now is the cult of the poster artistic.
Anonymous, c.1890

Advertisement is an absolute necessity
of modern life … [yet] still there is a
general feeling that the artist who
puts his art into the poster is déclassé –
on the streets – and consequently
of light character.
Aubrey Beardsley, 1894

Today, as neon lights spell out their
imperative messages to the public in
the city centres of London, Paris and
Tokyo, or television commercials issue
their thirty-second categorical
demands, it is hard to understand fully
the dominance of the poster as an
advertising medium in the second
half of the nineteenth century.

The main thrust of commercial
advertising campaigns is now
televisual, for the poster's role is largely
confined to enlivening long waits for
motorists in traffic jams, or cheering up
waiting passengers on the platforms of
underground stations, with artwork
heavily reliant on photographic
imagery.

In the 1860s, before the technical
innovation of colour lithography began
to liberate poster art, the hoardings of
European cities were given over
completely to bill-stickers, who pasted
black-and-white typographical
advertisements one upon another,
creating a monotonous palimpsest of
print. This sorry state of affairs began
to change when it first became
possible for serious artists to pause
from their strict pursuit of 'high art',
and undertake a wider range of
graphic commissions, combining both
Japonisme and the new invention of
colour lithography to create the
'golden age of the poster'. The
poster's impact was greatest in France,
where it intriguingly paralleled the
Impressionist painters' delight in the
rainbow palette of Japanese prints.

There are striking similarities between
the two processes of lithography used
by Western artists and the complex
woodcut technique employed by the
Japanese print-makers. Both achieved
dramatic effects by the bold use of
colour and flat colour areas, thick
outlines and simplicity of design.

The Japanese woodcut was essentially
a team effort. The artist who drew the
original design passed it to an
assistant who pasted the drawing on
to a plank of cherrywood cut across
the grain, which was then taken to a
block-cutter who cut different blocks
for each individual pigment up to as
many as sixteen, far more than is usual
in Europe. The blocks were kept in strict
ratio to each other by *kento* marks,
which ensure the different hues are
exactly in relationship with one
another.

Lithography was discovered by the
German, Aloys Senefelder, in 1798, and
was at first named 'Poly Autography'
from the Greek, meaning literally
'many originals'. Unlike most graphic
disciplines it is not an intaglio process
achieved by cutting *into* a surface, but
a process whereby the picture is made
on top of a surface, using the principle
popularly known as 'water-off-a-
duck's-back' or the antipathy of grease
to water. A drawing with special greasy
chalks and ink is made on a prepared
slab of limestone. The stone is then
washed with nitric acid, wiped with
gum arabic and dampened. When
printing ink is rolled on, it adheres to
the greasy chalks but not to the wet
stone. A palette of different colours
can be achieved by using separate
stones and superimposing one colour
upon another to produce a third.

Manet's lithograph of *The Cats'*
Rendezvous (41), a feline glimpse of
the roofs of Paris, can claim the honour
of being one of the earliest posters, as
it was used to advertise his friend
Champfleury's book *Les Chats* of 1868.
Its weakness is that the coarse
lettering, almost certainly added by
the printer, is not integrated into the
design (the example of the Japanese
print had not yet been fully understood
by Western artists). Japanese prints
had circulated since the 1850s but it
was in the 1870s that they really
began to influence the new art form of
the poster. They could be studied by
poster artists in exhibitions, galleries
and special numbers on Japan in
magazines such as *Paris illustré*.

At the very heart of the *ukiyo-e* print
business was one of its most popular
subjects, *kabuki*, the most junior of the
three major forms of Japanese drama
stemming from the more spiritual *noh*
theatre and the puppet drama *bunraku*.
Kabuki is traditionally said to have
begun in the Tokugawa era in the
early seventeenth century with female
performers who included a number
of ladies of easy virtue. Over the years
their activities became so scandalous
that from 1629 female performers and
dancers were banned outright. From
early on, women's roles in *kabuki*
dramas were played by men known as
onnagata, who can be identified by the
small square of fabric fastened around
their brows to cover their shaven
foreheads, as in a portrait of Sanogawa
Ichimatsu (42) by Sharaku (*fl*.1794–5).

43
Attributed to the Torii school,
Theatre signboard depicting scenes from the play *Nishikigi Sakae Komachi*,
*c.*1758.
Ink, colour and gold on paper,
177·6 x 97·2 cm
(70 x 38¼ in).
Museum of Fine Arts, Boston

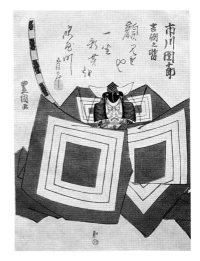

44
Utagawa Toyokuni,
***Ichikawa Danjuro VII in the Shibaraku Role of Kumai Taro*,**
1807.
Colour woodblock,
38·7 x 40 cm
(15¼ x 15¾ in)

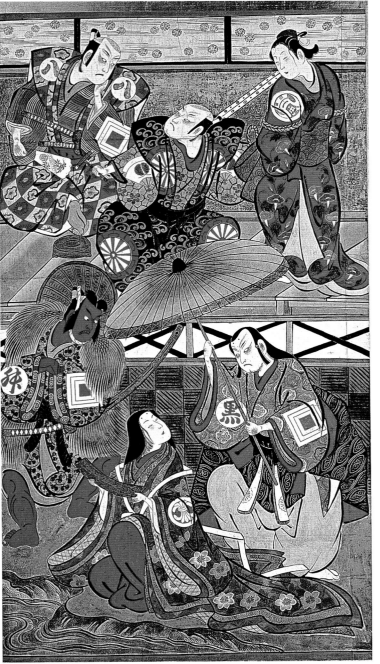

Entertainment always needs advertisement. A few rare signboards (*kanban*) for some *kabuki* performances survive, the earliest dating from 1758, acting as a poster and attracting the passing crowds to enter the theatre and enjoy the performances of leading actors (43). This signboard portrays two scenes from a drama. In the bottom half, the board tells one of the incidents befalling the poetess Ono no Komachi, who is threatened by the villain played by Danjuro IV, a member of one of the great theatrical dynasties, which survives today.

The sheer theatricality of the signboard prepares us for the dramatic work of such artists as Hiroshige, Kunisada, Kuniyoshi (*c.*1892–1953), Shunsho and especially Toyokuni (1769–1825; 44), whose portrayal of an actor striking a pose in an *otokodate* role (a role similar to that of Robin Hood – robbing the rich to help the poor) has just the bold simplicity of outline which so excited European artists. Such theatrical prints are brilliant records of individual performances, capturing the memorable moments when a climax in the dramatic action elicits a roar of applause from the fans as the action freezes for a minute or so. These prints would be passed from hand to hand in teahouses, thus serving an immediate purpose as 'fliers' to advertise actors or forthcoming performances, but coincidentally also preserving, like a fly in amber, the buzz and excitement of the *kabuki* stage. Single actor prints such as this were sold by hawkers to the audience.

One of the most important artists to portray the *kabuki* stage was Toshosai Sharaku, a mysterious figure appearing in 1794 and disappearing within a year without trace. In just nine months he produced 144 prints of actors appearing at the three *kabuki* theatres in Edo. He was particularly successful in capturing the grimaces and grotesque expressions which convey the actors' stage personae, and excelled at brutal close-up images, so cruel that it has been suggested that he was murdered by one of his sitters. Sharaku's powerful imagery is seen at its most effective in such noteworthy examples as the actor, Tanimura Torazo, in *The Loved Wife's Parti-Coloured Reins*, published in 1794 (45).

There were, of course, prints on other *ukiyo-e* subjects, many inspired by life in the chief centre of pleasure at Edo, the enclosed quarter of the Yoshiwara. On entering it the visitor was confronted with a complex hierarchy of merchants, waitresses, musicians, geishas and prostitutes. Off-duty actors and incognito samurai were often among the clients. The prints which record this society were many and various but included the depiction of such themes as Kunisada's *At the Dressing Table*, in which a woman muses on the aesthetic pleasures of the colour white, such as white chrysanthemums, white snow or just being a beauty with white skin.

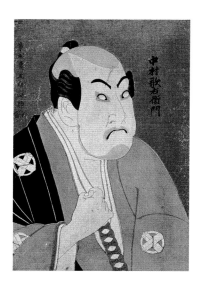

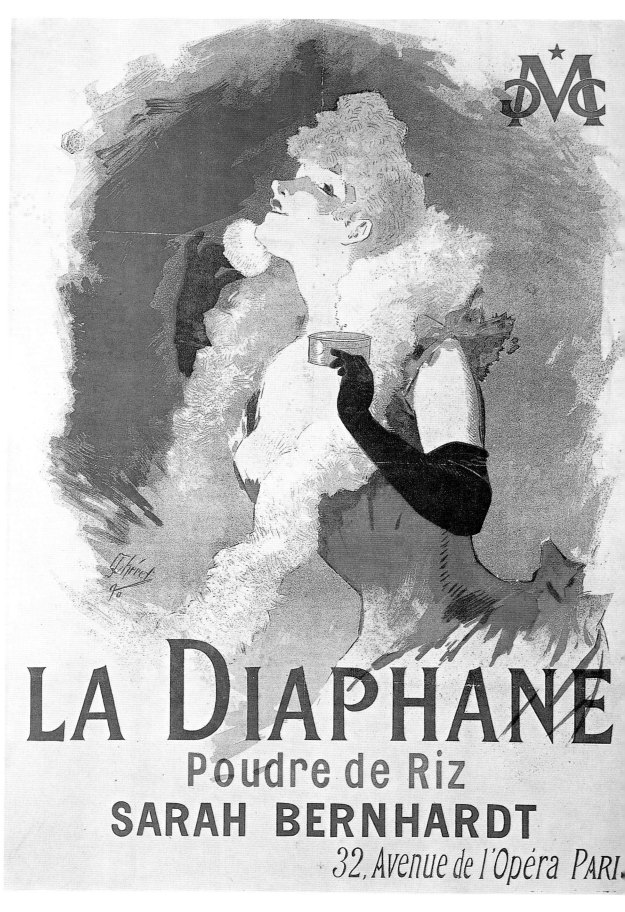

Japonisme

Such prints of *bijin* – beautiful women – not only captivated their immediate purchasers, but also found their way back to Europe, and in particular Paris, where they would inspire the first great practitioner of the art of poster design, Jules Chéret (1836–1932), who towards the end of his career defined his aims:

The poster artist must be a psychologist; he must have gone through a hard school and become familiar with the logical and optical laws of his art. He must invent something that will attract and excite even the average man when the street scene passes before his eyes as he walks along the pavement or drives past in his car; and nothing, I believe, is better suited to this purpose than a simple, charming and yet captivating picture in bright, yet harmonious colours.

Several of these aims were also described in an article of 1901 on Japanese art and the poster, in which the critic Raymond Needham described the essential qualities a poster required for success:

Take any representative Japanese print – a book illustration, a broadsheet or a theatre bill – and it will be found to embody all that a good poster should. One dominant idea is presented graphically, beautifully, the detail does not weaken, but actually enforces the motif.

45
Toshusai Sharaku,
*The Actor Tanimura Torazo,
as the Villain in The Loved
Wife's Parti-Coloured Reins*,
1794.
Colour woodblock,
37 x 24·9 cm
(14$^1_2$ x 9$^3_4$ in)

46
Jules Chéret,
La Diaphane,
1890.
Colour lithograph,
86 x 59 cm
(33$^7_8$ x 23$^1_4$ in)

47
Georges Goursat ('Sem'),
Palais de Glace,
c.1910.
Colour lithograph,
30 x 46 cm (11$^3_4$ x 18 in)

*There is not a superfluous line, the
colour scheme of flat tints is fresh and
striking but always harmonious. The
composition gives an idea of balance
and breadth, but affords no hint as
to how these qualities have been
obtained … The general effect is
decorative in the highest degree, may
be humorous and is certainly pervaded
by the 'hidden soul of harmony'.*

As a boy, Chéret was apprenticed to
a lithographer, and then worked in
London for seven years studying
developments in the processes which
enabled posters to be produced in a
larger format. More than any other
artist, he effected the change-over
from the old typographical poster to
the pictorial poster, in which female
charms demonstrate the classic
advertising dictum that sex sells. This
is demonstrated in posters for beauty
aids – one for soap and one for a face-
powder *La Diaphane* (1890; 46), to
which the great actress Sarah
Bernhardt lent her name – an early
example of the now familiar process of
celebrity product endorsement, and an
image that recalls the flat white make-
up of the geisha.

When Chéret began designing posters,
Napoleon III (r.1852–70) was
demolishing the old narrow streets
of Paris, and Baron Haussmann was
building wide boulevards with large
white buildings on either side. These
walls provided perfect sites for the
new flamboyant posters.

The citizens of Paris lived in public by
frequenting cafés, and at the hour of
the aperitif, half the population was
sitting at little tables on the pavement
watching the other half go by. Chéret's
posters provided the perfect background to the comings and goings of
Parisian life. Indeed, in an interview
with the English critic, Charles Hiatt,
Chéret maintained that for him,
posters were not necessarily a good
form of advertising but that they made
excellent murals. It was his great
achievement to take the visual
language of popular folk art, add the
delicate colours of the butterfly wings
and Japanese prints he kept by him
as he worked, and produce a new art
form. His posters of the 1890s were
aptly described by the contemporary
critic, Crauzat, as 'a hooray of reds,
a hallelujah of yellows and a primal
scream of blues'.

Chéret loved to portray the constantly
changing productions at popular music
halls such as the Folies-Bergère,
El Dorado and Olympia. At the time of
the *belle époque* (1865–1914), dancers
whirled across the stage in a tornado
of sound, created by the most famous
singers of their day, with loud orchestral accompaniment in the form of
a noisy clash of cymbals. Another
popular social activity was ice-skating
(47), portrayed both by Chéret and
Georges Goursat ('Sem'; 1863–1934).
Sem was the chronicler of the social
scene in Paris, Biarritz and Monte Carlo
before the First World War.

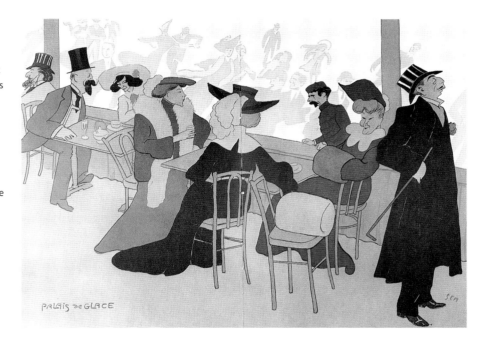

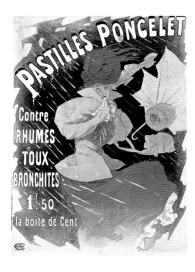

Japonisme

48
Jules Chéret,
Pastilles Poncelet,
1896.
Colour lithograph,
127·3 x 92·4 cm
(50⅛ x 36⅜ in)

49
Utagawa Toyokuni,
*Two Actors in a Snow
Scene, One Dressed
as a Woman*,
c.1814.
Colour woodblock,
37·4 x 50·8 cm
(14¾ x 20 in)

A number of Chéret's annual Christmas seasonal posters were entitled *étrennes* – literally, festive gifts – which frequently included Japanese toys, dolls, fans, masks, paper sparrows and goldfish. These posters enlivened the streets when shown on the 'Morrisy', round advertising columns invented in the 1860s as a device for displaying playbills, which can still be seen today. Oscar Wilde, after a visit to Paris in 1891, eulogized 'the charming kiosks', which, 'when illuminated at night from within, are as lovely as a fantastic Chinese lantern, especially when the transparent advertisements are from the clever pencil of M. Chéret.'

The public loved to collect Chéret posters in proof state before the letterpress was added, such as the poster for *Pastilles Poncelet* (48), in which the falling sleet forms a wintery comparison with Toyokuni's *Snow Scene* (49). Like Hokusai, Chéret lived to a great age, producing 1,200 posters in the course of his long career. According to a contemporary:

when he [Chéret] dealt with a stone already impregnated with yellow, blue or red ink, he projected a fine shower of colour that ... resulted in gradations and ranges of tones whose secret seemed impenetrable. He did it with the dexterity of a Japanese, while humming or chatting with his charming French gaiety..

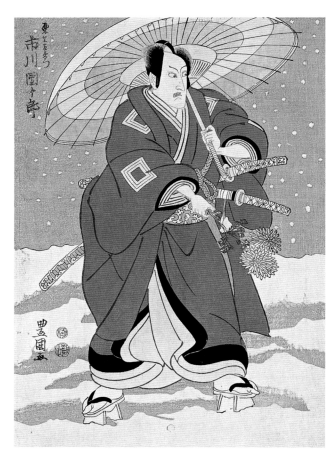

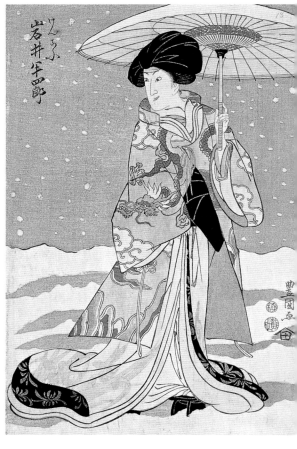

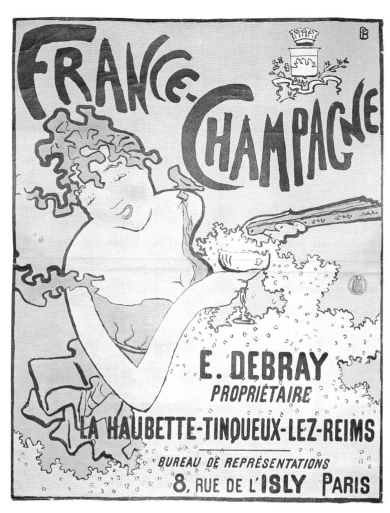

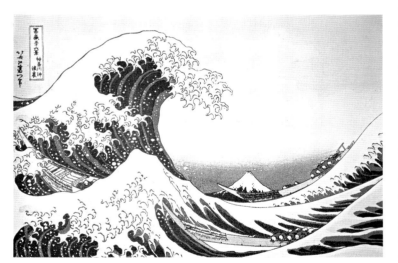

50
Pierre Bonnard,
France-Champagne,
1891.
Colour lithograph,
79·3 x 59·9 cm
(31¹⁄₈ x 23¹⁄₂ in)

51
Katsushika Hokusai,
Beneath the Wave off Kanagawa
(*The Great Wave*) from *Thirty-*
***Six Views of Mount Fuji*,**
c.1830–2.
Colour woodblock,
25·7 x 37·9 cm
(10¹⁄₈ x 15 in)

While Chéret was the father of the poster, 'admired by policemen and people of taste alike', the great master of the discipline was Chéret's pupil, Henri de Toulouse-Lautrec (1864–1901). His friend, Gauzi, said that Lautrec considered the Japanese his 'brothers' as they were closer to his restricted size and beside them he looked normal. Interviewed in old age, Chéret hailed Lautrec as his successor and heir, saying, 'Lautrec is a master'. Lautrec's initial interest in the poster discipline was not aroused by Chéret's work, however, but by that of Pierre Bonnard (1867–1947) and his *France-Champagne*, a prize-winning entry in a poster competition advertising a wine merchant (50). Bonnard's poster is appropriately awash with the bubbles of its product, a frothy sea from which emerges the model, a chic Parisienne borrowed from Chéret, fan in one hand, glass in the other, who giggles her way onto a poster perfectly 'on message' and nicely calculated to achieve its aim and sell its product – champagne. As a composition, Bonnard's poster brilliantly mingles lessons absorbed both from Gauguin (for example, his use of fluent black lines set against a vivid yellow paper; see 135) and the Japanese print. From the most famous of all Japanese prints, Hokusai's *The Great Wave* (51), Bonnard borrows and satirizes the stylized spray and transforms it into the bubbly froth of the champagne.

Impressed by the success of the poster *France-Champagne*, Lautrec sought out Bonnard to discuss poster design. It was an art form which Lautrec came to love and which he would completely revolutionize, steeped as he was in the world of the Japanese print, from which he acquired various stylistic mannerisms – bold outlines, trimmed edges and the use of a diverse range of flat colour.

Lautrec's name will always be associated with that of the music hall in the Montmartre area of Paris, the Moulin Rouge (52). The worldwide fame of the Moulin Rouge began on 6 October 1889, when it gave birth to the cancan. The club had become badly run down under its previous manager, and was given a face-lift by an enterprising businessman who turned it into a glittering dream palace, with rooms decorated in Oriental and Moorish styles, where people could dance in an open courtyard under the gaze of a huge wooden elephant. The arms of the mill, which gave the cabaret its name, still keep turning today. The hall's great attraction was a dance quadrille from the nearby music hall, Elysée-Montmartre. Its wild dancers vied with each other in the spectacle of the cancan, culminating in a jump in the air, an ear-piercing shriek and the splits.

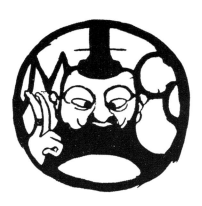

52
Henri de Toulouse-
Lautrec,
Moulin Rouge: La Goulue,
1891.
Colour lithograph,
191 x 117 cm
(75$\frac{1}{8}$ x 46$\frac{1}{4}$ in)

53
Keisai Eisen,
The Lonely Night House,
c.1848.
Colour woodcut,
36·5 x 25·5 cm
(14$\frac{3}{8}$ x 10 in)

54
Henri de Toulouse-
Lautrec,
*Self-Portrait as a Sword
Hilt (Tsuba)*, bookplate
for Maurice Guibert,
1894

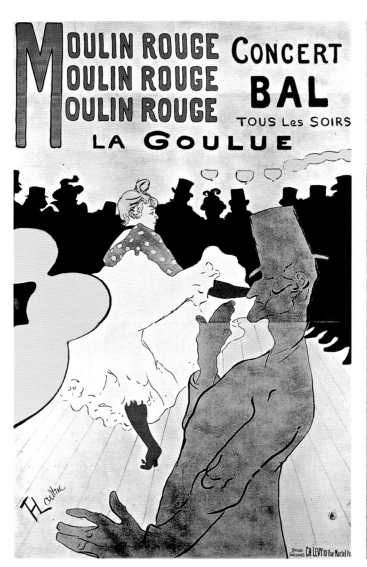

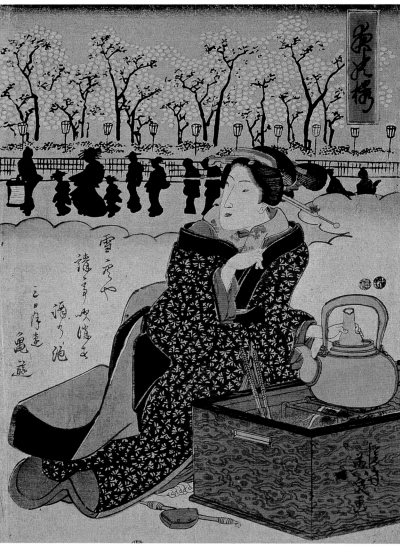

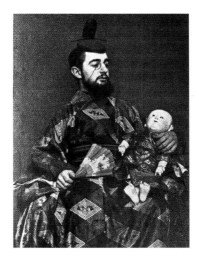

The female dancers, notably La Goulue and Jane Avril, competed with each other, and also danced with the remarkable double-jointed male dancer, Valentin le Désossé, which means literally, the Boneless Wonder. He is portrayed in the foreground while La Goulue dominates the centre of the dance floor surrounded by an admiring circle of spectators depicted in silhouette. Similar compositions using a distant frieze of silhouettes can be seen in Japanese woodcuts, an example being *The Lonely Night House* by Keisai Eisen, which shows the shadowy figures of a courtesan's entourage on a spring evening (53).

Lautrec was so enamoured of Japanese prints that he was prepared to exchange one of his own works for a coveted example. He sent to Japan for special inks and brushes, and designed his own seal-like monogram, derived from a Japanese source, a *tsuba* or sword hilt (54), and loved to dress up in Japanese costume (55). His favoured subject matter – popular entertainers, dancers and dance halls, bars and restaurants, prostitutes and their activities – have many affinities with themes often to be seen in Japanese prints, as for example, *Debauchery* (56).

Lautrec owed a particular debt to Utamaro, and there are obvious parallels between his *Elles* album (1896), the lithographic products of Lautrec's stay in the brothels of Montmartre, and Utamaro's works produced in the 'Houses of Pleasure' in the Yoshiwara. Lautrec owned a copy of Utamaro's erotic work, *The Poem of the Pillow*, which he had acquired from the de Goncourt brothers (57).

Lautrec's technical debts to Japanese prints were extensive. As Berthe Morisot once observed:

the imaginative and total integration of image and lettering into one decorative and instructive whole in his posters also owes much to Japanese prototypes.

From them he also gained his assurance in posing single figures in bold silhouette against a neutral background, as, for example, in the famous poster *Ambassadeurs: Aristide Bruant dans son Cabaret*.

The poster entitled *Divan Japonais* was made for a café which was transformed in 1893 by decorations of lanterns and bamboo chairs in what was considered to be the Japanese style (58). In the design of the poster, Lautrec decided to adopt Japanese principles of composition, cropping off the image by truncating the body of the singer, Yvette Guilbert, who is recognizable only by her distinctive black gloves.

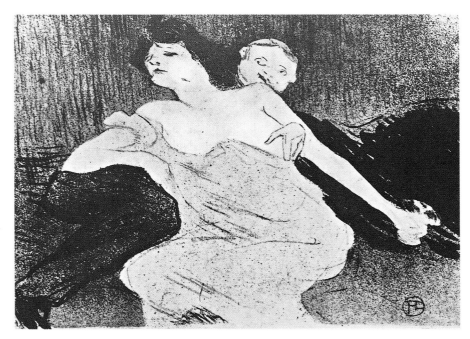

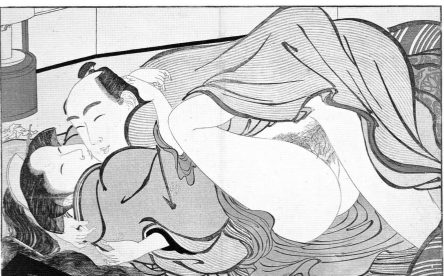

58
Henri de Toulouse-Lautrec,
Divan Japonais,
1893.
Colour lithograph,
81·5 x 62·3 cm
(32 x 24½ in)

59
Kitagawa Utamaro,
*Servant on the Verandah
of the Restaurant
Nakataya*,
c.1794.
Colour woodblock

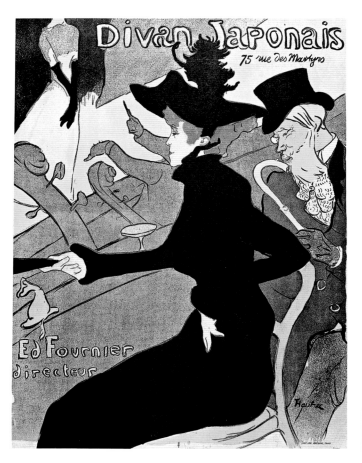

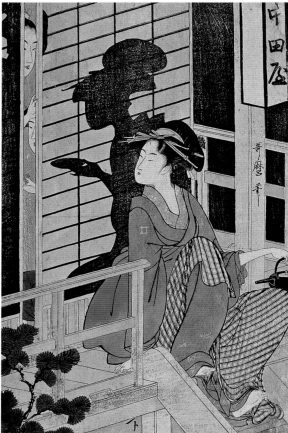

Years later Yvette Guilbert recalled the
venue:

*a little hall such as you may see in a
provincial café, with a low ceiling and
where at a pinch a hundred and fifty
or two hundred people might be got in
… a platform perched about five feet
above the floor made it necessary to
remember that I mustn't raise my
arms incautiously or I should knock
them against the ceiling. Oh! that
ceiling where the heat from the gas
footlights was such that our heads
swam in a suffocating furnace!*

Lautrec brilliantly conveys this feeling of
claustrophobia by cutting off Guilbert's
head completely, thus concentrating
our visual attention upon the elegant
seated figure of the dancer, Jane Avril.
The flat patterning, asymmetric
composition, elongated figures and bold
outlines reveal the influence of the
Japanese wood block, all elements to be
found in Utamaro Kitagawa's depiction
of a similar scene showing a servant on
the verandah of the restaurant
Nakataya (*c*.1794; 59). Although
Lautrec greatly admired Jane Avril, who
became a close friend, she complained
that Lautrec's posters of her always
made her look like a monster.

60
Henri de Toulouse-Lautrec,
Jane Avril au Jardin
de Paris,
1893.
Colour lithograph,
130 x 94 cm
(51⅛ x 37 in)

61
Utagawa Hiroshige,
The Benten Ford Across
the Oi River,
1858.
Colour woodblock,
35·3 x 24 cm
(13⅞ x 9½ in)

She may have been thinking of *Jane Avril au Jardin de Paris* (1893; 60), a work deriving its composition from Japanese prints, notably in the depiction of the double-bass player, whose face is half concealed by his hand that holds the instrument, which dominates the framing of the scene. It is rewarding to compare Lautrec's portrayal of the truncated hand with the bony knee of Hiroshige's oarsman in his *The Benten Ford Across the Oi River* of 1858 (61).

The notoriety that invariably surrounded the launch of Lautrec's posters put off many performers who still preferred to rely on Chéret for less innovative designs. One such figure was Loie Fuller, the most daring and original dancer of the 1890s. Her performances inspired poems from poets as diverse as Stephen Mallarmé, Arthur Symons and W B Yeats, while Chéret produced for her a poster printed in four colours of her famous *Fire Dance* in which she performed upon a stage of glass illuminated from all sides. A page of one of Whistler's sketchbooks vibrates with drawings inspired by her butterfly dance, which had a Japanese prototype. A fascinating contemporary of Fuller was Sadayakko, a Japanese actress (see also Chapter 7), who, with her company, was presented by Fuller at her theatre during the 1900 Paris exhibition.

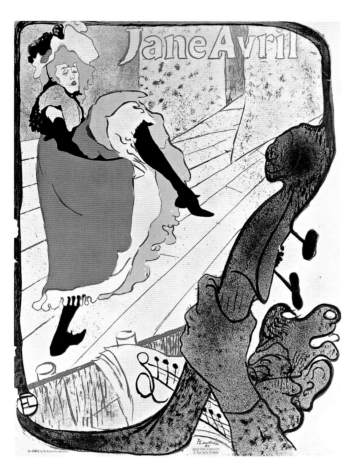

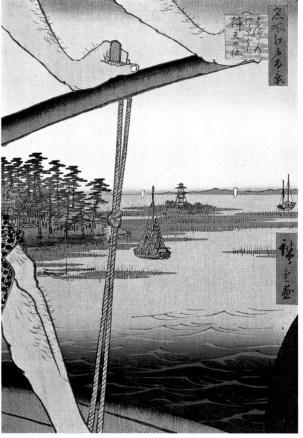

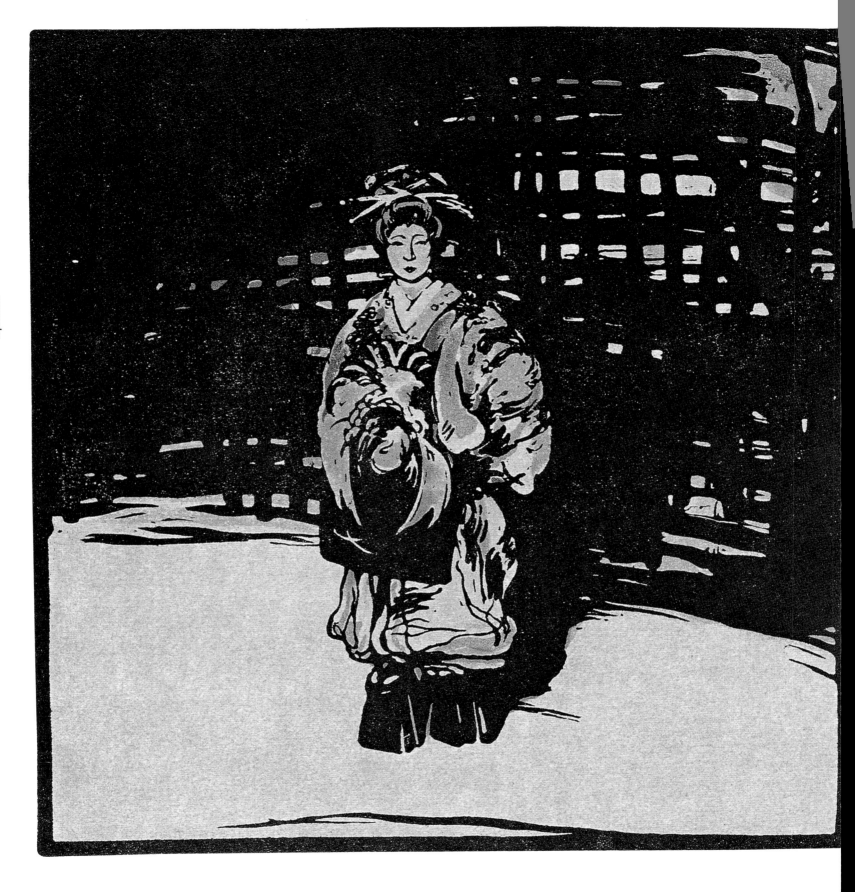

62
William Nicholson,
Sadayakko,
*c.*1900–1.
Colour lithograph,
image: 24·6 x 23·7 cm
(9³⁄₄ x 9³⁄₈ in)

63
Eugène Grasset,
La Vitrioleuse,
1894.
Colour lithograph,
59·4 x 43 cm
(23³⁄₈ x 17 in)

64
Jacques Villon,
Le Grillon,
1899.
Colour lithograph,
130 x 93 cm
(51¹⁄₈ x 36⁵⁄₈ in)

Sadayakko is seen here in a woodcut (62) by William Nicholson (1872–1949), one of the British poster artists known as the Beggarstaff Brothers.

Eugène Grasset (1841–1917), who would become a major French poster artist, began his career working under the architect Eugène Viollet-le-Duc (1814–79) on the restoration of the medieval walled city of Carcassonne in the south of France. He worked with great flair in an artistic discipline with similar problems to the poster, that of designing stained glass, and was also deeply influenced by the strong lines of Japanese prints. As a poster designer he met with mixed fortunes. In 1893 he interpreted the great actress Sarah Bernhardt as Joan of Arc. The Maid of Orléans was France's national heroine, and Grasset treated the subject with respectful dignity. The solemnity of the image did not meet with the unqualified approval of the actress, who wanted a more dramatic interpretation of her stage role, and demanded alterations which Grasset carried out with great reluctance, thus ending their collaboration. Grasset went on in 1899 to depict the terrifying image of a morphine addict injecting herself, and *La Vitrioleuse* preparing to throw vitriol at a target (63), which closely relate to the powerful close-up, large-scale heads of actors in performance by Toyokuni and particularly Sharaku (see 45).

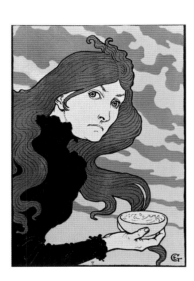

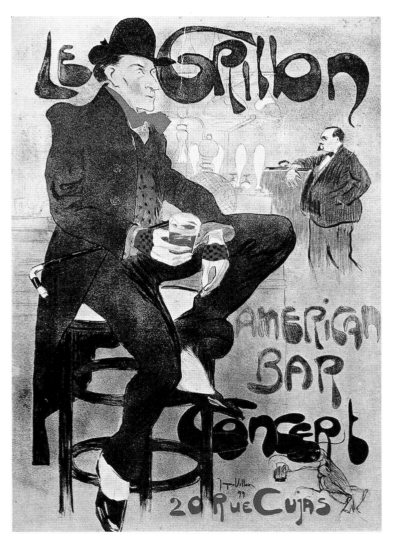

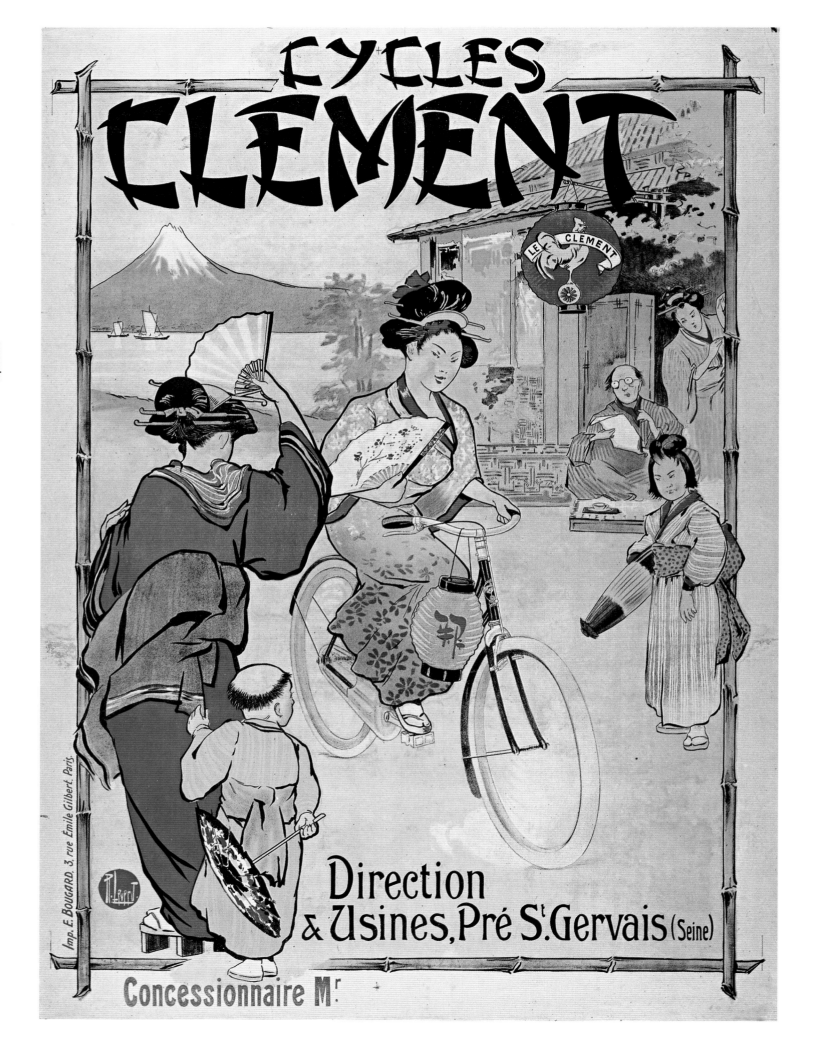

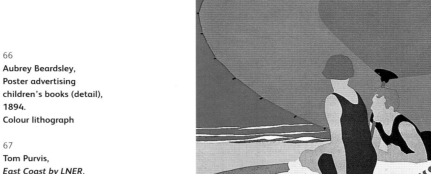

65
**Poster for Clement
bicycles,
*c.*1906.
Colour lithograph**

66
**Aubrey Beardsley,
Poster advertising
children's books (detail),
1894.
Colour lithograph**

67
**Tom Purvis,
East Coast by LNER,
1925.
Colour lithograph,
100.6 x 126.5 cm
(39⁵⁄₈ x 49³⁄₄ in)**

The artist, Jacques Villon (1875–1963), who would become one of the first abstract painters, created in 1899 a memorable Art Nouveau poster, *Le Grillon* (64). A friend of both Théophile Alexandre Steinlen (1859–1923) and Lautrec, whom he met at the Moulin Rouge, Villon's work has splendid power and originality, and its calligraphy is highly reminiscent of Japanese prints, especially in the striking lettering which draws attention to the smart 'American Bar' at the restaurant.

Among the most amusing and socially interesting themes of the turn of the twentieth century were posters of bicycles and typewriters. Two anonymous posters show intrepid Japanese girls, one actually wearing a kimono while cycling (65), while another uses a typewriter. For women, the bicycle, with its freedom of movement, of association and of dress, was a significant and liberating instrument. By featuring women, the manufacturer also implied to the contemporary viewer that the bicycle handled easily, and that 'femininity' was not lost, as some critics insinuated, but actually enhanced by riding a bicycle. Women were therefore not only portrayed, but idealized, in bicycle posters all over Europe and America.

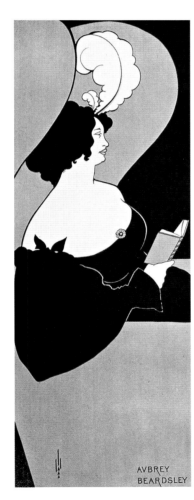

AUBREY
BEARDSLEY

All these artists shared one thing in common. They owed and acknowledged a great debt to the art of Japan. As in every aspect of the graphic arts which he essayed, Aubrey Beardsley (1872–98) introduced into his posters novel qualities of remarkable originality and his indebtedness to the Japanese print is clearly revealed in his placing of the figure and the flat treatment of patterns on garments.

Beardsley's delight in being deliberately perverse could take many forms. In 1894, great controversy was aroused by his poster for a rarefied double bill of new plays, one by the young poet W B Yeats at the Avenue Theatre. The comic journal *Punch*, unable to resist a pun, chaffed in mock Cockney, 'ave a new poster', and went on to regret that 'your Japanese Rossetti girl is not a thing to be admired …' Criticism was also levelled at Beardsley's poster for children's books where, indeed, the seated lady does seem a little *too* adult to be reading books for children (66). The tall upright format of the vertical panel on the left of both posters reflects Beardsley's love of Japanese art, and his study of 'pillar' prints – *hashira-e* – tall prints which could only be displayed in the formal alcove of the Japanese home like a hanging scroll painting, or on the side of a square wooden pillar.

The difficulties inherent in designing for such a tall and slim shape were just the type of challenge which Beardsley enjoyed. In an interview Beardsley claimed to prefer poster work to book illustration, remarking that although he personally had no great care for colour, he recognized that its use was essential for posters. For him poster work:

pays well and it's interesting. I enjoy the colour. I myself only use flat tints, and work as if I was colouring a map, the effect aimed at being that produced by a Japanese print.

With the greater ease of travel and more generous holidays of the twentieth century a growing demand arose for travel posters featuring in particular the attractions of seaside resorts. One of the last major figures to use Japanese-inspired themes in designing posters was the Scottish artist Tom Purvis (1888–1957). His poster for the London and North Eastern Railway with its vivid red parasol casting its protecting brown shade over two bathers wearing black costumes under a flawless azure blue sky (67), demonstrates the ongoing validity of a subject popular both in Japanese prints and advertising. Despite a lifetime's experience this is the dream we all have of the weather on Bank Holidays in England, the triumph of hope over experience, a wish to enter the always confident world of the poster where the sun always shines.

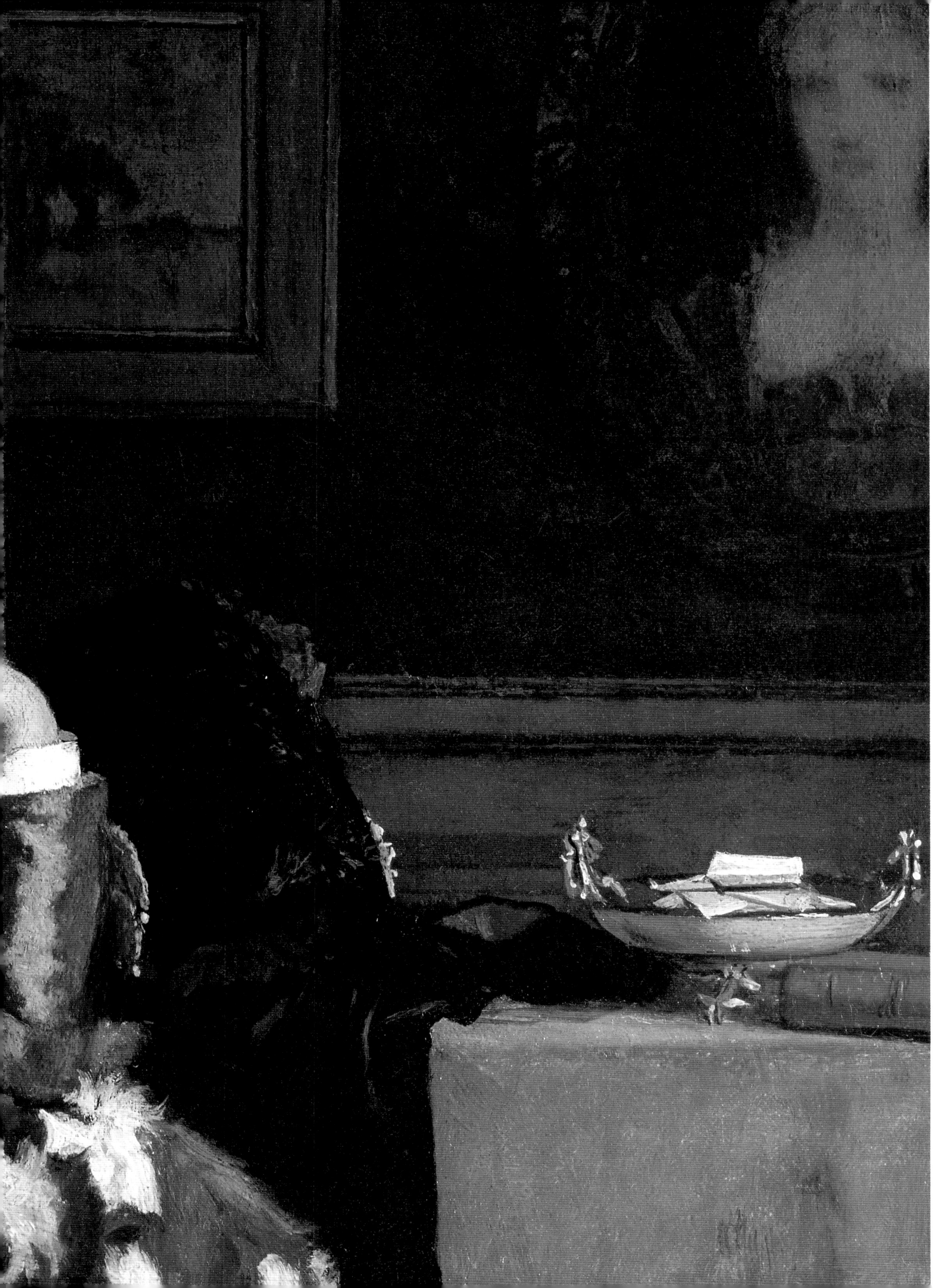

Chapter four: The Decorative Arts

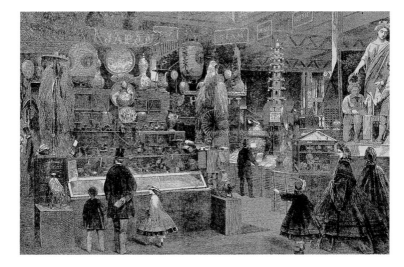

Previous page
Alfred Stevens,
The Duchess (formerly
known as *The Blue
Dress*), *c.*1880
(detail of 80)

68
*The International
Exhibition: The Japanese
Court* engraving from the
Illustrated London News,
1862

*Avoid the European and cleave to
the Oriental.*
W J Loftie, 1876

*The very 'marks' on the bottom of a
piece of rare crockery are able to throw
me into a gibbering ecstasy; and I
could forsake a drowning relative to
help dispute about whether the stopper
of a departed Buon Retiro scent-bottle
was genuine or spurious. Many people
say that for a male person, bric-a-brac
hunting is about as robust a business
as making doll-clothes, or decorating
Japanese pots with decalomanie
butterflies would be …*
Mark Twain, 1879–80

Although the shogunate regime of
Satsuma began to make overtures to
show goods in the 1851 exhibition in
the Crystal Palace, London, the times
were not propitious, and Japan was not
represented. By the time of the 1862
exhibition (68) a selection of Japanese
artefacts was made by the first British
diplomat in Japan, Sir Rutherford
Alcock. He had been the first
representative of the British Crown
in Edo since 1859 where he had collected 'a fair sample of the industrial
arts of the Japanese'.

The success of the exhibition was
marred by the untimely death of the
Prince Consort, but after the show
closed, both goods which had failed
to arrive in time and objects from the
display of prints, ceramics, textile
stencils and furniture were all bought
up by the Regent Street Oriental
Warehouse of Farmer and Rogers.
It was in this shop that Rossetti is
reputed to have introduced Whistler to
the manager Arthur Lasenby Liberty,
who was later to found his own famous
firm in 1875. Indeed Liberty's would
become the most important cross-
pollinating centre of the Aesthetic
Movement and Japonisme.

It was not until 1867 in Paris that
Japan officially participated in an
international exhibition. As was often
the case, the show was partly
motivated politically by the shogun
government which was on the brink
of collapse, but sought and found a
sympathetic supporter in France.

Japanese art also found its champions
in England. John C Robinson was an
immensely able administrator who
was largely responsible not only for
the Museum of Ornamental Art in
London, which eventually became the
Victoria and Albert Museum, but also
for making even the name South
Kensington, the area which still houses
the museum, virtually synonymous with
the decorative arts.

In 1855 he was laudatory in his
appraisal of the first Japanese
porcelain acquired before the
foundation of the museum in 1852:

*The Japanese porcelain is perhaps
distinguished by a purer taste in
design, the shapes of the pieces are
simpler and more elegant than the
Chinese, whilst in the painted
decoration, grotesque or fantastic
subjects are less affected; simple
renderings of natural flowers and
foliage, and elegant conventionalized
floral ornaments, being very frequent.
In colour, generally speaking, Japanese porcelain is fuller and richer in
effect than the Chinese.*

For its date this is a highly perceptive
appraisal of Japanese decoration and it
explains clearly the distinctive qualities
of the novel artefacts which both
Britain and the continent would so
greatly admire. This admiration would
soon reflect the truth of the old adage
that 'imitation is the sincerest form of
flattery' – however, some such
imitations would lead to extremely
strange and bizarre forms.

From the very beginning of the influx,
Japanese artefacts were copied all over
Britain and Europe – sometimes with
great sensitivity, sometimes with
appalling vulgarity or comic
misunderstanding of Japanese motifs.

This plagiarizing process is more
evident in the production of ceramics
than in any other discipline. The
reason for much of the great
popularity of Japanese wares lay in
their ability to present natural objects
in a completely novel manner. The
thought process was that by studying
and copying Japan, one could come to
a better understanding of one's own
place in nature. Throughout Europe,
wherever the ceramic disciplines of
pottery and porcelain flourished,
copying was rife and industrial
espionage thrived. Tracing the
resemblances and differences between
prototype and copy can lead to a
rewarding game of ceramic 'Snap',
providing immense entertainment for
the collector, dealer or art historian.
So successful, for example, were the
'Japanese' Royal Worcester Porcelain
pieces that a number of European
potteries copied them in large
numbers. Soon there stood on virtually
every 'what-not' or shelf throughout
the land, myriad vases and pots with
asymmetrical patterns of blossom, fans
and storks all proclaiming the stylistic
victory of Japanese design.

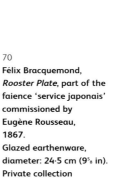

70
Félix Bracquemond,
Rooster Plate, part of the
faience 'service japonais'
commissioned by
Eugène Rousseau,
1867.
Glazed earthenware,
diameter: 24·5 cm (9⅝ in).
Private collection

69
Katsushika Hokusai,
Various Types of Birds
from the *Manga* vol. III,
1815.
Colour woodblock,
17·5 x 11·5 cm (7 x 4½ in)

The *Manga*, a particularly popular Japanese source from which Europeans borrowed motifs, has already been described (see Chapter 2). What exactly was in these fifteen volumes which made them so exciting? To turn the pages of the *Manga* today is to be transported back to two very different cities, the crowded streets of Edo – the capital of Japan – and Paris – the artistic centre of Europe – avid for visual novelty. The word *Manga* has been translated as 'drawing things just as they come', and the slim volumes do indeed provide a glorious hugger-mugger of random sketches, great landscapes, alternating with comic scenes in the bathhouse, some of which may well have influenced Degas. The architect and furniture designer, E W Godwin (1833–86), used illustrations from it of building methods and joinery. Exotic birds, fish, insects, animals and flowers provide an amazing cross-section of visual imagery (69). The possible decorative themes which can be used on pottery and porcelain are legion and sometimes conflict with European symbolism. Storks, for example, symbol of good luck and childbirth in Europe, represent happy old age in Japan, while the fox, a cunning villain in Europe, is regarded as a benevolent friend to the farmer whom he helps by eating the rodents that gobble up the grain.

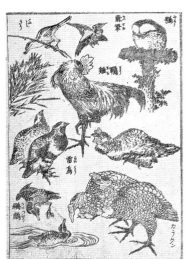

In the winter of 1866–7 Félix Bracquemond designed a faience 'service japonais' made at one of the twin factories of Montereau and Creil to the commission of the glass-maker Eugène Rousseau (1827–91), with such motifs as cocks with flowing tail feathers (70), fish, plants and insects copied after Hokusai's drawings in the *Manga* and other Hokusai books. The service was a great success, was reissued twice and was also much imitated by other factories. Today it is regarded as being the most important example of the influence of Japonisme in French decorative art of the nineteenth century. More immediately, the service was put to practical use at the dinner evenings of the Club Jinglar, an exotic Japoniste rendezvous at which frock coats and cutlery were supplanted by kimonos and *hashi* (chopsticks).

In England similar Japoniste activities first began when a new company, Royal Worcester Porcelain, was founded in 1862, under the leadership of a dynamic art director Richard William Binns, who held the post with great distinction until he reluctantly retired in 1897.

About 1870 the factory began to experiment with the new 'Japanesque' style, using an 'ivory porcelain body' which gave the chief modeller, James Hadley (1837–1903), a chance to show his virtuosity. The wares sometimes included little modelled figures which, when recessed in panels in the sides of vases, proved very popular with the public. Binns was instrumental in getting Royal Worcester to exhibit at Paris in 1867 and Vienna in 1873. At both shows Binns was not only active in selling wares, but also amassed a large collection of Oriental ceramics, principally Japanese, but also Chinese and Korean, which were taken back to Worcester and shown to the factory workers to inspire them. Sadly this vast collection of over 10,000 pieces was sold off in 1900 after Binns' death.

A high point of Binns' life occurred in November 1872 when the works were honoured by a visit from the Iwakura Japanese mission touring the country to study the industrial might of the West. The delegation included the Junior Prime Minister, the Minister of Finance and the Assistant Minister of Foreign Affairs. After a morning passed watching fox hunting (no doubt baffling for the Japanese for whom the fox is a benevolent figure), they must have welcomed being conducted round the factory by Binns himself. They took careful notes of all the processes which he described, at one point asking him to 'speak a little slower as the secretary could not write the description given fast enough'.

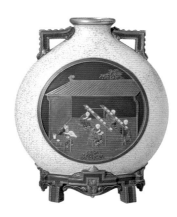

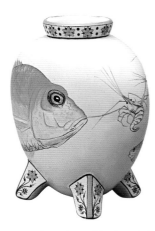

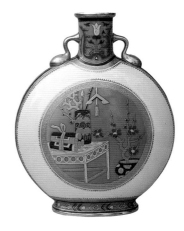

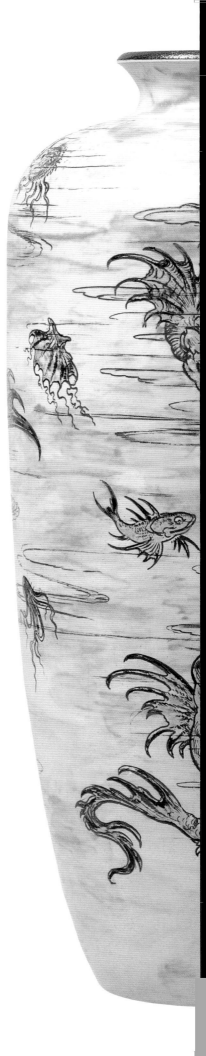

71
James Hadley,
Royal Worcester,
Pilgrim Vase showing Japanese
craftsmen at work,
1872.
Porcelain, moulded in relief,
painted and gilded,
height: 26 cm (10¼ in).
Victoria and Albert Museum, London

72
Christopher Dresser,
W S Coleman (decoration),
Minton & Co.,
Vase with fish and prawn tug-of-war,
1867.
Porcelain,
height: 27 cm (10⅝ in).
Private collection

73
Christopher Dresser (design),
Minton & Co.,
Moonflask,
c.1875.
Porcelain, imitating
approx. height: 30.5 cm (12 in).
Japanese *cloisonné*.
Private collection

74
Edwin Martin (design),
Martin Brothers Pottery,
Vase,
1898.
Saltglazed stoneware,
height: 31·3 cm (12¼ in).
Private collection

Binns' words would indirectly have strange effects, for within a few years the extraordinary situation was reached that Worcester's copies of Japanese wares were actually being *re-copied* by the Japanese themselves, not to mention by many European potteries.

The Art Journal eulogized the display of Royal Worcester Porcelain in the Japanese taste at Vienna as:

unique in design, quaint, without losing a certain eccentric beauty … There are many vases of various shapes designed by Hadley; an octagonal pair decorated with the story of the silk worm in bronze and gold … and a series of six pilgrim or gourd vases having for subjects **The Potter at His Wheel, The Oven for Burning the Clay … The Painting of the Wares [71], and The Making of Saggers.**

At Vienna, Royal Worcester wares jointly gained the first prize with Minton & Co., a firm which actually employed one or two Japanese artists in the design team headed by W S Coleman (1829–1904). Coleman was a leading figure of the Aesthetic Movement, and was for a time in charge of Minton's 'Art Pottery Studio' in Kensington Gore, London.

The library of Minton's design studio included books of Japanese prints of birds and flowers from the early 1860s. Minton also produced a range of wares in porcelain and earthenware based not only on prints but also on such diverse sources as Japanese lacquer, ivories and bronzes (72).

At its most feeble, Japonisme appeared in the traditional forms of the Western potter, with a profusion of Japanese motifs – pine branches, prunus blossoms and storks. Direct imitation of Japanese pottery by English manufacturers was rare, Royal Worcester's ware being inspired by Japanese work in metals and ivories, while Minton's most virtuoso work was their porcelain decorated with gilding and inspired by Japanese gold and silver lacquer, seen to advantage in a magnificent moonflask by Christopher Dresser (1834–1904) dating from 1875 (73).

A very different creative team from the Royal Worcester factory or Minton's was provided by the first British studio potters, the Martin Brothers, who between 1873 and 1914 produced their highly distinctive saltglazed stoneware called Martinware at Fulham and on the banks of the Grand Union Canal at Southall, Middlesex.

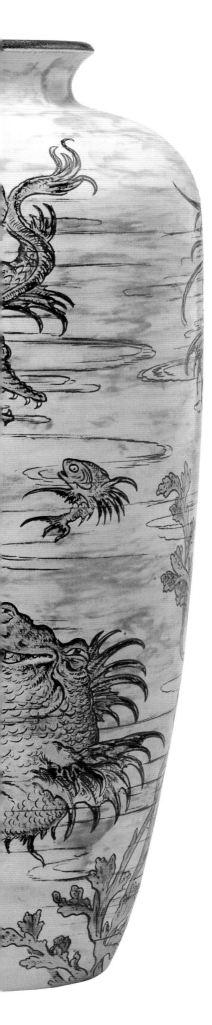

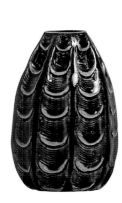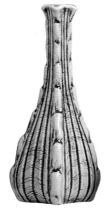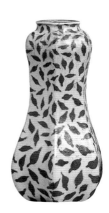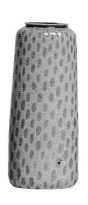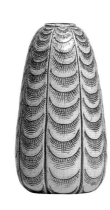

There were four brothers involved in the team. Robert Wallace Martin (1843–1923) was the founder, sculptor and leader of the brotherhood, Edwin Bruce Martin (1860–1915) was the draughtsman, and Walter Fraser Martin (1857–1912) was the potter and chemist responsible for glazes and firing the kiln. The fourth brother was Charles Douglas Martin (1846–1910), the salesman and manager of the shop, whose business methods were, to say the least, rather unusual. He was always afraid of industrial espionage when visitors came to pry, and when some Japanese visited the shop he was quite sure that they wanted to copy key pieces and hustled them out as quickly as possible, much relieved that they left without taking any wares with them.

In 1874 Lady Laura Trevelyan gave the brothers a Japanese book with woodcut illustrations which whetted their taste for the style and led them to acquire books of Japanese designs well into the 1880s. Their 'canal bank' style was a predictable development from copying the typical Japanese motifs of nature. By the mid-1880s they had adopted a form of decoration based on the flowers, insects, reeds and grasses of the canal bank, and this was joined by the more grotesque motifs of extraordinary birds and fish. Edwin's designs now included a strong Japanese influence, with writhing dragons and sea monsters (74).

In 1900 Edwin, Walter and Charles visited the International Exhibition in Paris, making a beeline for the ceramic section to look at the work of Alexandre Bigot (1862–1927), Félix Auguste Delaherche (1857–1940), Lachenal and others. They enjoyed the work of the recently deceased potter, Jean Charles Cazin (1841–1901), and other examples of the stylized organic forms which were so popular in continental Art Nouveau. On their return they began to produce some of their finest work; vases and bowls inspired by the forms of marrows, gourds and melons, with remarkable surface textures which often reproduced the skins of fish or lizards, thus imitating the notion of bonding flora and fauna when embellishing an individual pot – a characteristic of Japanese decoration (75–79).

A keen artist-collector was the Belgian painter, Alfred Stevens (1823–1906), a friend of Baudelaire, Manet and Degas who specialized in portraits of elegant women in intimate boudoir scenes with titles such as *The Porcelain Collector* (1868). He developed an influential wealthy clientele ranging from the Vanderbilts of New York to the actress Sarah Bernhardt, who studied painting in his popular atelier for women, and was his sitter on a number of occasions. He frequently used his own luxurious home as a setting, for it was furnished with fine things. Indeed he was, as the great aesthete, Comte Robert de Montesquieu, once observed, one of the first to appreciate the brilliant and bizarre charms of Far-Eastern bibelots.

75–9
**Martin Brothers Pottery,
Vases,
1897–1914.**
Saltglazed stoneware,
tallest height: 14 cm (5½ in).
Private collection

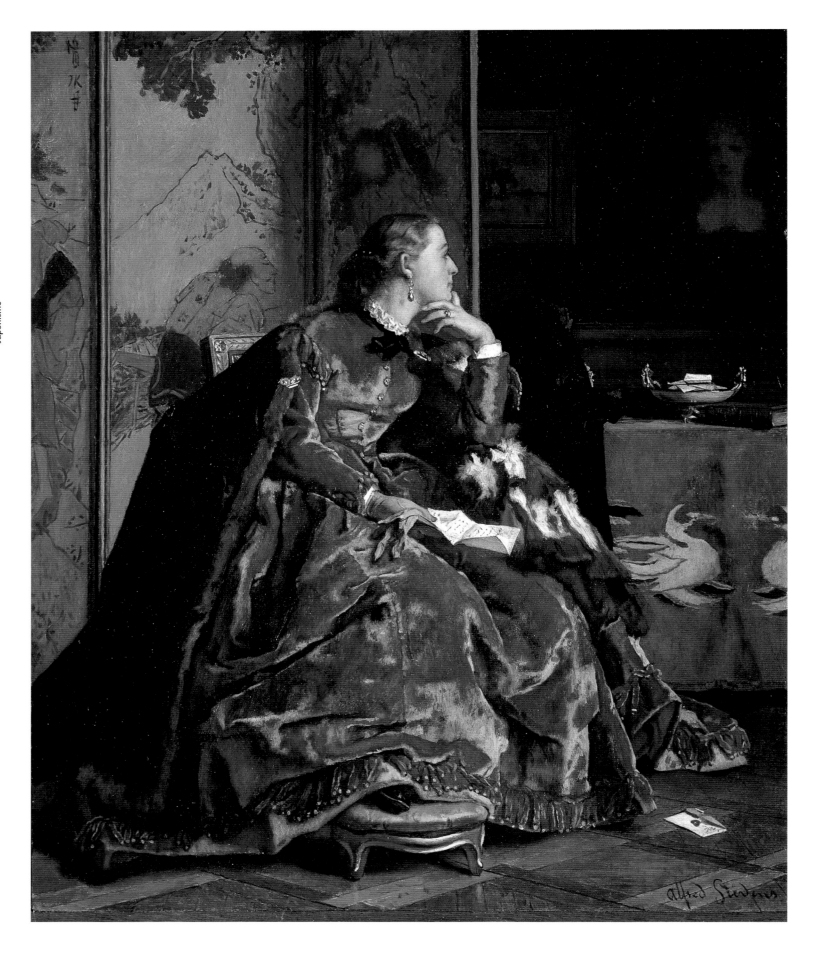

80
Alfred Stevens,
The Duchess (formerly
known as *The Blue Dress*),
*c.*1880.
Oil on wood,
31·9 x 26 cm
(12½ x 10¼ in).
Stirling and Francine
Clark Art Institute,
Williamstown, MA

81
James Tissot,
Children in a Garden,
*c.*1882.
Cloisonné enamel
on copper,
height: 25 cm (9⅞).
Musée des Arts
Décoratifs, Paris

Stevens' fantastic *Salon Japonaise* was described by Edmond de Goncourt in the journal of Saturday 13 March 1875:

Knowing that I am an amateur of things Japanese, he opens up his Japanese room. It is decorated with two rolls of paper with a gold background on which are two carts, each carrying a gigantic bouquet of flowers – the gift of a young man to his fiancée. Japanese art is certainly full of charming conventions! In order to conceal the geometrical regularity of the wheels the artist has broken up his design by means of a cloud of dust, a cloud of golden dust.

In *The Duchess*, or *The Blue Dress*, Alfred Stevens' pensive model sits before a Japanese screen on which we see Fuji's classic cone (80).

The portrait painter, James Tissot, in the late 1870s designed a service of *cloisonné* enamels, some of the most attractive Japoniste constrictions to the decorative arts. A fine example is the vase 'en gaine', *Children in a Garden* (81). It is not known why in the late 1870s he should embark on such a new venture.

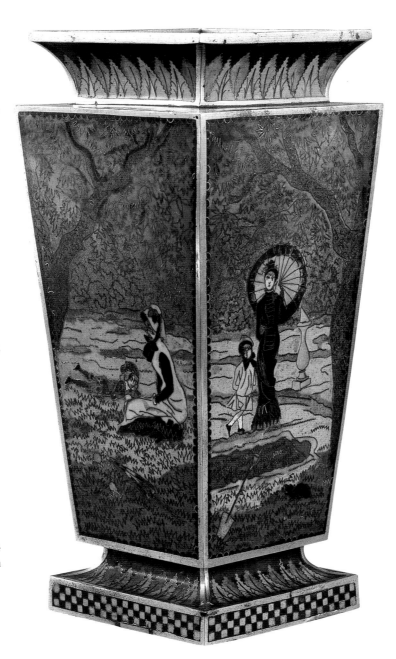

The process of making such *cloisonné* wares was fraught with the nerve-racking stress of keeping all the dividing wires absolutely taut until after the piece had been fired, as well as other technical difficulties. Fortunately new techniques for making small-scale pieces were evolved by the well-known French jeweller, Alexis Falize (1811–98). Falize became interested in the subject after seeing Sir Rutherford Alcock's collection in London in 1862. The exquisite quality of Falize's *cloisonné* enamel jewellery can be seen in his necklace and pair of earring pendants (82), which utilize motifs that Falize admitted tracing and copying from Japanese print albums.

The widespread dissemination of Japoniste sentiments was music to the ear of the great impresario of both Japonisme and Art Nouveau – Siegfried Bing. He opened his Oriental Art Boutique in Paris in 1875, where it became a meeting place for the exchange of ideas on Japan, which also found an airing through Bing's journal *Le Japon Artistique*, which ran for thirty-six issues from 1888 to 1891 in French, German and English editions (83).

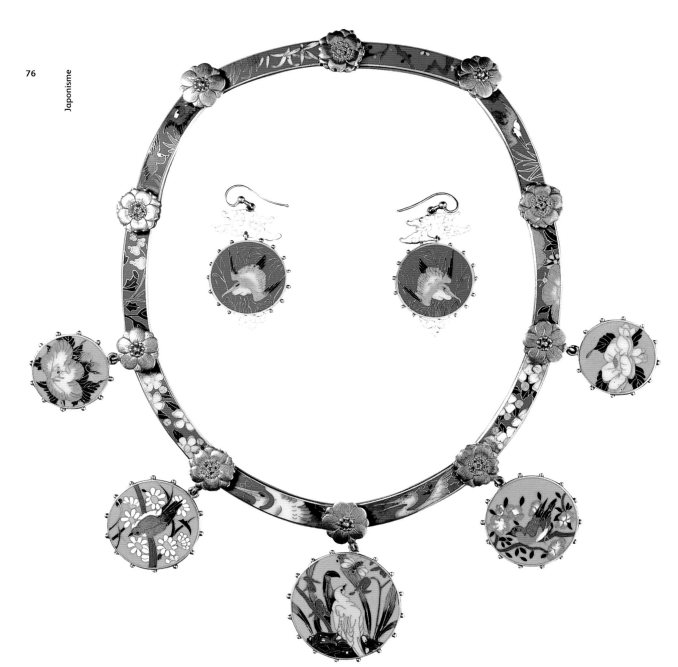

82
Alexis Falize,
Necklace and earring
pendants in the Japanese
style with joints disguised
by gold rosettes,
1867.
Cloisonné enamel,
diameter of largest
medallion: 3.5 cm (1^3_8 in).
Ashmolean Museum,
Oxford

83
Cover of Siegfried Bing's
journal *Le Japon
Artistique*, May 1888

In the issue of May 1888 Bing wrote:

*The Japanese artist is convinced
that nature contains the primordial
elements of all things and, according
to him, nothing exists in creation, be
it only a blade of grass, that is not
worthy of a place in the loftiest
conception of art.*

The intense study of the dynamic
forces of nature was also the
inspiration which motivated Emile
Gallé (1846–1904) who produced
some of the finest Art Nouveau
furniture. Gallé, deeply influenced
by Japanese prototypes and theories,
was one of the greatest of all artists
to work in the medium of glass.
He first began at a small pottery
works in 1874 experimenting with
stoneware and porcelain, often
embellished with dandelions, orchids
and chrysanthemums using opaque
glazes on simple, somewhat clumsy
forms. On turning to glass-making in
the 1880s Gallé used floral or insect
motifs, and drew inspiration from
many sources, notably Japanese art
and nature. He was to produce many
of the most beautiful of all Japoniste
works of art in a material unfamiliar
to the Japanese – glass.

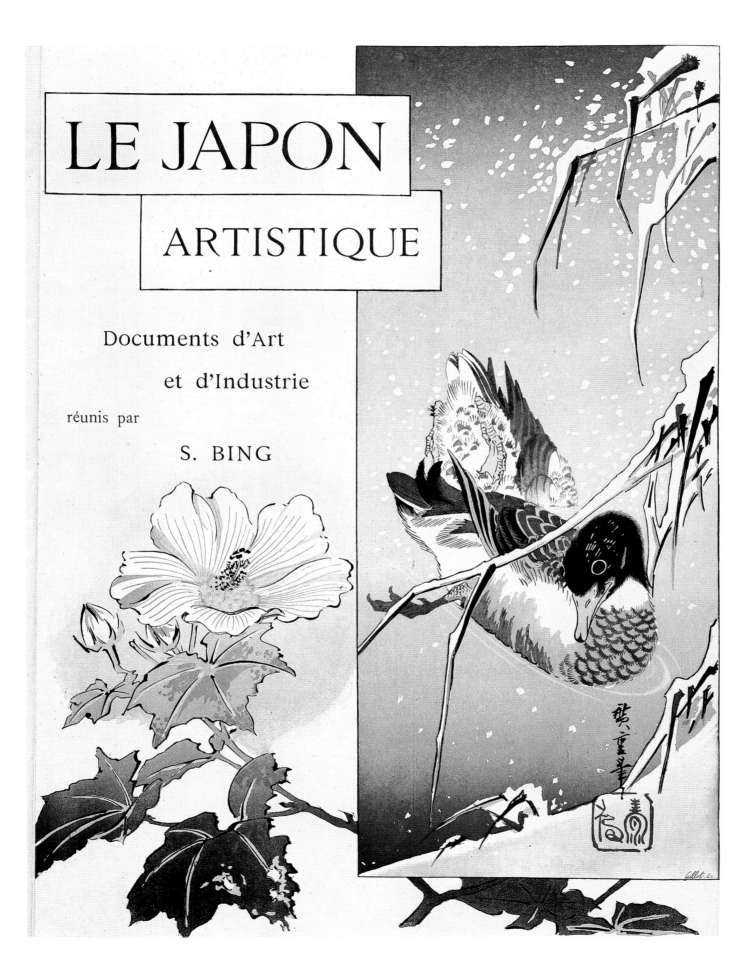

84
Emile Gallé,
Vase made for the
Paris Exposition,
c.1900.
Amber glass with etched
decoration,
height: 47 cm (18¹₂ in).
Victoria and Albert
Museum, London

85
Emile Gallé,
Model of a crystal vase
with pine branches,
1903.
Watercolour and
graphite,
49·5 x 32·2 cm
(19¹₂ x 12⁵₈ in).
Musée d'Orsay, Paris

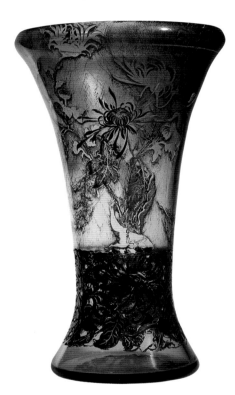

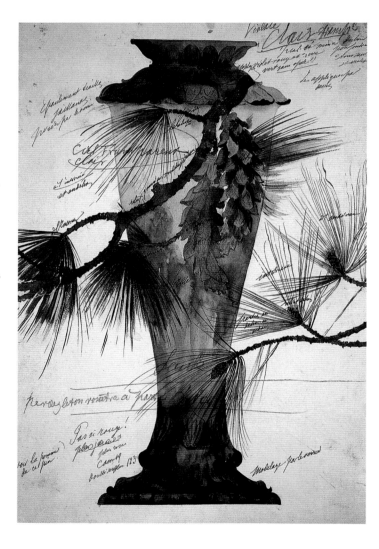

Some of his most moving small-scale pieces are his *vases de tristesse* and *verreries parlantes* – small exquisite pieces, subtly textured and decorated to reflect the mood of the inscriptions with which they were etched. Such pieces were always intended to be handled, and to do so is a great privilege. Examples exist with quotations from Villon, Baudelaire and Victor Hugo – brief, terse phrases like a *haiku* that juxtapose the image on the glass and the poetry, the dual influence of Japonisme and the French literary tradition. A trained botanist, Gallé looked to plants and flowers for inspiration, as in this large vase, carved, etched and engraved with chrysanthemums (84).

For a really masterly example of Gallé's method of work, it is rewarding to turn to an original design for a pine-bough vase, the pine being a symbol of longevity (85). This is a telling exercise in turning a two-dimensional drawing into a three-dimensional object, just as the cone holds the seed of the future.

86
Daum Brothers,
Vase with poppy,
c.1900.
Glass,
height: 20·4 cm (8 in).
Bröhan Museum, Berlin

87
Eugène Rousseau,
Vase with carp,
c.1878.
Glass, encased and
engraved,
height: 17·8 cm (7 in).
Walters Art Museum,
Baltimore

88
Katsushika Hokusai,
Carp in a Pool,
c.1833.
Colour woodblock,
23·2 x 28·7 cm
(9³⁄₈ x 11¹⁄₄ in)

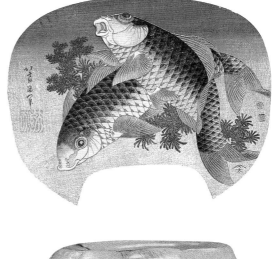

Gallé began the decorative application of glass to electric lighting, producing lamps in the form of flowers with light fittings concealed by half-open petals. After Gallé's death in 1904 the making of Art Nouveau glass continued to flourish in Nancy, for following in Emile Gallé's wake, like silver stars in a *pâte de verre* glass firmament, are the work of his followers, Victor Prouvé (1858–1943), who painted a famous portrait of Gallé, and the brothers Auguste (1853–1909) and Antonin Daum (1864–1930; 86). In Paris a spectacular glass was produced by Eugène Rousseau, who excelled at aquatic subjects (87). This vase recalls many Japanese treatments of the theme of carp moving though swirling waters, such as the woodcut by Hokusai (1833; 88).

Japan's influence began to be seen further and further afield. All over Europe in the late 1880s, from Cracow to Copenhagen, Japanese motifs triumphed, and irises and lizards, dragonflies and fish began to appear in any area not swamped already by asymmetric patterns. Nor was Europe the only continent to succumb to the charms of Japanese design. In Russia the Imperial Porcelain Manufacture at St Petersburg used the eagle motif from Hiroshige's *Eagle over Fukagawa* (89) to embellish the rim of a white porcelain jar (90). Another Russian piece using a Japanese theme is a vase decorated with a heron standing under blossom from the Imperial factory made in 1892.

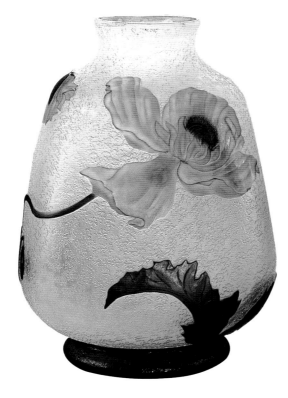

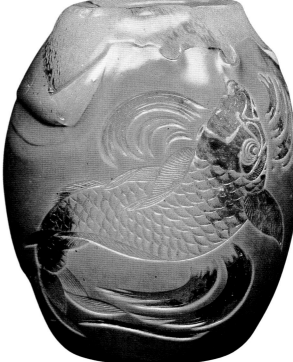

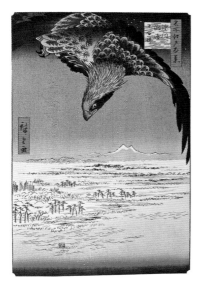

89
Utagawa Hiroshige,
Eagle Over Fukagawa from
One Hundred Views of Edo,
1857.
Colour woodblock,
33·8 x 23·1 cm
(13¼ x 9⅜ in)

90
Imperial Porcelain
Manufacture,
Jar with eagle decoration,
1913.
Porcelain,
height: 31·6 cm (12½ in).
The Hermitage,
St Petersburg

91
Arnold Krog for the Royal
Porcelain Factory,
Copehagen,
Vase,
1888.
Porcelain,
height: 35·7 cm (14 in).
Museum für Kunst und
Gewerbe, Hamburg

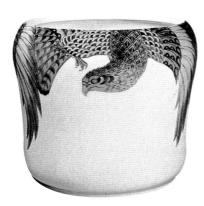

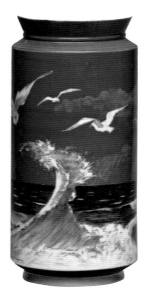

This motif is echoed by several manufacturers, notably at the Bing & Grondahl Copenhagen factory by Pietro Krohn who in 1888 designed an ambitious and original 'heron service'. A porcelain vase made in 1888 by Arnold Krog (1856–1931) of the Royal Porcelain Factory, Copenhagen, with underglaze painting of seagulls and waves echoes the conventional depiction of the waves of Hokusai and Hiroshige (91). Krog, an architect and painter with leanings towards the decorative arts, had visited England, Holland and France where he met Siegfried Bing who had just returned from the Far East laden with treasures.

Another major creative force involved with Japonisme was Théodore Deck (1823–91), an artist-potter and one of the most innovative figures in the ceramic business in France during the Second Empire. Born in Guebwiller, Alsace, he established himself in Paris in 1856 to make decorative earthenware and eventually became art director at Sèvres, but never lost touch with his native Alsace. Deck was an eclectic 'style cruncher', gathering images from both the Far East and his preferred Near East. Throughout his career Deck and his large design team experimented with stoneware, porcelain, tin-glazed earthenware and flambé glazes. Another of his factory's specialities were extensive tile panels derived from a wide range of Far Eastern design sources.

Surviving panels include decorations for a verandah depicted with gracefully drooping wisteria (a plant only recently introduced from Japan into Europe), flowering cherry blossoms, butterflies and two Mandarin ducks, symbolic of marital bliss. In the foreground are water lilies, one of the favourite subjects of the modern style, which anticipate by a decade the emergence at Giverny of Monet's magnificent visual celebration of the flower. Deck's most famous bathroom mural, an extensive series of variations on the always popular theme of cranes, was designed for the Villa Schlumberger for Deck's friend and patron, the textile manufacturer Jean Schlumberger (92). He was one of the new generation of wealthy factory owners who were also patrons of the arts. Such figures facilitated both the arts and local commerce by backing activities such as the weaving, textile and printing industries which flourished in Alsace, and also wallpaper-making which was the main industry of the town of Mulhouse.

As early as 1868 the Mulhouse firm of Scheurer, Rott & Co. was one of several enterprising manufacturers to see market possibilities in printing and exporting woollen fabrics to the Japanese market. They were the product of as many as sixteen rollers which each added a different colour or pattern to the fabric as it was threaded through the ingenious machines.

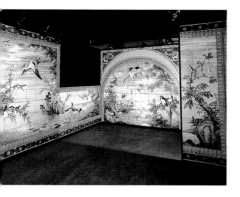

92
Théodore Deck,
Bathroom tile scheme
from the Villa
Schlumberger,
1876.
Ceramic tiles.
Musée de Florival,
Guebwiller

93
Proof impression for
textile destined for
Japan,
mid-1860s.
Pigment on paper.
Musée de l'Impression
sur Étoffes, Mulhouse

The fabric, plain at first, ended up covered with such familiar Japanese motifs as waves, branches, flowers (93) and inevitably Mount Fuji. The fabrics were inspired probably by Japanese silks which were greatly admired in Europe. Under this stimulus emerged a thriving two-way market between France and Japan. It seems therefore fitting that Lyon should own a textile called *A Chrysanthemum*, one of the symbols of imperial Japan, made in the mid-nineteenth century from satin, silk and strips of gold paper. Siebold brought it back from Japan after his second trip there and sold it in the 1880 sale of his collection at Munich, where it was acquired for the Lyon museum.

Surprisingly, although motifs such as stylized bird and flower forms were favourite themes of the fine and decorative artist, William Morris (1834–96), his only recorded remark on the subject of Japanese art and textiles is in a letter of October 1877 to his friend the dyer, Thomas Wardle, to say, 'I saw a piece of Japanese tapestry yesterday of silk very delicate in manufacture and fine in colour.'

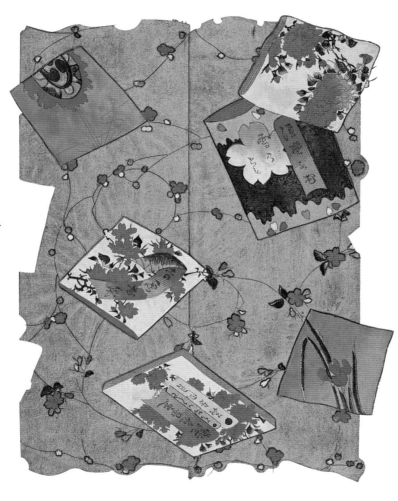

Edmond de Goncourt, on the other hand, was not only interested in Japanese artefacts, but also collected a number of European textiles designed using Japanese themes. After his death on 16 July 1896 he left instructions that the collection should not be left to the cold maw of a museum to be gaped at by unfeeling passers-by, but dispersed at auction to give individual purchasers the same pleasures and pains of collecting and ownership which had been enjoyed by himself and his brother Jules. Ironically, Edmond's wishes would not be fully realized for at one of the resultant sales in 1897 some significant pieces were purchased for the Lyon Museum, notably an embroidery on tabby silk showing two old men looking symbolically at the setting sun, a symbol of eternity, leaving behind them pine trees, cranes and turtles, emblematic of longevity (94).

The weaving of silk, so associated with the city of Lyon since the Middle Ages, was celebrated by the opening of a major museum on the theme in 1890. The museum's real beginnings, however, can be traced back to the Great Exhibitions at London in 1851 and Paris in 1855, 1867, 1878 and 1889. At these events shrewd purchases for the future museum were made by one of its leading advocates, the economist, Natalis Rondot. From the start, wise and imaginative acquisitions were made that accentuated the new enthusiasm for Japanese silks.

94
Cranes Flying Across the Setting Sun, Watched by Two Venerable Old Men,
c.1850–60.
Japanese silk, painted and embroidered with silk and gold thread.
Musée des Tissus, Lyon

95
The Swallows,
1894.
Silk (detail).
Musée des Tissus, Lyon

96
Sortie de bal, or mantle worn over ballgown, created by Worth, engraving from a prospectus for the Exposition Universelle at Lyon,
1894

97
Edward Chandler Moore, Tiffany & Co.,
Coffee pot, creamer and sugar bowl,
c.1877.
Silver, with various base metals applied,
tallest: 21·5 cm (8½ in).
Victoria and Albert Museum, London

98
Emile Auguste Reiber, Christofle & Co.,
Vase and cover,
1867.
Copper inlaid with silver, on a gilt bronze stand,
height: 30·5 cm (12 in).
Victoria and Albert Museum, London

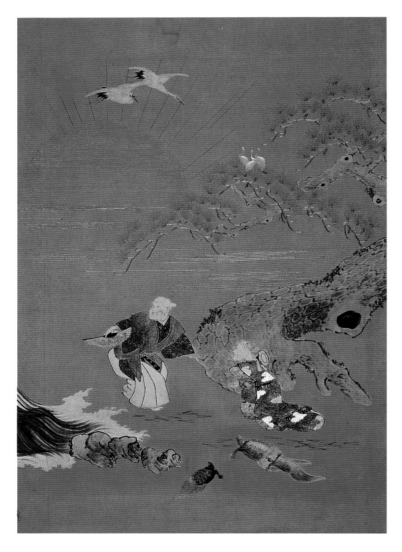

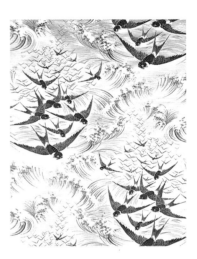

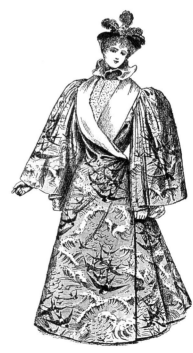

In 1894 the great couturier Charles Frederick Worth (1825–95) ordered a fabric named *The Swallows* (95) and used it to make an evening cloak for a ball (96). It was also shown at an important exhibition in Lyon and was subsequently acquired by the museum there. The motifs of swallows and waves (used as a powerful background here) often occur in Japanese art.

The jewellery manufacturer, Tiffany & Co., was founded in 1834 by Charles L Tiffany (d.1902), father of the legendary Louis Comfort Tiffany (1848–1933; see Chapter 9). In 1850 Charles opened a branch of the business in Paris which from 1860 specialized in Japanese styles and motifs. An intriguing example of the Japoniste style is the coffee pot, creamer and sugar bowl set made by Edward Chandler Moore (1827–91), Tiffany's leading independent designer who had visited the Paris Great Exhibition of 1867 (97). There he became fascinated by Japanese sword furniture, and mastered the technical skills needed to make a varied palette of coloured alloys from copper, gold and silver. Moore, appointed director of Tiffany's silver department in 1868, was an avid collector of Japanese metalwork. His knowledge of Japanese technique enabled him to impart a polychrome hammered surface on this pitcher and other pieces which resembled that possessed by Japanese 'crackle' pottery.

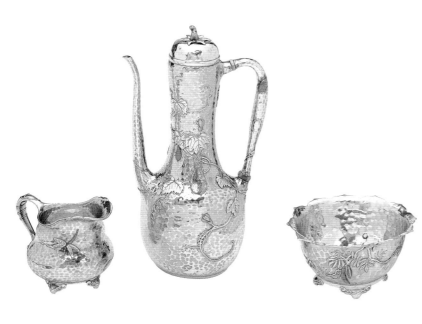

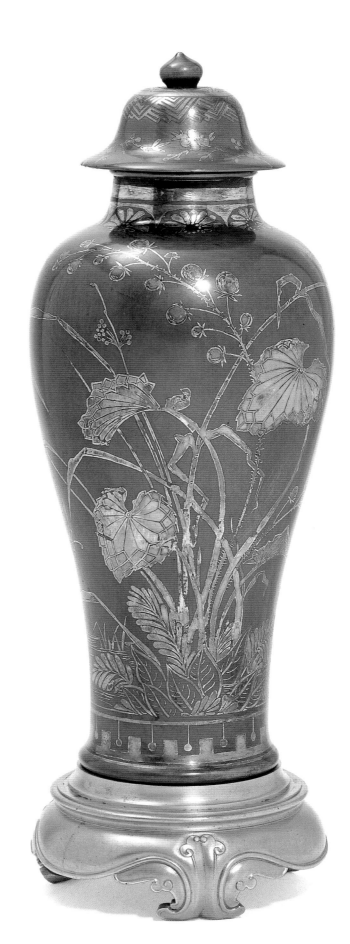

Siegfried Bing commented that in such pieces 'the borrowed elements were so ingeniously transposed to serve their new function as to become the equivalent of new discoveries', a point neatly demonstrated by the dragonfly on the creamer, which appears to have been borrowed directly from a page in Hokusai's *Quick Lessons in Simplified Drawing* (1812), demonstrating how to draw dragonflies (see 203). Perhaps fortunately, Britain could not compete in such stylistic struggles because its strict hallmarking laws forbade the mixture of precious with base metals, leaving Tiffany with little opposition to contend with and enabling him to create some of the most innovative metalwork of the century.

Tiffany's did not, however, have the field entirely to themselves. A vase and cover of 1867 (98) was designed by Emile Auguste Reiber (1826–1893), who was one of the most important of early Japonistes. The design for the inlaid silver on this vase may well have come from the *Useful Drawings for Art and Industry* of 1859 by Auguste Delâtré (1822–1907), which included eighteen engraved plates of Japanese birds, flowers, insects, marine life, samurai and landscapes by Hokusai.

Great department stores also helped to disperse Japanese artefacts. In his novel *Au Bonheur des dames* (1883), Émile Zola describes the world of a department store which he modelled on Parisian stores such as Le Louvre and Au Bon Marché. The owner of Zola's fictional shop had begun his business with:

a small bargain counter covered with faded bric-a-brac [which now] overflowed with old bronzes, old ivories, old lacquers … Few departments had had such modest beginnings, and now it had a turnover of thousands of francs a year, and stirred up all the Far East, where travellers ransacked temples and palaces. Four years had been enough to attract the entire artistic clientele of Paris.

In the decorative arts the cult of Japan continued to flourish even after it had lost its exotic novelty and when the whiplash lines of Art Nouveau reigned supreme. Japonisme survived because it offered a more lasting means of translating natural forms into a decorative style, a pursuit shared by potters, metalworkers, textile designers and above all by manufacturers, who all shared an eager enthusiasm to create variations, copies and imitations of Japanese novelties, which sold and sold and sold.

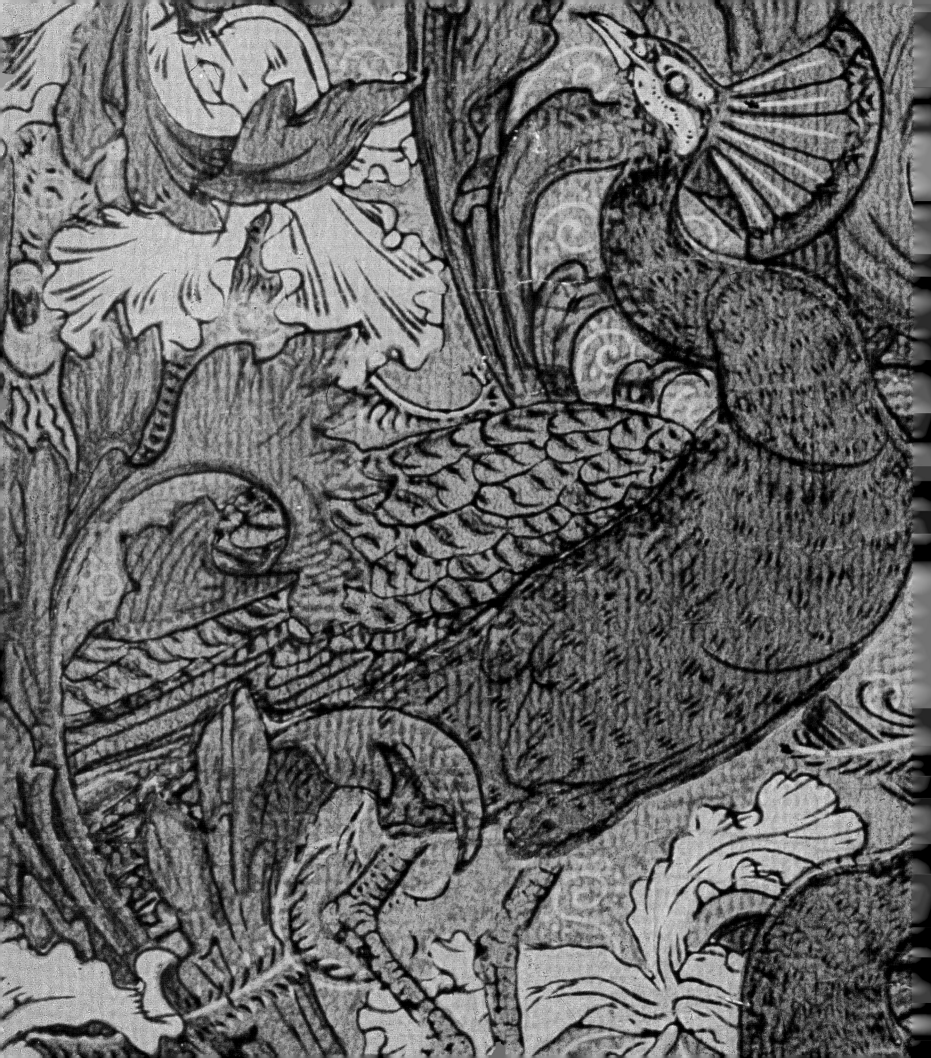

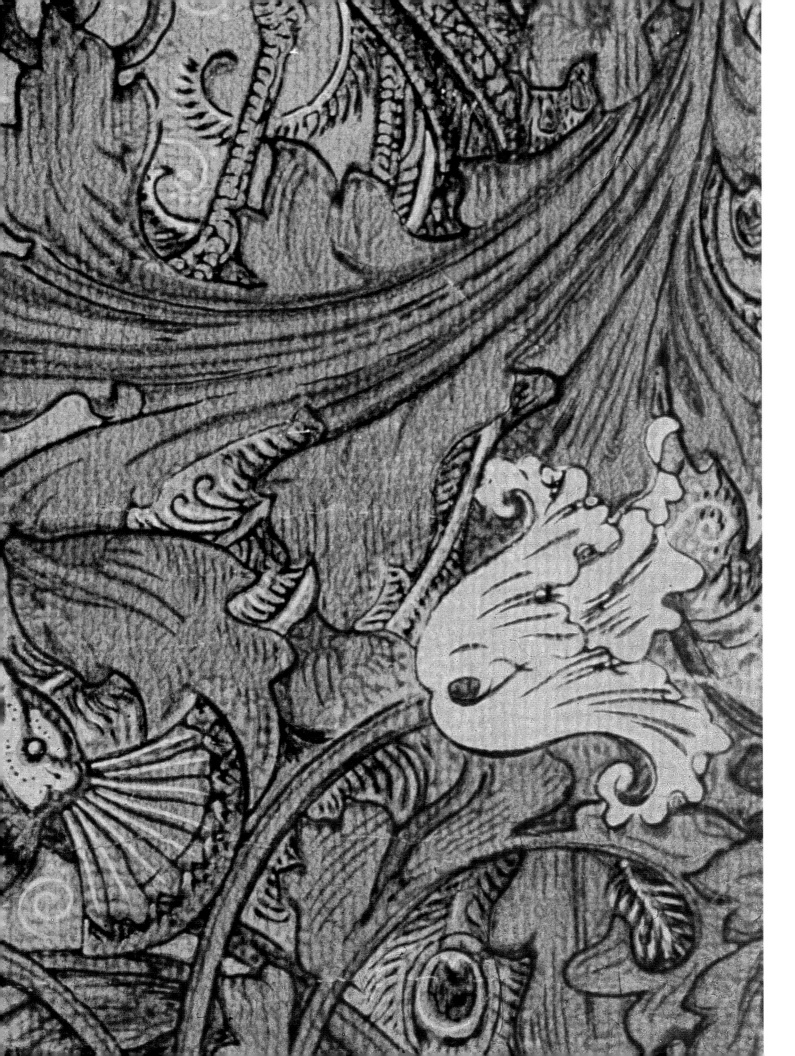

Previous page
Walter Crane,
Peacock Garden
wallpaper
(detail of 111)

99
E W Godwin,
Anglo-Japanese
Drawing Room
Furniture, **engraving**
from *Art Furniture*, **1877**

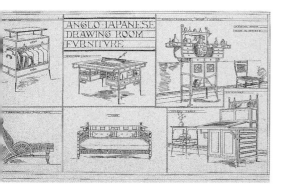

100
William Nesfield,
Folding screen of six
panels with twelve
Japanese paintings
of birds and flowers,
1867.
Ebonized wood with gilt
and fretted decoration
and painted panels of
Japanese paper,
height: 208 cm (82 in).
Victoria and Albert
Museum, London

Remember that the most beautiful
things in the world are the most
useless; peacocks and lilies for
example.
John Ruskin, 1851–3

The first trade agreement between
Great Britain and Japan was signed
in 1859. From that moment Japanese
goods began to flow into England, not
only via London but also through ports
such as Bristol, where Japanese prints
made one of their first recorded
appearances in England in 1862 on the
walls of the home of a talented young
Bristolian architect and writer, Edward
William Godwin. Godwin was an
eclectic genius, passionately interested
in subjects as various as the history
of costume, Greek art and stage
design. He drew constantly in a series
of small sketchbooks remarkable for
their clarity and precision. For such
a man, already deeply versed in
the European decorative tradition,
the discovery of Japanese art was
a novel and exciting aesthetic
revelation. He soon acquired not
only prints but fans and books,
and particularly prized two slim
volumes of Hokusai's *Manga* showing
Japanese techniques of construction,
joints and carpentry, which would
prove immensely influential on his
later career as a furniture designer.

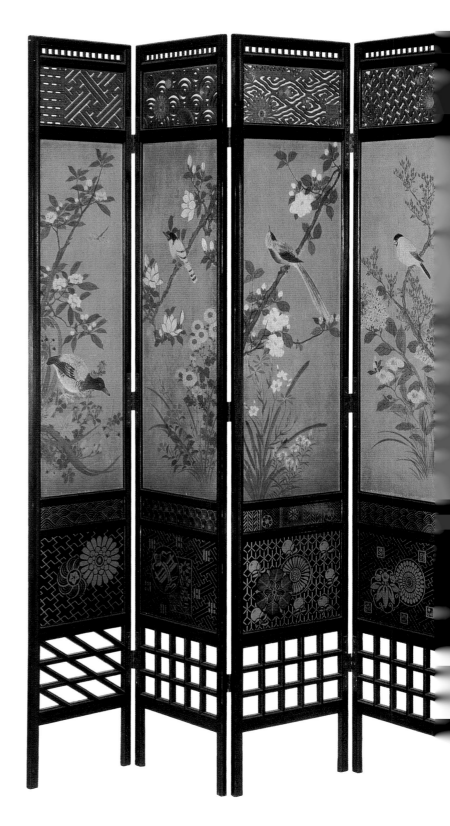

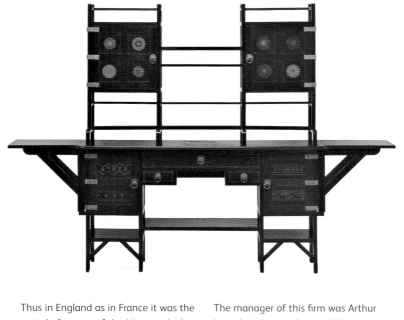

101
E W Godwin,
William Watt,
Sideboard,
c.1885–8.
Ebonized mahogany
with painted decoration;
silver-plated handles
and fittings,
height: 184 cm
(74³⁄₈ in).
National Gallery of
Victoria, Melbourne

Thus in England as in France it was the arrival of a copy of the *Manga* which really triggered public interest in the art and artefacts of Japan. In England that interest would be primarily reflected in the decorative arts, in France in the fine and graphic arts.

From the *Manga* in the mid-1860s Godwin drew the inspiration for the design of his 'Anglo-Japanese' furniture, ebonized black sideboards and tables which reveal his profound understanding of Japanese concerns for space and volume, asymmetry, reticence and restraint (99). This appreciation led him to decorate his home in a restrained yet highly original manner, revolutionary for the high Victorian era. He painted the walls in plain colours, hanging on them a few Japanese prints, and placed some Persian carpets on the bare boards.

Godwin's early interests were also heightened by the display of Japanese lacquer, bronze and porcelain shown at the London International Exhibition held at South Kensington in 1862, which was collected by the British Minister in Japan, Sir Rutherford Alcock. After the exhibition closed, the firm of Farmer and Rogers sold off some of the exhibits and other goods that had failed to arrive in time.

The manager of this firm was Arthur Lasenby Liberty, who in 1875 was to establish his own firm. Liberty & Co. would become celebrated for its stocks of both Japanese and Art Nouveau artefacts.

As with any new fashion, enthusiasm for Japonisme spread by word of mouth. The Jewish painter, Simeon Solomon (1840–1905), wrote to his friend the poet, Swinburne, in 1863 and described the home of his friend the architect, William Eden Nesfield (1835–88):

His rooms are in Argyll Street near mine, and he has a very jolly collection of Persian, Indian, Greek and Japanese things that I should really like you to see … he is an intimate friend of Albert Moore.

The work of both Nesfield and Moore was greatly influenced by Japanese artefacts. A spectacular example of this influence at work is provided by a six-fold screen designed by Nesfield in 1867 as a wedding present for his business partner, the famous architect, Richard Norman Shaw (1831–1912), with whom he shared offices from 1863 to 1876 (100).

The screen displays a sophisticated knowledge of Japanese motifs. Twelve painted panels depict birds perched on blossoming branches of chrysanthemums, lilies, pinks, peonies and magnolias. They are surrounded by incised, ebonized wooden frames, separated at the top with strips of open fretwork and a band of gilded and carved Japanese motifs. The screen is elaborately inscribed with a four-line stanza:

*All are Architects of Fate
Working on these walls of time
Some with massive deeds and great
Some with ornaments of Rhyme
Richard and Agnes Shaw AD 1867.*

The gilded bands of asymmetric decoration are composed of the Japanese patterns *sayagata* (key fret motif), *uzumaki* (spirals), family crests known as *tomo-e* and the auspicious Asian symbol of the swastika, all handled with great technical flair.

The question as to where Nesfield and James Forsyth (who made the screen) had acquired such knowledge is an intriguing one. It can perhaps be partially explained by a study of *Grammar of Chinese Ornament* by Owen Jones (1809–74) which was published in a limited edition of 300 in 1867. The more unusual motifs of the screen could also have been borrowed from Japanese ceramics and textile stencils. Such goods were all obtainable at Farmer and Rogers's Oriental Warehouse in Regent Street.

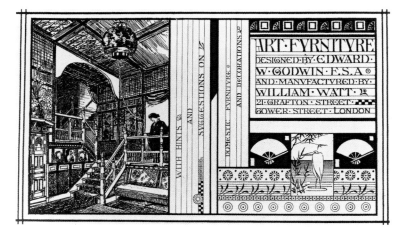

102
Walter Crane,
***Eleven, Twelve, Ring
the Bell*** from ***One, Two,
Buckle My Shoe*** **of the
'Six-Penny Toy' series,
1869**

E W Godwin became one of the shop's most regular customers. As a practising architect he possessed a keen appreciation of the architectonic qualities of Japanese art. In 1867 he designed the famous sideboard which he had made for his mistress, the actress Ellen Terry.

Its rectilinear form and plain dark panels, covered with embossed leather, possess a simplicity remarkable for its date, when ornate over-decoration flourished in Victorian furniture design. At least ten of these sideboards were created, the example illustrated here, dating from 1885 to 1888, being probably the most elaborately decorated of them all (101). The upper cupboard doors are stencilled with gold chrysanthemums, the lower ones with geometric decorations.

Ellen Terry and Godwin had two children, a daughter, Edith Craig, and a son, Gordon Craig who would become a great theatrical designer. In her memoirs Ellen Terry recalled that in her children's nursery:

they were allowed no rubbishy picture books but from the first Japanese prints and fans lined the nursery walls while their English classic was Walter Crane.

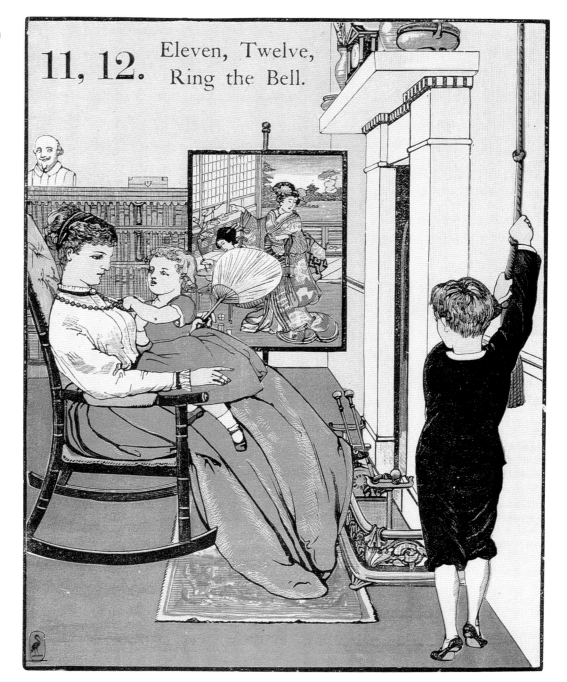

103
E W Godwin and
William Watt,
frontispiece and title
page from *Art Furniture*,
1877

104
E W Godwin, attributed
to William Watt,
Gong and stand,
1877.
Oak, iron and bronze,
height: 82·6 cm
(32¹₂ in).
Walker Art Gallery,
Liverpool

Ellen Terry is referring to illustrations in a nursery rhyme book by Walter Crane (1845–1915), *One, Two, Buckle my Shoe* (1869) from the 'Six-Penny Toy' series. The illustration to *Eleven, Twelve, Ring the Bell* (102) shows an 'Aesthetic' interior: a mother is sitting on an Anglo-Japanese-style chair, holding a Japanese fan, and a screen is decorated with an enlarged Japanese print design. Walter Crane (1845–1915) was a great admirer of 'things Japanese', acknowledging 'Japanese colour prints' as 'an important factor' in the evolution of his style, and owning some prints by Toyokuni which had been given to him by a family friend returning from Japan in about 1867. Just to complete the picture, or, rather, the 'Japanese print', Godwin's friend Whistler gave both Ellen and the children kimonos.

Godwin always enjoyed a close association with Liberty's, which he described as an 'Anglo-Japanese Warehouse'. He bought from it his own household furnishings and also probably such items as the six carved ivory monkeys of Japanese make, closely resembling *netsukes*, which he used as handles on his 'Monkey' cabinet. This was made for his own use, probably by William Watt, in walnut inset with four Japanese boxwood plaques. Japanese carved wood panels were included in Liberty's stock, and by 1881 special designs and sizes could be ordered from Japan 'to any character of drawing'.

The use of actual Japanese materials in this new type of furniture may also help to explain the title 'Art Furniture', a term first used in 1868 by Charles Locke Eastlake in his influential book *Hints on Household Taste* to describe furniture made under the direct control of the designer rather than pieces produced by semi mass-production methods in factories.

In 1877 the furniture-maker, William Watt, published a catalogue entitled *Art Furniture Designed by Edward W Godwin F.S.A. and Manufactured by William Watt With Hints and Suggestions on Domestic Furniture and Decorations* (103). Godwin's frontispiece is the most Japanese of all his interior designs. He was keenly aware of new publications on the designs of Japan, and was fascinated by Aimé Humbert's *Le Japon illustré* (1870), a record of a year's stay in Japan in 1863–4. From an illustration in it Godwin designed a gong and stand probably made by William Watt (104). Gongs or bells were articles always in demand in large Victorian houses to summon people for meals. The gong's shape derives from the Japanese *torii*, freestanding gateways which are an imposing feature of Shinto shrines.

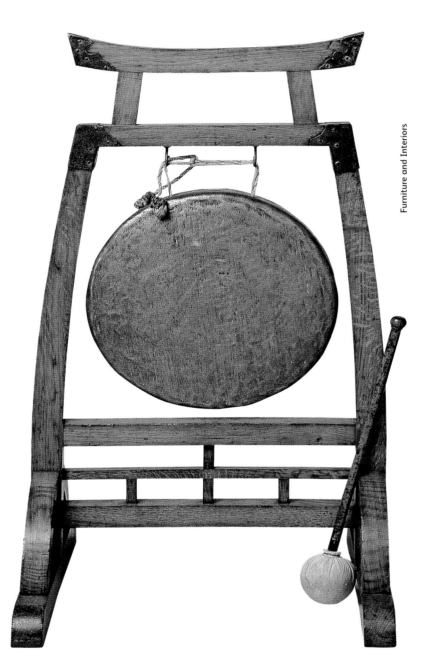

105
James Abbott McNeill
Whistler,
*Rose and Silver: The Princess
from the Land
of Porcelain*,
1863–4.
Oil on canvas,
199·9 x 116·1 cm
(78⅝ x 45¾ in).
Freer Gallery of Art,
Smithsonian Institution,
Washington, DC

A great friend of Godwin's and fellow enthusiast for Japanese art was the Gothic revival architect of Cardiff Castle, William Burges (1827–81). His review of the Japanese exhibits displayed in the 1862 Exhibition in *The Building News* positively glows with enthusiasm:

If the visitor wishes to see the real Middle Ages he must visit the Japanese Court, for at the present day the arts of the Middle Ages have deserted Europe and are only to be found in the East ... these hitherto unknown barbarians appear to know all that the Middle Ages knew but in some respects are beyond them and us as well.

Some of Burges's own collection of Japanese prints survive in the Victoria and Albert Museum, pasted into five scrapbooks. To turn their pages is an exciting experience, enabling us to share vicariously with Burges and Godwin the thrill of seeing for the first time the exotic patterns and bold designs of Japan, which as a wallpaper designer Godwin particularly enjoyed. On a page in one of his sketchbooks we can study his careful drawings of Japanese crests or *mon*.

One evening in May 1863, Burges chaired a meeting of the Architectural Association on Japanese Art. A lecture on 'The Prevailing Ornament of China and Japan' was given by Christopher Dresser, a young man who was to play a remarkable role in the dissemination of knowledge of Japan.

Dresser, a fine example of the phenomenon of the Victorian polymath, first studied at the Government School of Design run by Sir Henry Cole in Kensington. There he encountered such major names in the design field as Richard Redgrave (1804–88), Matthew Digby Wyatt (1820–77), Gottfried Semper (1803–79) and, most notably, Owen Jones, then engaged upon his *Grammar of Ornament* (1856), a book to which Dresser contributed several designs. From South Kensington he went to Germany, becoming a Doctor of Philosophy at the University of Jena. All seemed set for an academic career and a fulfilled life of fellowships and publications. As a botanist, however, his knowledge of the infinite variety of natural patterns provided the basis for a highly successful career as a freelance designer. He was indeed a born eclectic, able to turn his hand to anything, and has left an amazingly varied design legacy. His first exposure to Japanese artefacts took place in the 1862 International Exhibition, at which he made more than eighty drawings. This was Dresser's first contact with international exhibitions, which would later loom very large in his creative activities.

At the 1867 Minton stand in Paris, for example, he introduced the effect of adapting enamel techniques on to porcelain. In a more light-hearted vein and with equal facility he could draw semi-humorous grotesques of bats, cats, cranes, ducks, beetles and other insects. From the mid- to late 1860s he designed for Wedgwood and Minton (see 72 and 73) and from the mid-1870s for Elkington & Co., the silverware manufacturers.

In 1876 he visited the Philadelphia Centennial Exhibition and also actually went to Japan for a short visit of four months as representative for the South Kensington Museum and agent for Tiffany & Co., New York, and to advise the Japanese on their export trade, visiting sixty-four potteries and dozens of manufacturers of different wares. He took hundreds of photographs, and on his return his own designs, particularly for pottery and metalwork, were radically altered, becoming far more abstract as a result of his greater understanding of Japanese materials and aesthetics.

In his 1882 publication, a still very readable and amusing study, *Japan, its Architecture, Art and Art Manufactures*, Dresser wrote:

I firmly believe that the introduction of the works of Japanese handicraftsmen into England has done as much to improve our national taste as even our schools of art and public museums ... for these Japanese objects have got into our homes, and among them we live. I do not wish to destroy our art and substitute for it the Japanese style ... we may borrow what is good from all peoples; but we must distil all we borrow through our own minds.

From the time of its very first arrival in Europe, Japanese art was greeted with enthusiasm for its novel approach to the applied arts – where applied arts were of equal importance as fine art in creating a Japanese aesthetic. This was of particular importance in Great Britain where John Ruskin (1819–1900) and William Morris had been concerned with re-creating medieval craft techniques of the Gothic era, and with spreading the gospel that the decorative arts were a vehicle of spiritual and aesthetic redemption for the common man.

This process, surprisingly, seems to have absolved Ruskin and Morris from making pronouncements of any type on the alien artefacts from Japan. It was left to the Pre-Raphaelite critic, W M Rossetti, to make one of the first major critical responses upon the subject after a visit to the 1862 Exhibition, when he remarked, 'the very best fine art practised at the present day in any corner of the globe, is the decorative art of Japan,' while his brother Dante Gabriel delighted in Japanese designs:

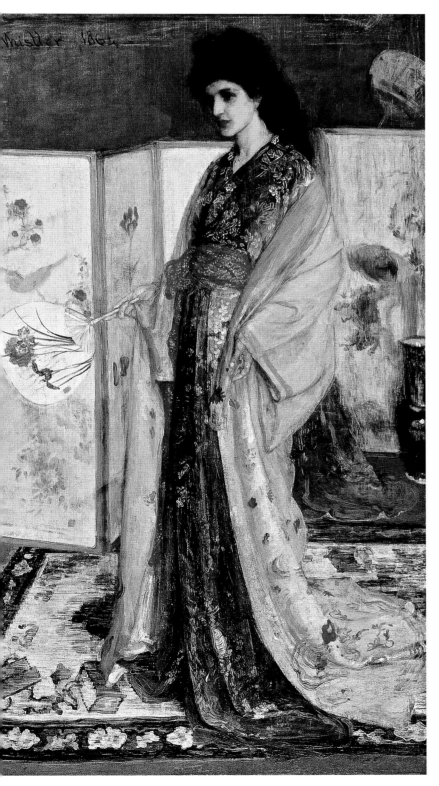

their enormous energy, their instinct for whatever savours of life and movement, their exquisite superiority to symmetry in decorative form, their magic of touch and impeccability of execution …

These views found support from the critic, Sidney Colvin, who, when criticizing the 'pseudo-Hellenic' style of paintings by Whistler's friend, Albert Moore, claimed that more perfect colour than Moore's could be found 'on a thousand fans, screens and painted hangings of Japan'. Predictably, Whistler also put his own individual spin on the received opinion of the difference between fine and applied art, declaring:

The painter must also make of the wall upon which his work is hung, the room containing it, the whole house, a Harmony, a Symphony, an Arrangement, as perfect as the picture or print which became a part of it.

Whistler's belief in his own axiom would be tested in the most controversial event in the history of Japonisme, *The Peacock Room* imbroglio. It begins in 1864 with the creation of arguably the most successful of Whistler's paintings using Japanese props, *Rose and Silver: The Princess from the Land of Porcelain* (105). The richly costumed figure of the princess wearing Japanese dress stands before a four-fold screen, behind which upon the wall hangs a *uchiwa* fan. Another fan with a design of irises is held in the princess's hand. The sumptuous colour and exotic background recall Rossetti's sensual female portraits.

The painting was exhibited at the Paris Salon and hung 'on the line', a good position which must have pleased Whistler, since it marked his first official recognition in France. Criticisms of the work varied from the caustic 'un pastiche chinois' to Gautier's alliterative observation concerning the blue-and-white Chinese carpet upon which 'the princess poses upon a pavement of porcelain'. After the first showing of *The Princess* in London at the International Exhibition of 1872, the painting was acquired by Frederick Richards Leyland (1831–92), a Liverpool shipping magnate and dilettante of music and the arts who played a major role in Whistler's life.

A great admirer of the work of Rossetti and Whistler, Leyland not only collected their paintings but also became fired by their enthusiasm for blue-and-white Chinese and Japanese porcelain, and, guided by the leading ceramic dealer, Murray Marks, he became one of a group of obsessive collectors.

One of the problems involved in collecting ceramics in large quantities is how to store and display your treasures. In the morning and billiard rooms at the home of fellow collector, Aleco Ionides, at 1 Holland Park, Leyland saw a remarkable quasi-Japanese installation devised by the architect, Thomas Jeckyll (1827–81). The fireplace in the morning room was especially remarkable for its serried rows of blue-and-white pots surmounting a cast-iron grate surround, devised by Jeckyll utilizing the shapes of Japanese *mon* (106).

As his collection grew, Leyland also began to dream of creating a similar 'palace of art' in his newly acquired and very grand town house, 49 Prince's Gate, Kensington. In one room, the dining room, he would unite Whistler's painting of *The Princess* with his porcelain collection in an imaginative and inspired setting. Leyland believed that a happy colour-contrast solution for the background to the display could be created by using the sumptuous red leather (then believed to be seventeenth-century Spanish, now thought to be eighteenth-century Dutch), which had already been used elsewhere in Ionides's house by Jeckyll. At one end of the room would hang the *Princess*, while facing her a prominent place was reserved for the *Three Girls*, another work commissioned by Leyland from Whistler, which sadly would never be completed.

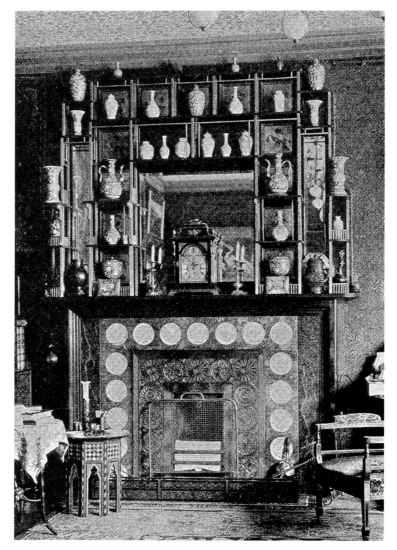

In April 1876, Mrs Leyland passed on to Whistler a fateful enquiry:

Jeckyll writes what colour to do the doors and windows in the dining room … I wish you would give him your ideas.

These were ominous words in view of what was to follow: all was sweetness and light until the moment when *The Princess* was hauled into position, the blue-and-white porcelain arranged on the shelves, and Whistler was asked to comment on the effect by Leyland. Whistler felt that the red flowers on the leather, which were painted and not embossed, 'killed' the tones in his painting. Leyland gave permission for the flowers to be painted yellow and gold, and for the red border of the rug to be trimmed. Whistler was still not completely satisfied, and Leyland agreed to him adorning the wainscoting and cornice with a 'wave pattern'.

Business problems now intervened for Leyland. His fleet, the Leyland Line, was entering into the Atlantic trade, and he had to leave London to stay in Liverpool during the summer months of 1876, to supervise events. He left, assuming the decoration of the room to be virtually completed. But Whistler, in his patron's absence, was inspired to create a far more radical treatment of the room.

107
James Abbott McNeill Whistler,
Shutters from *Harmony in Blue and Gold: The Peacock Room*,
1876–7.
Oil paint and metal leaf on leather, canvas and wood.
Freer Gallery of Art, Smithsonian Institution, Washington, DC

108
James Abbott McNeill Whistler's room,
2 Lindsay Road, Chelsea, 1867–8

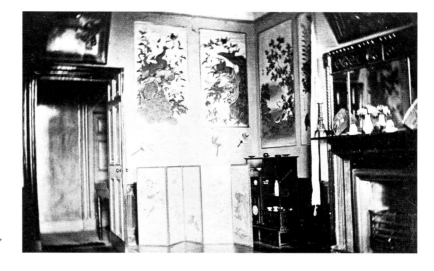

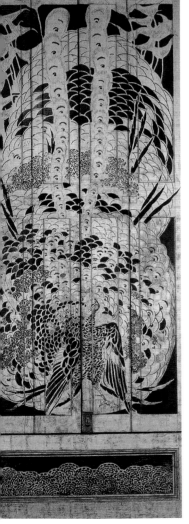
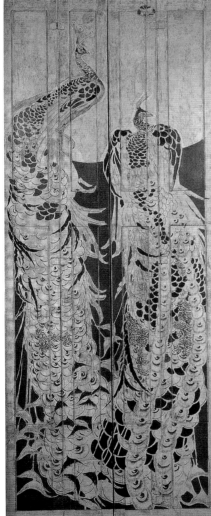
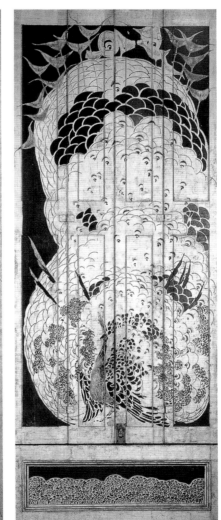

Whistler covered the ceiling of the room with 'Dutch metal', an imitation gold leaf, over which he painted a lush pattern based on peacock feathers. He gilded the walnut shelves and embellished the inner sides of the wooden shutters with four gorgeous peacocks whose vast sweeping trains derived from Japanese sources (107).

Exactly why peacocks should be so much on Whistler's mind must remain a mystery, although the birds have always been a popular subject in both the East and the West. It is worth being aware that the peacocks in Rossetti's back garden menagerie would have been all too audible to Whistler's ear, and that Whistler owned fifteen Japanese pictures of 'birds of many varieties and of the richest plumage'. An old photograph (108) tells us that at one time Whistler had three large Japanese paintings of peacocks hanging in his own rooms at 2 Lindsay Row, Chelsea. Such subjects were common throughout the Edo era, and birds were frequently depicted on screens by such artists as Ogata Korin (1658–1716), one of Japan's greatest decorative painters. Korin's birds provide a fascinating contrast with Whistler's – the former's shimmering yet perfectly restrained – Whistler's so animated and full of movement. While evidence of Whistler's contact with such a screen must remain conjectural, he may have seen a print by Hiroshige (109), which in its composition relates closely to the paintings on the shutters.

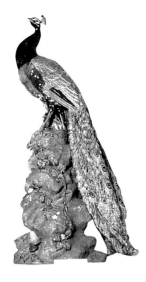

109
Utagawa Hiroshige,
Peacock and Peonies,
1833–5.
Colour woodblock,
38·7 x 17·1 cm
(15¹⁄₄ x 6³⁄₄ in)

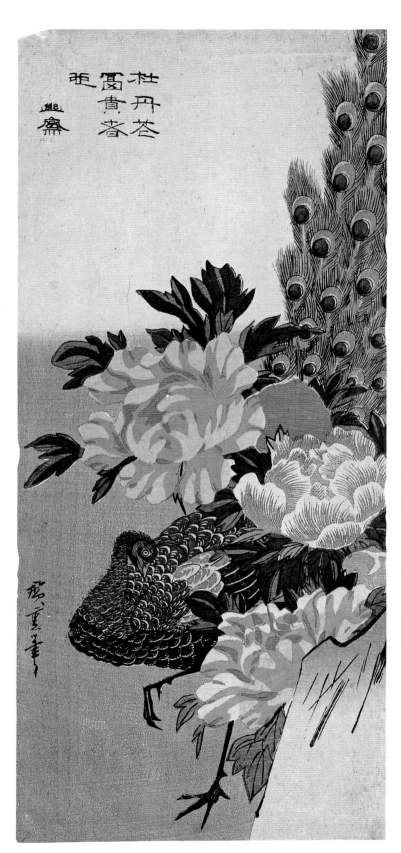

It is pertinent to ask *why* Whistler should have selected the peacock as the dominant component in his decorative scheme for Leyland's room. The theme had in fact been in his mind for some time, for as early as 1873 he had suggested a decorative scheme involving peacocks for the dining room of Aubrey House, Campden Hill (also in London), belonging to the banker W C Alexander, who rejected it because of its expense. Clearly the concept remained at the back of Whistler's mind, and his interest was fostered by several factors. The Pre-Raphaelites, attracted by its sonorous colours, often used the bird in paintings, as for example in Rossetti's large peacock next to King David in his triptych in Llandaff Cathedral, while Edward Burne-Jones (1833–98), Arthur Hughes (1832–1915) and Frederick Lord Leighton (1830–96) painted peacocks in their easel pictures. Ceramic peacocks also abounded, Minton producing a life-size bird in 1876 (110).

In 1880 Walter Crane designed a mosaic frieze of peacocks in Leighton House, and later in 1889 the sumptuous wallpaper *Peacock Garden* (111). Whistler would certainly have been aware of two contemporary decorative room schemes using the peacock theme extensively. The best surviving example is happily still on public display in the Victoria and Albert Museum. Dating from 1869, it was originally called the Dutch Kitchen or Grill Room. It is now called the Poynter Room after its designer Sir Edward Poynter. In it a frieze of peacocks surmount the tiles, which include two large panels above the grill depicting the birds.

Another peacock scheme, at Frederick Lehmann's house at 15 Berkeley Square, was designed by the architect, George Aitchison (1825–1910), the peacock frieze being executed by Whistler's friend, Albert Moore, in 1872. Surviving sketches reveal Moore's peacocks modestly trailing their trains rather than flaunting them as do Whistler's (112).

110
Minton & Co.,
Ceramic peacock,
1876.
Glazed ceramic,
height: 154 cm
(60⅝ in).
Potteries Museum and
Art Gallery, Stoke-on-
Trent

111
Walter Crane,
Peacock Garden wallpaper (detail),
1889.
Victoria and Albert Museum, London

112
Albert Joseph Moore,
Cartoon for the Peacock Frieze at
15 Berkeley Square,
1841–93.
Charcoal and white chalk on brown paper,
46 x 154.9 cm
(18 x 61 in).
Victoria and Albert Museum, London

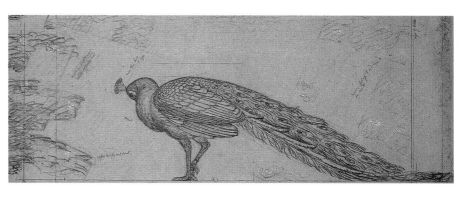

113
Satsuma faience vase
and stand, plate XII,
from Audsley and Bowes,
The Keramic Art of Japan
vol. 2, 1875

One of the best-known and most often cited Oriental sources for Whistler's peacock is to be found in George Ashdown Audsley and James Lord Bowes's *The Keramic Art of Japan* (1875). As an avid ceramic collector it is highly probable that Whistler saw this book, and was also influenced by the plate from it showing a large Satsuma faience vase with dragon handles and stand (113). Whistler almost certainly saw this vase, which belonged to a close friend of Leyland.

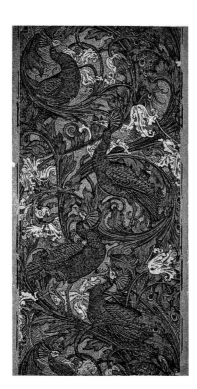

As the painting of the Peacock Room progressed, artistic circles in London buzzed with stories about the painter and his methods. Whistler, a brilliant publicist, held press conferences in the completed room. He actually issued a pamphlet, copies of which were distributed at Liberty's and several London shops, that audaciously welcomed the public to Leyland's house; he himself had not yet been allowed by the artist to judge the work for himself. When at last Leyland saw the room he was understandably irate at the complete reversal of his own preferred colour scheme, and the resultant disappearance of the red 'Spanish' leather under the brilliant blue and gold of Whistler's decorations. Leyland also disliked the creation of the peacocks on the shutters. When the shutters are drawn at night their sweeping trains swirl in cascades of golden feathers silhouetted against a background of gold leaf.

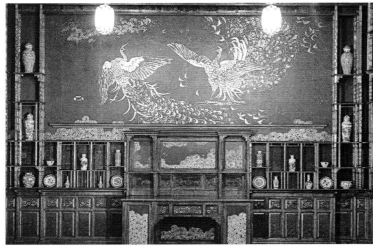

114
James Abbott McNeill
Whistler,
*Harmony in Blue and Gold:
The Peacock Room*,
1876–7.
Oil paint and metal leaf on
leather, canvas and wood,
Room dimensions:
4·2 x 10 x 6 m
(13 ft 9³⁄₈ in x 32 ft 9³⁄₄
in x 19 ft 8¹⁄₄ in).
Freer Gallery of Art,
Smithsonian Institution,
Washington, DC

115
James McNeill Whistler,
*Blue and Silver: Screen
with Old Battersea
Bridge*,
1871–2.
Distemper and gold paint
on brown paper laid on
canvas and stretched
on back of silk,
195 x 182 cm
(76³⁄₄ x 71⁵⁄₈ in).
Hunterian Art Gallery,
University of Glasgow

These peacocks were not part of the original commission, however, and Leyland wrote:

The peacocks you have put on the back of the shutters may possibly be worth (as pictures) the £1,200 you charge for them but … I certainly do not require them and I can only suggest that you take them away and let new shutters be put up in their place.

What really rankled with Leyland was Whistler's arrogance in inviting the general public into Leyland's home without asking his permission.

As always, financial concerns exacerbated the situation. Whistler had in mind a fee of two thousand guineas, a sum he felt barely paid for the work. In Whistler's day a pound was worth twenty shillings sterling, and a guinea twenty-one shillings. Only tradesmen were paid in pounds, whereas gentlemen's fees were settled in guineas. The prickly artist felt deeply insulted, accepting payment of one thousand pounds with very bad grace. On the blank wall opposite *The Princess*, he painted two magnificent peacocks – one the patron, scrabbling under his claws a pile of silver coins, the disputed shillings, while the other bird, the artist, shrieks a proud defiance – providing a commentary on his relations with Leyland (114).

Godwin wrote one of the most vivid accounts of the room's final appearance:

The scene is wonderfully dramatic, so dramatic in fact as to make one fancy that a story might well be wrapped up in it. There is a haughty tremulous rage in one bird, the very feathers seeming to shake, a seeming secured partly by a shower of gold dots, and partly by force of drawing in the raised and recurved tail … the other bird, the one of the emerald eye which would make us tremble for the life of the raging cock if once roused to retaliate. There is, indeed, more of Aristophanes, more of the Greek satirist, here than of Japanese drawings on fans, or trays, or crapes. The birds are, in fact, human peacocks after all … not those of the ornithologist nor the peacocks of the zoo.

Godwin amusingly refers here to the play *The Birds* by Aristophanes implying that patron and artist are both inhabiting 'Cloud Cuckoo Land'.

It is to his eternal credit that Leyland kept the room as Whistler left it, and made no attempt to erase the visual satire from the walls. He continued filling the shelves with porcelain until his death, aged sixty, in 1892.

Whistler loved painting as night was falling, as did the Japanese artists whom he admired, whose favourite motif in Edo was painting the Sumida river at dusk or when fireworks lit up the night sky. He passed long hours contemplating the river either from his Chelsea window or skimming along the Thames at twilight in a skiff rowed by his faithful but abused follower, Walter Greaves, who once observed: 'To Mr Whistler a boat was always a tone, to us it was always a boat.' A painting which celebrates Whistler's love of the Thames at dusk took shape on a Japanese screen. In London, as in Paris, Japanese screens had become both fashionable and readily available by the 1870s. Whistler himself purchased a two-panelled screen depicting flowers and birds by a contemporary Japanese artist, a woman named Nampo Osawa. Whistler adapted the screen by using the back as a support for a composition of his own entitled *Blue and Silver: Screen with Old Battersea Bridge* (115). In this experiment, as in his Nocturnes, Whistler reveals his remarkable assimilation of Japanese aesthetic principles.

In a letter of 1868 to Henri Fantin-Latour (1836–1904), Whistler described his aims:

It seems to me that colour ought to be, as it were, embroidered on the canvas, that is to say the same colour ought to appear in the picture continually here and there, in the same way that a thread appears in an embroidery, and so should all the others, more or less according to their importance. Look how well the Japanese understand this.

After 1877 Whistler was never to see his masterpiece *The Peacock Room* again, although he had not yet finished with the predominant colours of the room, gold and silver. They make a spectacular reappearance in the room decor on which he collaborated with his friend E W Godwin at the 1878 Paris international exhibition. Their work took the form of a stand for the furniture-maker, William Watt, which prominently featured *The Butterfly Cabinet* surrounded by other pieces of furniture.

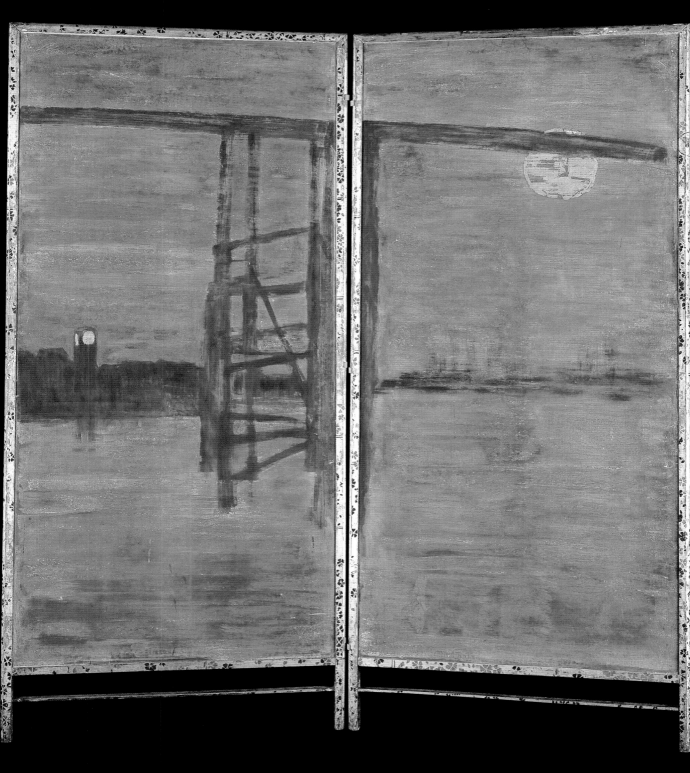

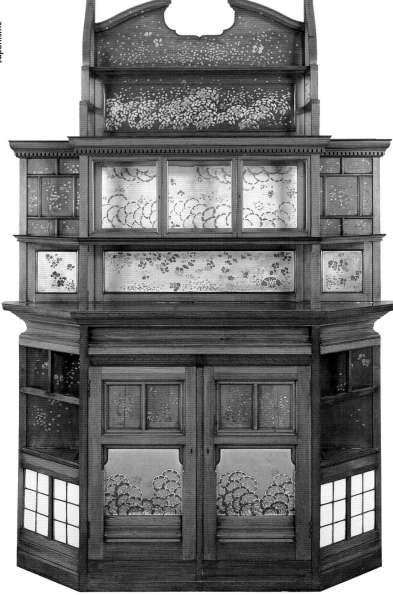

116
E W Godwin
*Harmony in Yellow and
Gold: The Butterfly
Cabinet*,
1877–8.
Oil on mahogany with
yellow tiling, brass
moulding and glass,
height: 303 cm
(119¹⁄₄ in).
Hunterian Art Gallery,
University of Glasgow

The cabinet was made in bright mahogany and painted in yellow and gold, which led Whistler to entitle it as a *Harmony in Yellow and Gold: The Butterfly Cabinet* (116), but was described by one critic as 'an agony in yellow', and the stand by another as the 'Primrose Room'.

One American visitor vividly described the effect:

yellow on yellow, gold on gold, every-where. The peacock reappears, the eyes and the breast feathers of him, but whereas in Prince's Gate it was always blue on gold, or gold on blue, here the feather is all gold, boldly and softly laid on a gold-tinted wall … The feet to the table legs are tipped with brass, and rest on a yellowish brown velvet rug. Chairs and sofas are cover-ed with yellow, pure rich yellow velvet, darker in shade than the yellow of the wall, and edged with yellow fringe.

Today the originality of 'The Butterfly Suite', is only known to us by its central feature, *The Butterfly Cabinet*. The cabinet was originally designed as an overmantel for a fireplace of bright mahogany with a painted decoration of Japanese cloud motifs and butterflies in shades of yellow and gold. The lower part immediately after the exhibition was converted from a fireplace to a cupboard with doors painted by Whistler, the form in which it survives today.

When Whistler and Godwin visited the Paris exhibition in 1878 it is intriguing to speculate whether they were ever confronted by the saffron yellow cabinet (117) exhibited by Madame Duvinage, widow of Ferdinand Duvinage, who ran her husband's firm, Duvinage & Harinkouck, from after his death in 1874 until 1882. In her workshop she strove to emulate the virtuoso craftsmanship of the great *ébénistes*, the de luxe cabinet-makers of the eighteenth century. The over-whelmingly ornate surface of the cabinet is smothered in a rich jumble of stylistic borrowings from Japan of dragons, phoenixes, swallows, the inevitable butterflies and chrysanthemums. The approach was a very different one from that of Godwin and Whistler who both had a sensitive understanding of decoration and spatial proportion.

An alarming example of the Japonisme style, can be seen in the cabinet designed and manufactured by Gabriel Viardot in 1888 (118). There are relatively few purely Japanese elements apart from the panels, for the rest of the cabinet is a strange mixture of both Chinese and Vietnamese elements, perhaps reflecting the fact that Vietnam (formerly Indo-China) was then one of France's most important colonies.

Nevertheless, the jury in the 1888 exhibition awarded Viardot a gold medal, praising particularly his 'Japanese furniture always extremely interesting for its tonality and perfect execution'. It provides an interesting comparison with the very different aim of Godwin's Anglo-Japanese works.

Japanese folding screens, like Japanese prints, provided a powerful visual stimulus for Western artists. Although lacquered screens were probably exported from Japan in quite large numbers from about 1630 to 1700, most were converted into furniture and very few survived intact. Like many of the most highly esteemed artefacts, screens possess both practical and aesthetic qualities. Uniquely adaptable into a variety of settings, screens function as freestanding partitions defining space, whether of an intimate or public nature. Folding screens vary from two to ten panels, but the most common format is a pair of six-panel screens. The design on a pair of screens may form a single composition when the screens are placed side by side, usually with complementary subjects such as landscapes of the spring and autumn. Themes linking screen with screen created exquisite visual conundrums as to which panel to emphasize by altering its position to make it more or less dominant, almost like a chime of bells.

117
Madame Duvinage,
Cabinet,
c.1878.
Rosewood, marquetry
of ivory, copper, brass,
pewter and bronze,
height: 130·4 cm (51⅜ in).
Musée d'Orsay, Paris

118
Gabriel Viardot,
Cabinet,
1888.
Carved walnut with
gilt bronze mounts,
Height: 162·6 cm
(64 in).
Victoria and Albert
Museum, London

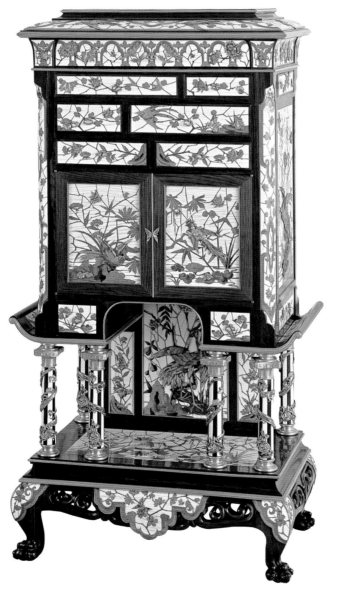

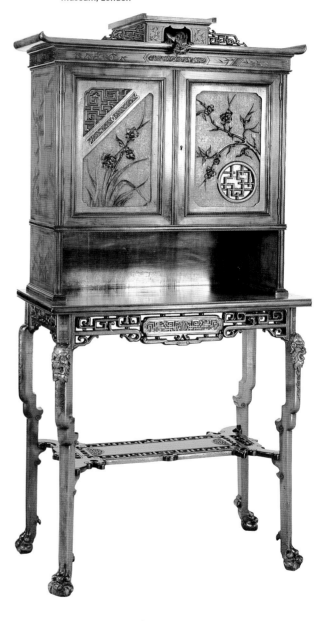

119
Attributed to Walter
Crane, Royal School of
Art Needlework,
Folding screen,
1875–6.
Wool thread on cotton
and silk,
151 x 59·7cm
(59¹₂ x 23¹₂ in).
Private collection

It was not, however, until the last decades of the nineteenth century that Western artists embraced the screen's potential as a form of household decoration. There were some memorable 'variations on all too familiar themes', such as the four-panel screen depicting peacocks possibly designed by Walter Crane and executed by the Royal School of Art Needlework (119). Alongside a three-panel screen with Japanese motifs, this was made for the famous Centennial Exhibition of 1876, Philadelphia. Crane reinterpreted decorative themes from the Far East, especially in the aquatic border at the bottom of the composition. Encouraged not only by the Royal College, but also by the Morris circle's enthusiasm for embroidery, Anglo-Japanese screens continued to thrive throughout the 1880s.

In France one group of young artists in particular would be greatly concerned with the screen as a pictorial discipline, the group were called the Nabis, the Hebrew word for 'prophets', because of their proselytizing belief in promoting art as a form of decoration. In 1887 Édouard Dujardin hailed in *La Revue indépendante* the coming of a new art form which he named *cloisonnisme*, the pictorial equivalent of the recently established school of Symbolist literature, the creation of which he accredited to Louis Anquetin (1861–1932). Other members of the group included Paul Sérusier (1863–1927), a follower of Gauguin, Pierre Bonnard, Édouard Vuillard (1868–1940) and Maurice Denis (1870–1943).

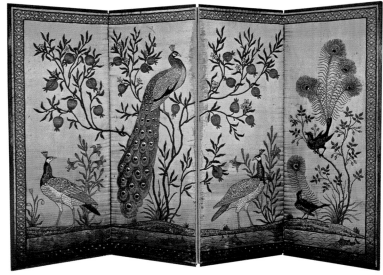

Art as decoration was a sentiment which possessed a great appeal for Bonnard who, in his first interview, proclaimed: 'Painting must, above all, be decorative.' Bonnard became known as the 'Nabis très japonard' because of his love of Japanese prints. Of them he said, 'what I had before me was something fully alive and also extremely skilful.' The Japanese taught him that 'it was possible to translate light, form and character with nothing but colour, without resorting to shading'. Bonnard was the first of the group to take on the problems of a folding screen. In 1891, at the Salon des Indépendants, he exhibited four panel paintings showing women in a garden at different seasons of the year, each panel the same size but composed as a separate entity. While not strictly speaking a screen, this work prepared the way for one of Bonnard's most famous works, the four-fold panel *Nursemaids' Promenade* (120), a composition which floats effortlessly across all four panels, linked only by the boy's hoop and the line of waiting cabs at the top of the composition, which was also issued in lithographic form.

120
Pierre Bonnard,
Nursemaids' Promenade
with Frieze of Carriages,
1895.
Colour lithograph,
150 x 200 cm
(59 x 78³⁄₄ in)

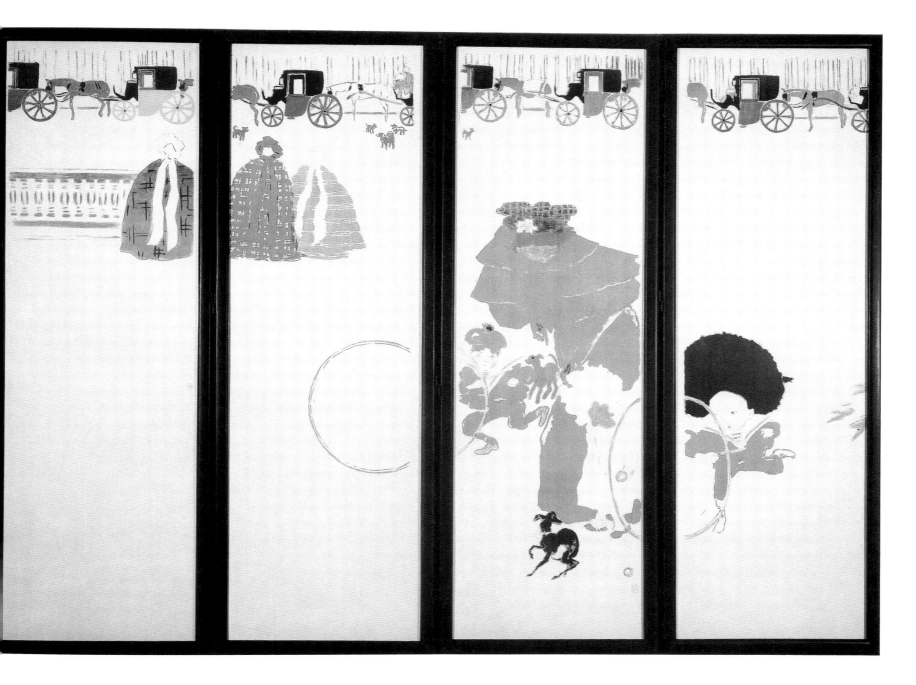

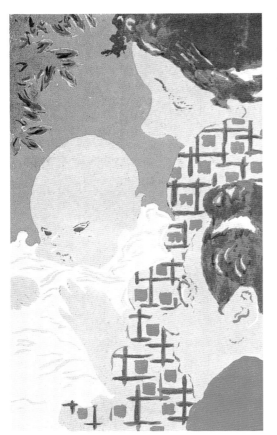

121
Pierre Bonnard,
Family Scene from an
album of *l'estampe
originale*,
1893.
Colour lithograph,
31·2 x 17·7 cm
(12¹₄ x 7 in)

Bonnard really loved Japanese prints. He delighted in their bright flat colours, and we may surmise especially the work of Kunisada and the domestic scenes of Utamaro so delightfully reflected in Bonnard's colour lithograph, *Family Scene* (121) of 1893. The work is inspired by the same ongoing human instinct to love and cherish childhood that is present in Utamaro's *Sankatsu and Hanhichi With Their Baby* (122) of a century earlier.

Bonnard's friend, Vuillard, is especially remembered today for his intimate easel paintings that capture the charm of scenes drawn from everyday life. He lived for much of his life in Montmartre among the ordered confusion of his mother's dressmaking shop, divided by screens which were in frequent use to provide privacy while garments were altered, while swatches of brightly checked fabrics were everywhere. His love of Japanese prints was to express itself not only by wearing a kimono and tacking prints to the wall, but also by owning a Japanese screen.

In the early 1890s Vuillard enjoyed several commissions for decorative panels for such patrons as Alexandre Natanson, the editor of *La Revue blanche* and his wife Thadée, the belle of the *belle époque*, who kept the gossip mills of the *beau monde* turning for years.

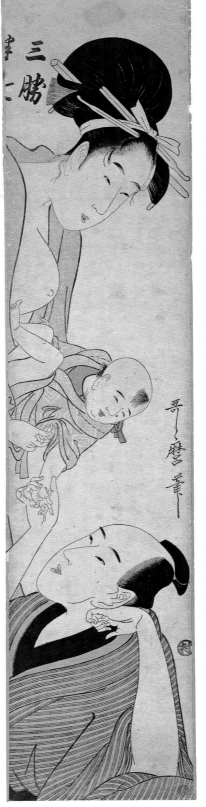

122
Kitagawa Utamaro,
*Sankatsu and Hanhichi
With Their Baby*,
*c.*1790.
Colour woodcut,
62·2 x 14·9 cm
(24¹₂ x 6 in)

In the dining room of their luxurious new home he painted for them nine decorative panels of the Tuileries Gardens and the Bois de Boulogne. A great feature of this area are the well-ordered parks where children played among the trees under the watchful eyes of their nursemaids, who formed the unaware models for the later screen of 1894 painted in distemper on canvas, entitled *The Nursemaids*, *The Conversation* and *The Red Sunshade* (123). These everyday scenes of women gossiping on park benches while children play among the trees were organized on Japanese design principles, which build up large compositions by letting the eye rove from a single image to diptych to triptych to polyptych, the nearest analogy in Western art being provided by the individual panes which make up stained-glass windows.

Differing dates and locations are claimed as witnessing the beginnings of Art Nouveau, that most varied of all artistic styles. Details of its many manifestations were spread by a wide variety of international journals, a few of them being *L'Art moderne* (Brussels), *L'Art décoratif*, *Art et décoration* (Paris), and *Die Jugend*, *Simplicissimus* (Munich). One of the most influential of these journals was *L'Art nouveau*, edited by Siegfried Bing, a name already familiar from his patronage of Japanese art, who in December 1895 opened a gallery in Paris of the same name.

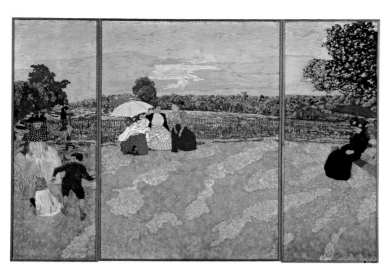

In every land there was a desire for a new start for art with the abolition of the old divisions between the fine and decorative arts. The continuing influence of Japan is evident in the emphasis placed upon asymmetry and simple outlines, and the study of exotic birds and flowers.

Many artists in Europe and America would create screens in the exciting years of the Art Nouveau movement, when the decorative arts flourished dramatically. One such artist was the polymath Emile Gallé. Gallé first worked in glass (see Chapter 4), but in 1884 turned his attention to furniture, believing that the same decorative style, based on natural forms, should apply to all the furnishings of a house. He first became attracted to the subject by the colourful variety of grained woods he discovered in a lumber yard where he had gone to obtain wood for the base of a glass vase. The experience alerted him to the pictorial possibilities of marquetry, and it was this quality that intrigued him and that can be seen in much of his furniture, which uses applied floral decoration in various woods often signed 'Gallé' vertically in the Japanese manner.

With the consummate skill acquired from his work with glass and metals, Gallé went on to produce such masterpieces as the remarkable bed with a marquetry headboard depicting a giant moth whose wings are drawn over a star-filled sky. The theme of dusk is echoed by the foot of the bed with the colours of dawn (124). Many of Gallé's pieces of furniture are decorated with flowers, landscapes and quotations from his favourite poets. A work table (125), for example, bears the inscription, 'Work is Joy at the House of Gallé'. This optimistic and very Morrisian slogan was tested by the fact that at the time of his death in 1904 his works at Nancy were employing over 300 men. For Gallé the Japanese influence continued through his friendship with a Japanese botanist called Takashima who studied forestry at Nancy. Their discussions led to the ironic comment of a critic called E de Vogue who wrote about Gallé: 'Let us be grateful for the quirk of fate which caused a Japanese to be born in Nancy.'

At the 1900 Paris exhibition, the high watermark of Art Nouveau, the reactions of the artistic establishment took various forms. The vice president of the jury for the awards in the exhibition was the forward-thinking Sir George Donaldson, who wanted to familiarize English designers and manufacturers with the 'new art' of Europe.

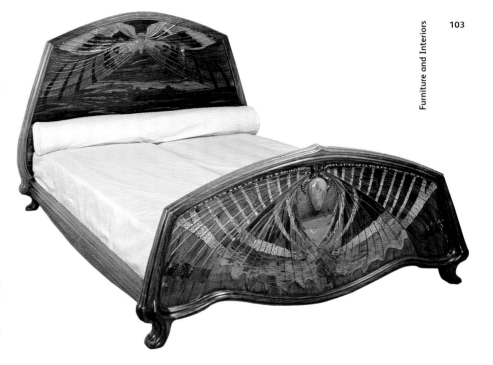

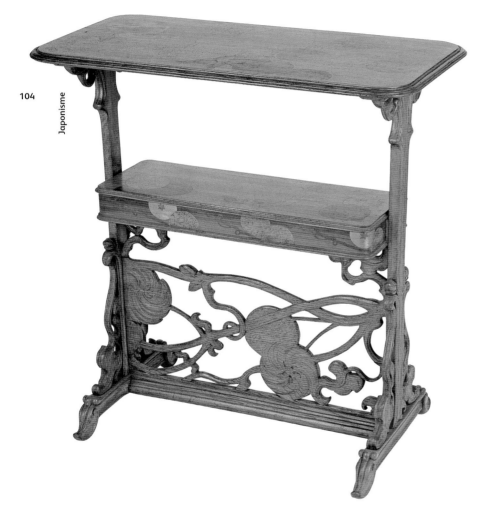

125
Emile Gallé,
Work table,
1899–1900.
Carved ash and walnut
with marquetry of
various woods,
height: 70 cm (27½ in).
Victoria and Albert
Museum, London

126
Louis Majorelle,
Cabinet,
c.1900.
Mahogany and oak veneered
with kingwood and amboyna,
enriched with carving and
marquetry of pearl, amboyna
and sycamore.
Victoria and Albert Museum,
London

Realizing that no public funds would be available to purchase controversial work he generously decided to present a number of pieces of furniture, pottery and metalwork to what is now the Victoria and Albert Museum. His gifts included an inlaid cabinet (126) by Louis Majorelle (1859–1926), another brilliant member of the Nancy School, and the Gallé work table already mentioned. Unfortunately, however, immense prejudice was easily whipped up against the new style, dubbed the 'cult of the ugly' and a 'strange decorative disease' by Walter Crane, then Principal of the Royal College of Art. Other critics preferred to call it the 'noodle' style, descriptive both of its Japanese borrowings and decorative effects. So great was the volume of criticism that the offending artefacts were quickly removed from public exhibition in the museum, when they were shown there in 1901. Today, ironically, they are treasured as major examples of the furniture of their time.

By the early twentieth century the always changing Western perception of what was truly inspirational in Japanese culture would be radically altered by the work of a new generation of architects and designers. They would be concerned not with the ornamental tradition, but with the Japanese sense of architectural proportion, and a new realization that everything in a Japanese house is determined by rule.

The Czech artist and writer, Emil Orlik (1870–1932), visited Japan several times between 1900 and 1921 and wrote two important essays on Japanese woodcuts, noting that:

The feeling for clear articulation in the Japanese colour woodcut impressed me the very first time I came across it. Horizontal lines always stand in an interesting relation to the verticals … Japanese painters … have even developed a grille-motif of posts or trees in the foreground, middle distance, or background to specify artistic effect.

These concepts would take memorable shape in both buildings and furniture, and the continuing contest between Anglo-Japanese and Japonisme would take new forms in Frank Lloyd Wright's America (see Chapter 9), and Charles Rennie Mackintosh's (1868–1928) Scotland, exemplified in an amazing large chair or very small semicircular settle (127) from the Willow Tea Room made in 1904 which vividly looks forward to the abstract tenets of the new twentieth century.

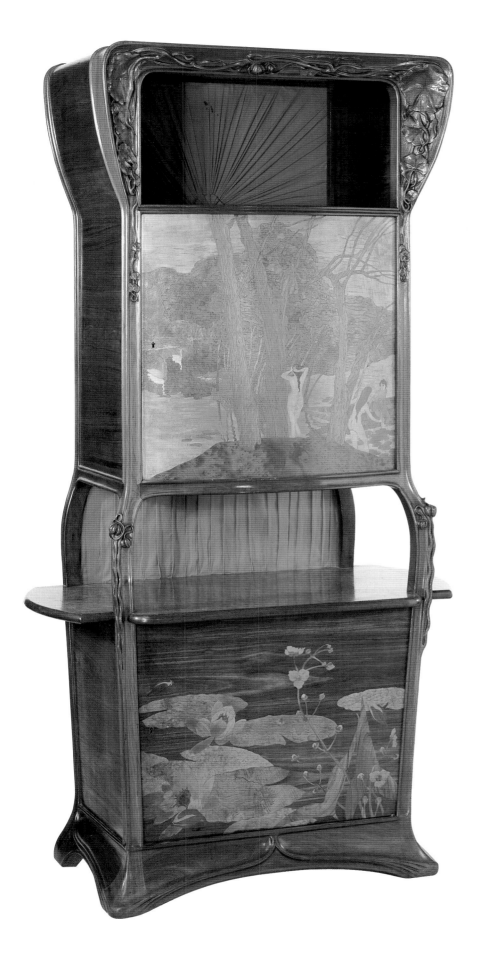

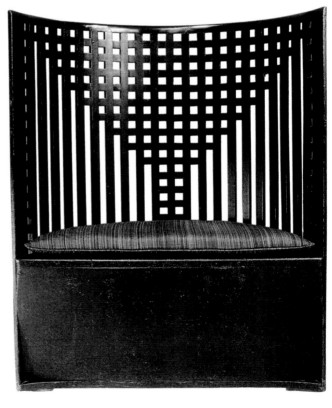

127
Charles Rennie Mackintosh,
Chair,
1904.
Ebonized oak,
re-upholstered with
horsehair,
height: 118·2 cm
(46½ in).
Glasgow School of Art

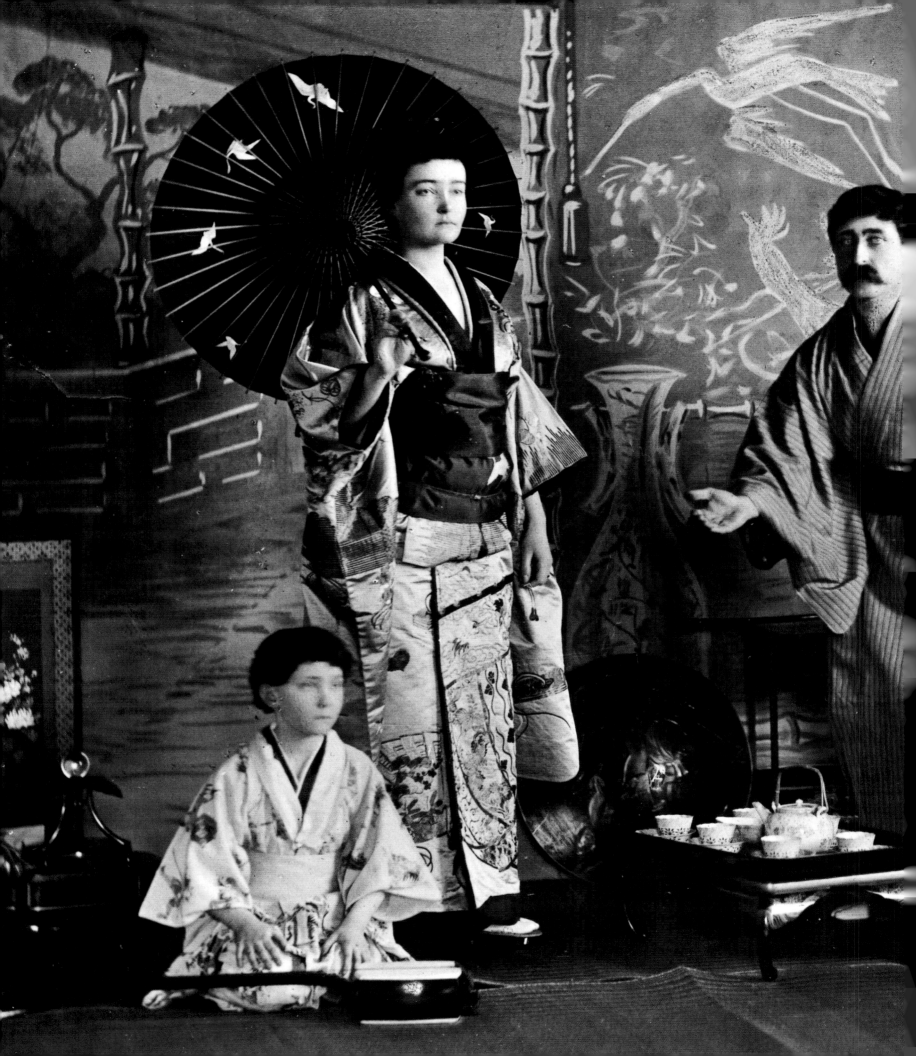

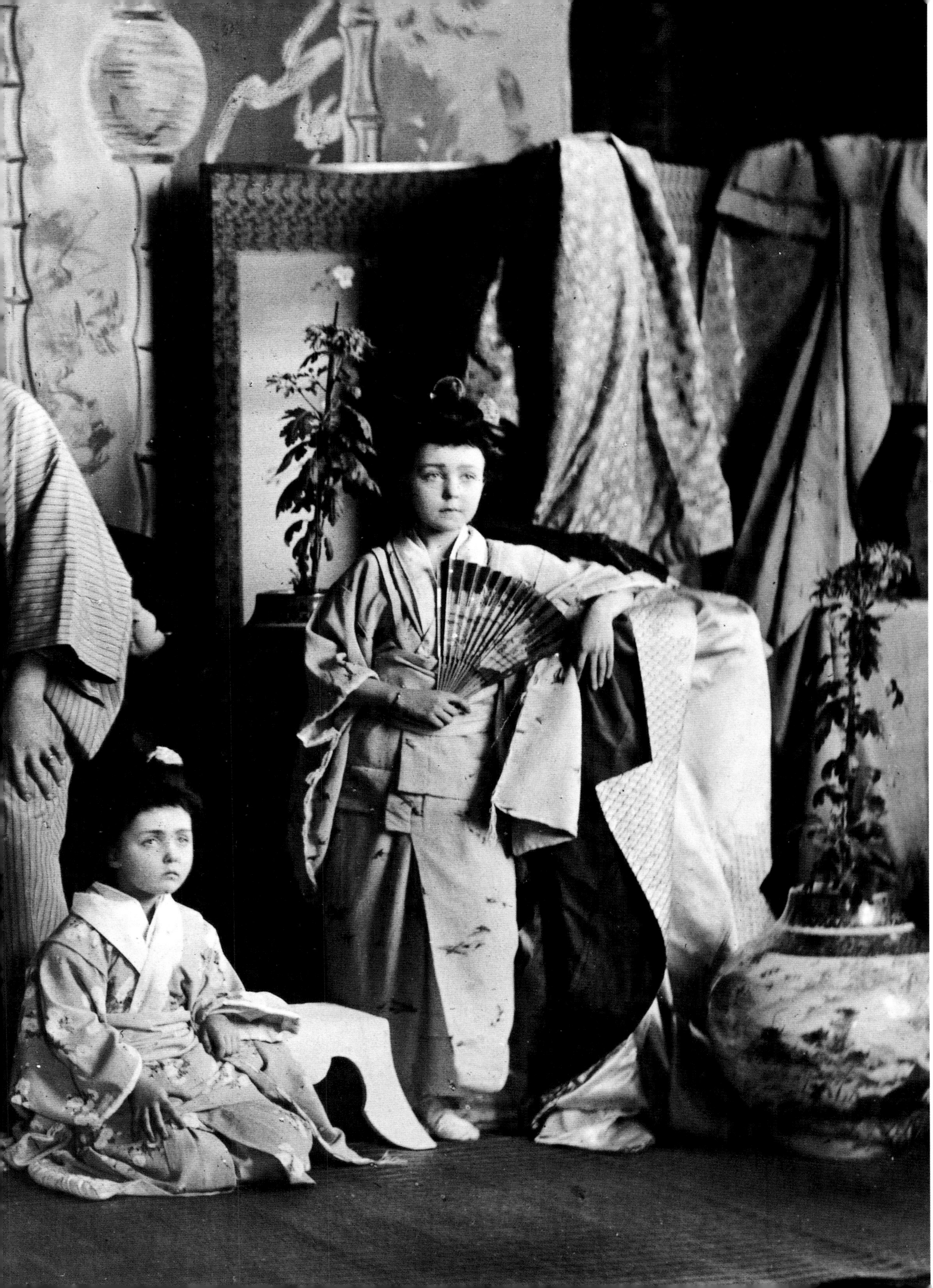

Previous page
**The Duke and Duchess
of Connaught and their
children dressed in
Japanese costume and
taking part in a Japanese
tea ceremony,
c.1890**

*The story of the beautiful is already
complete – hewn in the marbles of the
Parthenon – and embroidered, with
birds, upon the fan of Hokusai at
the foot of Fujiyama.*
J A M Whistler, 1885

In his novel *Pierre and Jean*, written
between June and September 1887,
Guy de Maupassant once again used
a literary device at which he excelled
by letting his description of a room
crowded with Japanese bric-à-brac
establish a mood. A young widow,
Jean, wants to impress his fiancée, and
he and his mother decorate a room in
his new apartment with:

*Japanese lanterns. Mother and son
had put as much imagination into this
room as they were capable of. With its
bamboo furniture, oriental figures and
vases, gold sequined silks, transparent
blinds of glass beads like drops of
water, fans fixed to the wall to hold
back curtains; with its screens, swords,
masks, cranes made of real feathers,
and all its knick-knacks in porcelain,
wood, paper, ivory, mother-of-pearl
and bronze, this room had the
pretentious and mannered
appearance which unskilled hands
and untrained eyes bestow upon
objects requiring the utmost tact,
taste and artistic training.*

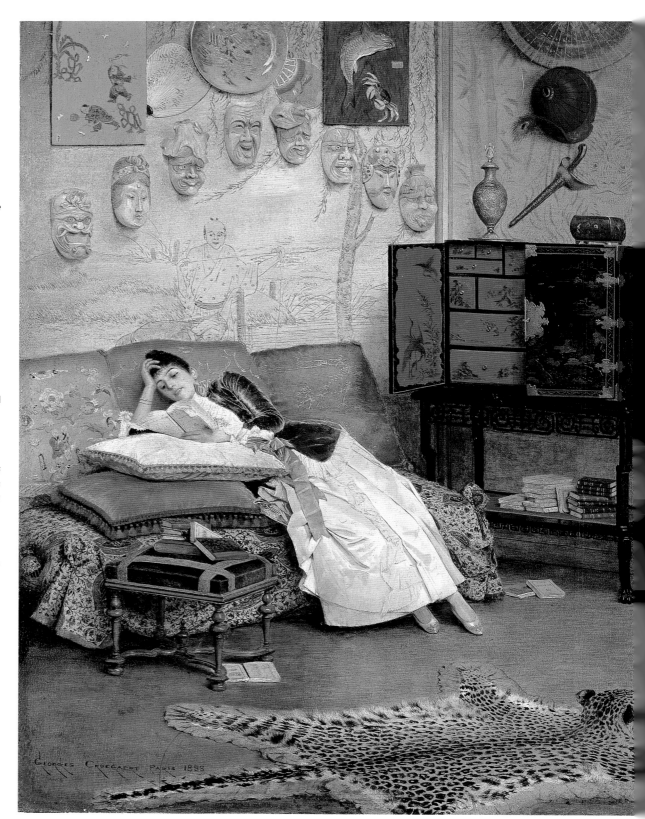

128
Georges Croegaert,
The Reader,
1888.
Oil on canvas.
Private collection

129
Kitagawa Utamaro,
*Women on the
Ryogoku Bridge*,
1795–1800.
Colour woodblock,
36·5 x 75 cm
(14³₈ x 29¹₂ in)

De Maupassant in this passage is subtly asking the question why the presence of Japanese artefacts could at one and the same time produce aesthetically pleasing and appallingly vulgar effects. In discovering why this is so we must look again at the importation of goods from Japan, and the standard of export wares deemed suitable for the barbarians in the outside world. By the 1880s acute artistic perceptions were becoming swamped by the popular mania for paper lanterns, fans and masks. Japanese motifs spread like a rash on everything from cheap trays to biscuit boxes. Fans, kimonos, screens and porcelain enlivened the 'artistic' rooms of the day, creating a decor of varying quality. An excellent example of a room of this type is provided by *The Reader* (1888; 128) by Georges Croegaert (1848–1923). In it we see a young Parisian lady who is, one may surmise, an avid reader of the extensive literature of Japonisme, and also a keen collector. Japanese objects jostle for our attention in her studio, including an awesome array of *noh* theatre masks, the obligatory fans and parasols, *kakemono* (hanging scrolls), lacquer panels and a valuable lacquer cabinet.

In the course of Japan's history both folding and fixed fans played a varied role. The importance of the fan went far beyond its practical use of keeping its bearer cool. Fans feature in a wide range of court and social activities; and were also used for the military purpose of making signals on the battlefield.

Fans figure largely in the disciplines of the theatre, dance and in the sumo wrestling ring, in which the referee, *gyoji*, controls the bout using a folding fan of a type known as a *gumpai uchiwa* (military fan). Today such fans can still be seen in use in the ceremonies, displays and bouts of the sumo ring. Fans were also created in large numbers for the 'fans' of famous *kabuki* actors by specialized artists such as Kunisada.

The growth of *ukiyo-e* woodblock printing during the Edo era provided a great stimulus to the development of fans of all types. Certain *ukiyo-e* print-makers were noted for their ability to create captivating fan shapes, notably Utamaro, whose *Women on the Ryogoku Bridge* (three sheets from a set of six; 129) shows women using a variety of both fixed *uchiwa* and folding *ogi* fans.

As Japanese fans began to be exported in large numbers in the 1860s, European artists began to experiment in painting on fan-shaped supports. Surprisingly, Whistler himself made no experiments in actually painting within the discipline of the fan shape, although fans do appear in his other work as background accessories, for example, a folding fan tucked behind a mirror frame, or a parasol in the grate, acting as a screen and indicating that the painting depicted a summer scene, as in the winter a fire would occupy the grate.

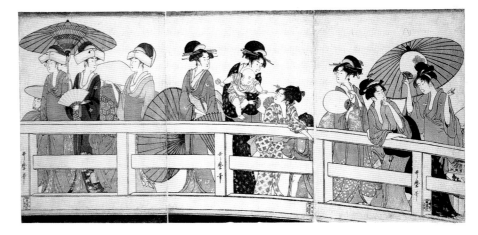

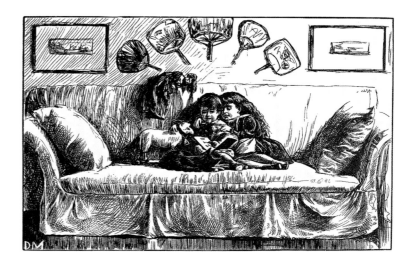

130
George Du Maurier,
Reading Without Tears,
from *Punch*,
February 1869

131
Simeon Solomon,
Lady with a Japanese Fan,
1865.
Watercolour,
41 x 35·5 cm
(16¼ x 14 in).
Grosvenor Museum,
Chester

A friend of Whistler from student days in Paris was the cartoonist, George Du Maurier (1834–96), who, in a cartoon for *Punch* dating from February 1869, showed his children seated on a sofa above which hang five *uchiwa* fans displayed very much like a military 'trophy' on the wall (130). Such casual displays of both fixed and folding fans were widely popular among aspiring followers of fashion at all social levels. The fan – cheap, frivolous, flirtatious and univer-sally available – became a badge of commitment to the arts for those of both high and low degree throughout the last quarter of the nineteenth century.

Close rivals to Whistler's *Symphony in White, No 2: The Little White Girl* (see 19), for the distinction of being the first paintings by a Western artist to depict a woman holding a Japanese fan, were two works by Simeon Solomon, who was an important figure in the nascent Aesthetic Movement. In one work, *Lady with a Japanese Fan* (131), Solomon's model sits posed against a background of *tatami* matting (Japanese floor covering) and a screen on which can just be discerned a stork. Behind her are Japanese Arita ware plates and two vases, one containing the obligatory aesthetic lily.

The painting, which dates from 1865, shows the model dressed in a Chinese robe but holding a Japanese fan, with a distinctive design of fans upon it. In another work of the same date the model is posed against a wall embellished with two *kakemono* paintings.

By the 1870s their cheapness and easy availability led to the visual triumph of fans in Europe and America. Curio shops selling both screens and fans abounded. Whether arranged symmetrically or casually in clusters, or attached to a screen, fans could enliven any room, arranged upon dado rails, or pinned to walls, and Whistler, as always, got in first with the idea of sticking fans to the ceiling. Nor was their more usual purpose forgotten, for as a writer in Oscar Wilde's journal, *The Woman's World*, observed in 1887, 'in the hot summers that have become the fashion, [we] fan ourselves, without regard to sex or condition, with Japanese fans.' As early as 1880, when George Du Maurier advised Frank Burnand to put 'Japanese sixpenny fans here and there on the walls' for the set of his play *The Colonel* satirizing Whistler, they had become an aesthetic cliché in England. In France, however, they still had a dramatic role to play.

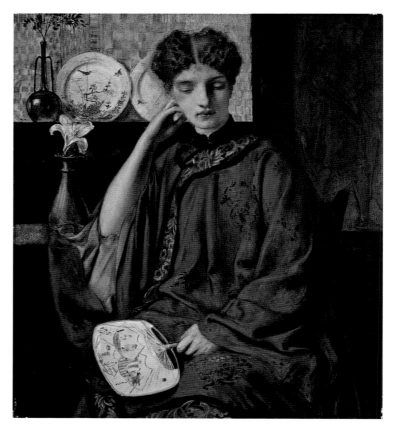

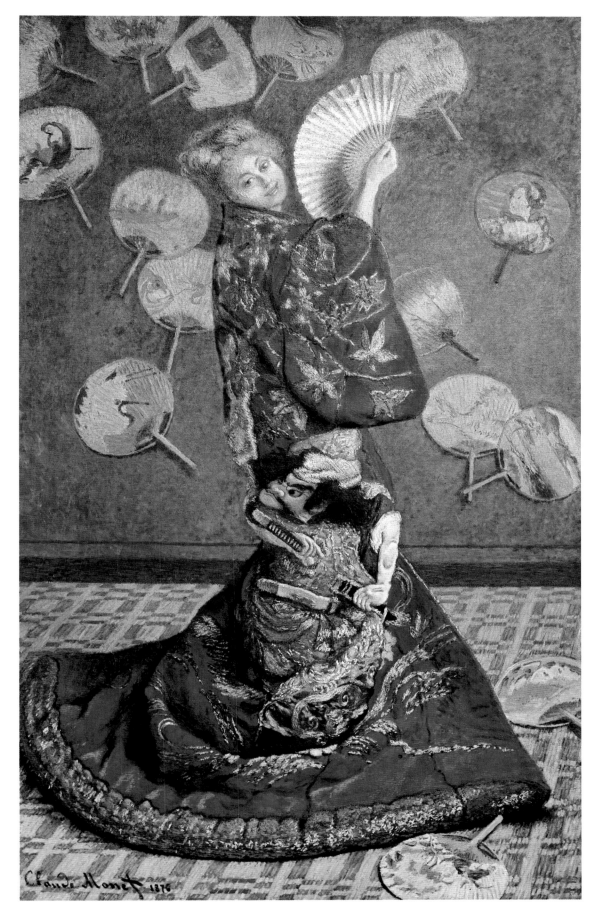

Claude Monet,
La Japonaise,
1876.
Oil on canvas,
231·6 x 142·3 cm
(91$^1_8$ x 56 in).
Museum of Fine Arts,
Boston

Artists used fans to decorate both their studios and their paintings, and Édouard Manet used a display of fans as an amusing visual ingredient in the portrait of Nina de Callias on a settee in a studio entitled *The Lady with the Fans* (1874). The sitter was a famous society hostess, renowned for her salons which, for more than fifteen years, were crowded with artists, musicans and writers. But while the fans in Manet's painting provide a striking background, they are eclipsed by the cascade of fifteen colourful fans which emblazon the wall of Claude Monet's studio in 1876. Before them stands his wife in a provocative pose clad in a *kabuki* actor's discarded robes. One fan, in particular, is of note, seen behind her left shoulder it portrays a 'tug of war' between a fish and a prawn, a theme also used by Christopher Dresser (see 72).

The painting *La Japonaise* (132), when first exhibited, met with both fierce criticism and great success, and would later gain iconic status. While the painting was in progress Monet wrote to his friend, Phillipe Burty (1830–90), saying that the *kabuki* actor's robes were 'superb to do'. But forty years later he was to describe the painting as 'une saleté' – a piece of filth – for reasons we can only guess at, but which may be connected with the embroidery of the figure of a warrior who seems to be fighting his way out of the woman's body.

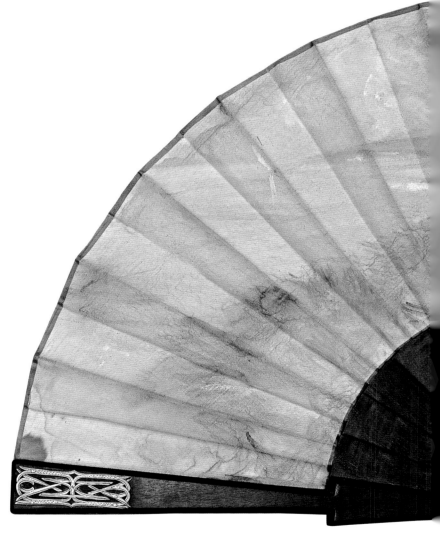

133
Jean Louis Forain,
Dancer With a Rose,
*c.*1885–90.
Watercolour on linen.
Dixon Gallery and
Gardens, Memphis

Madame Monet is wearing a blonde wig, and clearly enjoying the fun of dressing up. The fan that she is holding is, however, not Japanese, but a red, white and blue tricolour fan of a type often used by Parisians at 14 July celebrations. The dancer's pose may owe something to Monet's friend, Théodore Duret, who had visited Japan, and wrote with knowledge of the entertainment at a famous Kyoto teahouse:

The Japanese dancer is covered from head to foot in a large, richly coloured robe whose lowest folds form a circle around her. She changes position very slightly while dancing … her dance is all in character; it consists, above all, of the movement of the head, the upper part of the body and the arms. Our dancers first danced singly [using] a fan or a parasol to mark or accentuate their pose.

The enormous demand in Europe and America for Japanese fans radically altered production methods. Mass-production techniques were brought in from the early 1860s when vast quantities of fans were exported in order to satisfy the ever-growing demand for 'something Japanese'. Before the floodgates really opened with the end of the Edo era in 1868 and the accession of the Meiji emperor, fans and prints provided a novel visual stimulus to a whole generation of European artists.

The mingling of diverse traditions provided a challenge which particularly appealed to Edgar Degas, who formed an extensive collection of Japanese prints, including at least fifteen drawings by Hiroshige, two triptychs by Utamaro, sixteen albums of miscellaneous prints, and various loose sheets by Hokusai, Utamaro, Shunsho and others, while a framed diptych of *Women at the Bath* by Kiyonaga once hung in his bedroom. The influence of this collection can be particularly clearly seen in the twenty-five paintings by Degas which took the form of fans. They were painted on two main occasions, three in the year 1868, and the remainder mainly around 1879, when he began enthusiastically to plan for the fourth Impressionist exhibition, where a room would be totally devoted to fan-shaped paintings. But although other artists were asked, in the end at the exhibition only five fans by Degas, four by Jean Louis Forain (1852–1931) and twelve by Camille Pissarro were shown on what proved to be the only occasion on which Degas exhibited this aspect of his art.

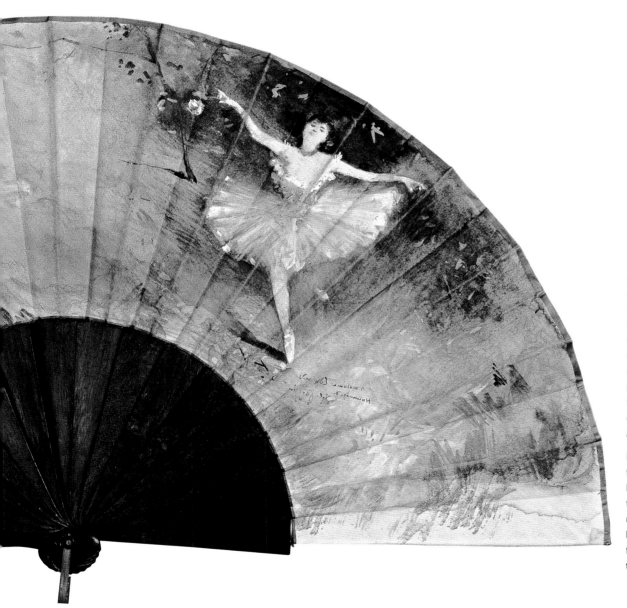

Degas's disciple, Jean Louis Forain, however, soon became a particularly successful creator of fan-shaped compositions. Forain was a man of great enthusiasms, a passionate admirer of Degas, a lover of ballet and of Japanese prints, several examples of which can be seen hanging on the walls of his home in a photograph taken in 1892 on the occasion of his marriage. Forain's *Dancer With a Rose* (133) demonstrates his abilities at their best.

Rather surprisingly, given the fan's intrinsic frivolity, it was the seriously minded Camille Pissarro who would create most fan-shaped compositions, exhibiting them in the fifth and eighth Impressionist exhibitions. In 1885 Pissarro grumbled that he 'had got to churn out fans because times are hard and for the moment one can only find a market for them, one mustn't count on paintings'. He experimented with the difficult shape to great advantage, creating such rural idylls as *Peasants Planting Pea Sticks* (1890; 134).

Paul Gauguin was also fascinated by the fan shape and owned an example by Pissarro, which he lent in 1879 to the fourth Impressionist exhibition mentioned above. Gauguin, always hard up, painted no fewer than thirty fans in his career probably because they sold well owing to their small size.

134

Camille Pissarro,
Peasants Planting Pea Sticks,
1890.
Gouache and black chalk
on grey paper,
39 x 60.2 cm (15³⁄₈ x 23³⁄₄ in).
Ashmolean Museum, Oxford

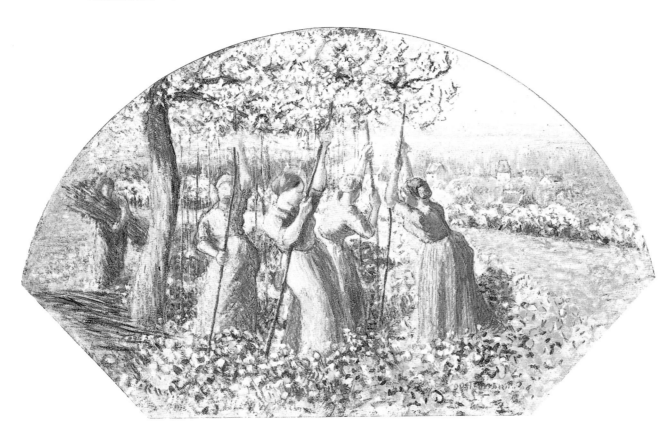

135

Paul Gauguin,
The Dramas of the Sea:
A Descent into the Maelstrom,
1889.
Lithograph on yellow paper,
17·5 x 27·6 cm
(7 x 10⁷⁄₈ in)

The most memorable of Gauguin's fan-shaped compositions, *The Dramas of the Sea: A Descent into the Maelstrom* (135), is based upon Sadahide's colour woodcut of *The Seaweed Gatherer* (136). In a lithograph on zinc, printed on yellow paper from a series of eleven, Gauguin, with brilliant inventiveness, has taken the basic fan shape, turned it upside down, and used its sloping sides to suggest the giddying depths of the whirlpool's sloping walls. The semicircle at the top of the print has been used to suggest the calmer waters of the more distant sea. The boat and sailor caught in the maelstrom suggest the theme of Edgar Allan Poe's story, *A Descent into the Maelstrom* (1841) and the climax of Victor Hugo's *Toilers of the Sea* (1867), while Gauguin has borrowed from Sadahide the figure of a man plummeting downwards threatened by the dark and angry waves and the inevitable progress towards the centre of the vortex of water.

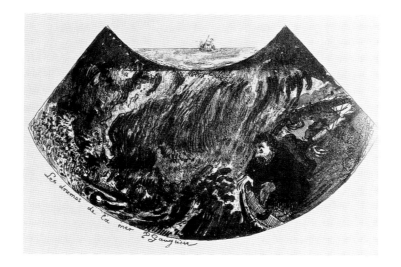

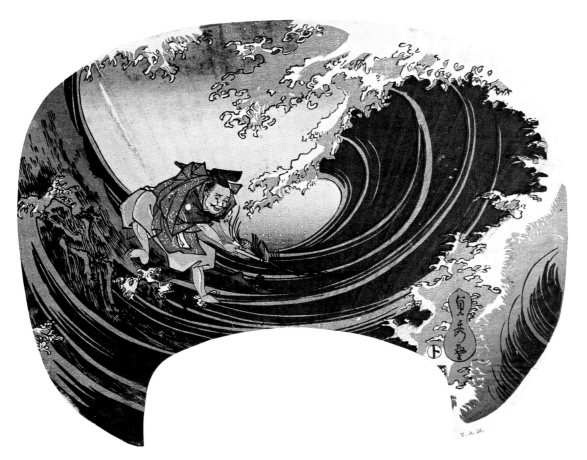

136
Sadahide,
The Seaweed Gatherer.
Colour woodblock,
22·9 x 28·6 cm
(9 x 11¼ in)

The aesthetic artist and illustrator, Walter Crane, was given some prints by Toyokuni by a family friend who had returned from Japan, and subsequently he acknowledged 'Japanese colour prints' as 'an important factor' in the evolution of his bold linear style and flat and delicate colours. These are seen to advantage in his 'Shilling Series'. Crane provided a visual pun on the artist's name, and he used the bird as his signature in the same way that Whistler used the butterfly. The most extraordinary mixture of all Crane's 'exotic' images of the Middle and the Far East, particularly Japan, is provided by *Aladdin; or The Wonderful Lamp* (1875; 137). One page shows an Arabic princess dressed in a kimono and *geta* (Japanese sandals), attended by Japanese maids and servants holding a Japanese fan and parasol. Architectural details reveal Japanese motifs in the lacquer screens of the doors and in painted tiles. A vase with hydrangea is seen in the foreground arranged in the Japanese manner.

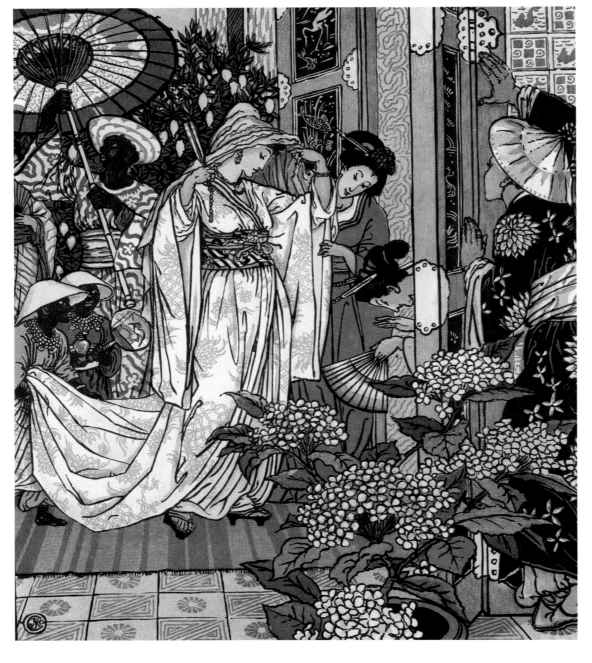

Sales of fans in the 1870s went from strength to strength, but with an inevitable decline in quality. The brilliant colours which created such a violent contrast to the subtler shades of the natural pigments used by the early masters were due to the importation of Prussian Blue from the West, a new chemical pigment which was accompanied by a crude aniline red, a regrettable manifestation of Japanese interest in imported colours. In 1876 Whistler's friend, E W Godwin, who had long advocated 'a fitting disposition of Japanese fans as an alternative … decoration for dining room walls', now warned against 'the common paper fan of today … impregnated with the crudeness of the European's sense of colour'.

Despite these warnings the craze continued, and in their fixed form the cheap paper *uchiwa* were by the 1880s made literally in millions in Japan specifically for the export market. In 1891 the combined total of folding and rigid fans exported from Japan reached the astounding total of nearly sixteen million. As the caption for a *Punch* cartoon by Harry Furniss put it:

Twopence I gave for my sunshade,
A penny I gave for my fan,
Threepence I gave for my straw hat –
forrin made –
I'm a Japan-aesthetic young man.

137
Edmund Evans, after
Walter Crane,
*Aladdin; or The
Wonderful Lamp,* from
the 'Shilling Series',
1875.
Colour woodblock,
27 x 23·5 cm
(10⅝ x 9⅜ in)

The Grossmith brothers' classic novel of suburban life, *The Diary of a Nobody*, serialized in *Punch* in 1888 and published in book form in 1892, has a passage in which Carrie Pooter beautifies 'The Laurels, Upper Holloway' by tacking up a few fans, a fashion which was by then, to use the slang of the day, already 'old hat'. By the time Henry James wrote his *What Maisie Knew* in 1897, Mrs Beale gives Maisie a Japanese fan to hang up, but neither lady is sure where to put it. In 1894, Rudyard Kipling also turned to exotic associations of the fan to conjure up a 'decadent' milieu in his poem 'The "Mary Gloster"' when the dying sea captain says to his son:

*The things I knew was proper you
wouldn't thank me to give,
And the things I knew were rotten
you said was the way to live.
For you muddled with books and pictures, an 'china an' etchin's an' fans,
And your rooms at college was beastly
– more like a whore's than a man's...*

A craze began for amateurs painting fans. The materials for doing this appeared in the form of assembled fans void of decoration, and manuals on the art of composing and painting fans. Fan shapes were everywhere; mantelpieces groaned with Christmas cards with asymmetrical forms and fan-shaped vignettes with such popular themes as cherry blossom or sparrows. Fans were also put to commercial use, with free fans advertising shops and luxury goods. In *Fans of Japan* (1894) Charlotte M Salwey describes the way in which:

fans find their way into almost every drawing-room and boudoir in our Western Hemisphere, and are twisted up with wool and silk and tawdry materials, and repainted by the modern Goth. They are set in fireplaces and windows as summer screens, put to all sort of tortures, for letter racks and tidies, and devoted to uses for which they were never intended.

Their use as a symbol of status in society was vividly described in the rural classic, *Lark Rise to Candleford*, by Flora Thompson, an autobiographical account of English village life at the turn of the century, published in 1945, in which she describes:

the homes of ... newly married couples illustrated a new phase in the hamlet's history ... there were fancy touches hitherto unknown ... Japanese fans appeared above picture frames and window curtains were tied back with ribbon bows.

The parasol, like the fan, found an appropriately warm welcome when introduced into Europe in the 1860s. Its arrival on the fashionable scene created an instant vogue. Light and elegant, it could be used to protect an elaborate hairstyle, hide the modest bearer from unwelcome glances or, alternatively, prove an effective aid to coquetry, although its main use was to protect its users from the hot rays of the sun.

Parasols feature significantly in several major paintings of both the Aesthetic and Impressionist movements. For portrait and figure painters it provided a dramatic background for a beautiful face and delicate female complexion. As a compositional device it was elegantly used by Tissot in his portraits of his mistress Kathleen Newton.

In 1886, fashions, especially in Britain, became very elaborate; ribbon bows appeared near the handles while the sunshades themselves became 'daintily puffed veils at the end of sticks'. Carved animals and insects featured on the handles, which could be as big as billiard balls. By the end of the century ladies carried their parasols closed while gentlemen had the tightly rolled umbrella without which no English businessman's costume was complete.

The parasol briefly occupied a central place in the artistic concerns of Whistler, who was a friend of Sir Henry Cole, the first director of what is now the Victoria and Albert Museum. He obtained for Whistler in 1873 a commission to execute two mosaic panels to join thirty-five portraits of artists already installed in arcaded niches. Unlike the other designs, Whistler's would be of women and depict 'a Japanese art worker'. One of Whistler's own suggestions for this project depicted a woman decorating a parasol, while in a second pastel she is shown decorating a fan. However, Whistler failed to enlarge his drawings to the requisite size desired and the project was never realized.

Fortunately for posterity, some related drawings for this commission do survive, of which one of the finest is *The Japanese Dress* (138), a pastel which Whistler himself described as 'a very brilliant drawing and of beautiful colour – Gold – & blue & violet – in short a sparkling business altogether'.

Whistler also used parasols in several of his most 'Japanese' landscape studies of the early 1870s, such as *Battersea Reach from Lindsey House*. But his most important compositions using both parasols and fans as props were the *Six Projects* dating from 1868, commissioned by Leyland, Whistler's most important and difficult patron (see Chapter 5).

In the *Six Projects*, four of the six compositions are horizontal in format and show ladies in Tanagra-style classical draperies standing by the sea with Japanese fans and parasols. The paintings were all given different titles such as *Symphony in Blue and Pink*, which indicate the predominant colours of the picture. To establish the key colour notes a strip of fabric of the appropriate colour was inserted into the slats of the parasol or fan held by the model.

118

139
Katsushika Hokusai,
Group With Umbrellas
from the *Manga* vol. I,
1812–14.
Colour woodblock,
17·5 x 11·5 cm
(7 x 4¹₂ in)

138
James Abbott McNeill
Whistler,
The Japanese Dress,
1888–90.
Pencil, chalk and pastel on
brown paper,
26·6 x 17·9 cm
(10¹₂ x 7 in).
Davison Art Center,
Wesleyan University, Boston

140
Édouard Manet,
*Queue in Front of
the Butcher's Shop*,
1870–1.
Etching,
16·8 x 13·7 cm
(6⁵₈ x 5³₈ in)

The paintings were designed to form a frieze in Leyland's music room, for he was an accomplished pianist and first suggested the word 'nocturne' to Whistler as a generic term for his night scenes. Although the projects were never completed, they mark a turning point in Whistler's career, enabling him to synthesize his various interests – Japonisme, classicism and the analogies between music and painting – into a coherent aesthetic of his own.

In addition to the main type of parasol, the *kinugasa*, there were also more elaborate parasols designed for the export trade, the *komori-gasa*. It is surprising that in Europe and America there do not seem to be any examples of parasols designed by artists, with one predictable exception, a parasol designed by Whistler for his great friend and taxing client, Lady Archibald Campbell, known as Lady Archie. It was well known that Whistler's monogram and the prominent pair of butterflies depicted on it immediately identified it as his signed work, and by implication hinted at an intimate relationship between the creator and the user. The design consisted of six pale green leaves enclosing seven darker leaves around a central flower. Washes of pale green and cream hint at the subtlety of the final effect.

Given our universal interest in weather, the parasol, sunshade and umbrella have surprisingly been relatively little studied. As a subject they are often shown in use in Japanese prints, Hiroshige, in particular, being fascinated by the way humans behave during the downpours of the rainy season or heavy falls of snow. In Hokusai's *Group With Umbrellas* (139) we possess one of his insights into human discomfort. This print may in part have inspired Édouard Manet's *Queue in Front of the Butcher's Shop* (1870–1; 140), a poignant memory of the siege of Paris when rats joined dogs and cats on the menu.

Renoir, most chauvinist of artists, had strong reservations about copying Japanese prints, complaining that:

Japanese prints are certainly very interesting, as Japanese prints – in other words as long as they stay in Japan. A people should not appropriate what belongs to another race; in so doing, they are apt to make stupid mistakes. There would soon be a kind of universal art, without any individual characteristics.

This prophetic disclaimer apart, Renoir seems to have at least looked at the same subject from the *Manga* when working on his major painting, *The Umbrellas* (c.1881–6; 141). It is one of his most puzzling pictures, perhaps because of a four-year gap which took place between working on both halves of the canvas – the half containing the umbrellas being left until last. Maybe he had just mislaid his umbrellas?

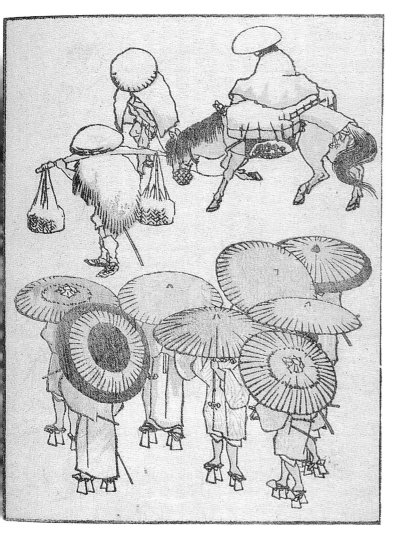

141
Pierre-Auguste Renoir,
The Umbrellas,
c.1881–6.
Oil on canvas,
180·3 x 114·9 cm
(71 x 45¼ in).
National Gallery, London

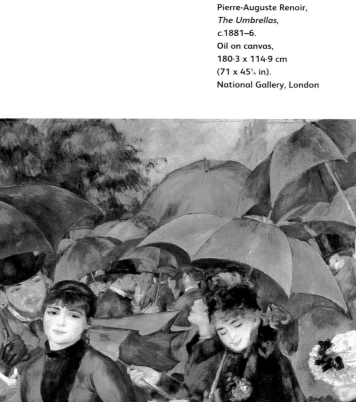

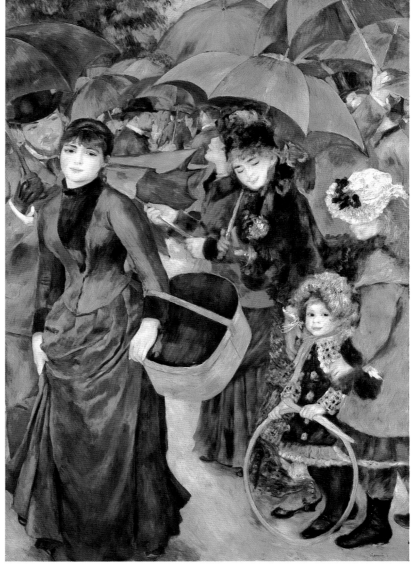

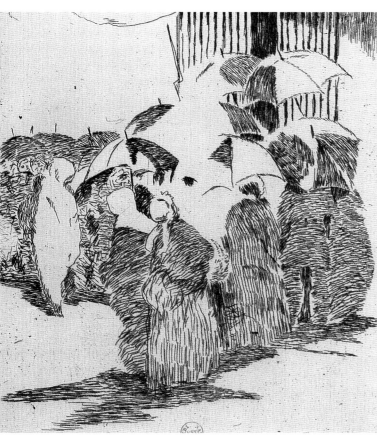

Fans, Parasols, Combs, Pins, Kimonos

142
Front cover of *Vogue*
magazine, April 1917

143
Ernst Ludwig Kirchner,
*Girl Under Japanese
Umbrella*,
c.1909.
Oil on canvas,
92·5 x 80·5 cm
(36³⁄₈ x 31⁵⁄₈ in).
Kunstsammlung
Nordrhein-Westfalen,
Dusseldorf

144
Vitaldi Babani,
Chrysanthemum Kimono,
c.1905.
Musée de la Mode et du
Costume, Paris

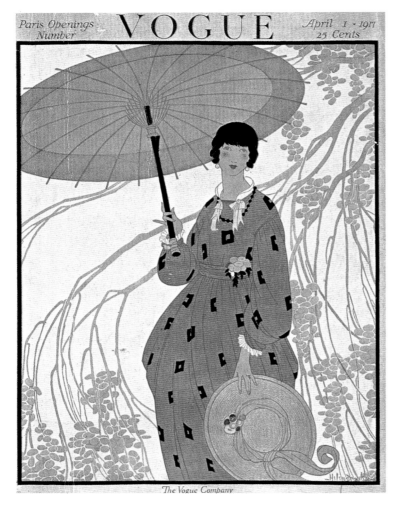

In the twentieth century the parasol would continue to surface as a decorative accessory, as in the cover for American *Vogue* for April 1917, with its use of the Japanese motifs of trailing cherry-blossom branches before which posed the willowy figure of an American, rather than a Japanese, beauty (142). The parasol also found a powerful interpreter in the German Expressionist artist, Ernst Ludwig Kirchner (1880–1938), who used a parasol in his vibrant *Girl under Japanese Umbrella* (*c*.1909; 143).

Both fans and parasols featured in the studios of European artists at the height of the craze for Japonisme and so also did the kimono (literally meaning 'the thing worn'), a garment which dates back over three hundred years. During this time various techniques for dying and painting developed, including Yuzen, a starch-dying technique named after Yuzen Miyazaki (*fl*.1688–1704). Yuzen was a famous dye master who began to use rice-paste as the 'resist', a substance that is applied to part of the fabric to prevent it taking up the dye.

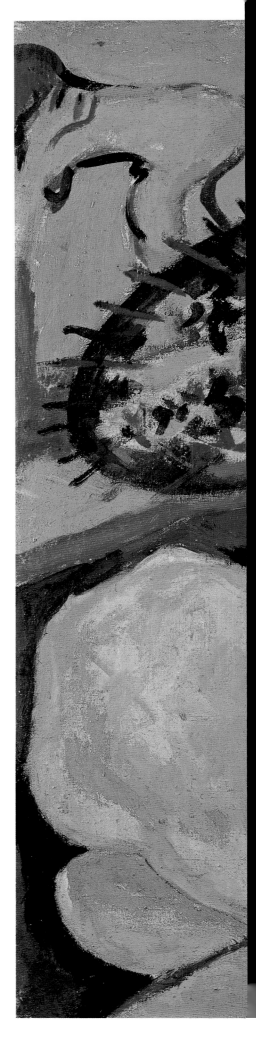

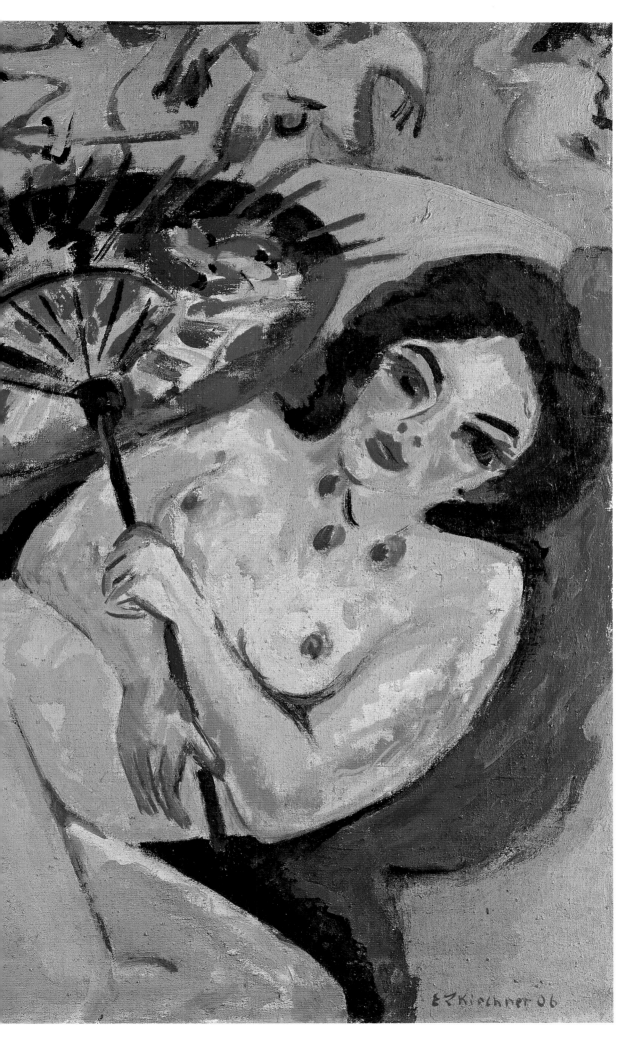

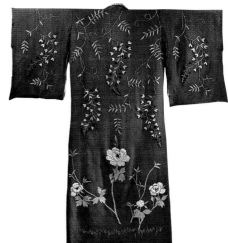

This technique started a revolution in the dying of freestyle designs, as dyers could easily depict landscapes, flowers, leaves and birds on silk textiles. The structure of a kimono as a cloak suspended from the shoulder provides a large area upon which to create a pictorial effect. Another nuance of the word kimono implied 'things to carry' and the make-up of the garment in crude but accurate terms can be compared to that of Western 'sandwich' men. Another more flattering analogy can be cited comparing the wearer with an easel and the garment with a blank canvas, upon which are created a design appropriate to each season, with such traditional motifs as cherry blossoms, chrysanthemums, bamboo, pine branches and running water. This example (144) of a kimono was from the shop on the Boulevard Haussmann in Paris founded by Vitaldi Babani in 1895, whose 'robes d'interieur japonaises' were greatly sought after by fashionable ladies. His talent for publicity led to the opening of workshops and branches as far afield as Kyoto and Constantinople.

We gain a good idea of such works seen through European eyes through the paintings of the Amsterdam-based Impressionist artist, George Hendrik Breitner (1857–1923), who loved to paint women in kimonos.

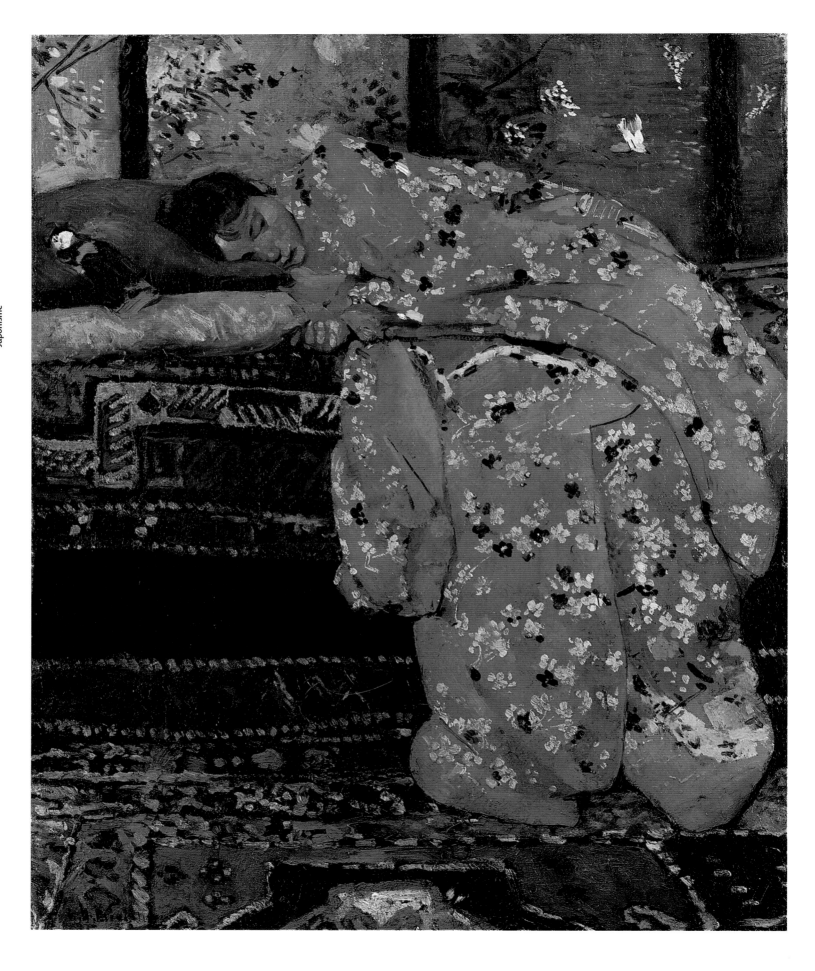

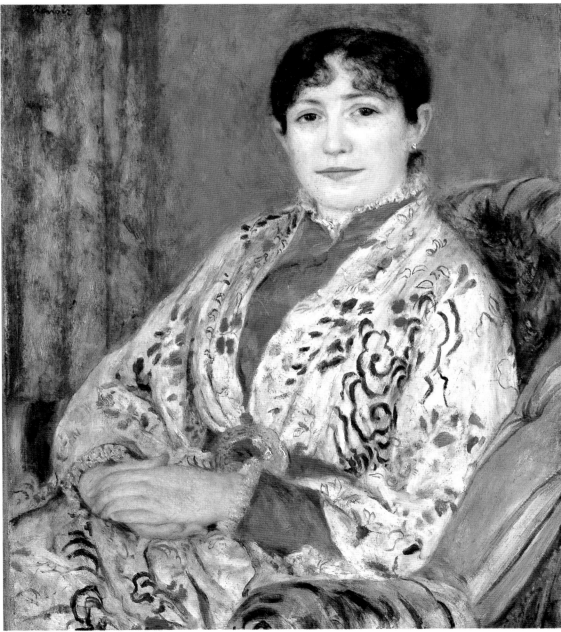

145
George Hendrik Breitner,
Girl in Red Kimono,
*c.*1893.
Oil on canvas,
85 x 52·2 cm
(33½ x 20½ in).
Haags Gemeentemuseum,
The Hague

146
Pierre-Auguste Renoir,
Madame Hériot,
1882.
Oil on canvas,
65 x 54 cm
(25½ x 21¼ in).
Hamburg Kunsthalle

147
Miss Turner,
Gown,
*c.*1872.
White silk, printed and
embroidered with
chrysanthemums and fans.
The Kyoto Costume Institute

He created many 'variations on a theme' with models wearing either a white or a red kimono elaborately embroidered with cherry blossoms and birds (145).

In the studios of Europe and America, quite apart from its use as an exotic prop, the kimono was also to provide a vital ingredient in seductive aspects of the battle of the sexes, lending a new dimension to the phrase 'why not slip into something a little looser?' In the process the garment could suffer many modifications from its traditional form, for the Japanese use of a kimono with its tight, waist-encircling *obi* (sash) can be restricting rather than liberating. Nevertheless, in the 1880s the garment was utilized by fashionable European ladies as a *robe de chambre* because of its comfort. In the portrait of *Madame Hériot* (1882), Renoir, trained as a decorative porcelain painter, clearly delighted in the related task of painting the silk embroidery worn by the wife of the director of the Grands Magasins du Louvre, who sits comfortably installed in an armchair (146). She wears a kimono which has clearly been adapted to fit her, made up from silk produced in Japan in the last years of the Edo era. A very similar fabric was used in England *c.*1872 by Miss Turner, a court dressmaker, to create a dress with a bustle (147).

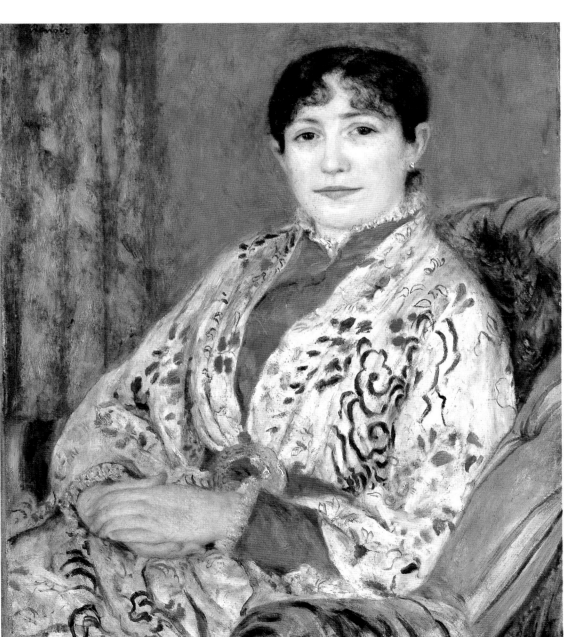

148
Amaryllis du Japon,
1890–1.
Colour lithograph,
129 x 93 cm
(50³₄ x 36⁵₈ in)

The voluptuous appeal of Japanese silks and kimonos also ensured that they featured frequently in the literature of Japonisme. J K Huysmans, who took such perverse delight in pinning down artistic styles, describes in an early working-class novel, *The Vatard Sisters* (1879), how his hero, Cyprien Tibaille, expresses a longing 'to embrace a woman dressed as a rich circus artiste, under a wintry, yellow-grey, snow-laden sky, in a room hung with Japanese silks …' Guy de Maupassant, who, as we have seen, had such a sharp eye for the more kitsch aspects of the fashion, describes in his most famous novel, *Bel Ami* (1885), how the 'hero', Duroy, an unprincipled social climber of boundless ambition, is excited by the sensual aspects of the garment:

Duroy sat and waited, waited for some time. At last a door opened and Madame de Marelle ran in, wearing a pink silk Japanese kimono embroidered with a gold landscape, blue flowers and white birds … he found her very attractive in her soft, brightly coloured kimono, less elegant than Mme Forestier in her white negligée, less endearing, less dainty, but more exciting, more seductive … What he wanted to do most with Mme Forestier was to lie at her feet or kiss the delicate lace of her bodice and breathe slowly the warm scented air between her breasts. With Madame de Marelle, he was conscious of a definite, animal, sensual desire, which made his hands tingle, to stroke the soft curves of her silk wrapper …

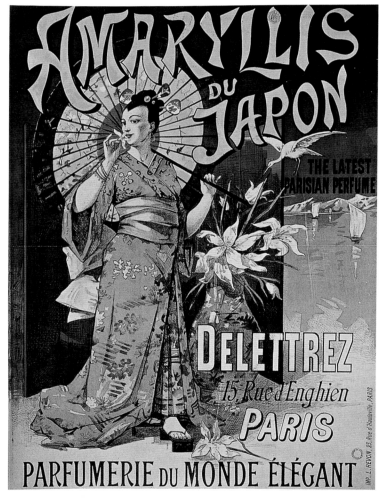

Scent, so powerfully evoked in this passage, was also advertised by a poster *Amaryllis du Japon* (1890–1), which one can easily imagine Duroy purchasing during one of his amorous campaigns (148).

A painting very close in mood to de Maupassant's novel was *The Japanese Woman* (149) painted in 1875 by Hans Makart (1840–84) who usually specialized in exotic themes from the Middle East. Makart may have been drawn to a Japanese theme by the popular success of the Japanese section of the International Exhibition held in Vienna (1873). Many splendid Japanese items were on view at this exhibition, and it is possible that the combs and kimono the model is wearing were acquired at that time. In the painting a very Rubenesque Austrian lady is posed semi-nude in a kimono while still retaining her Japanese hair pins. Her head and bust are shown against a bedraggled parasol made of feathers. She teases a bird by holding its nest which still contains eggs, thus arousing the ire of the rejected parent bird who complains at the window, creating a complex symbolic conundrum worthy of investigation by the famous Viennese doctor, Sigmund Freud.

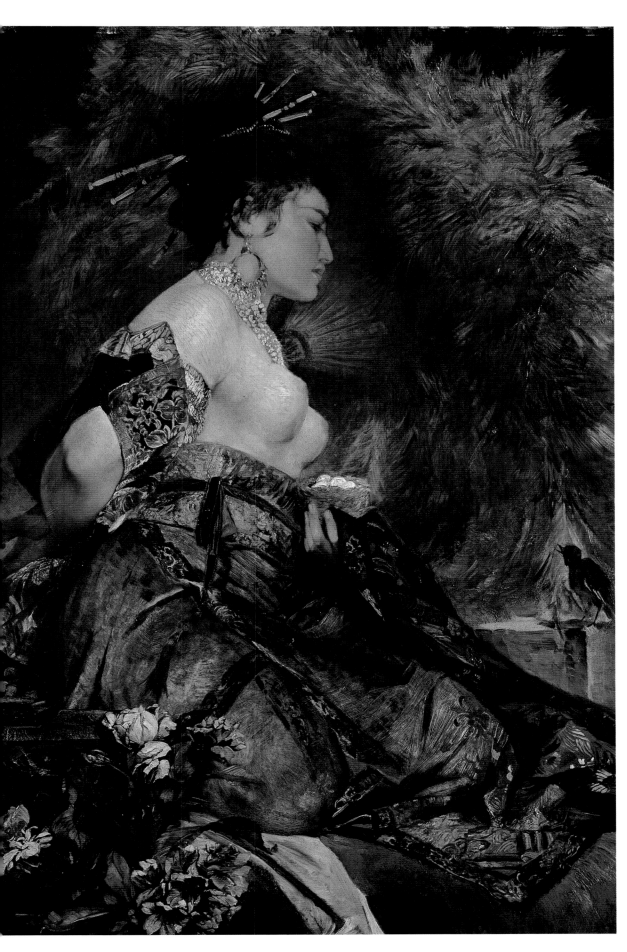

Hans Makart,
The Japanese Woman,
1875.
Oil on panel,
141 x 92·5 cm
(55¹₂ x 36³₈ in).
Oberösterreichisches
Landesmuseum, Linz

Makart's friend, Gustav Klimt, was also
a collector of Japanese art and owned
an impressive collection of *noh* theatre
costumes and kimonos. The Austrian
art journal *Ver Sacrum* frequently
published articles on such themes as
'The Spirit of Japanese Art' (Ernst
Schurr, 1899), from which Klimt learnt
much on the design of bold patterns
derived from butterfly wings and
peacock feathers. Photographs of
Klimt's studios survive showing walls
crowded with Chinese and Japanese
scrolls, and samurai armour. Klimt
enjoyed working in a smock (a kimono-
like garment of his own design) made
up in a Japanese-inspired textile by his
friend the designer and architect Josef
Hoffmann (1870–1955). Like Godwin
and Hoffmann, Klimt was also
fascinated by Japanese heraldic
mon, filling several sketchbooks with
drawings. Some of the *mon* were
subsequently transformed in his
paintings, which utilize abstract
patterns recalling butterfly wings and
peacock feathers. Klimt made much
use of gold leaf in his backgrounds of
brilliant colours, perhaps derived from
seeing examples of screens of the
Rinpa school founded by Ogata Korin,
one of Japan's greatest decorative
artists.

150
Gustav Klimt,
Expectation from
the *Stoclet Frieze*,
1905–9.
Tempera, watercolour,
gold, silver and bronze
leaf, chalk and pencil
on paper,
**193 x 115 cm
(76 x 45¼ in).
Museum für Angewandte
Kunst, Vienna**

151
René Lalique,
Butterfly Combs,
1904–5.
Carved horn, gold and
enamel,
**9·5 x 10 cm
(3¾ x 4 in).
Private collection**

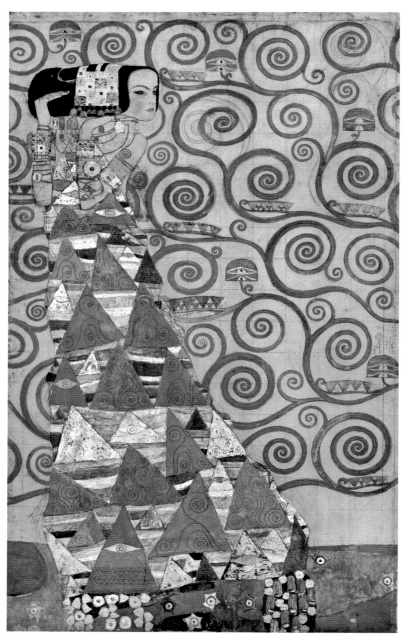

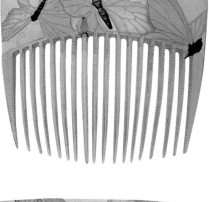

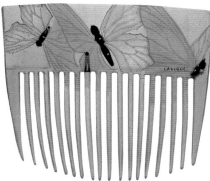

In 1905 Adolphe Stoclet, a Belgian millionaire, asked Hoffmann to design a palace in Brussels. Hoffmann commissioned Klimt to paint a frieze in the dining room (150). In it the figures of a man and a woman emerge from elaborate foregrounds and backgrounds made up of flakes of gold and semi-precious stones. The patterns vary from close-set studies of flowers in bloom to geometric triangles and rectangles. Although Klimt also deeply admired the Byzantine mosaics at Ravenna in Italy, the Japanese influence was important. Today these deeply sensual paintings are familiar as reproductions all over the world.

A Japanese theme which Klimt, a great womanizer, must have felt particularly attracted to was the 'search for the fashionable beauties of Kyoto or Edo'. This ongoing quest for ideal female beauty occupied print-makers, who struggled to cope with the bewildering frequency with which famous beauties changed fashions. When the hairstyle needed a change it was not uncommon for the engravers to set into the cherry plank small squares of a much harder wood onto which new hairstyles could be cut, thus prolonging the life of a block four or five times. The same beauty could be portrayed with an up-to-date, fashionable hairstyle, and such insets saved time and money.

152
René Lalique,
Drone With Umbels
hair comb,
*c.*1901–2.
Carved horn, gold and
enamel,
16 x 11·5 cm
(6¹⁄₄ x 4¹⁄₂ in).
Calouste Gulbenkian
Museum, Lisbon

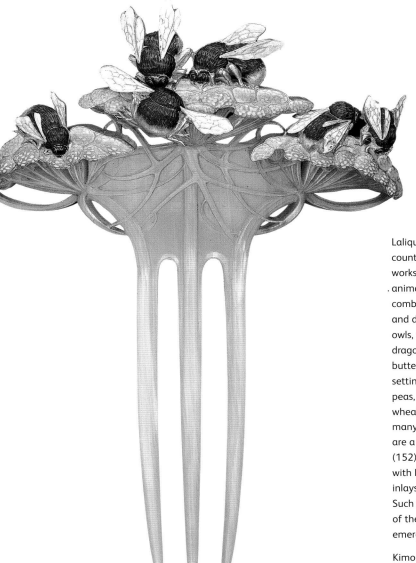

The chief accessories were the fan, comb and the hair pin (*kogai*), the latter being not only ornamental but also, depending on how many were worn, a mark of distinction and rank in the world of the geisha. Between 15-cm (6-in) and 30-cm (12-in) long, like a knitting needle, the top is surmounted with a gold, silver or copper knob which can take the form of amulets, flower buds, nuts or little bells. The ornamental hair comb, which was such a feature of Japanese women's dress, became a vital ingredient of the extremely high coiffures of the fashionable woman of the West. This set a challenge to many jewellers of the time, who also turned their attention to the manufacture of hat pins, which played a useful function at such outdoor pursuits as the races, regattas and garden parties then so popular.

Western jewellers, such as Henri Vever and René Lalique (1860–1945) in Paris and Louis Comfort Tiffany in New York, conscious of their own virtuosity, not only manufactured splendid pieces for practical wear, but also created *objets de vitrine* – stunningly beautiful display pieces. A splendid example of such a luxurious object is provided by Lalique's *Butterfly Combs* (151), carved on horn with gold and enamel, on which the insects jostle for our attention. These examples are carved in low relief to produce an impression of insects thronged in a swirling mass. One can imagine the consternation which greeted such a realistic effect of butterflies set against the elaborate hairstyles of the day.

Lalique had been brought up in the country and loved nature. From his workshops flowed a wide variety of animal and vegetable forms, set in combs, hair grips, breast pins, clasps and diadems. A strange menagerie of owls, affronted peacocks and bees, dragonflies, crawling beetles and butterflies was worked into elaborate settings of anemones, orchids, sweet peas, cherries, pine tree branches, wheatsheafs and wisteria. Among his many spectacular jewelled ornaments are a *Drone With Umbels* hair comb (152) in which six drone bees in gold, with light blue and black enamel inlays, sit on wild carrot flower heads. Such items reflect the artistic vision of the time and the ideals of the emergent Art Nouveau movement.

Kimonos, sunshades and Japanese ornamental accessories were also greatly in demand in the West as costumes at fancy dress balls, a popular fashionable diversion of the 1880s. In Henry Somm's paintings *Elegant Lady in a Japanese Garden*, and *A Procession of People in Japanese Costume* we get a glimpse of this type of 'dressing up' party. Even the British royal family took part in a variant of this type of entertainment known as a *tableau vivant*, as an engaging photograph of about 1890 of the Duke and Duchess of Connaught and their children in Japanese costume reveals (see pp.106–7).

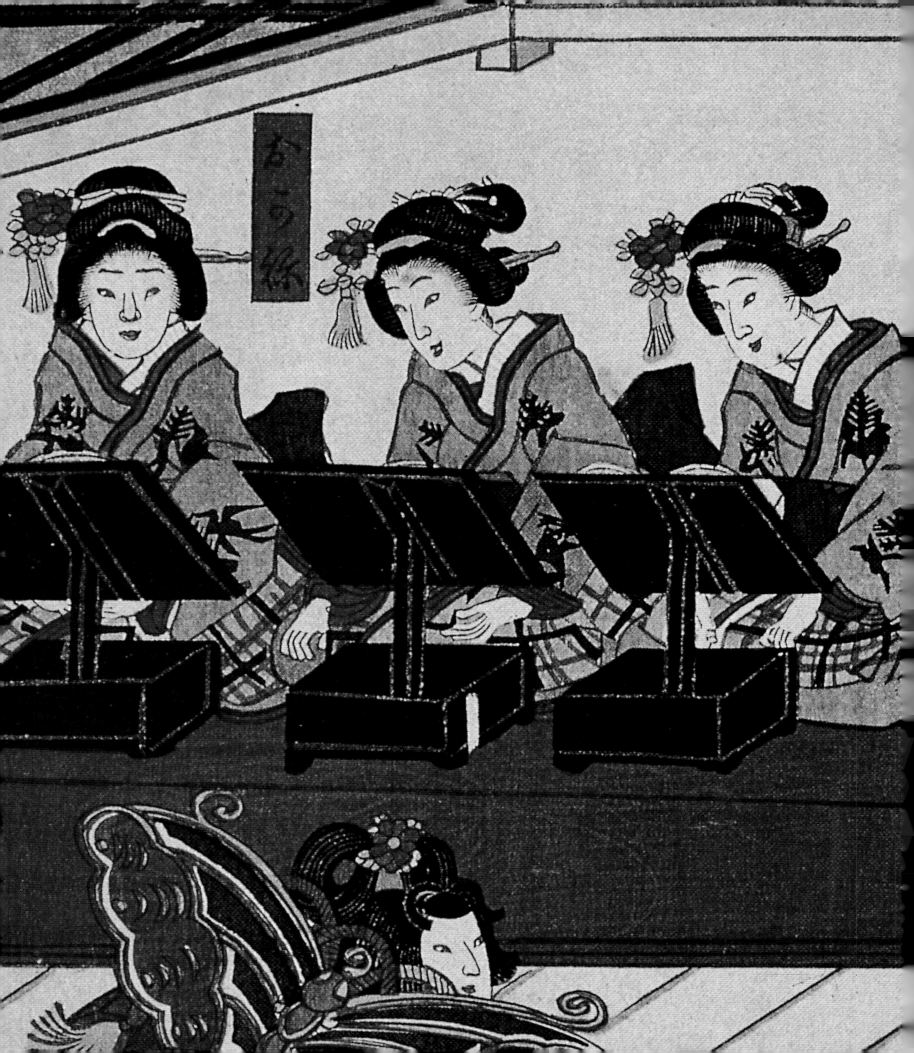

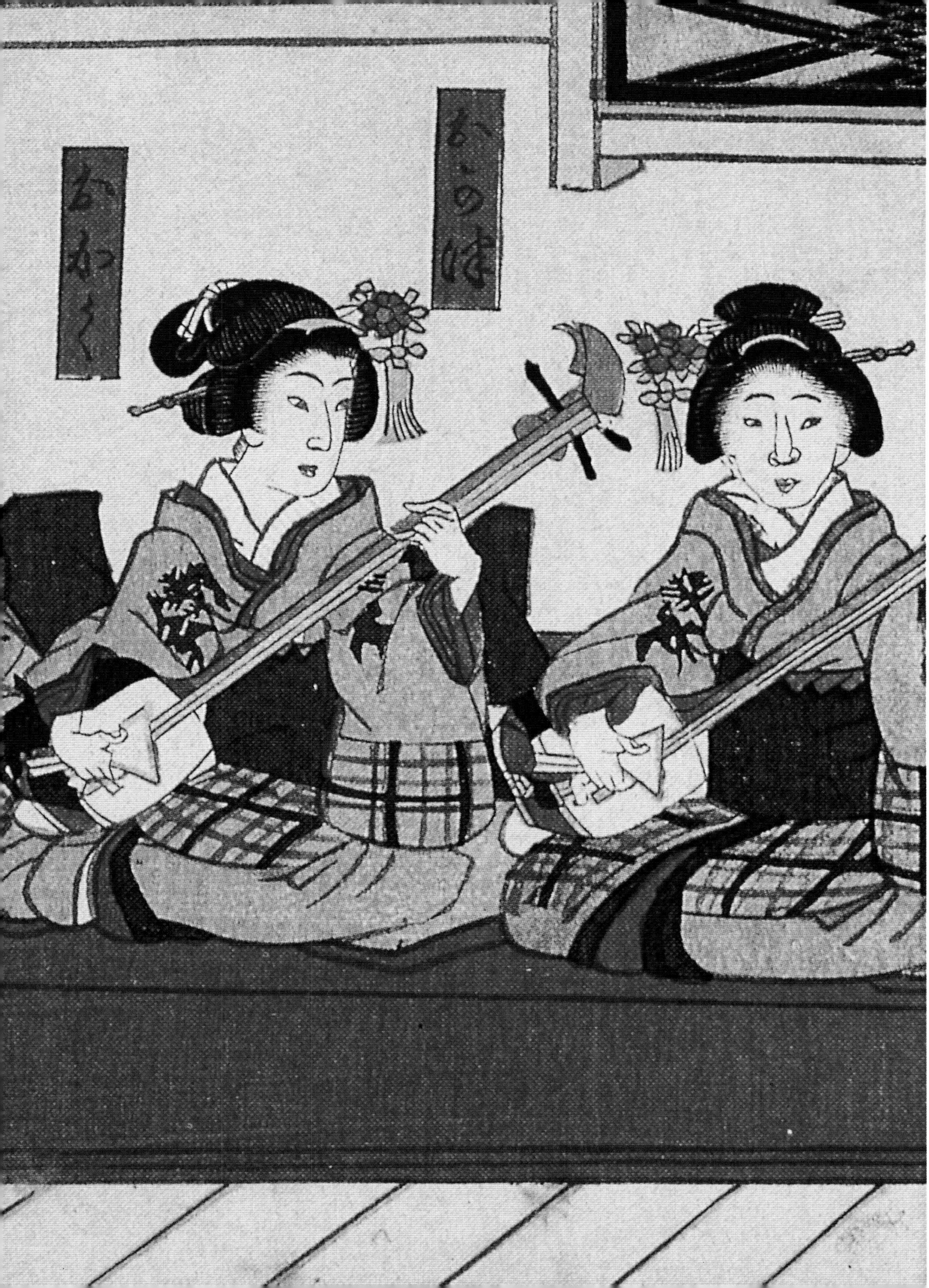

Chapter seven:
The Novel, the Stage and the Opera

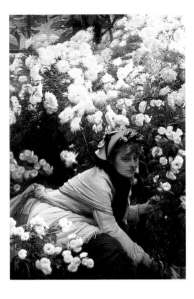

153
James Tissot,
Chrysanthemums,
c.1874–5.
Oil on canvas,
118·6 x 76·2 cm
(46¾ x 30 in).
Clark Art Institute,
Williamstown, MA

Previous page
**Baichoro Kunisada
and Oko Kunisada,
The Matsumotoro
Theatre in the Tokyo
Pleasure District, 1870**
(detail of 172)

'Japonaiserie forever'.
The de Goncourt Brothers, 1867

Everything is Japanese now.
*Alexandre Dumas (*fils*), 1887*

**Rog-a-by bebby off in Japan
You jus' a picture off of a fan.**
John Luther Long, 1900

Japonisme, generally considered as a phenomenon which only affected the visual and decorative arts, also influenced the novel, the stage and the opera. As a style, Japonisme coincided almost exactly with the Impressionist movement but also with the French school of naturalistic fiction which centred on Émile Zola, who vied with the de Goncourt brothers for recognition as a leader of the new 'realist' or naturalist school, and also as a collector of Japanese prints. He was once described by Edmond de Goncourt as being 'an engine greased for industrial labour', an analogy which refers to his role as the great chronicler of the lives of the working class and lower bourgeoisie. He preached the value of obtaining sociological insights by the accumulation and careful documentation of material facts.

Zola's passion for the meticulous recording of detail to achieve authencity led him, so it is said, to have been deliberately run over by a hansom cab in order to describe the experience exactly.

While not all of his followers would go to quite such drastic lengths, they nevertheless shared a belief that they should use every effort to obtain accurate descriptions for the backgrounds to their stories. Such 'realism' has been amusingly defined as 'truth to the observed forms of life (especially when they are gloomy)'.

Not all writers known as 'realists' relished the label. Gustave Flaubert, in particular, disliked being so categorized, describing himself as 'a rabid old Romantic – or a fossilized one, whichever you prefer'. Yet some of the greatest exponents of realist doctrines were his disciples, the de Goncourt brothers and Guy de Maupassant. De Maupassant loved clutter and enjoyed describing the details of a crowded room, or an artist's studio laden with Japanese gee-gaws, a device tellingly used in *Bel Ami*, written in 1885. In the novel the hero becomes nervous and apprehensive when his new mistress announces that she is coming to see his sleazy 'bed-sit' in a working-class quarter of Paris. He decides the room needs redecoration:

As soon as he had finished his newspaper work, he planned the rearrangement of his room to receive his mistress and conceal as far as possible the poverty of the flat. He had the idea of pinning on the walls small Japanese knick-knacks, and he laid out five francs on a whole collection of rolls of coloured crinkly paper, little fans and screens, with which he hid the worst stains on the wallpaper. On the window-panes he stuck transparent pictures, boats on rivers, flocks of birds against a background of red skies, women in brightly coloured costumes on balconies, and processions of little black dwarfs over snow-covered plains. His rooms, which were just big enough to hold a bed and chair, soon began to look like the inside of a Chinese lantern. He considered the result satisfactory and spent the evening sticking on the ceiling birds cut out of the coloured plates he had not yet used. After that he went to sleep, lulled by the whistles of the trains. Next day ... [his mistress] was charmed by the dazzling colour of the prints, exclaiming, 'What a delightful room!'

Vying with the popularity of Japanese artefacts was the craze for a flower – the chrysanthemum, which began even before the publication of Pierre Loti's best-selling novel, *Madame Chrysanthème*, firmly established the flower as a popular symbol of Japan. This popularity is reflected in one of the most beautiful works by James Tissot (153). The flower is referred to in Marcel Proust's *Remembrance of Things Past*, when his hero Charles Swann is captivated by the *demi-mondaine* Mme Odette de Crécy's apartment, with its:

huge Japanese lantern ... and a long rectangular box in which bloomed, as in a hothouse, a row of large chrysanthemums, at that time still uncommon, though by no means so large as the mammoth specimens which horticulturists have since succeeded in producing.

Swann was irritated by the sight of these flowers, fashionable in Paris throughout the late 1880s. Odette pins Charles down:

in one of the many mysterious little alcoves ... [she] installed behind his head and beneath his feet great cushions of Japanese silk which she pummelled and buffeted as though to prove that she was prodigal of these riches, regardless of their value ... she drew his attention now to the fiery-tongued dragons painted on a bowl or stitched on a screen ... or a toad carved in jade.

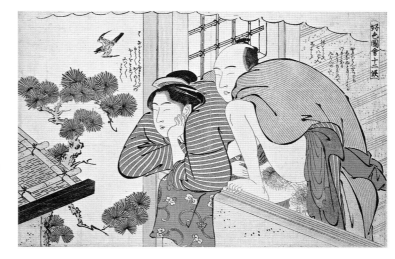

154
Katsukawa Shunsho,
Lovers on a Balcony from
the series *The Twelve
Hours of Lovemaking,*
c.1800.
Colour woodblock,
24·8 x 37·4 cm
(19³⁄₄ x 14³⁄₄ in)

In 1887 Alexandre Dumas (*fils*) enjoyed a huge success with his play, *Le Francillon*. One exchange in the play gained immense publicity. A guest at a fashionable dinner asks his hostess for the recipe of the salad they had eaten that evening, to which the hostess replies that she calls it a Japanese salad, as 'it must have a name, and everything is Japanese nowadays'.

These words 'everything is Japanese nowadays' rapidly became a widely used catchphrase. Later in Proust's novel the hero, Swann, while passing an evening at the Verdurins', is deeply bored by a fellow guest, Mme Cottard, who, despite having not yet seen *Le Francillon*, gushes unceasingly about it, saying, 'wherever I go I naturally find everybody talking about that wretched Japanese salad. In fact one is begin-ning to get just a little tired of hearing about it.' Remorselessly, Mme Cottard continued, swayed by the power of the catchphrase, which for the duration of the 1880s demonstrated that Japon-isme had become, as a contemporary critic remarked, 'no longer a fashion, it's an infatuation, a folly'. It was a craze, and one which had some inter-esting effects on literature of the time.

As the enthusiasm for Japanese art spread like a contagious virus across Europe, Edmond de Goncourt's annoyance grew. Anticipating Oscar Wilde twenty years later, he began to grumble that the subject had become vulgarized and over-popularized. On 29 October 1868 he protests:

The taste for things Chinese and Japanese! We were among the first to have this taste. It is now spreading to everything and everyone, even to idiots and middle-class women. Who has cultivated it, felt it, preached it, and converted others to it more than we; who was excited by the first volumes and had the courage to buy them?

In the first of our books En 18 .., [Eighteenth-Century French Painters] a description of a mantelpiece with Japanese ornaments brought us the honour of being called Baroque fools, people without taste, and caused Edmond Texier to demand that we be committed to Charenton [the lunatic asylum which had housed the Marquis de Sade].

But despite these groans, a recurring cry of all collectors, Edmond continued to acquire works at fever pitch. On 30 October 1874 with his friend, Burty:

we went to inspect the arrival of two shipments from Japan. We spent hours in the midst of those forms, those colours, those objects in bronze, porcelain, pottery, jade, ivory, wood and paper – all that intoxicating and haunting assemblage of art. We were there for hours, so many hours that it was four o'clock when I had lunch. After these debauches of art – the one this morning cost me more than 500 Francs – I am left worn out and shaking as after a night of gambling.

I came away with a dryness in the mouth which only the sea water from a dozen oysters could refresh. I bought some ancient albums, a bronze … and the gown of a Japanese tragedian on whose black velvet there are gold dragons with enamel eyes clawing at each other in a field of pink peonies.

By 1883 de Goncourt's obsession with collecting Japanese art had reached new and worrying levels. On 29 December, reviewing the purchases he had made in the passage of the year, he wrote describing 'madness, a sexual passion for things Japanese. This year I have spent 300,000 francs on them – all the money I have made.'

On 17 July 1884 he writes of his envy of the dealer, Siegfried Bing, who 'will have seen almost all the art of China and Japan pass through his hands'. Bing was not only a dealer in Japanese art, he also edited the influential journal *Le Japon Artistique*, which was published in thirty-six issues from 1888 to 1891 in French, German and English (see 83). The periodical's influence continued long after it stopped publishing; Gustav Klimt, for example, buying a complete set in 1906. Bing also organized several exhibitions of Japanese prints, the most important being held at the École des Beaux-Arts in Paris in 1900; others were at the Fine Art Society in London in 1890, and Boston in 1894. Bing went on to become one of the great impresarios of the next new artistic movement, Art Nouveau.

On 28 December 1886 de Goncourt attended a party where he met another leading figure in the dissemination of knowledge of Japanese art, Tadamasa Hayashi (1851–1906), who first came to Paris in 1878 when he was employed at the Exposition Universelle as a translator. In 1884 he set up in Paris as a dealer and researcher. He was at the heart of Parisian cultural activities and became virtually the father of the study of Japanese art history in Europe, and thus a congenial spirit for Edmond de Goncourt.

A few days later, on 5 January 1887, Edmond gave a lunch party, one of the guests being the etcher, Félix Bracquemond, who earlier in the mid-1870s had first acquired a copy of Hokusai's *Manga*, and brought it to the attention of French artists and writers. After the lunch Edmond noted:

I have Bracquemond and the sculptor Rodin to lunch today. Rodin, who is full of fawnishness, asks to see my Japanese erotics, and is full of admiration before the women's drooping heads, the broken lines of their necks, the rigid extension of arms, the contractions of feet, all the voluptuous and frenetic reality of coitus, all the sculptural twining of bodies melted and interlocked in the spasm of pleasure [154].

Japonisme

155
Édouard Manet
Portrait of Émile Zola,
1867–8.
Oil on canvas,
146 x 114 cm
(57¹₂ x 44⁷₈ in).
Musée d'Orsay, Paris

Zola shared the de Goncourts'
enthusiasm for erotic prints, and the
staircase of his home was lined with
the kind of print that he chose to call
'my furious fornications'. Zola always
needed a new artistic cause to
champion, and an ideal contentious
issue presented itself in Édouard
Manet's works, which in the 1860s had
become synonymous with scandal and
ridicule, leading Manet to erect his own
'pavilion' in a shed at the World's Fair
held in Paris in 1867. There he showed
fifty of his paintings, some of which
were attacked for their resemblance to
the popular imagery of crude penny-
plain and twopence-coloured prints,
which are still produced in France
today in the town of Épinal in the
Vosges. Zola defended Manet's work
in a 23-page article published on
1 January 1867 in the *Revue du XXe
siècle*, a eulogy written after visiting
the artist in his studio. In this article
(subsequently published as a book)
Zola suggested, in defence of Manet's
works, that it would be much more
interesting to compare his bold
simplified style of painting with
Japanese prints, which resembled
Manet's work 'in their strange
elegance and their magnificent
patches of colour'.

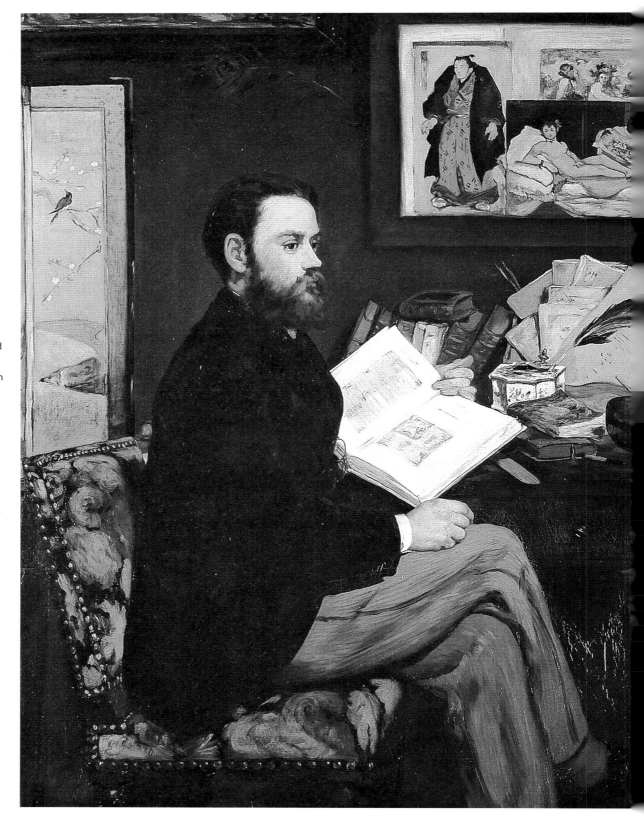

156
Sadahide,
*Englishman Sorting
Fabric for Trade at
Yokohama*,
1861–2.
Colour woodblock,
35 x 25 cm (13³⁄₄ x 9⁷⁄₈ in)

157
Édouard Manet,
Nana,
1877.
Oil on canvas,
149·9 x 115·6 cm
(59 x 45¹⁄₂ in).
Kunsthalle, Hamburg

Zola's portrait by Manet (155), probably begun in the autumn of 1867, is full of both clear and coded references to the interests of both artist and sitter. These range from the Japanese screen seen on the left which became a familiar prop in Manet's studio, to 'short-hand' references to his principal artistic interests. These are represented by three prints pinned or stuck casually to a board at the top right of the painting, which refer both to Manet's love of the painter Velázquez (1599–1660) and a shared interest in the Japanese print, apparent in the woodcut of *The Sumo Wrestler Onaruto Nadaemon of Awa Province* by Kuniyaki II (1835–88). Manet's own work is represented by a graphic version of *Olympia* (1863), the painting which Zola had stoutly defended in his article, shown prominently displayed among the clutter of books and brushes on a small table. The eyes of all the figures in these three prints are directed towards the sitter Zola, as if to acknowledge the writer's role as defender of Manet's interests. Manet may have adopted this compositional device from one of the prints by Sadahide (1807–*c*.1873) depicting foreign visitors to Yokohama, such as the *Englishman Sorting Fabric for Trade at Yokohama* (156), whose thoughts have strayed to his wife so far away in reality, but symbolically present in the cartouche (for similar fabrics see 93–95).

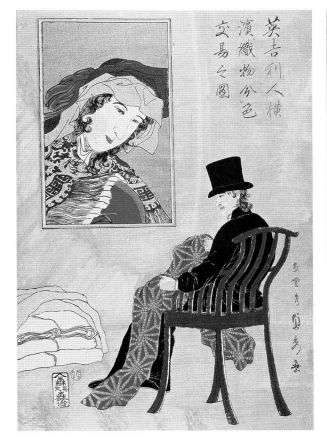

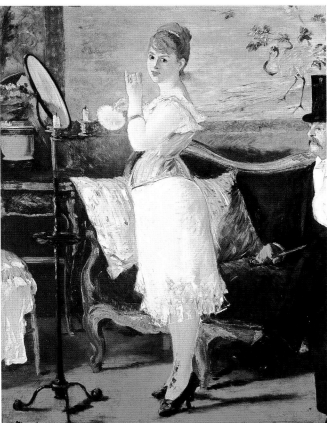

Some years after painting his portrait of Zola, Manet painted a 'portrait' of the prostitute, Nana (157), in Zola's *L'Assommoir* of 1877. The geisha and the courtesan were favourite themes of the Japanese print, and Manet also clearly welcomed the opportunity to treat similar potentially popular subjects. In the painting Nana looks over her shoulder at a gentleman visitor, cut off by the edge of the picture in the Japanese manner. She gazes at us seductively with her back to her caller. On the wall behind her is the same screen decorated with cranes, which appears in Manet's earlier painting of Zola. Here the presence of the cranes in the screen provides both a visual and verbal pun, for the word *grue* ('crane') was also commonly used to describe a courtesan. Nana's small head, long neck and white slip, despite her plump stature, make a jocular visual reference to the 'crane'.

Such meticulous descriptions of squalid, yet erotic interiors captured the popular imagination, as would an incident which became one of the most famous of love stories. Everyone today is familiar with the story of Puccini's *Madame Butterfly*, Cio-Cio-San, and her desertion by Lieutenant Pinkerton. It was based upon a nineteenth-century true story of Yamamuru Tsuru. She attempted suicide after being deserted by an English merchant who had fathered her child and later returned to enrol his son in the American missionary school in Nagasaki. It was first published as *Madame Butterfly* in 1901 by John Luther Long.

This all-too-familiar story of love and betrayal when combined with the clash between the cultures of East and West is unforgettable. These tragic events are all wrapped up with the axiomatic assumption of Western superiority that falling in love with a white man entailed. This theme still continues to hold an extraordinary fascination for dramatists, film-makers and composers, producing such contemporary variants as the recent musical, *Miss Saigon*. Tales of betrayed trust and desertion move us, just as they did Giacomo Puccini when he wrote the music for his opera in 1904. To understand the background to *Madame Butterfly* it is rewarding to trace its antecedents, right back to the time when the English navigator, Will Adams, settled in Japan in 1600 and took a Japanese wife with whom he had two children. Ever since then, the relationship between Western men and Japanese women has inspired fantasy and speculation. But while the sexual mores of the two societies differed widely, not all male visitors to Japan abandoned their partners completely, for some married and settled down either temporarily or permanently in Japan.

Variations of these human dilemmas continued throughout the nineteenth century. One interesting story, little known in the West, can be studied in the life of Charles Wirgman, the war artist for the *Illustrated London News*.

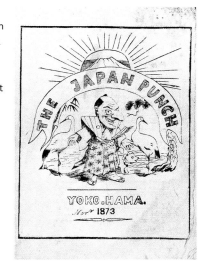

158
**Charles Wirgman,
Cover from *The Japan
Punch*, 1873**

Wirgman is remembered affectionately in Japan for his humour, manifest in his comic publication, *The Japan Punch*, published intermittently between 1862 and 1887 (158). *The Japan Punch* was very popular among Westerners in the treaty ports, as were such sketchbooks as *Artistic and Gastronomic Rambles in Japan from Kyoto to Tokyo by Tokaido* (1872). That there was also a tender side to Wirgman's personality is revealed in a number of watercolour sketches of such subjects as Japanese women, notably several sensitive studies of his wife, of whom unfortunately very little is known (see 174).

Ever since 1785, when Philip James de Loutherbourg had staged at Covent Garden in London the pantomime *Omai, or A Trip Round the World* in the wake of Captain Cook's explorations in the Pacific, the exotic East provided a popular theme for stage shows. For European composers the romantic East was also always a trump card to play from the time of Gluck's *Le Cinesi* (*The Chinese Ladies*), a lavish *chinoiserie* production staged in Vienna in 1754 with crystal and transparent decor in the Chinese style, to Giuseppe Scarlatti's *L'Isola disabita* (*The Desert Island*) in 1757. This slapstick farce with mock Chinese words, a Chinese beauty and a handsome Dutchman proved a huge success, not least because of the scenery, costumes and mockery of Chinese customs.

A century later, the visual enthusiasm for *chinoiserie* themes had given place to a demand for subjects presented with the wrappings of Japonisme fostered by a vast public demand for traveller's tales, poems and dramatic and musical celebrations of Japan. Musically the first Western celebration of a specifically Japanese theme took place as early as 1872 in Saint-Saëns's obscure but engaging third opera *La Princesse jaune* (*The Yellow Princess*), which was first performed at the Opéra Comique in Paris, but was not a success. This was perhaps because it had only two characters, and the exotic atmosphere is largely evoked by means of pentatonic melodies.

It may also have arisen because the piece was not, as is misleadingly suggested in the title, set in an exotic foreign land, but in the much more familiar locale of Holland, and was really a satire on the national passion for collecting all things Japanese. The story concerns the love between the heroine and her boring cousin, the pedantic Cornelius, who is completely obsessed with Japanese artefacts, and has unfortunately fallen in love with a girl portrayed upon a fan. Disillusionment sets in with a dream which reveals to Cornelius the restricted nature of Japanese life, and tells him that what he really needs is a beautiful Dutch girl. With such a fustian plot it is hardly surprising that the opera only received five performances and has rarely been revived.

Japonisme had very differing effects on different artists, and the same applied even more to composers and writers. In 1878 a Japanese fantasy by Ernest d'Hervelly opened to packed houses in Paris, while at the Opéra during the same year a 'Japanese ballet' proved equally successful. Both these events no doubt relied on spectacle but they show the potential which existed for musical extravaganzas.

It was at first within the covers of a successful novel that the artistic cross-pollination of Japan and Europe, first on the page and later on the stage, effectively took place. Its author was Pierre Loti, the *nom de plume* of Louis Marie Julien Viaud, a French naval officer who eventually left the French navy to specialize in stories of passionate but transient romance in exotic Oriental settings.

Published in 1888 as *Madame Chrysanthème*, the story takes the form of a diary kept by Pierre (the author), a naval officer on the *Triomphante*, forced to stay at Nagasaki from July to September while his ship underwent repairs. In its entries Loti describes the process by which officers of foreign navies were permitted to enter into temporary marriages with geishas, a convenience which could be easily terminated with the expiration of the husband's stay, an arrangement of which, as Loti ironically observes, the officers of the American, British and French navies enthusiastically availed themselves.

During his two months with his 'geisha' Chrysanthemum, Loti comes to know her intimately and becomes, in a detached way, more amused than charmed by her childlike, playful gaiety, 'a little creature made to laugh yet easily saddened'. He captures her personality in a passage describing a walk through Nagasaki with her friends:

All five of them hold hands, like little girls out for a walk … Seen from behind, they're very fetching, these dolls, with their hair so nicely done, and their tortoiseshell combs so prettily arranged … As with all Japanese women, the backs of their little necks are delicious … In the bazaars our girls make lots of purchases every evening. Like spoiled children they want everything – toys, combs, belts, flowers. And then they all give one another presents, with pretty, girlish little smiles. Bluebell, for example, chooses for Chrysanthemum an ingeniously conceived lantern in which shadow puppets, set in motion by a hidden mechanism, dance round and round the flame.

In return, Chrysanthemum gives Bluebell a magic fan which can show, according to your inclination, either butterflies flitting among cherry blossom or monsters from beyond the grave chasing one another among black clouds …

In the well-known teahouses, where we round off our evening, the little serving girls welcome us when we arrive with an air of respectful recognition as one of the groups who are living the high life in Nagasaki. There we chat brokenly, often losing the thread, in miniature gardens lit by lanterns, beside goldfish ponds with little bridges and little islands and little ruined towers.

Loti apologized to his readers for the style of this last sentence regretting that 'in describing this land one is tempted to use the word "little" six times in a line'.

An oil painting, *L'Ameya: The Sweet Stall* (1892; 159) by Robert Blum (1857–1903) records a shopping spree very similar to that described by Loti. Blum's painting first appeared as an illustration to *Japonica* by Sir Edwin Arnold accompanied by a commentary describing the virtuosity of the sweet stall owner who was able to use molten sugar just like a glass-blower to create edible toys.

159
Robert Blum,
L'Ameya: The Sweet Stall,
1892.
Oil on canvas,
63·7 x 78·9 cm
(25 x 31 in).
Metropolitan Museum of Art, New York

160
Felice Beato,
Game of Shuttlecock,
1868.
Hand-painted albumen print

Such popular genre subjects taken from street life as *Game of Shuttlecock* (160) were also the delight of the busy photographer, Felice Beato. Beato's photographs (and those of his many imitators) provide remarkable visual records of the childlike games beloved by Chrysanthemum and her friends, which Loti began to find juvenile rather than charming. Unable to suffer fools gladly and swiftly bored with the liaison, Loti leaves – his last illusions about the love affair being shattered by the sight of his discarded girlfriend happily counting her money and testing the coins with a hammer 'with the competence and dexterity of an old money lender'.

Loti retired from the French navy in 1883. He had not, however, yet finished with all his Japanese material. In 1883 he had attended a ball at Edo and used his memories of this event to describe a scene in *Japoneries d'automne* (*Autumnal Memories of Japan*, 1889):

They're a little too bedecked with gold braid, these numerous Japanese gentlemen – ministers, admirals, officers, officials of one kind and another – all in their party outfits … And then how oddly they wear their tailboards. No doubt their backs were not designed for this sort of thing. Impossible to say where the impression comes from, but I find all of them, always, in some elusive way bear a marked resemblance to monkeys.

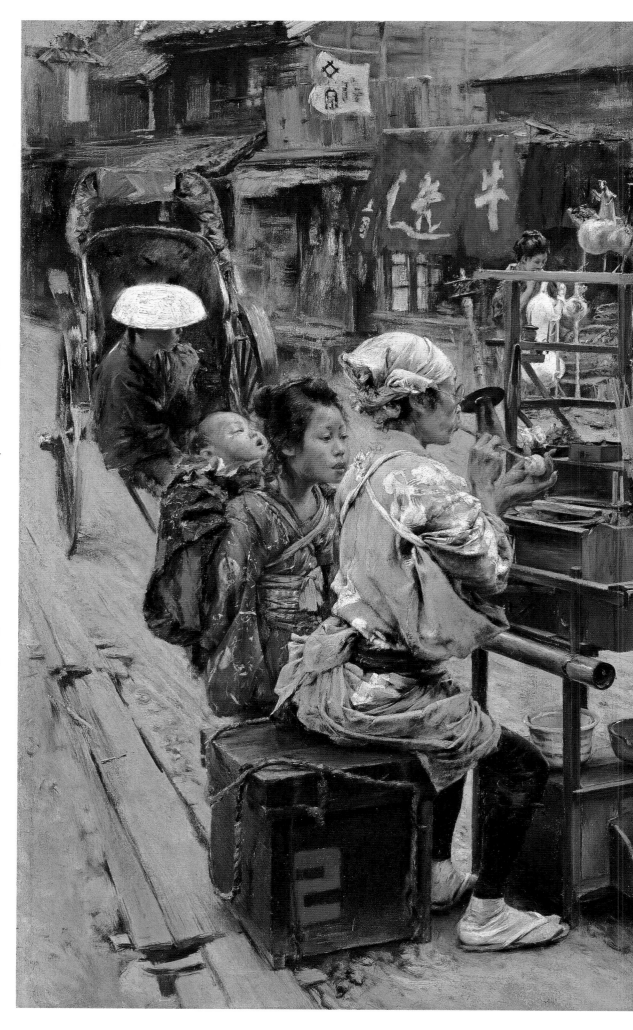

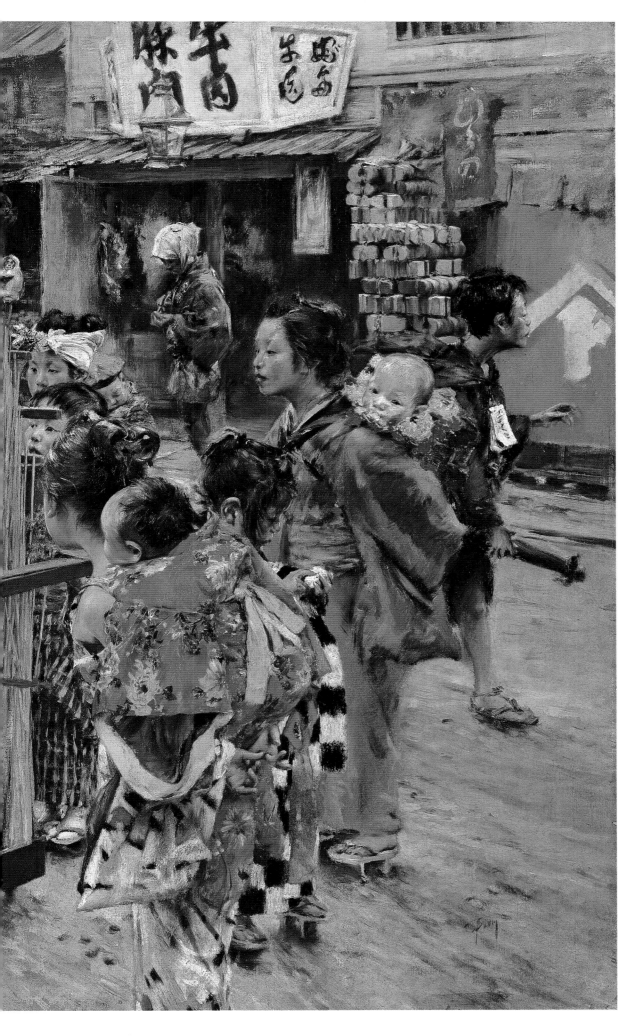

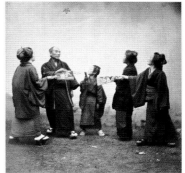

Such crude racist analogies, which recall both the *singeries* of eighteenth-century French art and post-Darwinian prejudices (present elsewhere in Loti's work), were particularly disliked by the liberal-minded painter, Félix Régamey (1844–1907), who had visited Japan with Émile Guimet, founder of the great museum which bears his name in Paris. Régamey embarked on a protracted disagreement with Loti over the moral implications of his novel. Their arguments reached a climax after 1893, when the composer, André Messager wrote and conducted an opera based on Loti's tale. Régamey published his own version of the story in 1894, entitled *Le Cahier rose de Madame Chrysanthème* (*The Pink Notebook of Madame Chrysanthemum*), told by the heroine in the form of an intimate journal.

It was, however, the circus ring which was to inspire one of the most important and spectacular renditions of the theme. In November 1892 Henri de Toulouse-Lautrec visited a show entitled *Papa Chrysanthème* at The New Circus, an elegant establishment in the Rue Saint-Honoré. He made many strikingly Japanesque sketches, notably a large drawing in which the hair, hat and dress of the lady take on bizarre shapes, while the dancer bends her body backwards to create a sharply exaggerated curve.

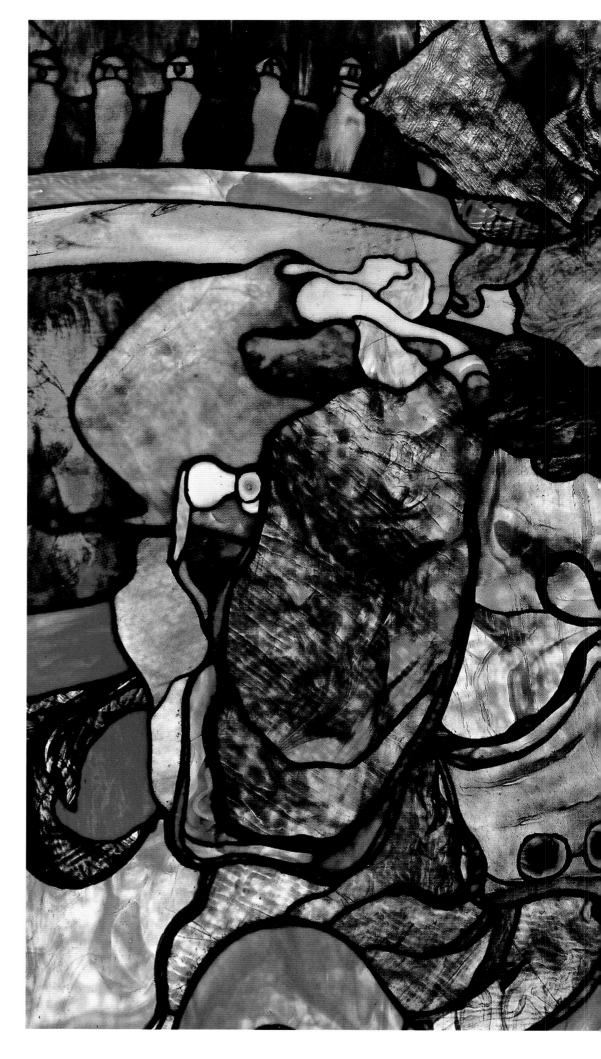

161
Henri de Toulouse-
Lautrec,
Tiffany & Co.,
At the Nouveau Cirque,
Papa Chrysanthème,
1895.
Marbled glass,
120 x 85 cm
(47¼ x 33½ in).
Musée d'Orsay, Paris

Japonisme

The broad handling of the subject
suggests that it was probably first
thought of as a design for a poster,
but the black outlines also suggest that
stained glass was a favoured option
from the beginning. The title yet again
cashed in on the success of Loti's
novel, which had made the very word
'chrysanthemum' synonymous with
both Japan and exoticism. This
particular variant of the oft-told tale
was a nautical fantasy of a prince who
returns to Japan with a European
fiancée, who presents herself at court
in a ceremonial dance in the centre of
the ring. In Toulouse-Lautrec's sketch
of the scene, an overdressed lady with
a huge hat gazes across the ring at the
spectacle, watched by five gentlemen
wearing evening dress – the 'stuffed
shirts' of the title, *Clowness and Five*
Stuffed Shirts, whose hairstyles have
a distinct resemblance to Oriental 'pig-
tails'. For this number the circus ring
was transformed into a pool, dotted
with water lilies and lotus leaves, and
dancers using diaphanous veils and
coloured electric lights in imitation of
Loie Fuller (a flooded ring is still used
to create a similar effect at the
Blackpool Tower circus).

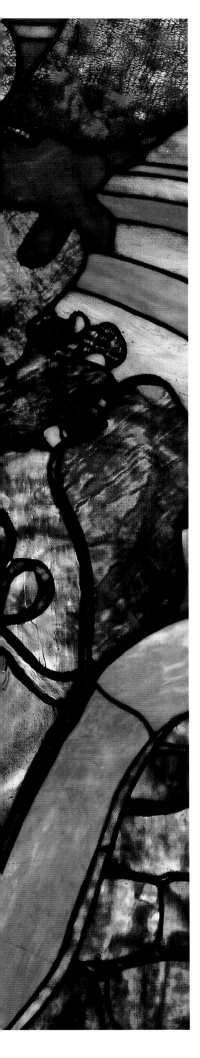

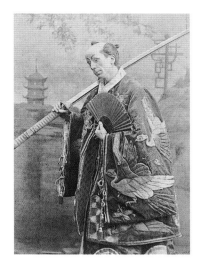

On a visit to New York in the early 1890s the entrepreneur, Siegfried Bing, discovered the art workshops of Louis Comfort Tiffany and was immensely impressed by the new forms of stained and decorative glass that Tiffany named 'favrile' glass. Here, he sensed, was a major attraction for his new salon dedicated to the novel themes of Art Nouveau. Impressed by the remarkable effects that could be obtained in this exciting new medium, he commissioned the Nabis group of artists – among them Bonnard, Vuillard, Denis, Sérusier and Félix Vallotton (1865–1925), together with Toulouse-Lautrec, to supply a series of cartoons for stained glass. For his contribution to the scheme Toulouse-Lautrec recalled his drawings of three years earlier of *Papa Chrysanthème* and realized how well his design, with its bold, broad lines, would adapt into the supportive 'leading' needed in a stained-glass composition (161). Tiffany's craftsmen brilliantly interpreted Lautrec's studies and the resultant glass panels formed the opening display in Bing's new salon. In a review of the show in *La Revue Blanche*, Jacques Émile Blanche singled out Lautrec, 'who has composed the loveliest, and the most modern, of decorative motifs out of a circus scene and a harlot's hat'. With its bold design, and extremely Japanese composition, the panel became one of the most remarkable examples of Japonisme's influence upon the decorative arts.

These themes would seem at first very far from the stock-in-trade of the famous British partnership between the composer Arthur Sullivan and librettist William Schwenck Gilbert, aided by the indispensable impresario, Richard D'Oyly Carte, who together created with reforming zeal a new genre of English operetta. In 1881 Aestheticism had provided Gilbert and Sullivan with the ideal contemporary subject to satirize in *Patience* in Bunthorne's song of confession: 'I do *not* long for all one sees that's Japanese.' Four years later, in 1885, the cult for Japan provided the perfect target for their greatest satirical partnership, which took the form of *The Mikado* or *The Town of Titipu*. By 1885 plentiful evidence existed for any theatrically aware impresario that virtually any show with a Japanese theme had a good chance of success. This was manifest in such musical extravaganzas as *The Japs* or *The Doomed Daimyo*, performed at Bristol on 31 August 1885 and at the Novelty Theatre in London, which was basically a conjuring show. Much more successful was *The Great Taykin*, a 'Japananza' in one act with music by George Grossmith, produced at Toole's Theatre under Toole's management on 30 April 1885 and withdrawn on 6 August after eighty-seven perfor-mances. Its female characters enjoyed such excruciating names as Kissi-Missi and Tickle-Ing.

The production of *The Mikado* on 14 March 1885 was a much more important event, which really ensured the popularity of Japanese art in England and America, by making gentle fun of it. Gilbert himself described the initial moment of inspiration for the piece, when:

an executioner's sword hanging on the wall of my library – the very sword carried by Mr Grossmith at his entrance in the first act – fell off the wall and suggested the broad idea upon which the libretto is based [162].

The libretto of *The Mikado* created the land of Titipu, a 'topsy-turvy' mirror of England, dressed 'à la japonaise'. In reality there was nothing Japanese in it except the Lord High Executioner's name Ko-Ko, which means pickles, and a single pseudo-Japanese tune in Sullivan's music, accompanying the entrance of the Mikado: 'Miya sama, miya sama, On n'm-ma-no mayé ni' etc. The tune is almost identical with the war song of the Imperial Army to which the troops went to battle in 1868 and saw the victory of the Meiji emperor over conservative warlords opposed to the opening up of Japan. Years later a Japanese visitor pulled Sullivan's leg by telling him that it was 'the foulest song ever sung in the lowest teahouse in Japan'. In reality the stirring words describe the waving of the imperial banner of silken brocade, as a signal for the chastisement of rebels.

Characters in The Mikado
sketched by the
illustrator 'Henry Stephen
'Hal' Ludlow (1851-1930).
The costumes include
those worn by the 'Three
Little Maids from School'
– Peep-Bo, Yum-Yum and
Pitti-Sing. At the bottom
left, the Lord High
Executioner, played by
George Grossmith,
brandishes his sword.

163

*Afternoon Tea at the
Japanese Village in
Knightsbridge* from
The Graphic,
13 March 1886

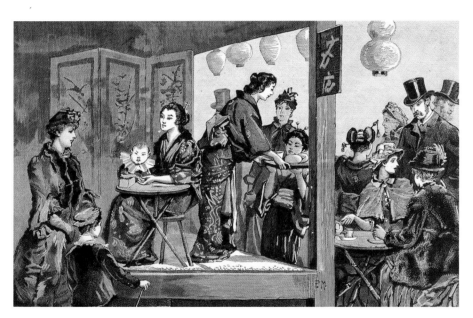

When Katisha threatens to reveal that Nanki-Poo is not a second trombone player but the son and heir of the Mikado, the other characters sing loudly to overpower her voice the Japanese words, 'O NI! bikkuri shakkuri to! oya! oya!' – a non-Japanese farrago of words which may be translated as 'You devil! with fright! with hiccups! hey! hey!'

The first lines of the operetta conjure up the popular enthusiasm for imported goods and things Japanese:

If you want to know who we are
We are gentlemen of Japan
On many a vase and jar
On many a screen and fan …

A stickler for accuracy in his productions, Gilbert visited one of the popular attractions of the 1880s, what we would call today a 'theme park' in the form of a Japanese village run by a showman named Tannaker in Hyde Park, London, near the top of Sloane Street (163). A flyer for the show gives the entrance charge, one shilling for adults, and children six pence. It announces 'New and Novel Entertainments' at 1, 3, 5 and 8 p.m., and proclaims it to be the only Japanese village in Europe, warning the public that since its establishment, 'many wretched imitations have sprung up in provincial towns. Beware of impostors and imitators.'

The poster proclaims grand entertainments: '… streets of houses, shops, temples populated by Japanese men, women and children showing their everyday life', and Gilbert was delighted when he found in the teahouse an authentic Japanese girl. Despite the fact that her English was limited to 'Sixpence please' (the price of a cup of tea in Knightsbridge), she was able to instruct his 'three little maids from school' in the correct furling and unfurling of their fans to denote wrath, delight or homage.

The sets were created by Hawes Craven, a leading theatrical designer, who worked for most of Sir Henry Irving's productions. The costumes were by Wilhelm (William John Charles Pitcher; 1858–1925), the leading theatrical costume designer of the day. Wilhelm's designs for *The Mikado* show Gilbert's collaboration in their insistence on the accurate representation of Japanese dress (164). Gilbert boasted that the costumes worn by the principals were genuine and original Japanese ones of ancient date:

the magnificent gold-embroidered robe and petticoat of the Mikado was a faithful replica of the ancient official costume of the Japanese monarch; the strange-looking curled bag at the top of his head was intended to enclose the pigtail.

Such costumes can be seen in a poster by John Hassall (1868–1948) for a touring version of the show (165).

141

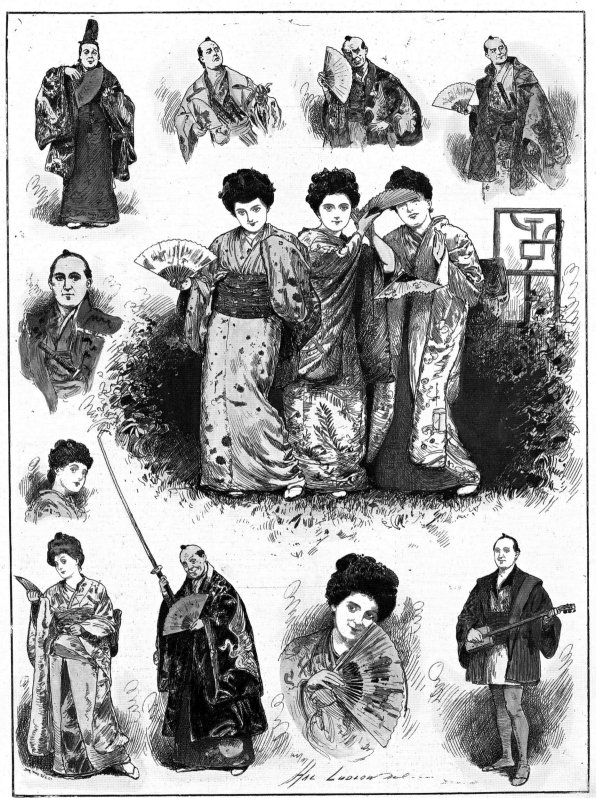

The Mikado (Mr. R. Temple).
Nanki-Pooh (Mr. Durward Lely).
Katisha (Miss Brandram).

Pooh-Bah (Mr. R. Barrington).
The "Three Little Maids from School" (Misses Sibyl Grey, L. Braham, and Jessie Bond).
Ko-Ko (Mr. G. Grossmith).

Ko-Ko (Mr. G. Grossmith).
Yum-Yum (Miss L. Braham).

Pish-Tush (Mr. F. Bovill).

Nanki-Pooh (Mr. Lely).

SKETCHES FROM "THE MIKADO" AT THE SAVOY THEATRE.

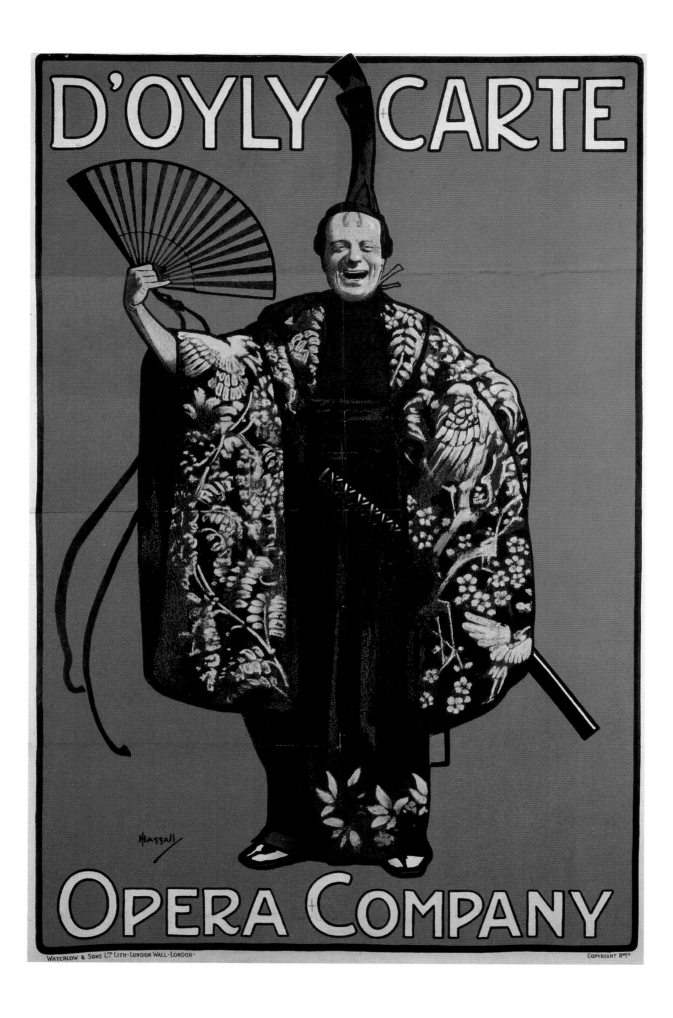

165
John Hassall,
Poster for *The Mikado,*
D'Oyly Carte Opera
Company,
1905.
Colour lithograph,
50·8 x 31·8 cm
(20 x 12¹₂ in)

Antique suits of armour were brought over from Japan only to be found useless because they would not fit any man taller than 1·4 m (4 ft 6 in). Later Gilbert enlisted a male dancer to teach the company proper Japanese deportment, posture and carriage. They were shown how to use fans and to apply Japanese make-up, and how to make the curious hissing sound which passes for laughter among high-born Japanese ladies. The supervision of costumes and of incidental dances was undertaken by a member of the staff of the Japanese Legation in London.

But although Gilbert strove his hardest for accuracy of dress, his private opinions about the Japanese craze are best summed up by the lines about:

The idiot who praises with
enthusiastic tone,
All centuries but this and every
country but his own

Over the whole production hung the long-standing problems of copyright wars between England and the United States of America. This complicated issue meant that any foreign author's work was fair game. Until 1891 printers and publishers did as they liked with the work of English authors; pirate productions abounded and no redress was available. As Arthur Sullivan remarked of the American judges, who decided against appeals to stop unauthorized performances: 'It seemed to be their opinion that a free and independent American citizen ought not to be robbed of his rights of robbing somebody else.'

The material for the costumes was supplied by the famous shop, Liberty's, who sent a team to Japan to study materials and designs and were rewarded by an advertisement for 'Liberty Art Fabrics' in the programme of the first performance in London on 14 March 1885. Liberty's also loyally refused to sell a duplicate set of fabric to an American named Duff, who was rushing to secure the American copyright by bringing out a pirated production of the piece in New York before the official production. Duff's agent went on to Paris, but Richard D'Oyly Carte (the long-suffering manager of the company) had already purchased every Japanese costume in the city, declaring, 'I don't mind how much money I spend to smash Duff!'

The subsequent secret rush to New York by the official company in order to open before the pirated version and secure American copyright led to intense public interest. During the winter of 1885–6, Madison Square Gardens housed a 'Mikado' village with demonstrations of silk weaving. The music of the show became immensely popular throughout Great Britain and her empire, and right across America wherever a military band went, selections from *The Mikado* were played. As the *Daily Telegraph* commented on the first night of *The Mikado* in 1885: 'We are all being more or less Japanned.'

The show ran initially for no fewer than 672 performances at the Savoy and 430 in New York between 1885 and 1886, and a number of touring companies spread not only the fame of Gilbert and Sullivan's operetta but also a taste for things Japanese both across America and around the world.

An amusing finale to the triumphant progress of *The Mikado* was provided in 1907 by the heralded arrival of Prince Fushimi on an official visit to England. Japan had just beaten Russia in the War of 1906 and politicians anxious to create a good impression on the imperial visitors, as so often happens, fell over backwards in threatening to ban performances of the piece. Questions were inevitably asked in the House of Commons, prompting a debate which sounds just like Gilbert at his best:

Mr Faber: Is it not a fact that the
playing of the music of The Mikado on
board ships of war and by regimental
bands has been forbidden? (laughter)
Is the Right Hon. Gentleman aware
that the action of the Lord
Chamberlain in this matter has made
this country ridiculous in the eyes of
the civilized world?
The Home Secretary: I strongly
protest against the last remark of the
Hon. member, and as regards the first
question, it has nothing to do with
my department.

A few years later, in January 1914, the first Japanese performance of *The Mikado* took place at the Imperial Theatre in Tokyo amidst the inevitable controversy, summarized in a leading Tokyo newspaper by an indignant 'old Fogey' who wrote:

an opera like this can only be a
national disgrace. If, however, we
reflect that this is the image of
Japanese women held by Westerners,
then this opera could be of some use
to us in showing how Westerners
think about Japan.

Another crisis for conservative lovers of Gilbert and Sullivan occurred in 1926, when the artist and aesthete, Charles Ricketts, was asked to design the costumes for a revival of *The Mikado* at the Princess Theatre in London. His superb designs were notable particularly for the way in which he stencilled the Japanese patterns on the costumes. Ricketts was delighted by the commission, particularly enjoying designing fantastic court dresses. He wrote:

The Geisha, Madam Butterfly, and
The Mikado have created a dreary
pink dressing gown style quite unlike
anything Japanese and I believe the
public would be startled by the
novelty of an entirely different
presentment [166].

166
Charles Ricketts,
Original design for *The Mikado*
from a souvenir of Richard
D'Oyly Carte's season of
Gilbert and Sullivan operas,
Princess Theatre, London,
1926.
Gouache over pencil

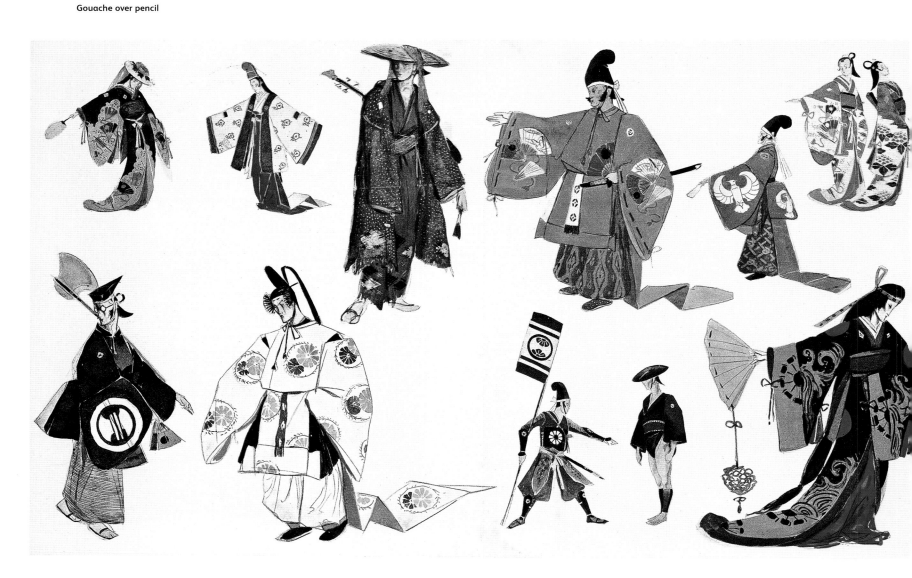

Dudley Hardy,
The Geisha,
1896.
Colour lithograph,
70 x 48 cm
(27¹₂ x 18⁴₅ in)

Startled the public certainly were and,
as with any attempt in Great Britain to
change a long-established and much-
loved tradition, also scandalized. *The
Globe* newspaper turned to verse to
parody the fact that:

*We've lost The Mikado; the scenes
we all know*
*Poo Bah and Yum Yum and the
schoolgirls must go,*
*With Katisha and also the cheerful
Ko Ko.*

The runaway success of *The Mikado* in
1885 created a demand for shows with
an exotic Japanese subject, and in 1896
The Geisha (167) was staged by the
great impresario, George Edwards, at
the Gaiety Theatre, London, starring
the inimitable Marie Lloyd, who sang
the role of the English girl, Molly
Seamore, visiting Japan. She foolishly
puts on the dress of a geisha, and thus
finds herself put up for public auction.
She is bought by a Japanese aristocrat,
who proposes to make the English girl
his wife, but Mimosa San, a 'real'
geisha, rescues the imprudent Molly.
Marie Lloyd's interpretation of the hit
song of the show was remarkable for
its innuendo:

*Ev'ry little Jappy chappies gone upon
the Geisha*
Trickiest little Geisha ever seen in Asia!
*I've made things hum a bit, you know,
since I became a Geisha*
*Japanese-y, free and easy Tea house
girl!*

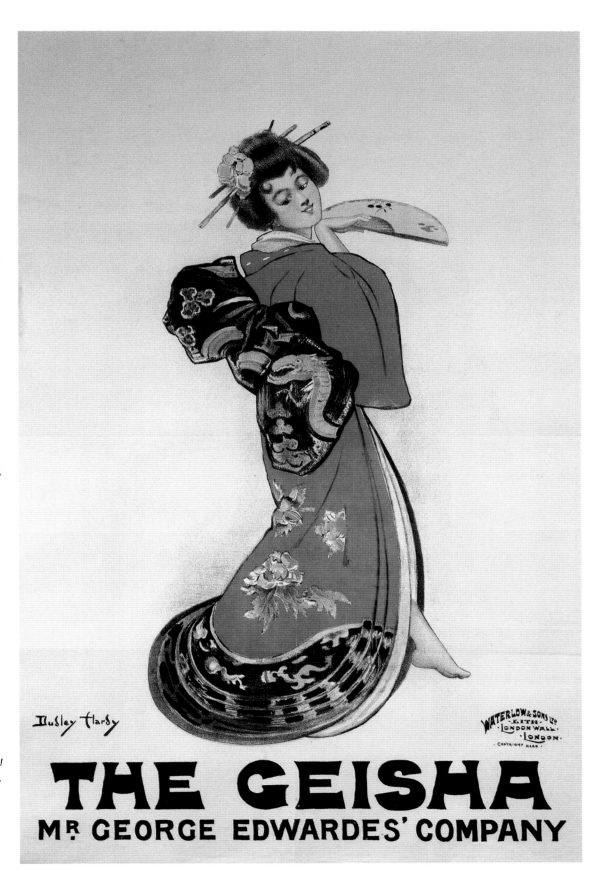

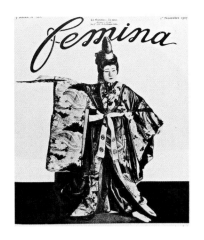

168
Madame Sadayakko on front page of *Femina*, 1907

The show was immensely successful, earning in its tours of the United Kingdom, America, Australia and Canada over two million pounds in the money of the time. Two jolly songs, *The Amorous Goldfish* and *Chin Chin Chinaman*, and two lovely sets, *The Teahouse of Ten Thousand Joys* and *A Chrysanthemum Fête in the Palace Gardens*, helped to pull in the public wherever the show was staged. The success of such a male chauvinist plot is remarkable when it is remembered that these were the years of the New Woman and the emergent suffragette movement.

In London, as in Paris, a tremendous interest in Japanese costume began to influence fashion and make its mark upon the musical and dramatic stage. In 1900 the celebrated actress, Réjane, wore a kimono which caused a sensation and led to the opening of a shop selling similar garments under the trademark 'Kimonos Sadayakko'. Sadayakko was a famous geisha with dramatic talents who had once enjoyed the patronage of the Japanese Prime Minister. She first appeared in the West in San Francisco (1899) with an all-male troupe and rapidly gained superstar status. In New York in *The Geisha and the Knight* she created a sensation by the removal of layers of kimonos to persuade monks to admit her into a temple.

In the Paris Exposition of 1900 she performed at Loie Fuller's theatre in a free adaption of Dumas's *The Lady of the Camellias* (*La Dame aux Camélias*), set in sixteenth-century Japan. Sadayakko's likeness can be seen in a memorable woodcut by William Nicholson (see 62). He was one of the many artists to try to portray her personality, ranging from the Dutch Fauve painter, Kees van Dongen (1877–1968), the German, Max Slevogt (1868–1932), and the young Pablo Picasso (1881–1973), who took up a commission to design a poster for her, for which four sketches still exist. Auguste Rodin begged her to sit for him, but she told him quite truthfully that she had no time. Sadayacco subsequently signed a contract with the shop Au Mikado to advertise a range of beauty products and perfumes. Frequently in the public eye in the pages of the leading fashion journal *Femina* (168), she became known in Paris as a Madame Chrysanthème figure, 'a Madame Butterfly become very Parisienne', whose products formed a remarkable finale to the years of 'kimonomania'.

Kimonos featured spectacularly in several dramatic presentations in Paris, notably *The Seller of Smiles* in the *Théâtre Japonais* (1888), *The Dream* (1890), and especially, *Madame Chrysanthème*, which was staged on 30 January 1893, fixing a stereotype of the geisha, although it was not the only work to deal with such a theme.

'Desertion' plays entertained readers and audiences in America and the West well into the twentieth century with such titles as *A Flower of Yeddo*, *The Lady of the Weeping Willow Tree* and *A Japanese Marriage*. A number of popular novels with Japanese settings were also published in America between 1880 and 1905, one notable title being *Honda the Samurai: a Story of Modern Japan* (1890) by William Elliot Griffis, America's best-known early interpreter of Japan's recent history. It was, however, Edward H House, who taught for twenty years in Tokyo, and edited the *Tokyo Times*, who was one of the first to write novels describing love affairs between Japanese women and Western men, notably his *Yone Santo, A Child of Japan* (1888). In the late 1870s House had adopted a seventeen-year-old girl, Koto Aoki, who was on the point of suicide after her marriage failed, a moving parallel between an incident in the novel and House's own life.

The first woman novelist to write stories with a Japanese setting was Winnifred Eaton Babcock. Born in Montreal in 1879, the author was the daughter of a Chinese mother but took the pen-name of Onoto Watanna and adopted a Japanese viewpoint when writing a series of love stories set in Japan that featured women of mixed Japanese and Western ancestry.

Floral titles flowed effortlessly from her pen, *The Wooing of Wisteria* (1902) being followed by *The Love of Azalea* (1904), but neither of them match her earlier novel, *A Japanese Nightingale* (1901), in which the heroine Yuki is of mixed blood and a geisha whose mother was deserted by a Dutch naval officer at Nagasaki. The plot in *A Japanese Nightingale* relates the eventful love affair between a wealthy American and a girl with an American father and a Japanese mother. The protagonist of the novel is a performer, 'hostess' and a hired 'wife' but her fate is far less tragic than that of Madame Butterfly. The story of *Madame Butterfly*, dealing as it does with similar themes, far exceeds these works of popular fiction as a work of art.

The writer, Lafcadio Hearn, was in a very different league. Of Irish-Greek parentage, he was educated in England. As the result of an accident in boyhood he lost the sight of one eye, which both made his appearance a little alarming and made him 'a bit of a loner'. In 1869 he settled in Cincinnati, working as a journalist and incurring scandal by living openly with a mulatto woman. In 1890 he went to Japan where he settled for the last fourteen years of his life. He married a Japanese woman, Setsu, and had a son, Kazuo (169).

169
**Lafcadio Hearn with his
wife and son, Kazuo, at
Kumamoto,
photographed in
1895**

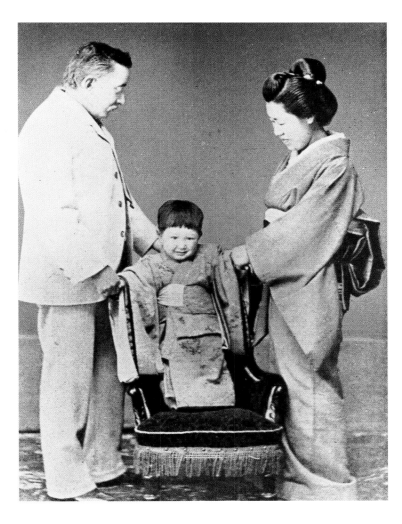

Hearn adopted Japanese dress, and although he never fully mastered the language, took the name of Yakumo Koizumi. From 1896 to 1903 he taught at Matsue and lectured on English literature at the Imperial University in Tokyo. To this day his work is underestimated in the West and he is remembered as a travel journalist, but in Japan he is revered as the first major writer from the West to interpret Japanese customs, mythology and landscapes sympathetically. He is famed particularly for his documentaries, notably *Glimpses of Unfamiliar Japan* (1894), *Out of the East* (1895) and *Japan: an Attempt at an Interpretation* (1904). Hearn had been unhappy and unsuccessful in the West and felt bitter at his failure, emotions that he purged in his exhilarated espousal of Japan and his belief in the moral and aesthetic superiority of Japanese culture.

The life of Madame Butterfly differed from its predecessors by the power of its simple story of seduction and unrequited love, based on a real incident. The story was written by John Luther Long, a successful Philadelphia lawyer and author. Besides *Madame Butterfly* he wrote the novels *Miss Cherry Blossom of Tokyo* (1895) and *The Fox Woman* (1899).

Long probably never visited Japan himself, but his sister had lived there as the wife of an American missionary in Nagasaki. She told Long about the tragic event in the true story of Madame Butterfly (Yamamuru Tsuru) and was able to confirm every incident in detail. Substituting an American naval officer for the English merchant, Long's story appeared in the *Century Magazine* in 1898 and was adapted for the stage in 1900 by the actor, manager and playwright, David Belasco.

Giacomo Puccini, the great Italian composer, once described himself as 'a passionate hunter of women, wild duck and libretti'. Soon after successfully launching *Tosca* in Rome in January 1900 he began to search for another story with exotic colour in order to inspire his established librettists, Illica and Giacosa, and his publisher, Ricordi. Puccini was consumed by a compelling personal motivation, the wish to vie with his great rival, the operatic composer, Pietro Mascagni. Mascagni had followed the sensational success of his *verismo* opera *Cavalleria Rusticana* with a tragic piece called *Iris*, with a Japanese setting, which was produced with great success in Rome in 1898 and Milan in 1899. The stage designs for the opera were remarkable, for the artist, Adolpho Hohenstein, had clearly done his homework, as the rod puppets in the first act were carefully based upon the Japanese *bunraku* puppet theatre.

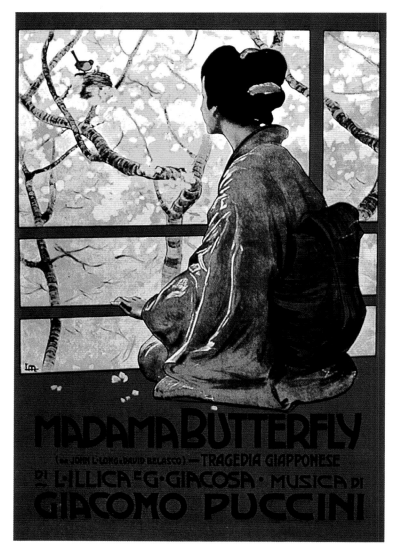

170
Madama Butterfly,
1904.
51 x 71 cm
(20 x 28 in)

Both the puppets and the geisha costumes produced a dramatic effect, added to by the musical novelties of the *koto* (a stringed instrument), bells, a tam-tam drum and gongs, all used in the travelling theatre scene in the first act, and the scene in the Yoshiwara in Edo in the second act.

The melodramatic plot of the opera tells the story of Iris (soprano), a beautiful young laundress, who is the only support of her blind father Il Cieco (bass). As dawn breaks over a small village near Mount Fuji, Iris awakes troubled by a nightmare, in which her doll had been attacked by serpents and monsters, a presager of ill omen. As the action develops, a performing troupe of actors, musicians and puppeteers arrives, and the young Osaka (tenor), a wealthy rake, and his friend, Kyoto (baritone), a brothel keeper, are attracted by Iris and attempt to abduct her. She continues to repulse Osaka, who helps Kyoto to imprison her in his brothel.

In a crowd scene Iris's voice is recognized by her father, who curses her and throws handfuls of mud at her as she tries to escape through the crowd. Shocked by his rejection, Iris jumps into the inflamed mob and is left for dead.

In the final act, set in the sewer below the brothel, some rag-pickers, thinking she is dead, rob Iris's body of her remaining finery. As she reflects on life the sun's rays warm her last moments and her soul ascends to heaven, in one of the most melodic moments in the work.

Consumed with envy at Mascagni's exotic Japanese theme, Puccini, while in London for the first British performance of *Tosca* at Covent Garden in June 1900, happened to see Belasco's play at the Duke of York's Theatre enticingly entitled *Madame Butterfly*, and with a glamorous leading lady, Blanche Bates. Although Puccini spoke almost no English, he rushed backstage on the opening night and, weeping copiously, asked him for the operatic rights to the play. Pinkerton's adage, 'it is easier to go to bed than talk', was a motto close to the heart of Puccini, who was himself a great womanizer. The heroine Cio-Cio-San's suicide by harakiri awoke all his dramatic instincts. Back in Italy, in order to create the right atmosphere, he undertook careful research of the exotic subject. He questioned artists and authorities on Japanese culture, transcribed melodies from records sent from Tokyo by his friend, the wife of the Japanese ambassador. When after some maddening delays he finally caught up with the performances by Sadayakko and her troupe in Milan, Puccini was deeply impressed by the gory finales of several *kabuki* plays in their repertoire.

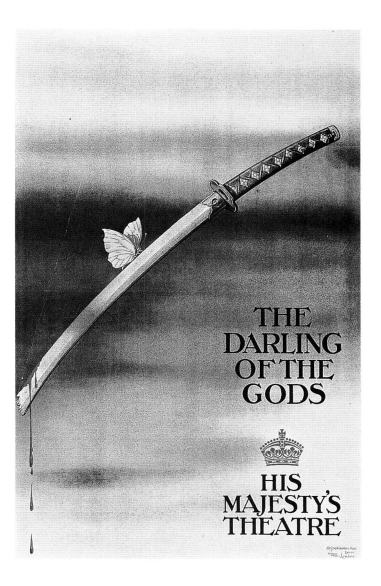

171
Makino Yoshio,
***The Darling of the Gods*,**
1903.
22.8 x 16.2 cm
(9 x 6²₅ in)

On a more lighthearted note Puccini's curiosity even extended to Gilbert and Sullivan's *The Mikado*, a vocal score of which was still to be seen at Puccini's hunting lodge, Torre del Lago, in recent years, with a pencilled Italian translation of two of the songs. Puccini also studied collections of Japanese songs. Almost half the first act alone is dedicated to building up an authentic Japanese atmosphere and echoes of genuine Japanese themes. In the second act he strengthened the percussion, using a tam-tam and Japanese bells, together with *campanelli a tastiere* (glockenspiels) and tubular bells.

The first night was held in La Scala, Milan on 17 February 1904. The evening was a legendary disaster, not even the haunting 'One Fine Day' pleasing the fickle Milanese audience, and the birdsong at dawn was greeted by the claque (supporters of Mascagni) with derisive farmyard imitations. Some judicious cuts were made and three months later, when presented in Brescia, the revised piece triumphed. The opera has grown in popularity ever since, forming links not only between music and drama and the East and the West, but also creating a spectacular example of the unexpected power of Japonisme to effect a marriage with the *verismo* world of Puccini and Italian opera, reflected in the spectacular posters by Rossi and Myerbach-Rheinfeld in the Ricordi archive (170).

The success of the American run of his play *Madame Butterfly* inspired Belasco to write another drama with a Japanese theme. In 1902 he produced *The Darling of the Gods* (171) with expensive authentic Japanese settings in its production, which he once again co-authored with John Luther Long.

Madame Butterfly and *The Mikado* have one quality in common which leads to their continuing success – they both provide immensely rewarding opportunities for costume and scenery designers. Recent years have seen such novelties as 'Black' Mikados and 'Mafia' Mikados set in Sicily, while at the Royal Albert Hall in London, the audience has enjoyed a performance of *Madame Butterfly* with the central amphitheatre set up as a Japanese raked garden in the first act and flooded in the second act.

It is perhaps appropriate to conclude these excursions into the dramatic presentation of the butterfly by enjoying its depiction in a print signed Baichoro Kunisada and Oko Kunisada of a Butterfly dance. Two geisha are shown playing the roles of butterfly maidens (172) at the Tokyo Matsumotoro Theatre in Edo in Horse year, while the stage musicians, also geisha, sit on a dais.

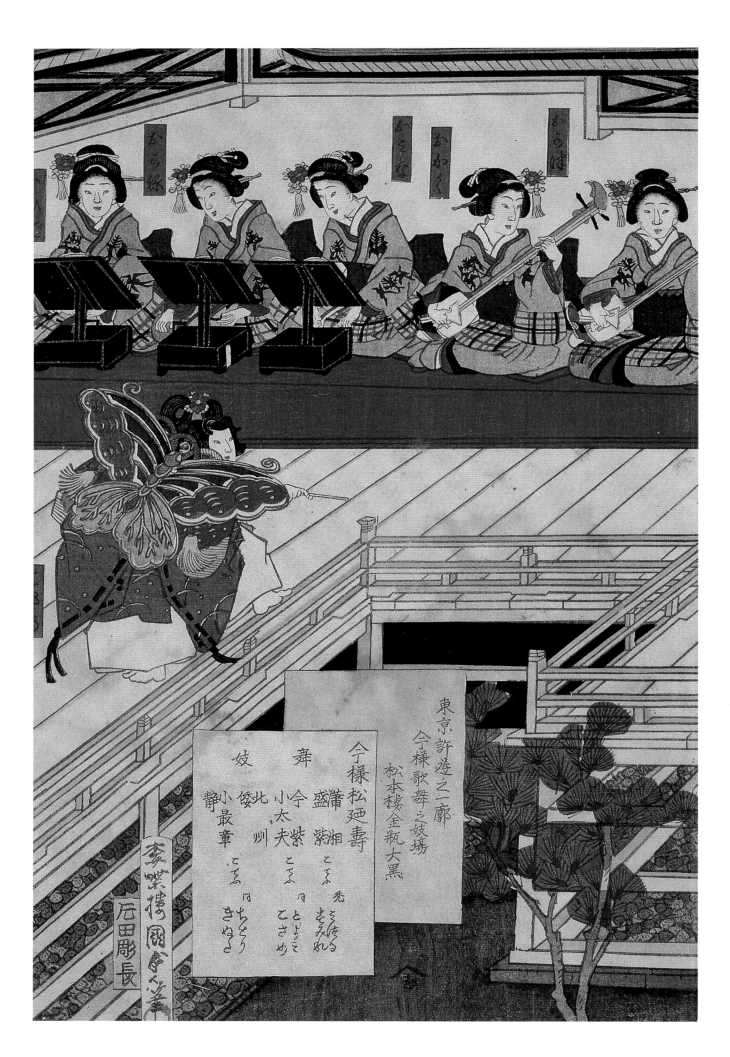

172
**Baichoro Kunisada
and Oko Kunisada,
*The Matsumotoro
Theatre in the Tokyo
Pleasure District*,
1870.
Colour woodblock,
36·5 x 25·4 cm
(14³⁄₈ x 10 in)**

173
**Dustjacket for Claude
Debussy's *La Mer*,
adapting a detail from
Hokusai's *The Great
Wave*,
1905.
35 x 54 cm
(13³⁄₄ x 21¹⁄₄ in)**

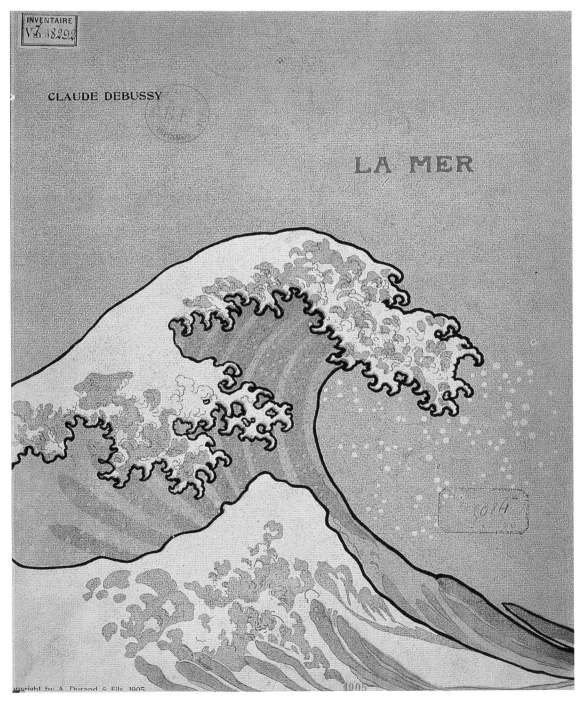

CLAUDE DEBUSSY

LA MER

There is also a direct link between classical orchestral music in the West and the Japanese print. Claude Debussy loved England, which he visited on several occasions. He began to compose the piano version of his composition, *La Mer* (*The Sea*), while staying at the island of Jersey from whence he wrote to his new publisher, 'The sea has been very good to me, and has shown me all her moods.' Debussy much admired Hokusai and suggested using a stylized detail of the famous print, *The Great Wave*, on the cover of the piano score, which was published in 1905. Later Debussy worked on the orchestral version of his score while staying at the Grand Hotel in Eastbourne in a room overlooking the sea. There, despite the distraction of a band playing selections from Gilbert and Sullivan, he finished the work. The orchestral score bore a reproduction of the crest of *The Wave* (173).

Today, a century later, Debussy's masterpiece continues to provide potent evidence of the creative force of Japonisme's marriage of East and West, a union which, although much disparaged, has inspired some great art and music.

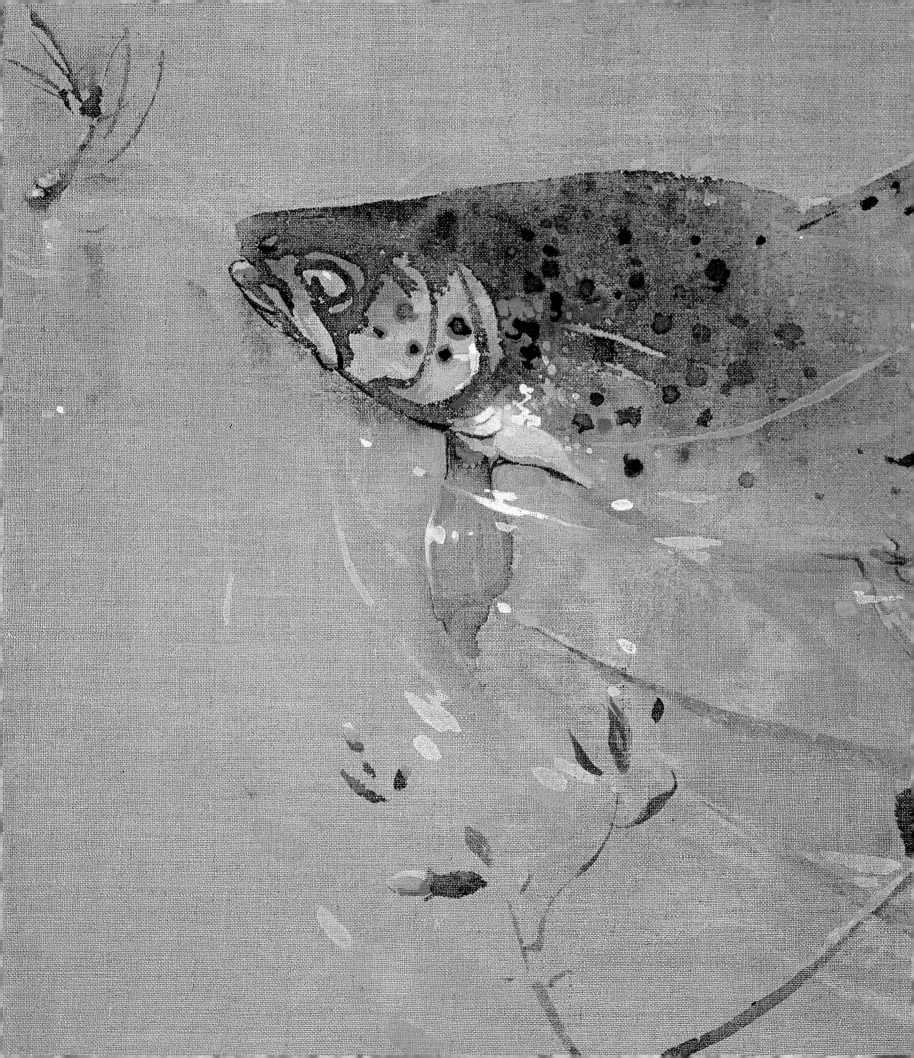

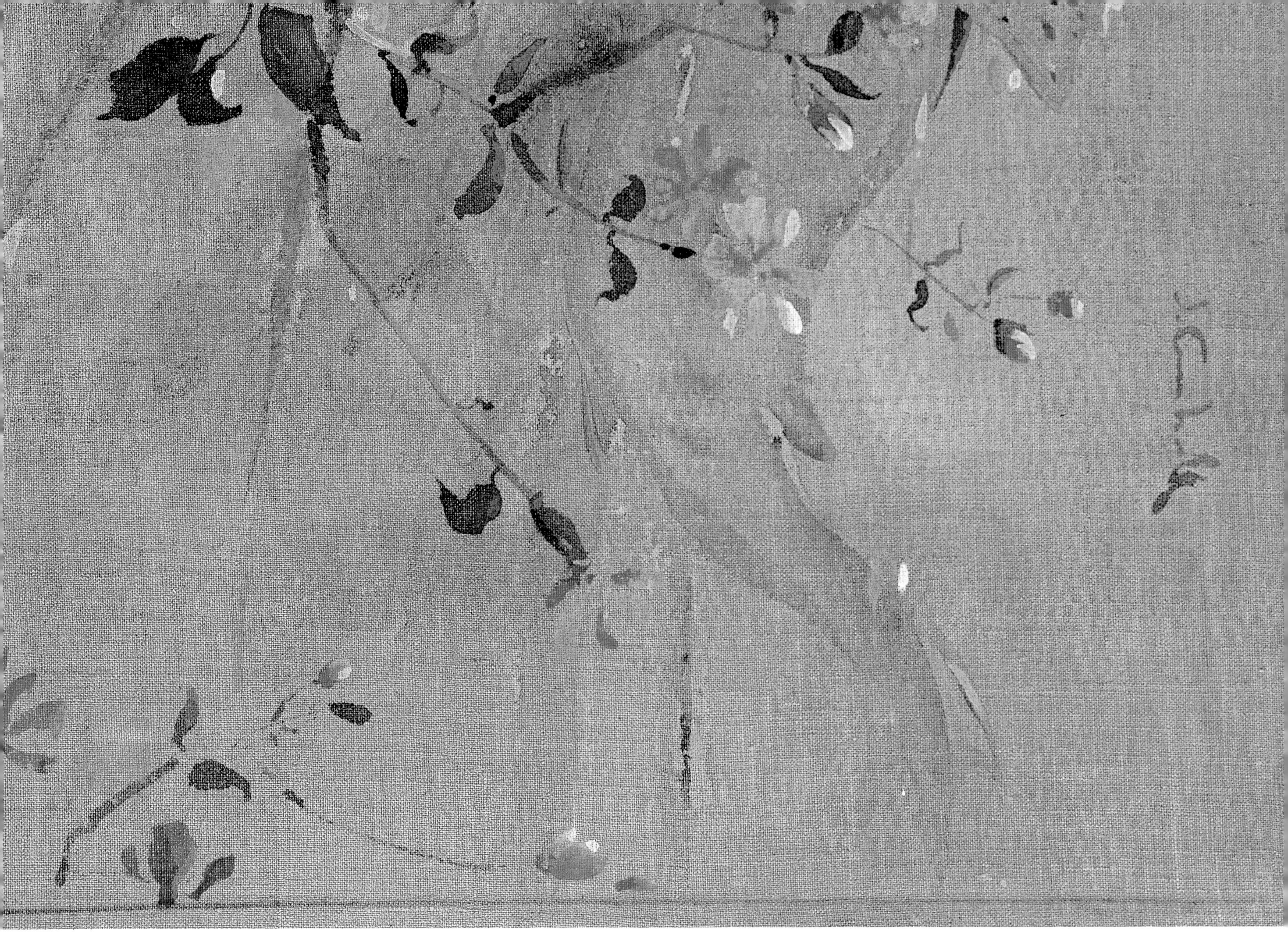

Chapter eight:
Visitors to Japan: Dream and Reality

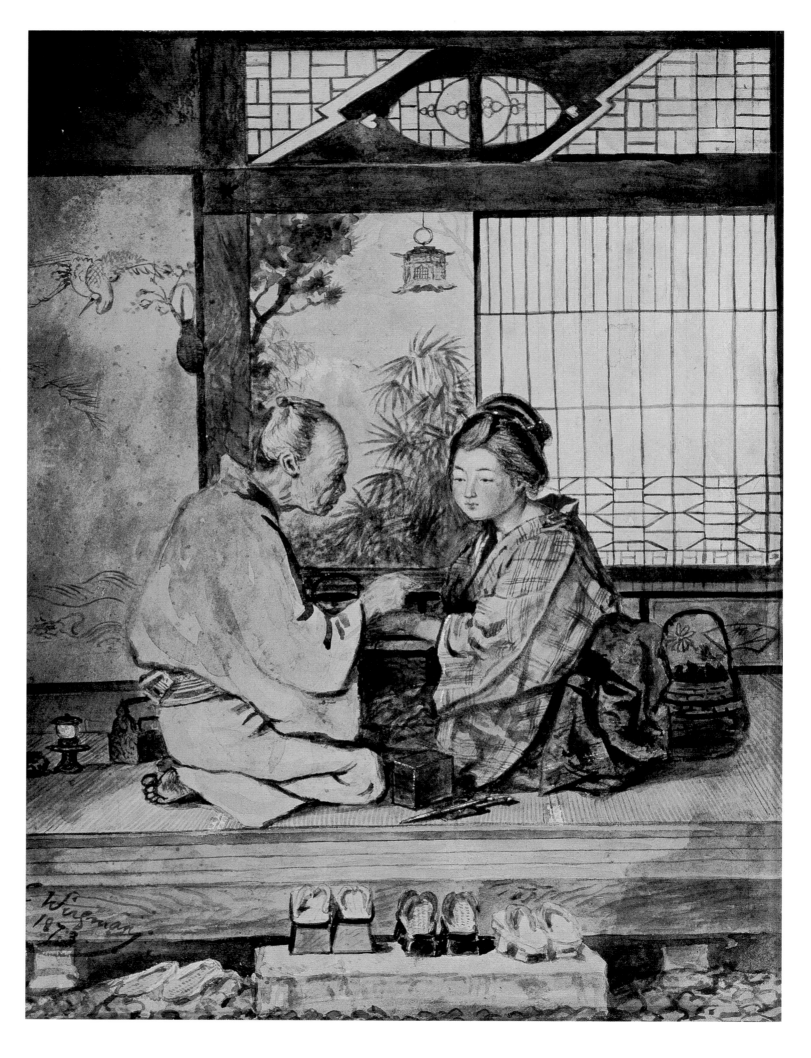

Previous page
Joseph Crawhall,
A Trout Rising **(detail
of 184)**

174
Charles Wirgman,
The Fortune Teller,
**1873.
Watercolour on paper,
40·4 x 30·8 cm
(16 x 12⅛ in).
Yokohama Museum
of Art**

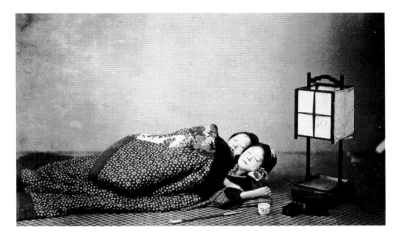

175
Felice Beato,
Sleeping Beauties,
**1868.
Hand-painted albumen
print**

*I no longer need to have Japanese
prints for I constantly tell myself
that I am in Japan here.*
Van Gogh, Arles, 1888

While Van Gogh found the imaginary
'land of Japan' he mentally
experienced at Arles an acceptable
alternative to actually visiting the
country, other artists, photographers,
collectors, writers and designers, for a
wide variety of reasons, needed the
stimulus of travel to Japan itself. All
shared the common motivation of
curiosity. They also possessed varying
reasons for the journey, from a wish to
expand the stock of a great shop and
other business endeavours to an
interest in comparative religion; from
a desire to provide a visual record of
every aspect of this strange land to a
wish to record the flora or fauna of the
country. Another potent factor was the
mysterious 'lure of the East', which still
remains today a major consideration in
our decisions about where to pass our
annual holidays. In the second half of
the nineteenth century this manifested
itself in the arrival of the first tourists
in Japan, who all had one thing in
common, a desire for pictorial
souvenirs as records of their stay. At
first such pictorial records could only
be created by the use of brush, pen
and the tools of the engraver.

One of the first artists to work within
these limits was the Londoner, Charles
Wirgman, who was only twenty-five
when he was sent to China in 1857 as
a war artist to cover the Opium Wars,
and then moved to Japan in 1861.
His vision of Japan comes down to
us today primarily via the engravings
after his drawings which appeared in
the *Illustrated London News*. These
vivid sketches became very influential
in forming the Victorian vision of
Japan. Like any skilled graphic
journalist, Wirgman's eye was constantly alert and he recorded vividly
such subjects as the temple of
Kamakura near the scene of the
murder of two British officers and
the subsequent execution of the
murderers, but also less disturbing
and more picturesque scenes, such as
The Fortune Teller (174).

While in China in 1860, Wirgman
met the photographer Felix Beato
(1830–1906), who was born in Venice
but trained in England and had
become one of the first war reporters
to use the new medium of
photography while working in Greece,
India, Egypt and the Crimea. In 1860
both men met while covering the
Opium Wars and the Anglo-French
military expedition which resulted
in the sack of the Summer Palace
in Peking. From China they travelled
independently to Japan where they
settled in Yokohama.

Beato arrived in 1863, and wrote an
entertaining article for the *Illustrated
London News* describing Wirgman's
house, which was packed with curious
Japanese visitors anxious to see
Wirgman painting in oils, a technique
not widely known in Japan. In 1862,
Wirgman, a jolly eccentric, founded the
humorous journal, *The Japan Punch*,
which appeared sporadically until 1887.
In 1863 he became one of the first
foreigners since Will Adams to marry
a Japanese woman (see Chapter 1).

In 1865 a business partnership was
formed entitled Beato & Wirgman,
Artists & Photographers, which lasted
until 1869. Beato covered the latest
news stories, including such major
events as the Battle of Shimonoseki in
1864 when the British navy shelled the
town in retaliation for earlier Japanese
retributive action in the Straits of
Shimonoseki. In a less belligerent spirit,
Beato also travelled the length and
breadth of Japan, capturing with his
camera the landscape and people,
subjects still virtually untouched by
Europeans. This work culminated in the
two-volume album, *Photographic Views
of Japan*, published in Yokohama in
1868, the first volume to record the
cities and landscapes of Japan in black
and white, including such classic views
as the Tokaido Road between
Yokohama and Fujiyama.

The second volume, *Native Types*,
comprised approximately 100 albumen
prints carefully hand-coloured by a
Japanese painter of such subjects as
Mother and Child and *Sleeping
Beauties* (175). In many of these prints
there are striking similarities in poses
and subject matter to *ukiyo-e* prints.
Indeed as in the West, the introduction
of photography was to prove a major
factor in the decline and fall of the
traditional woodblock print.

Beato's works were soon widely copied
by less skilful hands. The always
popular genre subject of two or three
young trainee geishas in rickshaws was
endlessly imitated for popular Western
taste. Described as 'Yokohama-shasin'
(Yokohama-photographs), they were
purchased in large quantities by
tourists. These were the type of prints
with which Carrie Pooter entertains the
guests in her home in Grossmith's
celebration of suburban life, *The Diary
of a Nobody*. Such photographs could
make the alien, but exciting, world of
Japan almost as familiar to the Pooters
in Upper Holloway, London, as aspects
of their own environment. Photographs,
created strictly for the export trade,
by their nature conveyed a sense of
the reality of daily life in the far-off
land of Japan.

Japonisme

176
Frank Dillon
The Stray Shuttlecock,
1878.
Oil on canvas,
90 x 120 cm
(35½ x 47¼ in).
Victoria and Albert
Museum, London

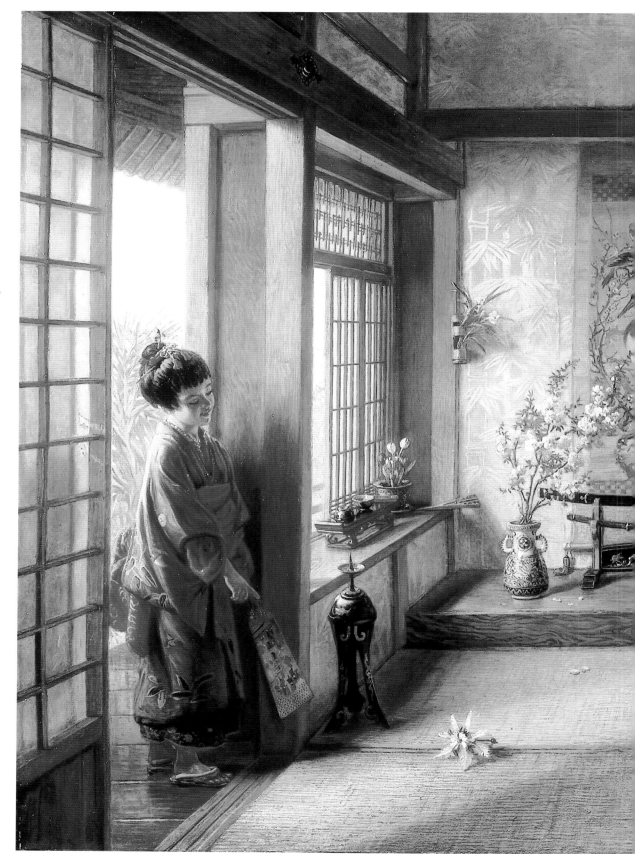

Woodcuts, however, conceived as a popular art form in Japan, during their passage to Europe, 'suffered a sea change, into something rich and strange'. *Ukiyo-e* prints, still very cheap to buy, could give to their purchasers the exciting frisson imparted by the ownership of works of art. Their novelty could also encourage bolder spirits to venture to Japan and either make their own paintings, or form collections of Japanese works which eventually entered museums. From Bournemouth to Birmingham, Cracow to Cambridge and Maidstone to Mulhouse, both major and minor collections of Japanese works were assembled during the late nineteenth and early twentieth centuries.

An early visitor to Meiji-liberated Japan was the English painter, Frank Dillon (1823–1909). A topographical painter who had worked in Egypt, Dillon was a friend of the Pre-Raphaelite, George Price Boyce (1826–97), who is known to have been very interested in Japonisme. Dillon visited Japan in 1875 and on his return to England painted several interiors, including *The Stray Shuttlecock* (176), which were crowded with correct Japanese props – *samisen* (a stringed instrument resembling a zither), scrolls and sword racks – many items being left to what is now the Victoria and Albert Museum. His paintings possess a certain charm, but are very obviously painstaking, while not wholly accurate, re-creations of Japanese rooms, for there is far more on show than would be the case in reality.

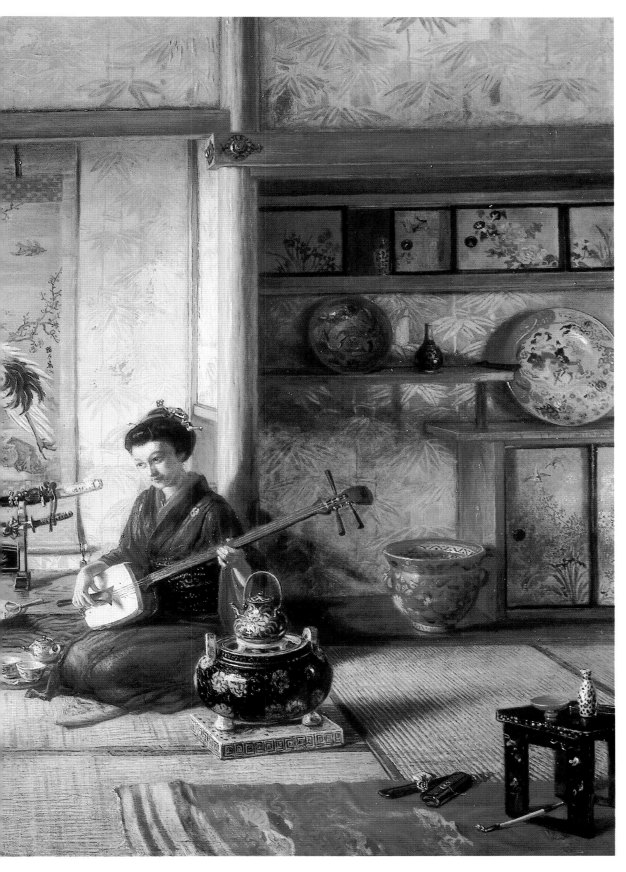

The presence of *zori* (outdoor sandals) symbolizes summer, while the shuttlecock represents the New Year, and therefore winter. In 1880 Dillon published *Drawings by Japanese Artists*, which included fifteen colour reproductions of Japanese paintings, and in the introduction a discussion of the use of decorative motifs such as flowers and birds, calligraphy and brush techniques.

For some liberated British women, the increasingly straightforward journey to Japan presented no real challenge, notably for the indefatigable botanical painter and illustrator, Marianne North (1830–90). She is remembered today by visitors to her memorial gallery in Kew Gardens, London, which displays 832 paintings arranged by her on the crowded walls. She visited Japan in 1876 and described in her journal her first glimpse of Fujiyama on 7 November of that year:

I watched the sun rise out of the sea and redden its top, as I have seen so well represented on so many handscreens and tea-trays … we drove out into the country, and took funny cups of yellow tea in a bamboo tea-house, with five pretty girls rather over four feet high, in chignons with huge pins, blackened teeth, and no eyelashes, laughing at us all the while.

(The custom of blackening teeth with iron dissolved in vinegar mixed with powdered gall nuts goes back to the ninth century, as does the practice of shaving eyebrows and repainting them higher up the face.)

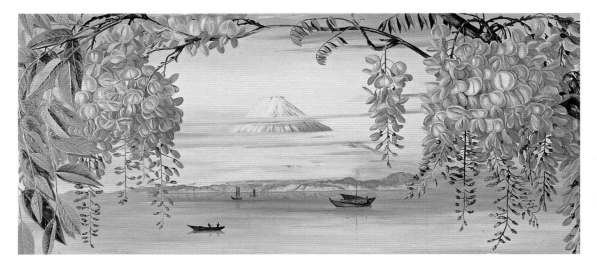

177
Marianne North,
Wisteria chinensis,
1875–7.
Oil on prepared paper
fixed to canvas,
30 x 45 cm
(11³₄ x 17³₄ in).
Marianne North Gallery,
Kew Gardens, London

During her all too brief stay, curtailed by an attack of rheumatic fever, she managed to paint a view of Fuji, seen through an arch of the climbing shrub *Wisteria chinensis* (177). Other paintings show the Hottomi Temple, Kyoto, among the pine trees and Japanese flowers. She enjoyed travelling about:

The railway went alongside the famous Tokaido road, and was full of interest. The rice and millet harvest was then going on, and the tiny sheaves were a sight to see. They piled them up against the trees and fences in the most neat and clever way, some of the small fan-leaved palm-trees looking as though they had straw petticoats on … At the last station one of the Japanese ministers got into our carriage in the costume of an English gentleman, chimney-pot hat included … and at Tokyo packed Miss C. and myself into two jinrickshas, a kind of grown-up perambulator, the outside painted all over with marvellous histories and dragons (like scenes out of the Revelation). They had men to guide them with all sorts of devices stamped on their backs, and long hanging sleeves. So we trotted off to the Tombs of the Shoguns.

Another redoubtable British lady traveller, Isabella Bird, visited Japan a year later in 1877, but found the experience already a little too tame. Like many other visitors in later years she reacted with suspicion to the industrial muscle of the new Japan, writing in her journal after spending just one day in the thriving commercial centre of Yokohama: 'I long to get away into the *real* Japan.' When she did manage to visit a small town called Yusowa, things were also unappealing as hundreds of people crowded round to enjoy the experience of seeing a Western lady eat lunch:

those behind being unable to see me, got ladders and climbed on to the adjacent roofs, where they remained till one of the roofs gave way with a crash.

A year earlier, in 1876, Émile Guimet, an industrialist from Lyon, landed at Yokohama accompanied by the painter Félix Régamey. Guimet, whose chief interest lay in the study of comparative religion, persuaded Régamey to accompany him as a 'human camera' to record religious rites and rituals. They had met up in the Philadelphia Centennial exhibition where an extensive display of Japanese items was on view, and then travelled on to Japan.

Régamey was already deeply interested in everything pertaining to Japan, which he had seen in the pages of the *Illustrated London News* (the journal for which he would later work himself), and he also made chromolithographic copies of prints by Hiroshige and Hokusai for a book on the poetess, Ono-no Komachi, by the Japanese enthusiast, Philippe Burty.

In three months of travels around Japan, Guimet and Régamey investigated the relationship between Buddhism and Shintoism. In temples and sanctuaries they observed the religious practices of the monks and studied the representations and gestures of the statues of gods, while also forming an important collection of ritualistic objects and ceramics. When they returned to France they collaborated on several books, notably *Promenades Japonais* (1878–80), a handsomely illustrated account of scenes of everyday life. They also contributed articles and illustrations to the Arts and Crafts journal, *Le Japon pratique*.

On his return to France, Guimet at first worked on setting up a museum in Lyon and then helped to arrange objects from the Far East in the 1878 exhibition at the Trocadéro in Paris, including forty paintings of religious subjects by Régamey.

In 1883 Guimet offered his extensive collection to the state, and subsequently the city of Paris donated a site for the building, which first opened in 1889 at the Place d'Iéna as a museum devoted to the religions of the world, and formed one of the attractions of the Exposition Universelle of that year. Subsequently the emphasis of the museum gradually became centred upon Asian art and an extensive library. Today the Musée Guimet, recently brilliantly modernized and rearranged, houses one of the finest Oriental collections in the world.

While great institutions such as the Musée Guimet will always gravitate to capital cities, local museums also play an important role in informing the public, a fact which often goes unrecognized. All over the West one can find many small collections of Japanese works often formed in the nineteenth century and left for the unexpected enjoyment of visitors. One of the most impressive small-scale collections of Japanese works in England is in the Maidstone Museum, Kent, where lived the Hon. Henry Marsham.

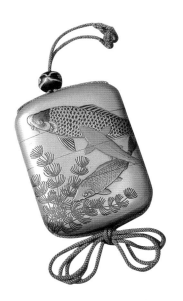
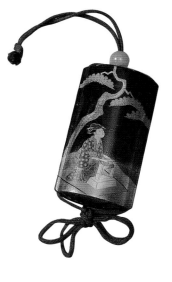

In the 1870s Marsham retired from the army in order to collect ceramics in Japan, which he bequeathed to Maidstone Museum in 1908, inspiring the Hon. Walter Samuel (son of Lord Bearsted, the founder of 'Shell' oil) to do the same with his excellent and varied collection of Japanese sword fittings, *netsuke*, *inro* (178), lacquer, books and prints which he left to Maidstone Museum on his death in 1924. Even more striking with its Japanese garden overlooking the sea is the Russell-Cotes Museum in Bournemouth, Dorset. In 1885–6 Sir Merton and Lady Russell-Cotes visited Japan and collected with immense enthusiasm. When they returned home Sir Merton recorded with pride that over 100 cases 'were filled by my wife and myself. Among the curios there were some rare and antique specimens of Japanese art.' The collection was initially displayed in the Royal Bath Hotel nearby during the construction of the Mikado Room with its ceiling depicting the Meiji emperor and empress.

Guimet's collecting activities were a part of his idealistic aims to make knowledge available to a wider public. For Régamey, a born romantic, the visit to Japan was the fulfilment of his wildest dreams, 'the age of gold, neither more nor less'. Everything enchanted him, from the tattooed rickshaw men to – inevitably – the geisha.

While Régamey romanticized Japan for many years after a brief visit of three months, other creative spirits dreamed of visiting Japan but avoided the actual journey. Foremost among such daydreamers was Oscar Wilde, who on his whistle-stop lecture tour of the United States of America in 1882, dreamt of new worlds still to be conquered. From San Francisco Wilde wrote home to say:

I feel an irresistible desire to wander, and go to Japan, where I will pass my youth, sitting under an almond tree, drinking amber tea out of a blue cup, and looking at a landscape without perspective …

To his friend and verbal sparring partner, Whistler, Wilde wrote with a more specific proposal: 'When will you come to Japan? Fancy the book, I to write it, you to illustrate it. We would be rich.'

Wilde wrote at the height of the aesthetic enthusiasm for the novel arts of Japan, although his own personal flirtation with Japanese art was not of very long duration. He did, however, write one poem in 1887, originally entitled 'Impression Japonaise':

The white leaves float upon the air,
The red leaves flutter idly down,
Some fall upon her yellow gown,
And some upon her raven hair

She takes an amber lute and sings,
And as she sings a silver crane
Begins his scarlet neck to strain
And flap his burnished metal wings.

She takes a lute of amber bright,
And from the thicket where he lies
Her lover, with his almond eyes
Watches her movements with delight.

While Japanese art still retained its capacity to surprise, Wilde responded to it with enthusiasm. He felt that there was a real kinship of attitudes between his own poetry and Japanese art, commenting on 'the influence which Eastern art is having on us in Europe, and the fascination of all Japanese work'.

Yet Wilde, always susceptible to the vagaries of fashion, soon sensed that the Occidental love for Japan would prove of limited duration. A close friend of his was the young Australian artist, Mortimer Menpes (1860–1938), Whistler's Australian assistant and biographer, who became godfather to Wilde's oldest son, Cyril. In 1887 Menpes visited Japan for eight months to learn 'all the methods of Japanese art'. On his return he exhibited 137 oils (179) and forty prints created in Japan, in the Dowdeswell Galleries, New Bond Street, London.

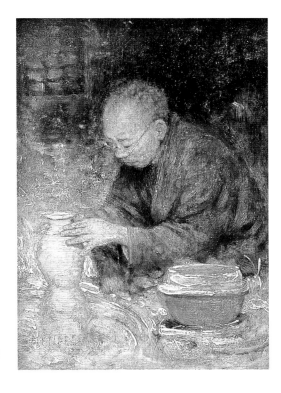

The exhibition was visited and reviewed by Wilde, who posed the question:

… do you really imagine that the Japanese people, as they are presented to us in art, have any existence? If you do, you have never understood Japanese art at all … One of our most charming painters went recently to the Land of the Chrysanthemum in the foolish hope of seeing the Japanese. All he saw, all he had the chance of painting, were a few lanterns and some fans. He was quite unable to discover the inhabitants, as his delightful exhibition … showed only too well. He did not know that the Japanese people are, as I have said, simply a mode of style, an exquisite fancy of art. And so, if you desire to see a Japanese effect, you will not behave like a tourist and go to Tokyo. On the contrary, you will stay at home and steep yourself in the work of certain Japanese artists and then, when you have absorbed the spirit of their style, and caught their imaginative manner of vision, you will … sit in the Park or stroll down Piccadilly, and if you cannot see an absolutely Japanese effect there, you will not see it anywhere …

As so often, Wilde is at his most profound when most paradoxical, here enraged by his disciple, Menpes, visiting Japan without his permission. It is impossible not to feel sorry for poor Menpes, who, characteristically, was also abused by Whistler. Undeterred, Menpes continued to be a passionate advocate of Japanese decoration, and his home, a house designed by the founder of the Century Guild, Arthur Heygate Mackmurdo (1851–1942), at 25 Cadogan Gardens, was described as a 'dream of Oriental beauty' with themed peony, camellia and chrysanthemum rooms. On a second visit to Japan in 1896, Menpes wrote:

I had taken with me very full plans and I gathered together the best artists and craftsmen that I could command … ceiling, doors, wallcoverings and windows were finished completely … by Japanese craftsmen. In two hundred packing cases their work was carried to London.

Menpes published his memories of Japan in *Japan, a Record in Colour* in 1901 with 100 colour illustrations. But in a few short years even Menpes had tired of the Japanese style and he sold the house in 1900, retiring to the sylvan delights of a Kentish fruit farm.

Wilde's satirical comments on Menpes's work provoked an outburst from Rudyard Kipling on his way to Japan in 1889:

Mister Oscar Wilde of the Nineteenth Century is a long-toothed liar. In an article … he, with his tongue in his brazen cheek, avers that there was no such a place as Japan – that it had been created by fans and picture books just as he himself had been created by pottery and fragments of coloured cloth. Never believe anything that Mister Oscar Wilde tells you.

Rudyard Kipling visited Japan in 1889 and again on his honeymoon in 1892. On his first visit he wrote a series of travel articles in the form of letters which he sent back to India for publication in the *Pioneer* newspaper in Allahabad. The eleventh letter includes descriptions of routine tourist excursions to potteries and workshops which are transformed by Kipling's humour, love of the grotesque and feeling for beauty.

For Kipling on that first visit, the experience of Japan was virtually love at first sight. His vivid reports on what he saw have been described 'the most graphic ever penned by a globetrotter', a description surely justified by this portrayal of a street in Tokyo after dark:

Half the town was out for a walk, and all the people's clothes were indigo, and so were the shadows, and most of the paper lanterns were drops of blood red. By the light of smoking oil-lamps people were selling flowers and shrubs – wicked little dwarf pines, stunted peach and plum trees, wisteria bushes clipped and twisted out of all likeness to wholesome plants, leaning and leering out of green-glaze pots … At a corner of a street, some rich men had got together and left unguarded all the gold, diamonds and rubies of the East, but when you came near you saw that this treasure was only a gathering of goldfish in glass globes – yellow, white and red fish, with from three to five forked tails apiece and eyes that bulged far beyond their heads.

A few days after his arrival Kipling visited a curio shop in Kobe to see its *netsuke* collections. *Netsuke* are small carved figures, designed to be used with the kimono, which is bound at the waist by a wide sash, the *obi*.

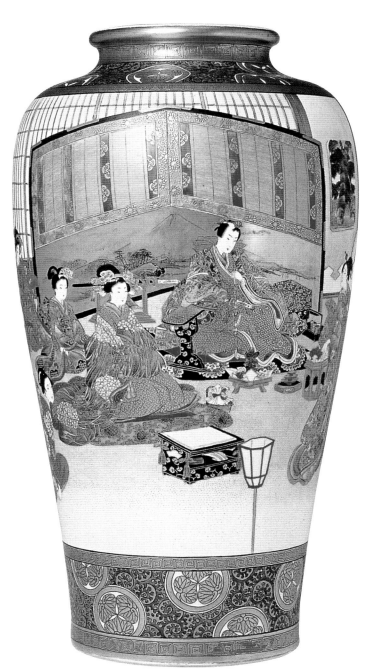

From the *obi* the *netsuke* is suspended and used as a 'toggle' from which to hang a wide variety of small boxes, *inro*, containing objects as varied as tobacco, ink pads, brushes, tea jars, seals, medicines and so on. Kipling greatly enjoyed:

the buttons and netsuke that … can be taken out and played with … the old man horribly embarrassed by a cuttle fish; the priest who makes a soldier pick up a deer for him and laughs to think that the brisket would be his and the burden his companions; or the dry, lean snake coiled in derision on a jawless skull mottled with the memories of corruption; or the Rabelaisian badger who stood on his head and made you blush though he was not half an inch long; or the little fat boy pounding his smaller brother, or the rabbit that had just made a joke, or – but there were scores of these notes, born of every mood of mirth, scorn and experience that sways the heart of man … [I] held half a dozen of them in my palm and winked at the shade of the dead carver!

On another occasion in Kyoto, Kipling visited a pottery, and a maker of *cloisonné* enamels. He recalled how:

the manager took us to see the potters [who] lived close to the kiln and had nothing pretty to look at.

It was different in the painting rooms which were reached by way of one or two Japanese gardens full of quaint flowers and the sound of the spring breezes. Here in a cabinet- like house sat the men, women, and the boys who painted the designs on the vases after the first firing. That all their arrangements were scrupulously neat is only saying that they were Japanese; that their surroundings were fair and proper is only saying that they were artists. A sprig of a cherry-blossom stood out defiantly against the black of the garden paling; a gnarled pine cut the blue of the sky with its spiky splinters as it lifted itself above the paling, and in a little pond the iris and the horsetail nodded to the wind. The workers when at fault had only to lift their eyes, and Nature herself would graciously supply the missing link of a design. Somewhere in dirty England men dream of craftsmen working under conditions which shall help and not stifle the half-formed thought. They even form Guilds … to bring about the desired end … Would they have their dream realized let them see how they make pottery in Japan … [180]

These references to the ideals of William Morris and the Guilds of the Arts and Crafts Movement came naturally to the pen of Kipling, who was the nephew of Burne-Jones. It is followed by one of Kipling's frequent expressions of regret that the virtuoso artistic abilities of the Japanese should be sacrificed to the pursuit of cheap export markets.

Such markets had arisen with the accession of the Meiji emperor in 1868 when great encouragement was given to plans to increase business overseas. The showcases to encourage export orders were provided by the prestigious world fairs held in America and Europe. The Satsuma pottery on show at such events was magnificent at its resplendent best, appallingly vulgar at its worst. Increased demand led to some of the major factories mass-producing Satsuma pottery of very poor quality to support the continuing existence of their master studios. Two distinct types of Satsuma evolved, the show pieces and the export wares. Kipling particularly disliked cheap Satsuma ware with a crackled white glaze, which he describes as having 'a golden smallpox upon it'. He pungently describes how:

the potters squat upon the floor making ormolu Satsuma for cheap shops at home. The barbarians want Satsuma and they shall have it, if it has to be made in Kyoto one piece per twenty minutes. So much for the baser forms of the craft.

The badness of the bad things I could describe at length: of the good I know only that they were desirable ... I saw others as good and as true as the eye could wish in blue, violet, imitation Imari, 'royal Keg' [Kutani] and half a dozen other varieties of the worked clay which ignorance debars me from naming.

Far from being ignorant, Kipling reveals a sophisticated discernment years ahead of his time, and a sensitive knowledge of the aesthetic sensibilities of Japanese taste and the dangers of over-elaboration.

After the pottery he visited the *cloisonné* enamel manufactory where he:

began to understand the cost of the ware when I saw a man working out a pattern of sprigs and butterflies on a plate about ten inches in diameter. With finest silver ribbon wire, set on edge, less than a sixteenth of an inch high, he followed the curves of the drawing at his side, pinching the wires into tendrils and the serrated outlines of leaves with infinite patience. A rough touch on the copper plate would have sent the pattern flying into a thousand disconnected threads.

Kipling was left with a mission – the resolve to save Japan from herself, saying, 'if they are left to themselves they will make *cloisonné* by machinery in another twenty years and build black factories instead of gardens'. This was the aesthetic dilemma of which Rudyard Kipling became so acutely aware during his visit to Kyoto in 1889 and so accurately described in the letters home.

On his second visit, his honeymoon trip, Kipling was less carefree, with less opportunity to enjoy parties at teahouses with pretty young girls, and he regrets that 'you cannot live on giggles'. Nevertheless the visit reveals Kipling's sensitivity to such great artefacts as the Daibutso in Kamakura, the great bronze figure of the Buddha. From his father, John Lockwood Kipling, an authority on Indian art and director of the museum at Lahore, Kipling had inherited a great empathy with depictions of the Buddha. At Kamakura he disliked the Western tourists' crass delight in being photographed sitting on the figure's lap. He read a naively worded notice deploring this practice put up by the priests at the shrine. and turned it into a poem with some memorable lines.

*A tourist-show, a legend told,
A rusting hulk of bronze and gold,
So much, and scarce so much, ye hold
The Meaning of Kamakura?*

*But when the morning prayer is prayed,
Think, ere ye pass to strife and trade,
Is God in human image made
No nearer than Kamakura?*

*Yet spare us still the Western joke
When joss-sticks turn to scented smoke
The little sins of little folk
That worship at Kamakura*

*The grey-robed, gay-sashed butterflies
That flit beneath the Master's eyes.
He is beyond the Mysteries
But loves them at Kamakura*

(181)

There were, of course, other English writers and artists of the 1880s and 1890s who visited Japan. But for some of them the experience did not quite live up to expectations. In Tennyson's poem the spell is broken when the Lady of Shalott looks out of the window at the real world, rather than observing its reflection in a mirror. So it was for the Scottish painters, Edward Atkinson Hornel (1864–1933) and George Henry (1858–1943), who visited Japan from 1893 to 1894. They were both members of the group 'the Glasgow Boys' from Scotland. Their visit was sponsored by the dealer Alexander Reid and collector, William Burrell, who were conscious of a growing Glaswegian interest in Japan and its culture. Before their departure Hornel stated that the reason for their visit was to go to see:

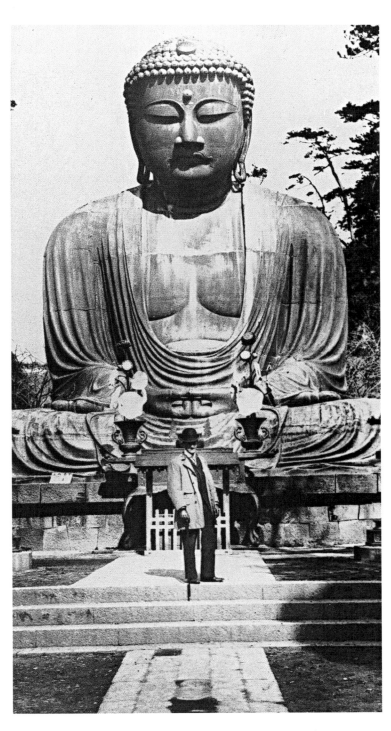

*a reed shaken by the wind, for those
acquainted even slightly with
Japanese art the words express
the spirit and motif of its dainty
achievements. Japanese art rivalling in
splendour the greatest art in Europe,
the influence of which is now
fortunately being felt in all the new
movements in Europe, engenders in
the artist the desire to see and study
the environment from which this great
art sprung, to become personally in
touch with the people, to live their life,
and to discover the source of their
inspiration.*

Unfortunately their visit was to prove a
less than ideal experience, for the spell
was broken for the two artists when
they too looked out of the window at
the real world of Japan, rather than
observing its reflection in the mirror of
the Japanese print. They both loathed
life in the missionary community where
they were billeted, complaining that:

*every second man you encounter
is a missionary, and your rest is
chronically broken by the
uncongenial clang of the church
bells, whose notes are as
unmelodious and distressing as the
music (so called) of the Japanese.*

They stayed at Nagasaki, Yokohama
and Tokyo, where they were disap-
pointed in an exhibition of works by
Japanese artists who had gone to
study painting in Paris and Munich,
and in Hornel's view had 'learned
their painting but lost their art!'

As these anecdotes show, artistic cross-
pollination could have its hazards, but
a work such as *Geishas in an Interior*
(182) has great charm despite Hornel's
very non-Japanese use of rich pigment.
Henry's watercolour paintings were
of course less opaque, and in a work
such as *The Koto Player* (183) he
successfully captures a memorable
musical moment.

For Henry the experience of visiting
Japan was a mixed blessing. A year
later, suffering from a bad case of
post-Japanese depression, he wrote to
Hornel, 'I have so little heart for these
d—d Japanese pictures that I am
seriously thinking of chucking the
whole thing up. I have not a bloody
cent.' He later recalled his visit to
Japan in less than enthusiastic terms:

*I painted landscapes there, both oils
and watercolour, and figures, from the
geishas, the most highly refined and
educated women in Japan; and in
both the same national feeling was
visible, the absence of any strong
contrast of colour. I had all my life
been trying for strong colour, tartan
landscape and vivid contrast.*

Their stay, which lasted nineteen
months was not, however, all doom
and gloom. Hornel certainly enjoyed
meeting his sitters, remarking:

*I love to remember them as a large
and happy family, clattering by in
the sunshine with smiling faces and
no thought of the morrow, to spend
the day mid plum or cherry blossom.*

Edward Atkinson Hornel,
Geishas in an Interior,
1894.
Oil on wood,
25 x 32 cm
(9$^7_8$ x 12$^5_8$ in).
Private collection

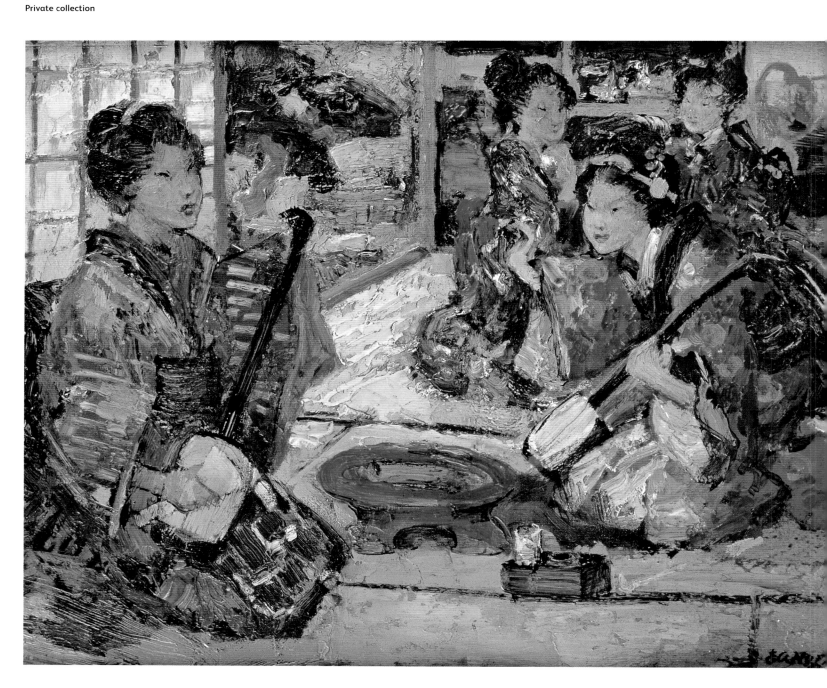

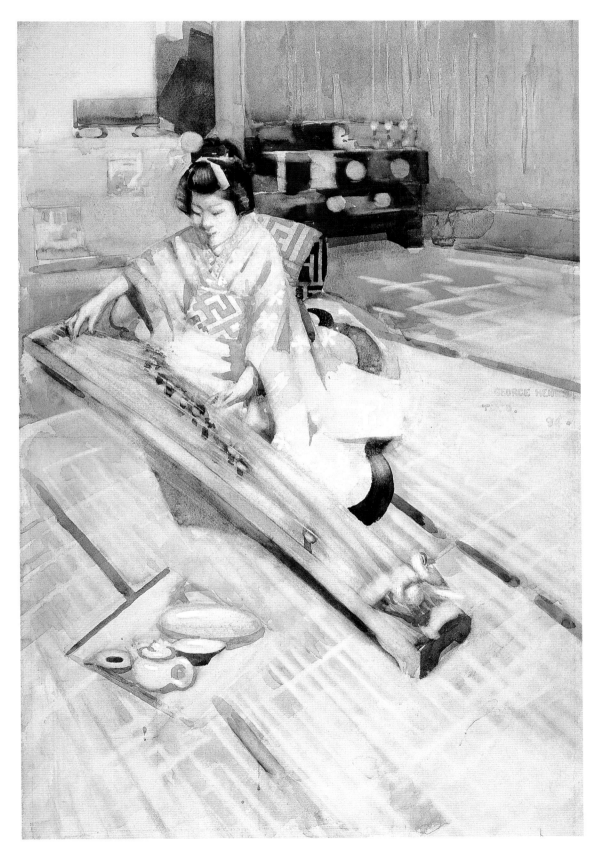

183
George Henry,
The Koto Player,
1903.
Watercolour,
67·9 x 45·1 cm
(26³⁄₄ x 17³⁄₄ in).
The Burrell Collection,
Glasgow

Hornel's 'welcome home' exhibition in Glasgow in April 1886 was a triumphant success with rave reviews and many sales. Henry continued for many years to relive the visual experience of Japan by working directly from the 'Yokohamashasin' photographs described earlier which he had bought in Japan. Both Henry and Hornel, like so many of the people discussed in this chapter, however short their visit to Japan, were never quite the same after the experience.

There were, of course, other poets and artists influenced by Japan, who never made the trip, notably another member of the 'Glasgow Boys' group, Joseph Crawhall, an exquisite animal artist. He excelled in such paintings as *A Trout Rising* (184). They successfully cross the border between Occidental and Oriental depictions of nature subjects to produce a highly successful blend of Caledonian and Japanese skills.

In the field of poetry there were other figures who came to know Japan solely via the medium of the Japanese print, including the now little-remembered figure of W E Henley, who wrote poems with such titles as *Ballade of a Toyokuni Colour Print*, and an evocation of the Thames – 'Under a stagnant sky' – which he dedicated to Whistler, whose work he consistently championed.

184
Joseph Crawhall,
A Trout Rising,
*c.*1907.
Watercolour,
25·7 x 36·8 cm
(10$\frac{1}{8}$ x 14$\frac{1}{2}$ in).
Hunterian Art Gallery,
Glasgow

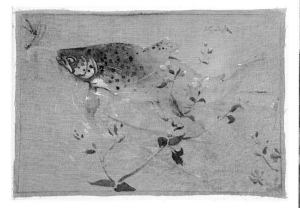

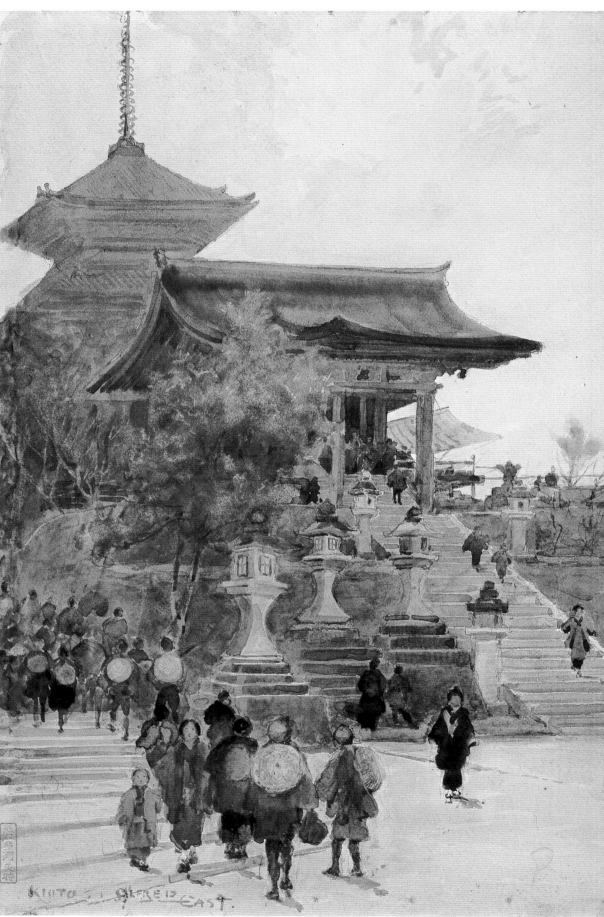

185
Sir Alfred East,
*The Entrance to the
Temple of Kiyomizu-dera,
Kyoto, With Pilgrims
Ascending,*
*c.*1889–90.
Watercolour,
36·8 x 26·1 cm
(14¹₂ x 10¹₄ in).
Victoria and Albert
Museum, London

186
Self-portrait of
Gabriel Veyre,
1898

A literary figure who did travel widely in Japan was Sir Edwin Arnold, author in 1881 of the popular if prolix *The Light of Asia*, editor of the *Daily Telegraph* in 1873 and one of the several well-known Englishmen to marry a Japanese woman. His collection of travel essays, *Japonica*, is embellished with photographs showing some of his lady friends, playing the *samisen*, flower-arranging and when disrobed, posing by a bath tub.

Sir Alfred East (1849–1913) was born at Kettering, Northamptonshire, where the Alfred East Gallery houses a fine collection of his work. He studied at Glasgow and in Paris under Adolphe William Bouguereau (1825–1905) and was influenced by the Barbizon school. Success led to friendship with such figures as Arthur and Emma Liberty and Charles Holmes, who would become in 1893 the founder of the highly influential magazine *The Studio*, which was always sympathetic to Japanese themes.

The Libertys were the owners of the famous shop in London, which from its conception had been closely associated with the cult of Japan, and a visit there during a world tour was irresistible. In 1889 the four enthusiasts, East, the Libertys and Holmes set off on a journey which inspired a book, *Pictorial Records of Japan* (1911), illustrated with numerous oils and watercolours by East and photographs by Mrs Liberty.

An attractive example of East's powers can be seen in his oil painting of Kiyomizu-dera, the 'must see' favourite temple on everyone's visit to Kyoto (185). From the little rivulet's three channels you can choose to drink a pledge promising either Health, Wealth or Long Life. East captures brilliantly the remarkable way in which the wooden structure juts out from the mountainside. Both East's oils and Mrs Liberty's photographs created records similar to those made by many visitors to Japan, but the still camera used by professional and amateur photographers alike would soon have a rival – the movie camera.

Visitors to the Villa Lumière, a splendid Art Nouveau house in Lyon, can capture something of the excitement which surrounded the making of the very first films in 1895 by the Lumière brothers, Auguste and Louis. The first films were entitled *Workers Leaving the Lumière Factory*, *The Gardener and the Hose* and *Arrival of a Train*. They presaged a race to demonstrate the new discovery of cinematography around the world. The Lumière brothers needed an Opérateur Lumière for the difficult job of presenting the new medium to audiences across the world, and also making films of distant lands and showing them as the journey progressed. In this way the thrilling new experience of cinematography could be virtually self-financing and excite audiences with an extended global vision.

The right man proved to be the extrovert figure of Gabriel Veyre (186) a young chemistry student always keen to don local costume. He was the perfect man for the job, at ease with audiences in North or South America, China, Indochina and Japan, where between October 1898 and February 1899 he made ten films with titles such as *Geishas in a Jinricksha* (see 246), *Japanese Dances*, *Rain Dance of Spring* and *The Rice Harvest*. These, the first films made in Japan, added real movement to the frozen reality of the photograph, a realization of the Lumière brothers' dream that their new invention would 'open the world to the world'. A few years later the first Japanese costume films would familiarize audiences the world over with the reality of Japan and the stirring historical figures of the samurai. Whether you went to Japan, or stayed at home and dreamt of it – the reality of the moving camera and the cinema would permanently change the outside world's perceptions of Japan.

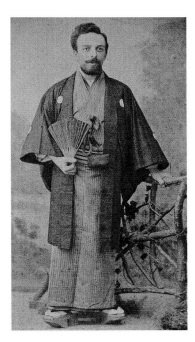

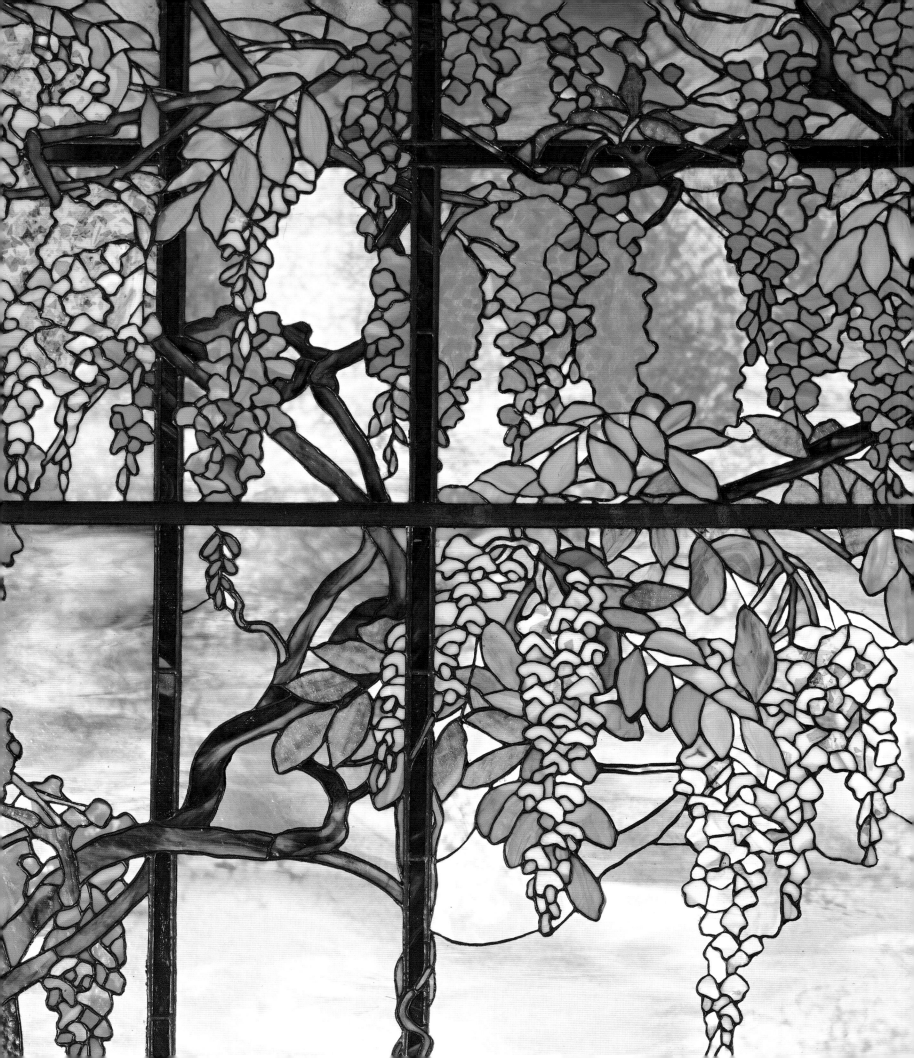

Chapter nine: The United States and Japan

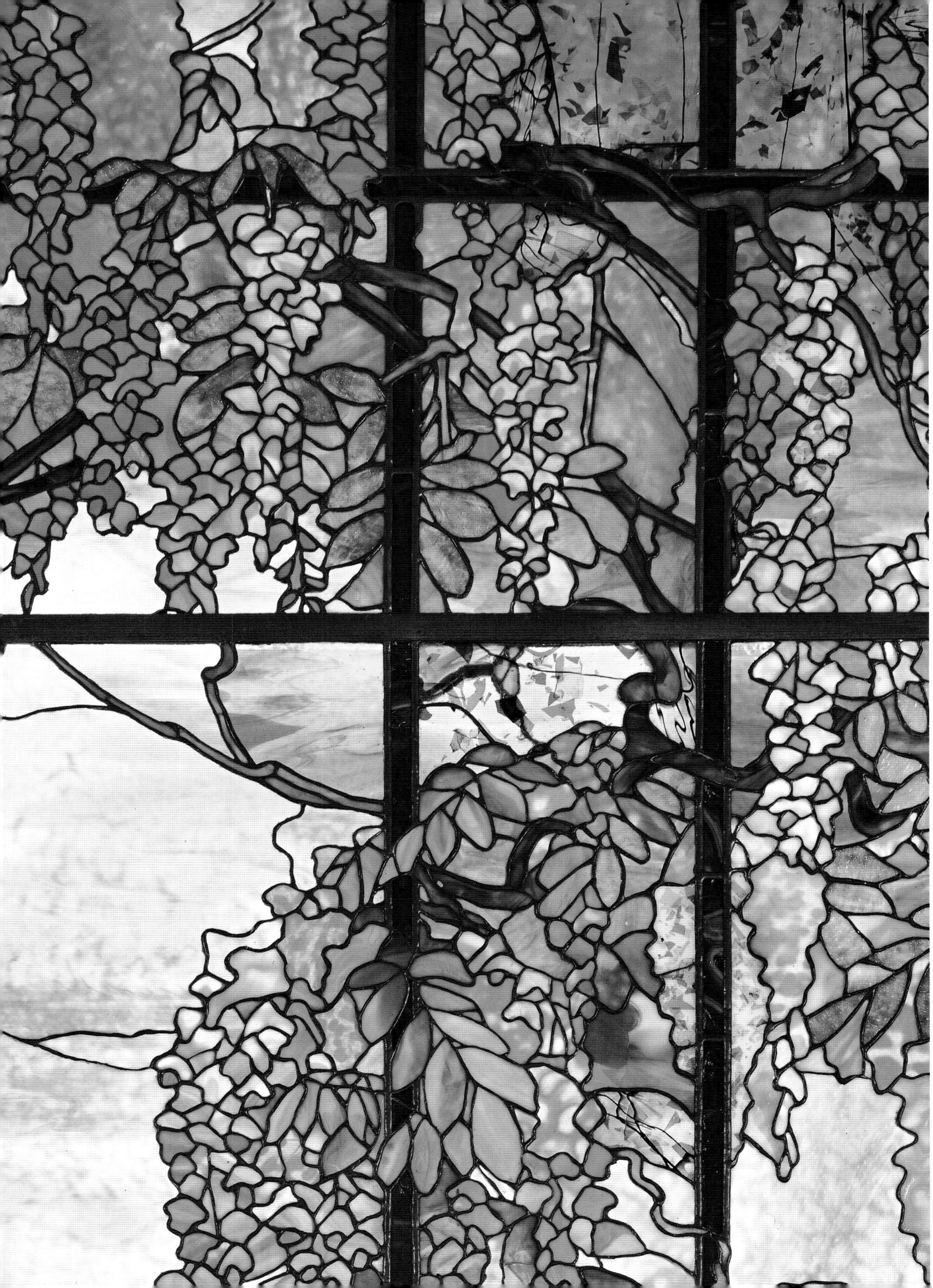

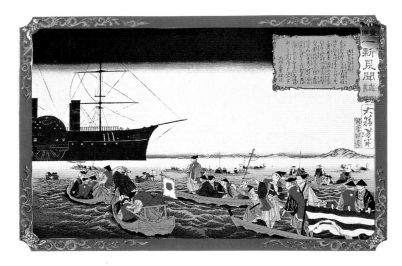

Previous page
**Louis Comfort Tiffany,
Tiffany Glass & Decorating Co.,**
View of Oyster Bay window from
the William C Skinner House,
New York
(detail of 191)

187
Taiso Yoshitoshi,
**Commodore Matthew Perry
arrives in Japan,**
*c.*1876.
Colour woodblock

188
Japanese Parlour at
**William H Vanderbilt
House, New York,**
photographed by
Christian Herter,
1883–4

I have never confided to you the extent to which the Japanese print per se has inspired me. I never got over my first experience with it and I shall never, probably, recover. I hope I shan't.
Frank Lloyd Wright 1954

When, in 1851, Herman Melville published his massive prose epic, *Moby Dick*, and launched the *Pequod* and Captain Ahab in search of the white whale in Japanese waters, he evoked the mysterious beauty of the endless unknown archipelagos which protected the impenetrable land of Japan from the outside world.

For Melville both the great white whale in *Moby Dick* and Japan itself possessed a powerful but enigmatic beauty, still unexplored and unknown. In the real world, however, the fateful initial contact with Commodore Perry (187) would set off an exchange of ideas and artefacts that, after slow beginnings, became a flood. In Japan itself, a reciprocal passion for the productions of America led in the early summer of 1860 to a Japanese delegation visiting America, on a mission to ratify the treaty brought about by Perry's visits.

The delegation visited several American cities. In New York they drove through crowded streets, watched by Walt Whitman who described the event in a poem originally entitled 'The Errand Bearers', but changed to 'A Broadway Pageant'. Its opening lines described the scene when:

Over the Western sea hither from Nippon come,
Courteous, the swart-cheek'd two sworded envoys,
Leaning back in their open barouches, bare-headed, impassive,
Ride today through Manhattan.

Many similar delegations would follow, but although America had initially opened up Japan, the terrible internal struggles of the American Civil War meant that interest in the new discoveries in Japan was at first restricted to a relatively small circle, and the boom only really began in the more peaceful decade of the 1870s, which saw the celebration of the centenary of the signing in Philadelphia of the Declaration of Independence in 1776. Fifty box-carloads of materials were shipped to Philadelphia to be displayed in the Japanese stand at the Centennial, the first Japanese-style building to be erected on American soil.

The display proved extremely popular, beginning an enthusiasm for Japanese prints, screens, bronzes and other types of metalwork, and the novelties of kimonos, fans and parasols. As knowledge of these artefacts spread across America 'from sea to shining sea', American tastes began to shift from the dominance of European culture to include a delight in things Japanese. Attempting to trace the influence of Japanese art is complicated by the emergence at precisely the same time, in the mid-1870s, of the eclecticism so characteristic of the Aesthetic Movement. This led to such uneasy bedfellows as the objects Charles Caryl Coleman (1840–1928) used in his *Still Life with Peach Blossom*. In this painting the Japanese theme was almost swamped by the ornate Turkish carpet which jostles for attention with a Japanese fan and peach blossom.

Such aesthetic problems were a familiar occupational hazard for Oscar Wilde, the 'Aesthete' and erstwhile champion of Japonisme, during his famous lecture tour. Enthusiasm for Japanese artefacts, and for American productions utilizing Japanese motifs, developed dramatically, ensuring the popularity of the cult for Japan in America. During the winter of 1885–6, Madison Square Gardens housed a 'Mikado' village with demonstrations of silk weaving, and subsequently a Japanese room appeared in virtually every New York home of artistic pretensions.

A particularly remarkable example was the Japanese parlour (188) of the William H Vanderbilt house on Fifth Avenue. It was the creation of the interior decorator and designer, Christian Herter (1840–83), with brilliant ornamental glass by John La Farge (1835–1910) depicting a fantastic peacock, 'a bird of Eastern fairyland', red lacquer beams against a bamboo frieze, walls hung with gold brocade, and lacquered shelves and cabinets galore to hold 'the rarest objects of *bijouterie* and *vertu*'.

Gustave Herter (1830–98) and his half-brother, Christian became well known as eclectic interior designers. The brothers were greatly taken by the Japanese works shown at the 1876 Centennial in Philadelphia. During the early 1870s Christian visited England and was probably exposed to the design ideas of E W Godwin. In the early 1880s the brothers created a number of pieces in the Anglo-Japanese style with which the name Herter became synonymous. Several pieces of their furniture closely echo Godwin's designs, but in a re-markable cabinet of 1880 Japanese and Gothic decorative themes are linked with superb effects to produce an outstanding example of what might be described as 'American-Japanese' furniture.

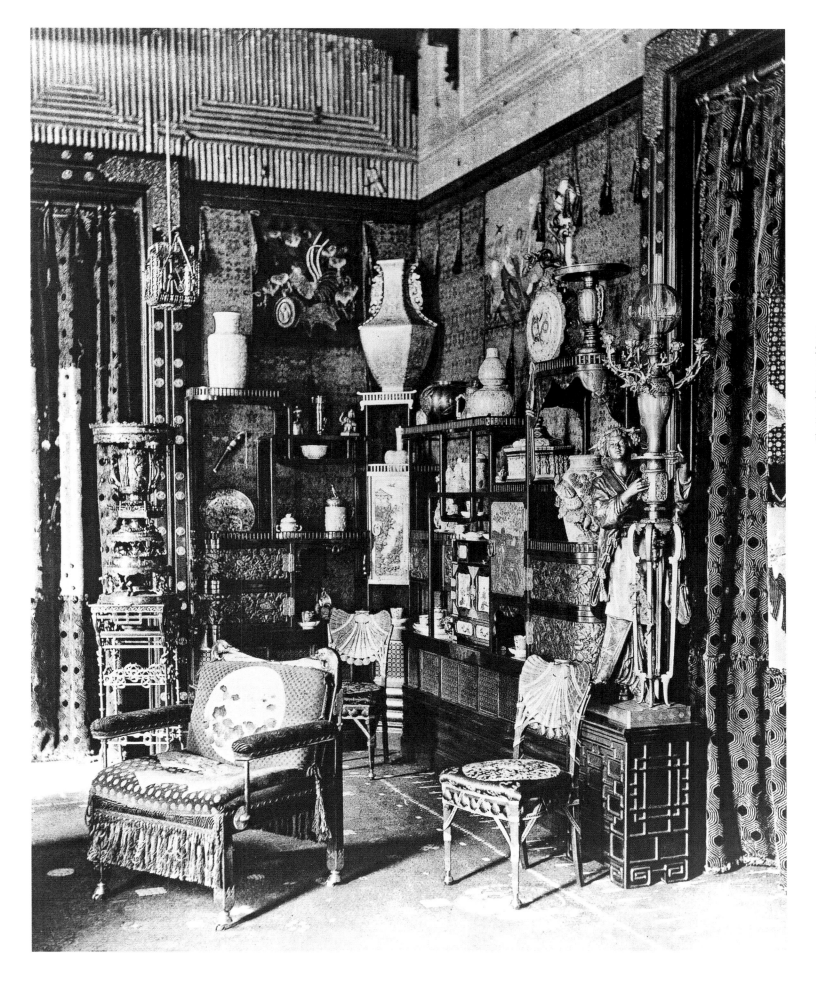

189
**Herter brothers,
Wardrobe,
*c.*1880–5.
Ebonized cherry wood,
inlaid woods and brass,
height: 199·4 cm
(78¹₂ in).
The Metropolitan
Museum of Art, New York**

190
**Artus van Briggle, Harriet
Elizabeth Wilcox
Rookwood Pottery,
Vase,
1896.
Sage-green clay,
height 30·4 cm (12 in).
Museum of Fine Arts,
Houston**

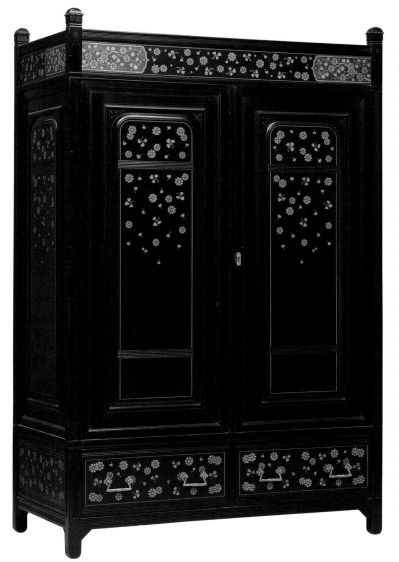

It is, however, surpassed by the restraint of the wardrobe (189), also of 1880, in which floral inlay of great distinction produces a work which ranks with the Nesfield screen (see 100). It was owned in the 1880s by the actress, Lillian Russell, who starred in Gilbert and Sullivan's *Patience*, in which Bunthorne, the 'Aesthetic Sham', confesses that he does 'not long for everything that's Japanese'. In spite of Bunthorne, the popularity of the new decorative vocabulary of Japonisme provided an incentive not just for American collectors but also for potters, glass-makers and textile and furniture designers.

The Rookwood Pottery, Cincinnati, was founded in 1880 by Maria Longworth Nichols, and in 1882 was given the ultimate 'aesthetic' accolade of a visit by Oscar Wilde. In 1887 Kataro Shirayamadani joined the company. He brought with him proficiency in the Japanese painting tradition, which led to the adoption by Rookwood of an instantly recognizable 'Orientalist' decorative style. The resultant productions of the pottery were stocked from the beginning by both Tiffany & Co. and Siegfried Bing. In 1900 the Victoria and Albert Museum bought from Bing a fine example of Rookwood ware, a vase decorated by Harriet Elizabeth Wilcox (*fl.*1880–1900). Another production of the Rookwood pottery was a vase in which the classic cone of Fuji is almost obscured by an arrangement of storks under a full moon (190).

In the ceramic painting craze which swept the country in the 1880s Japanese fans jostle for our attention with owls, peacock feathers, sprites and butterflies. Such collages of Aesthetic and Japoniste themes were also used extensively by the silver and jewellery businesses, Tiffany & Co., which were founded in 1834 in New York and in 1850 in Paris by Charles L Tiffany, the father of the legendary Louis Comfort Tiffany, an extravagant man with extravagant tastes who gradually took over both businesses in the 1860s and 1870s.

In the 1870s Louis Comfort Tiffany became particularly interested in the creation of glass which reproduced the appearance of ancient glass, and after years of experimentation patented an iridescent technique in 1880, the resulting vessels being decorated by trailing ivy leaves, lily pads, irises, dragonflies and peacock feathers. By good fortune, in 1879 Thomas Edison had invented the incandescent light-bulb at just the moment when over 300 tons of surplus material from the stained-glass workshops needed recycling.

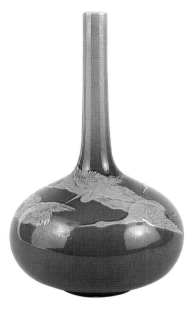

In this way the Tiffany leaded lamp was born and took the world by storm. Similar motifs were used in the lamps and windows which have become so associated with the Tiffany name. The firm traded as Tiffany Glass & Decorating Co. from 1890 and opened furnaces in Corona, Long Island.

Tiffany's virtuoso powers as a designer of secular stained-glass windows and lamps are shown to immense advantage in his vast windows in Philadelphia and the American wing of the Metropolitan Museum of Art, New York, in which he uses one of the most Japanese of floral motifs, hanging branches of wisteria (191).

Apart from extensive travels in Europe and North Africa, Tiffany's life for nearly half a century was passed in New York, then, as now, one of the most assertive cultural centres, not only in the United States, but also the Western world. Its wealthy citizens provided a roll-call of money and power and imaginative customers for innovative designs. 'Cometh the hour, cometh the man': with hindsight it seems inevitable that Tiffany in 1879 should write, 'I have been thinking a great deal about decorative work, and I am going into it as a profession … I believe there is more in it than in painting pictures.'

Aged thirty-one, Tiffany was encouraged in this new career by Edward Chandler Moore, his father's chief designer, who had first become fascinated by Japanese art at the Exposition Universelle in Paris of 1867. Moore joined the firm in 1868, and, because no adequate training for silversmiths existed in New York, he established a programme at the Tiffany workshop. He freely used Japanese themes in the decoration of silver and jewellery. A characteristic work of the company at this time is provided by a fan brooch of green, white, red and yellow gold, set with opals, which gained international acclaim, as did a silver jug of 1878 decorated with irises, exhibited in Paris at the Exposition Universelle the same year.

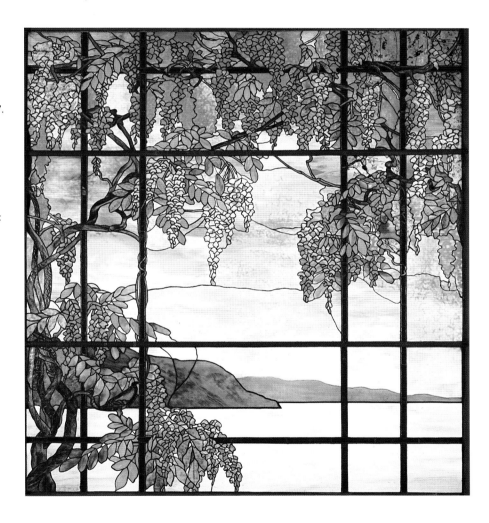

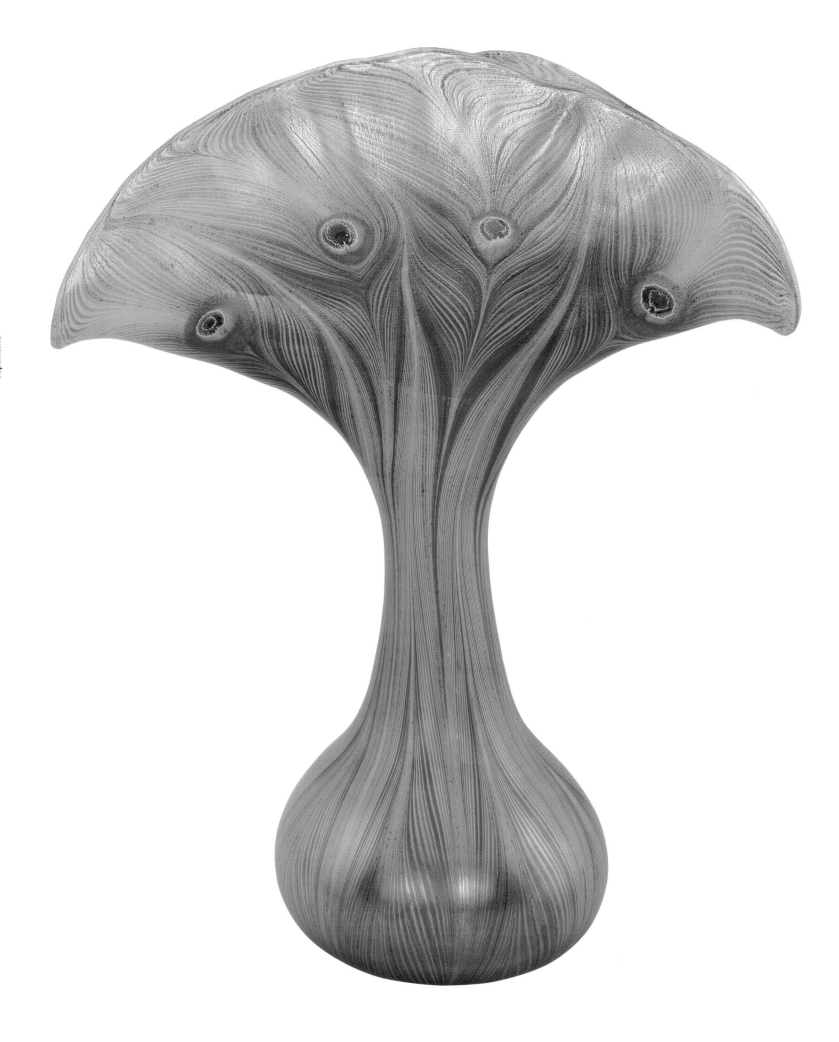

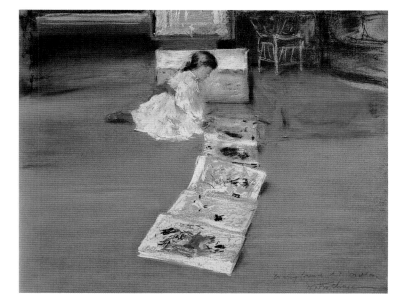

192
Louis Comfort Tiffany,
Tiffany Glass
& Decorating Co.,
Peacock Vase,
1893–6.
Favrile glass,
35·9 x 29·2 cm
(14¹⁄₈ x 11¹⁄₂ in).
The Metropolitan
Museum of Art, New York

193
William Merritt Chase,
*Shinnecock Studio
Interior*,
c.1892.
Pastel on paper,
40·6 x 50·8 cm
(16 x 20 in).
Private collection

From the 1870s Tiffany began to design the interiors of private and public buildings for such clients as the banker, J Pierpont Morgan, the railway tycoon, Cornelius Vanderbilt II, and the sugar magnate, Henry Osborne Havemeyer, for whose residence Tiffany created colourful glass mosaics and vases, one of which depicts the ubiquitous peacock theme (192).

While both the amateur and professional decorative artists of America found the visual cornucopia of ideas from Japan virtually inexhaustible, practitioners of the fine arts of painting and architecture looked to the lessons of the Japanese print not only for ideas but for discipline. A typical note was struck by the American Impressionist and friend of Claude Monet, Theodore Robinson (1852–96). His words can represent the thoughts of many American artists whose reactions to Japanese art were both muted and sensitive. He wrote:

My Japanese print points in a direction that I must try and take, an aim for refinement and a kind of precision seen in the best old as well as modern work. The opposite pole to the slap-dash, clumsy …

Robinson was writing in 1885, only thirty-five years after Hiroshige created *Fireworks over the Ryogoku Bridge, One Hundred Views of Edo* (1849–50), the print to which he is referring.

The mid-1880s were years in which the availability of the prints and the wide margins of profit realizable had created a great market opportunity for dealer and connoisseur alike, as de Goncourt recorded on 1 July 1893 after attending a dinner of Japanese enthusiasts at Véfours:

Bing talks today of the craze for Japanese prints among various American amateurs. He tells of selling a little packet of such prints for 30,000 francs to the wife of one of the richest Yankees, who in her small drawing room has an Utamaro facing the most beautiful Gainsborough in existence. And we admit to each other that the Americans, who are in the process of acquiring taste, will, when they have acquired it, leave no art object for sale in Europe but will buy up everything.

Bing and de Goncourt's admission was to prove prophetic, and from Boston to Chicago to San Francisco, major collections of prints were formed in those years, even more extensive than those still in Japan.

The three major American artists whose works were influenced by the print, Whistler in London, Mary Cassatt in Paris and Elihu Vedder (1836–1923) in Rome, could perhaps all be described like the painter John Singer Sargent (1856–1923) as 'American Express' Americans, who passed virtually all their lives as expatriates, coming to resemble characters far from home in a novel by Henry James, Edith Wharton or Frances Hodgson Burnett. That said, a key player in the process of making both Japonisme and Impressionist works popular in the United States of America was Mary Cassatt. Although most of her life was spent in France, her letters sped across the Atlantic to great purpose. She always retained close ties by correspondence with such influential long-standing American friends as the Potter Palmers and Mrs H O Havermeyer, the cheque-book and the force behind the acquisition of many major Impressionist paintings in the Metropolitan Museum of Art, New York, and the Art Institute of Chicago. Indeed late in her life Cassatt would declare, 'it has been one of the chief interests in my life to help fine things cross the Atlantic.'

Although Whistler and Cassatt will always be particularly associated with Japonisme, the genre was also practised to great effect by other American artists both well known and less familiar, including Winslow Homer (1836–1910), William Merritt Chase (1849–1916) and Maurice Prendergast (1859–1924).

The work of William Merritt Chase is still far too little known outside the United States. In *Shinnecock Studio Interior* (c.1892; 193), one of his most Japoniste paintings, Chase's daughter intently studies a volume of Japanese prints spread out upon the floor. From Chase too came one of the most sensual of all American versions of a woman wearing a kimono, a painting which vies with the work of Whistler in this genre. It shows the back of a semi-nude woman wearing a kimono seen from behind kneeling before a Japanese screen (194).

The Bostonian, Maurice Prendergast, was spiritually in tune with subjects from transient everyday life (the very definition of *ukiyo-e*). He loved to depict people enjoying themselves in such innocent pleasures as visiting Central Park in New York. He was born in Newfoundland, Canada, but the family moved to Boston in 1868 where he left school when very young. He never married and throughout his life was accompanied and supported by his brother Charles, a gifted frame-maker and also an artist. Prendergast made several long stays in Europe, the most important being a visit to Paris from 1891 to 1893, when he flirted with such sophisticated influences as the Nabis, Symbolist, Whistlerian, Art Nouveau and of course Japanese styles, developing from them his own highly innovative technique of watercolour painting.

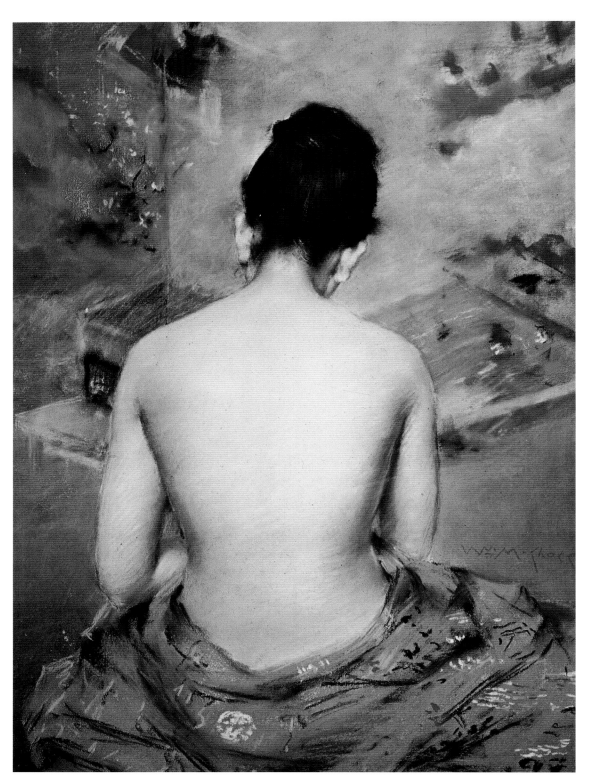

Two outstanding examples are provided by *Umbrellas in the Rain, Venice* and *Festival Night, Venice* (195). The two works date from eighteen months spent in Italy from 1898 to 1899, and although both umbrellas and Japanese lanterns are familiar props they are used here by the artist with consummate skill and to great effect.

To a greater or lesser extent these American artists all returned to America after foreign travel as students. Almost inevitably in London or Paris they saw collections of Japanese prints, which created an abiding interest in the subject. This process often took place at exhibitions all over Europe, beginning in London with the Japanese exhibition held at the Old Society of Watercolours in Pall Mall in February 1854, and again in 1862. These were followed by exhibitions in Paris in 1867 and 1890, Vienna in 1873, Philadelphia in 1876, and Chicago in 1893. These were all major exhibitions and there was a brisk exchange of works not only in Paris but also at The Hague and many other centres. This growing accessibility of prints at art dealers also took place all over America. In 1890 for example Almay's department store in Salem, Massachusetts, opened a Japanese section which led to further outlets in Boston and Newport.

195
Maurice Prendergast,
Festival Night, Venice,
1898–9.
Gouache on paper,
27·8 x 38·2 (11 x 15 in).
Courtauld Institute of Art
Gallery, London

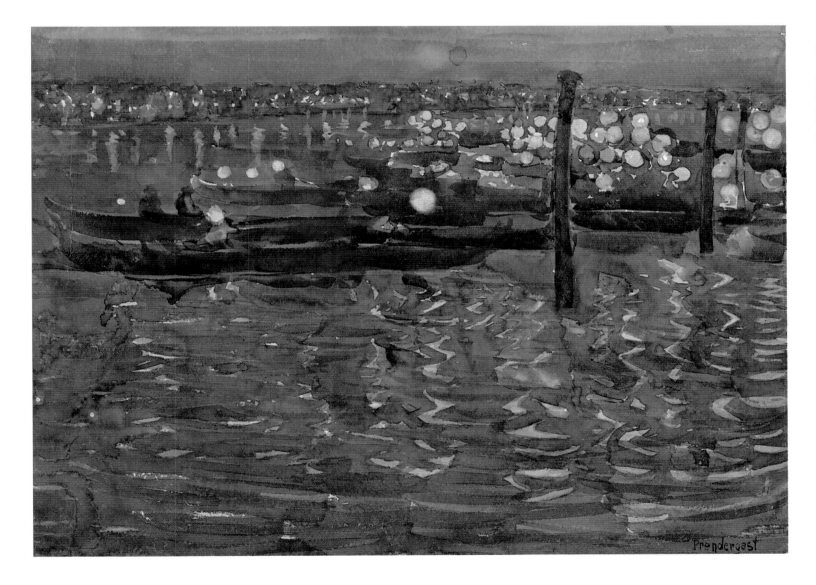

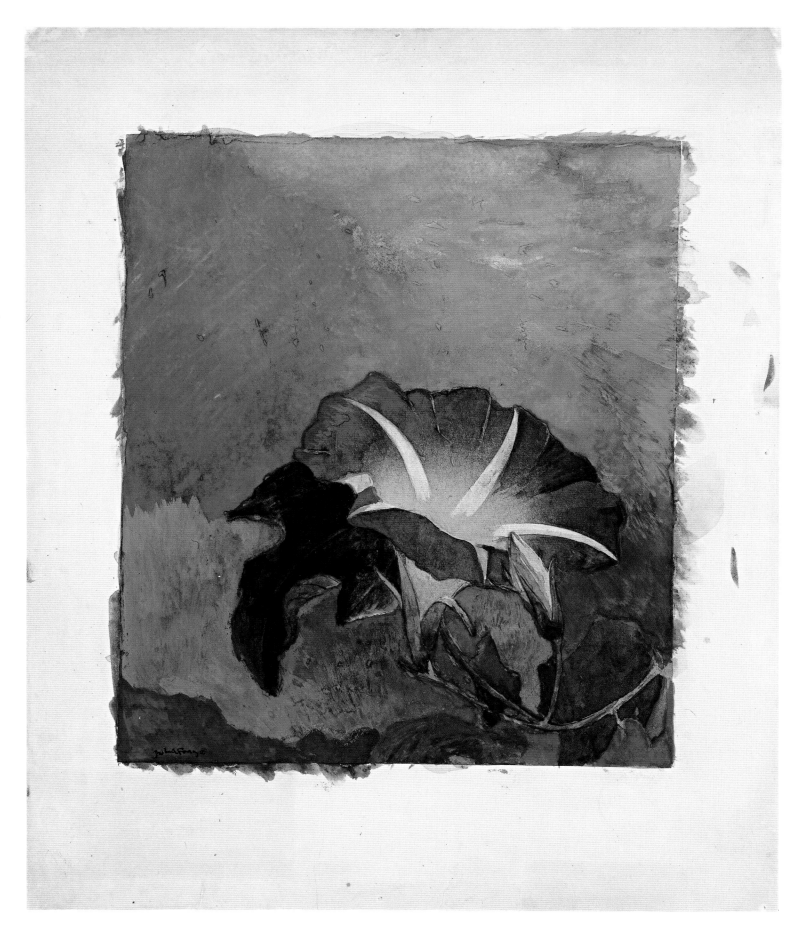

196
John La Farge,
Nocturne,
c.1885.
Watercolour, gouache
and charcoal on paper,
20·3 x 17·8 cm
(8 x 7 in).
The Metropolitan
Museum of Art, New York

197
Will Bradley,
The Serpentine Dancer,
1894.
Illustration for *The
Studio*

The moneyed ruling élite of railway tycoons and barons of industry and banking wanted spectacular results for the money they invested on furnishing their palatial homes. They acquired large decorative sculptures and paintings, and looked not to England and Aestheticism, but to Paris and the École des Beaux-Arts, the official French Academy, for inspiration. The term 'beaux-arts' is applied to works created by French-trained Americans, whose undisputed leader was the sculptor Augustus Saint Gaudens (1848–1907). His friend and colleague, John La Farge, already mentioned with the creation of the stained-glass window in Vanderbilt's *Japanese Parlour* (see p. 188), was trained as a painter. La Farge began collecting Japanese art at the start of his career, and later travelled to Japan in the 1880s and 1890s, painting many watercolours to illustrate his books on those journeys. In the late 1850s as a young student in Paris he had met Gautier, Baudelaire and the de Goncourts. La Farge was one of the most innovative minds in the American Aesthetic Movement, and demonstrated his lifelong debt to Japanese art in a watercolour, *Nocturne* (196). A typical polymath of the period, eminent as a landscape artist, collector and mural painter, he also became a stained-glass designer of great originality.

He began to experiment in this medium in 1875, after a visit to England in 1873 where he had studied the work of Morris & Co. La Farge was to take the art of stained glass in a different direction from medieval revivalism. His windows eschew painted glass, but use opalescent and streaked glass. In 1880 he established his own firm of interior decorators. In later years, after revisiting Japan, he returned to Japanese themes with new enthusiasm.

As we have seen in Chapter 3, the Japanese print played a major role in the design history of the poster throughout Europe. Americans from Henry James to Scott Fitzgerald and Gene Kelly have always loved Paris, and it is not surprising to find a school of American poster design which owes something to both Paris and Japan. This was true particularly in the case of Will Bradley (1868–1962). Often dismissed as being a mere Beardsley imitator, Bradley, like so many designers, was unable to resist the public's insatiable demand for peacock feather designs, of which he did several, most notably one for the Scribner publication, *The Modern Poster* of 1895–6. Bradley also produced one of the greatest designs depicting the virtuoso dancer Loie Fuller in one of her famous presentations *The Serpentine Dancer* (1894; 197) which recalls the swirling movement of the *kabuki* stage.

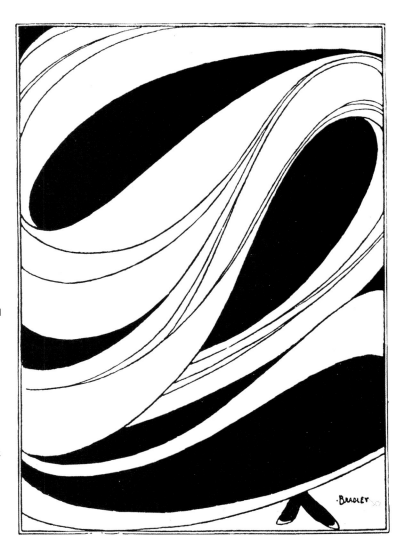

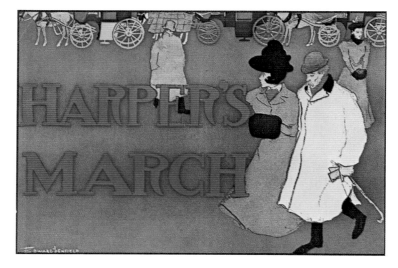

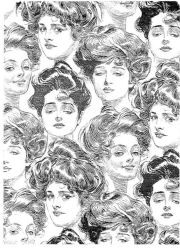

198
Edward Penfield,
Harper's March,
1897.
Colour lithograph,
35·6 x 48·3 cm
(14 x 19 in)

199
Charles Dana Gibson,
Design for Wallpaper
Suitable for a Bachelor
Apartment from *The*
Weaker Sex, **1903**

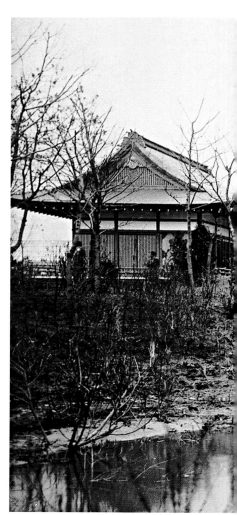

The work of Edward Penfield (1866–1925) for *Harper*'s magazine in the 1890s shows again and again both his admiration for Japanese prints and the influence of Lautrec's posters, particularly in the marvellously controlled use of 'spatter' and the 'bleeding off' technique seen so clearly in some of his finest designs. In 1892 the decision was made to design a new cover for *Harper*'s every month, reproducing them in a larger format as posters, a frequent feature in the life of many illustrators. Penfield designed each new monthly cover for the next six years. He was not averse to some direct 'cribbing' as, for example, *Harper's March* of 1897 (198) which compositionally is a straight 'rip off' from Bonnard's screen (see 120), showing a line of horse-driven cabs, using the same dramatic trimming of the image, borrowed directly from Japanese prototypes.

Charles Dana Gibson (1867–1944), like Chéret (see Chapter 3), was given the rare distinction of having a type of feminine beauty named after him – the Gibson Girl. She was fashionably dressed, incredibly poised and assured, and smiled but rarely laughed; the dream of American, or rather Anglo-Saxon, femininity.

Her charms were perhaps seen to most advantage in the remarkable *Design for Wallpaper Suitable for a Bachelor Apartment* (199). From 1894 to 1905 Gibson pictured her in a long series of drawings depicting her flirting and courting, playing croquet, set in the drawing-room, or promenading on the beach, all activities analogous to those of the geisha, although however strenuous the physical activity of a Gibson Girl, her bouffant hairstyle remained undisturbed. They played a distinct yet clearly related variation on the elaborate themes of the coiffeurs of the geishas, portrayed with their ornamental combs in the 'close-up' format adopted in the series of beautiful women by such an artist as Utamaro.

Japanese art not only played a highly important role as an influence on American artists, it was also a significant influence on American architects. In 1863 Sir Rutherford Alcock proclaimed that 'the Japanese have no architecture', a generalization which stuck and was often linked to the facetious judgement that 'Japanese gardening runs largely to gravel'.

As late as 1893, in virtually his only statement concerning Japan, William Morris declared that 'the Japanese have no architectural, and therefore no decorative instinct'. The events which gradually changed these ideas were the great International Exhibitions which introduced Japanese buildings and gardens to the West.

In the Philadelphia Centennial of 1876, a two-storey Japanese residence was much admired for its controlled use of space on a restricted site. This quality was emulated in the design of small detached houses on the Atlantic seaboard states, in such colonies as the fashionable Tuxedo Park in the Catskills. Another exhibition building to prove highly influential was shown by the Japanese at the World's Columbian Exposition in Chicago in 1893, a villa based upon the famous mid-eleventh-century Buddhist pavilion near Kyoto, known as the Hoo-den (Phoenix Hall; 200). The Chicago version had lightweight timber construction, deep roof overhangs, and a stress on horizontal lines. This was the first time that the young architect, Frank Lloyd Wright saw Japanese architecture, an experience which would prove of great significance for his work.

200

**The Japanese Pavilion,
Hoo-den, or Phoenix Hall,
on Wooded Isle, at the
Columbian Exposition
of 1893, Chicago**

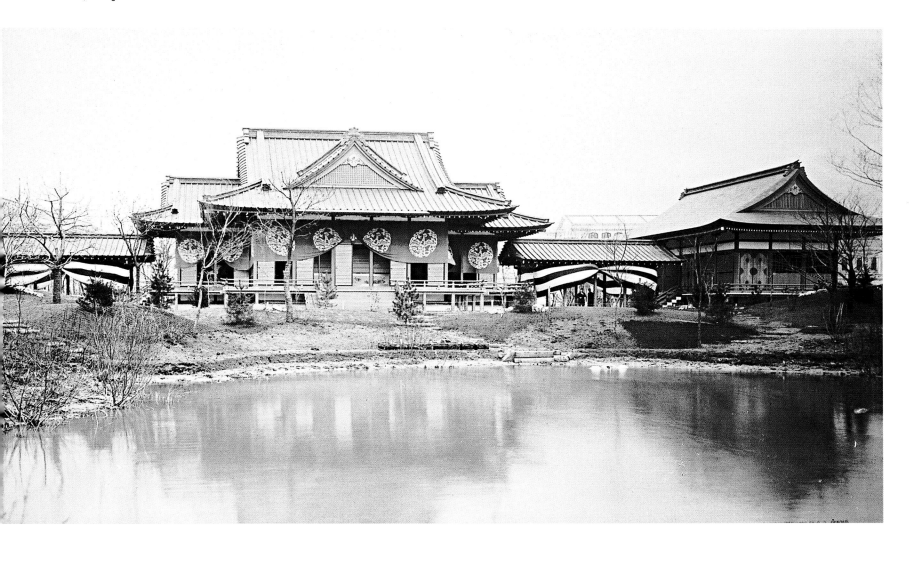

Japonisme

201
**Frank Lloyd Wright,
Warren Hickox House,
Kankakee, Illinois,
1900**

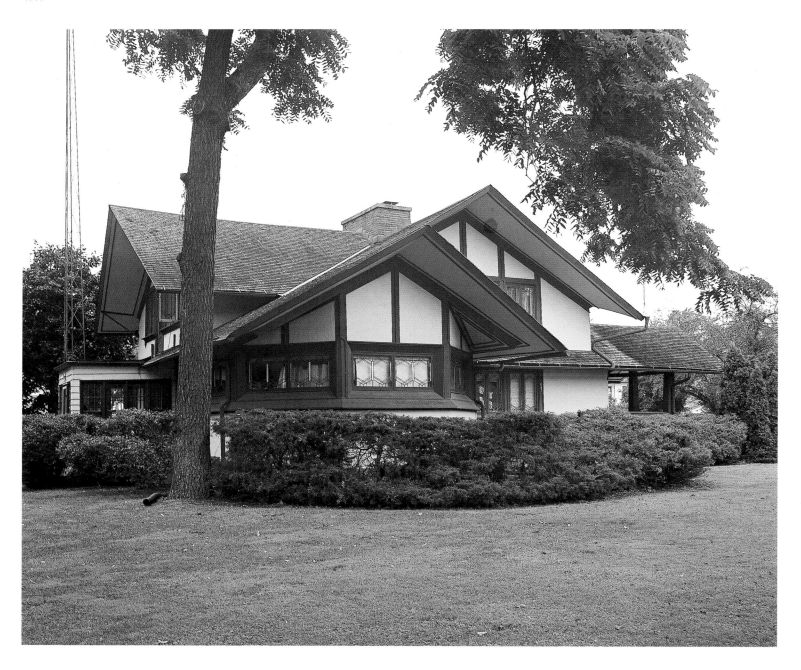

202
Arthur Wesley Dow,
Japanese Colour Prints,
1896.
Colour lithograph,
64·7 x 49·5 cm
(25¹₂ x 19¹₂ in)

Two years later Wright's design for the Chauncey Williams residence in the Chicago suburb of River Forest, included short walls and and a tall steep roof like a farmhouse in a Hokusai print. By 1900 Wright was borrowing directly from Japanese architecture, as seen in a house he designed in Kanakee, Illinois (201) which made use of predominantly horizontal lines, low-pitched roofs with deep eaves and the gables pushed forward at the apex, windows integrated within the half-timber framework, living-rooms opening on to terraces, and low-key, inconspicuous entrances. All these disparate Japanese elements have been completely assimilated into Wright's own architectural vocabulary.

Wright loved not only Japanese architecture but also the Japanese print, an interest which began in 1889, a moment that he later described with the nostalgic passion of a first love affair. Years later in 1932, he confided in his autobiography:

Ever since I discovered the print Japan has appealed to me as the most romantic, artistic, nature inspired country on the earth … If Japanese prints were to be deducted from my education, I don't know what direction the whole might have taken.

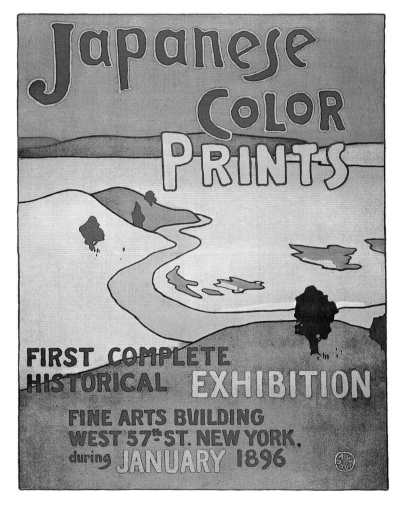

Among the many exhibitions of Japanese prints which Wright visited, one of the most important was held in New York in 1896 with a striking poster (202) by the artist, Arthur Wesley Dow (1857–1922). Dow was the protégé of the colourful figure of Ernest Fenollosa (1853–1908), one of the foreign experts brought in to modernize Japan during the Meiji era. Fenollosa was to become the foremost authority on Japanese art, and eventually the first curator of Oriental Art at the Fine Arts Museum, Boston.

For several years in the 1890s and 1900s Wright attempted to branch out as an independent architect, while also establishing himself as a dealer in Japanese prints, two very different pursuits which ran successfully in tandem although with the occasional ups and downs. These were often caused by him using his print collection virtually as currency, as he did on his return from his first visit to Japan in 1905. He had left Walter Burley Griffin (1876–1937), the future architect of Canberra, Australia, in charge of the Oak Park office, and on his return, dissatisfied with Griffin's performance, Wright paid him off with Japanese prints! The two men never spoke again. On his first visit to Japan in 1905 Wright stayed in the first Imperial Hotel, built in 1890 and designed by a Japanese architect, Watanabe Yuzuru (1855–1930), near the Imperial Palace in downtown Tokyo.

203
Katsushika Hokusai,
*Quick Lessons in
Simplified Drawing*,
1812–14.
Colour woodblock,
21 x 15 cm
(8¼ x 6 in)

Yuzuru had trained in Germany and created a grandiose Neoclassical design for the façade of a three-storey building which could cater for sixty guests in lavish comfort in a manner comparable with Brown's Hotel in London, the Ritz in Paris and the Waldorf Astoria in New York, and would become the social centre of Tokyo.

Wright made many further visits to Japan particularly during the years 1916–22, the lead-up to rebuilding the Imperial Hotel. Using what would be called today extensive networking, Wright eventually secured the contract, work on which began in 1919, delayed by the death of the Meiji emperor. The building was not completed until 1922, and survived both the Tokyo earthquake of 1923 and the bombing of World War II only for it to be demolished in 1968. It was partially reconstructed at the Meiji village in the Gumma Prefecture in 1976. C R Ashbee (1863–1942), the English architect, designer and romantic socialist, wrote of Wright in 1909, 'the spell of Japan is upon him … he feels the beauty and makes magic out of the horizontal line', an acute appraisal of much of Wright's work throughout his later career.

While very busy on architectural projects with the financial backing of the wealthy Spaulding brothers of Boston, Wright was able to acquire major examples of Japanese prints. On his return to America, after what would prove to be his final visit to Japan in July 1922, Wright made his last major transaction as a print dealer by selling a large collection to the Metropolitan Museum of Art.

Wright was always a great attraction on the lecture circuit, and from the printed versions of the talks which remain we can gain a good idea of his shifting interests in Japanese art. In a lecture of 1908, subsequently published as *The Japanese Print: An Interpretation* (1912), Wright declares that Japanese art:

is a thoroughly structural Art … the first and supreme principle of Japanese aesthetics consists in a stringent simplification by elimination of the insignificant.

As an exemplar of these words Wright was particularly fond of a little volume that illustrated 'diagrammatic studies of various plants, animals, nearly everything on earth' by Hokusai, entitled *Quick Lessons in Simplified Drawing* (1812–14; 203). It possesses a magical quality of simplification which Wright so admired, the discovery that everything can be broken down into circles, squares, rhombuses and triangles.

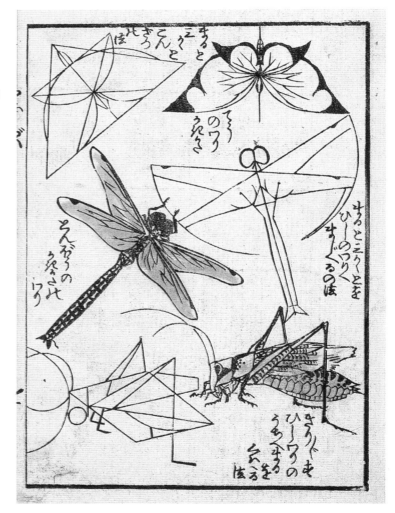

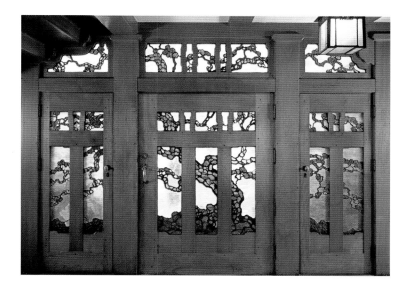

204
Greene and Greene,
The Tree of Life,
David B Gamble house,
Pasadena,
1907–9

Unfortunately, Wright was not always able to conduct his life with the serene simplicity that he admired, especially in the 1920s when his private life and career became a little 'blurred'. Whenever Wright was working in Japan at full stretch on the Imperial Hotel project making drawings for the builders, antique dealers besieged the lobby. His son, John, recalled:

Dad was buying so many works of Oriental art that vendors poured in every day and stood in line in the lobby of the hotel from morning until night. It kept him jumping from his stool at the drafting board to examine these antiques as they were presented to him.

Buying at such speed inevitably led to the acquisition of suspect works but, as in all stories unveiling forgery, it is not easy to ascertain exactly what transpired. Accusations were made that Wright had knowingly sold over-printed and revamped prints to innocent clients. The taint of the faked print led the closed community of Japanese print dealers to establish a vetting process, and not all Wright's works bore the association's seal of approval. Ironically, Wright had written to the Metropolitan Museum offering to lend a group of sixty well-executed 'vamps', 'true vampires convicted and generally admired as such', for an exhibition which would 'put the collector on his guard'.

After Wright ceased to visit Japan in 1922 the opportunity in the 1920s to play 'pass the parcel' with his 'mistakes' became very difficult. But throughout his life he continued to add to his own collection of Japanese art, and at his death at the age of ninety-one, he possessed about 6,000 prints, twenty large-scale folding screens and large quantities of textiles, ceramics and sculptures.

Today one of the most accessible of Wright's interiors is the living-room of the Francis Whittle House, Wayzata, Minnesota (1912–14), now installed at the Metropolitan Museum in New York, complete with its original textiles, Japanese prints on the walls and built-in furniture. Together they convey a magical feeling of uncluttered space so characteristic both of Wright's taste and of Japanese interiors. Another memorable Wright interior is the living-room of his own house at Taliesin, at Spring Green, Wisconsin. It provides a testimony to his strong perception of Japanese proportion and subtle understatement. Within it we glimpse Wright's 'sense of place', a demo-nstration of the abstract principles that E W Godwin had been among the first to perceive in Japanese art.

This unique fusion of carefully considered arrangements of furniture with ornament and ceramics can stand as a monument to the legacy of Japonisme to both the Arts and Crafts Movement and the Modernism of the twentieth century. Wright's work, the antithesis of the skyscraper, has a timeless validity.

The Greene Brothers, Charles Sumner (1868–1957) and Henry Mather (1870–1954), also owed the start of their successful careers as architects to seeing the Japanese displays at the Columbian Exposition, Chicago, in 1893 and in 1894 at the Midwinter Exposition, San Francisco. Working from their offices in Pasadena, they produced notable bungalows which in the light character of their building were distinctly Japanese in style. This is to be seen most impressively in their masterpiece for David B Gamble built in 1907–9, which now houses the Greene and Greene Library at 4, Westmoreland Place, Pasadena, California (204). Their successful buildings were amusingly described in the 1950s by the words of the founder of the Bay Region style, William Watson Wurster, 'Japanese houses are not best suited to Japan. They are more suitable for Honolulu and are best suited to California.'

An American who has done much since Lloyd Wright to make Japanese prints appreciated in America is a major figure from the world of popular musicals, novels and films. James Michener was the author of *Tales of the South Pacific* (1947), which achieved fame as the musical, *South Pacific*, and the drama, *Sayonara*. Some of his profits went to forming his great collection of prints now at the University of Honolulu in Hawaii. Michener's books on Japanese prints and on Hokusai's *Manga* provide a most readable and enjoyable introduction to Japanese prints. The position of Michener's collection, halfway across the Pacific in Honolulu, and a popular destination for Japanese visitors eager to practise their English, provides a symbolic and emotive link where West can meet East and East can meet West.

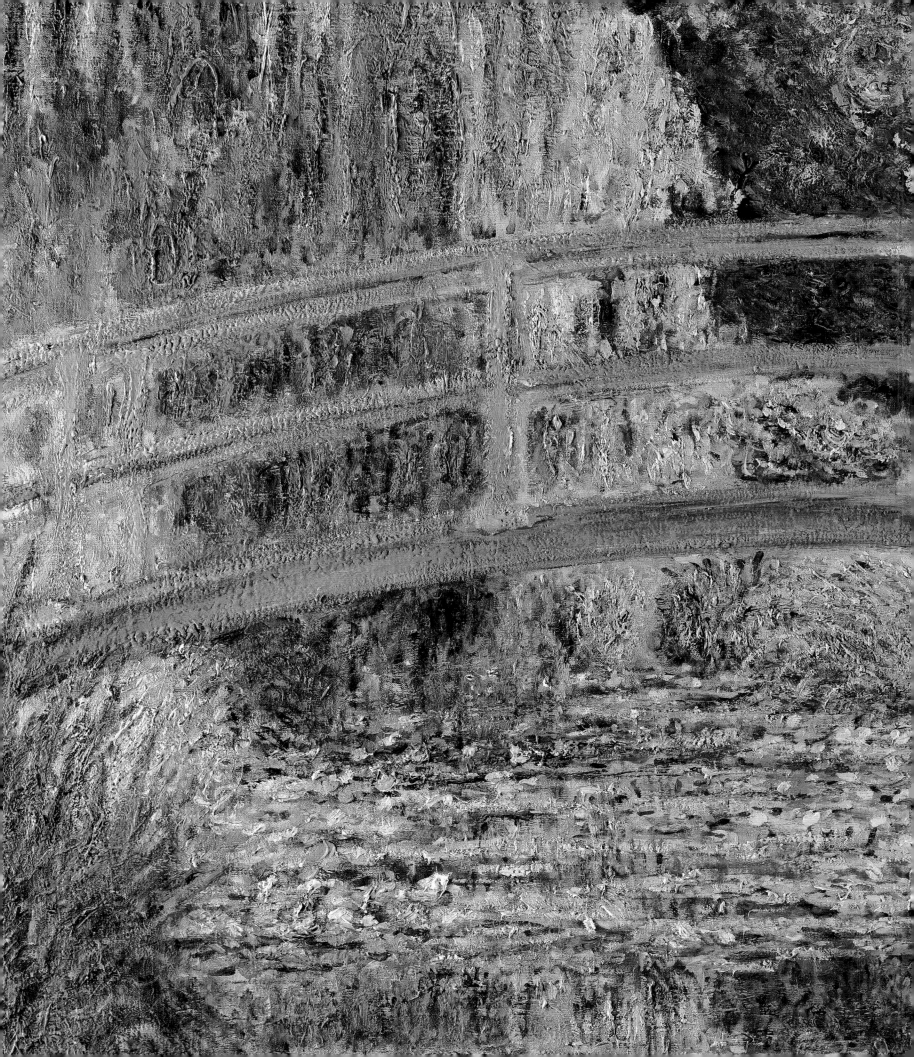

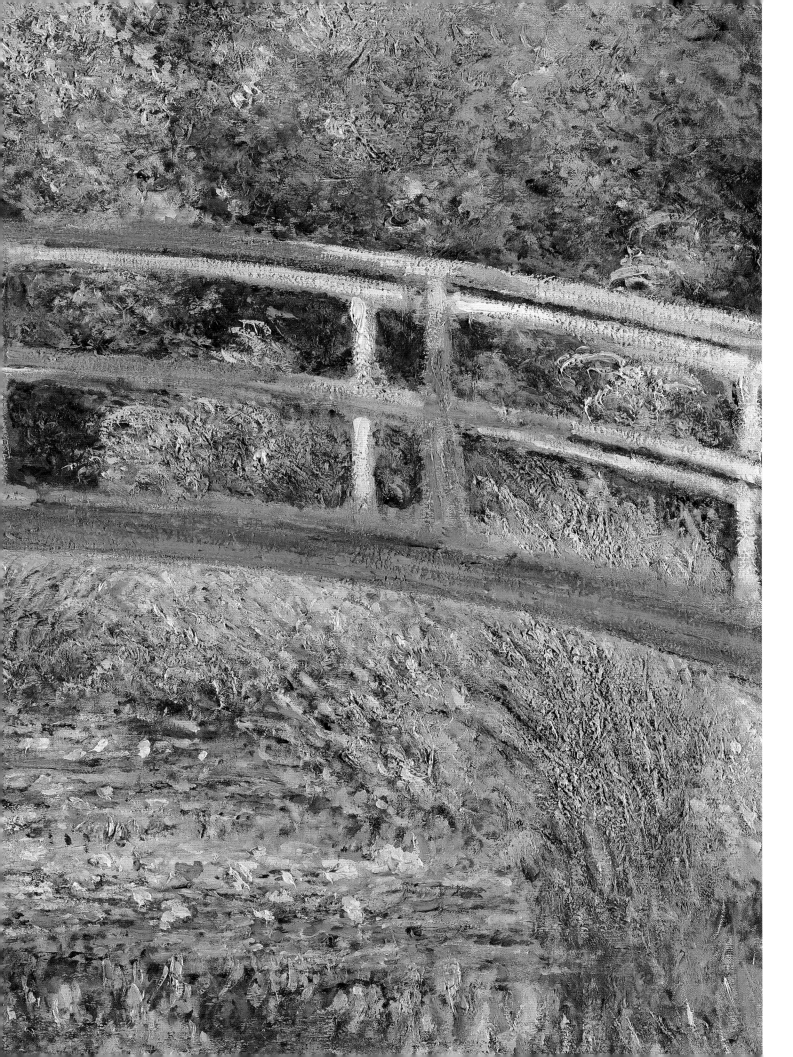

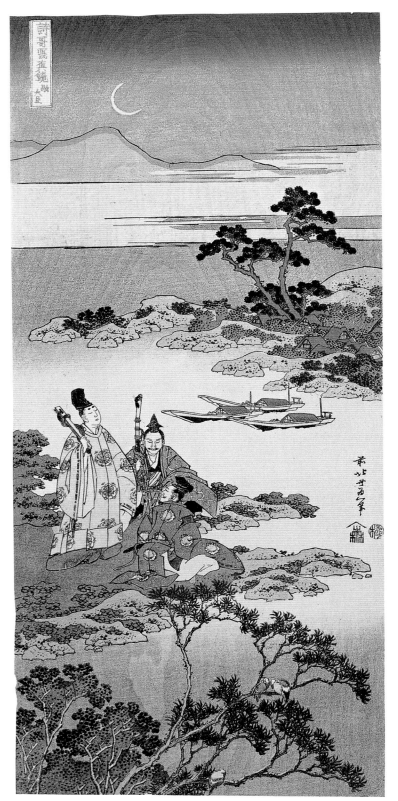

Previous page
Claude Monet
The Water-Lily Pond
(detail of 214)

205
Katsushika Hokusai,
Three Noblemen by
a Lake Under a Sickle
Moon,
*c.*1830–49.
Colour woodblock,
50·6 x 22·7 cm
(20 x 9 in)

Leaving my brush behind
In Edo
I set forth on a new journey
Let me enjoy all the famous views
In paradise.
Hiroshige, on his deathbed, 1858

A garden in Japan is a representation
of the scenery of the country.
Sir Josiah Conder, 1893

In a series of prints of the 1830s
illustrating *The Imagery of Poets*,
Hokusai depicts a scene that
symbolizes an ultimate aim of Japan's
first great religion, Shinto. It expresses
man's delight in the beauties of
nature, be it a splendid tree, striking
rock, waterfall, cliff or vista. Entitled
Three Noblemen by a Lake Under a
Sickle Moon (205), it depicts the
minister, Minamoto no Toru (822–95),
son of Emperor Saga, portrayed with
two other noblemen in the extensive
landscape garden he created next to
his palace near Kyoto. The large lake
in the garden was dug out and in
imitation of Shiogama Bay, filled with
water transported all the way from the
coast. A poem by Toru which describes
'boats floating on the water in bright
moonlight, shaded by the pines' may
have inspired Hokusai's print.

Landscape was slow to emerge from
being a mere background accessory in
figure groups, until the appearance of
Hokusai and Hiroshige. In the 1840s
a new more powerful censorship had
virtually banned courtesan and *kabuki*
prints. As a result pictures of famous
views and great highways such as the
Tokaido road became much in demand
and Hiroshige in particular came to
dominate landscape art. Both artists
would produce popular imagery
showing heroes or poets enjoying a
famous view, as seen in Hiroshige and
Kunisada's *View of Tago Bay* (206)
which portrays Prince Genji and a
lady companion who listens while
he evolves his poem which compares
the garden, with its two black conical
fishing nets, and the distant classic
silhouette of Fuji.

Another example of the garden
emerging from the landscape and vice
versa is provided by Hokusai's *The Poet*
Abe no Nakamaro Gazing at the Moon
From a Terrace (207). The Japanese
nobleman, Abe no Nakamora
(698–770), when only sixteen
accompanied a delegation from Japan
to China to obtain the secrets of the
Japanese system of recording time.
Although warmly received by the
Chinese emperor he was refused
permission to return home. The rest
of his life was passed in China where
he eventually became a regional
governor. His life was always to be
passed in exile, yearning for his
homeland in Japan.

206
Hiroshige and Kunisada,
View of Tago Bay,
1857.
Colour woodblock,
each: 36·8 x 24·8 cm
(14¹₂ x 9³₄ in)

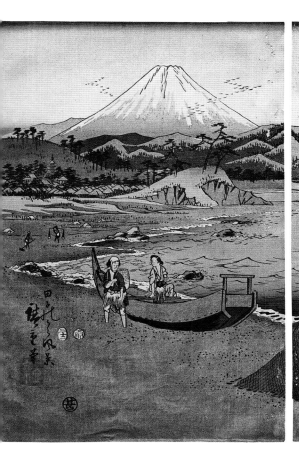
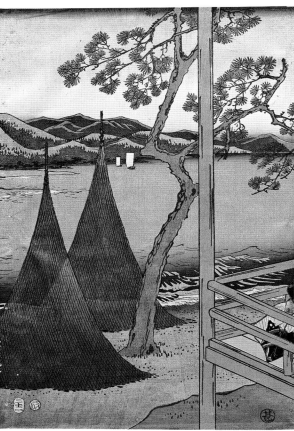
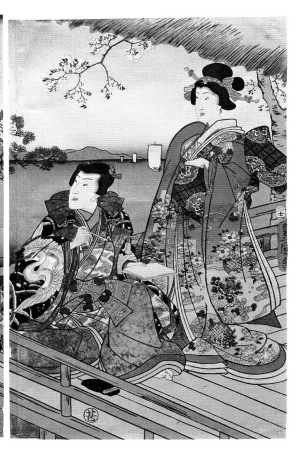

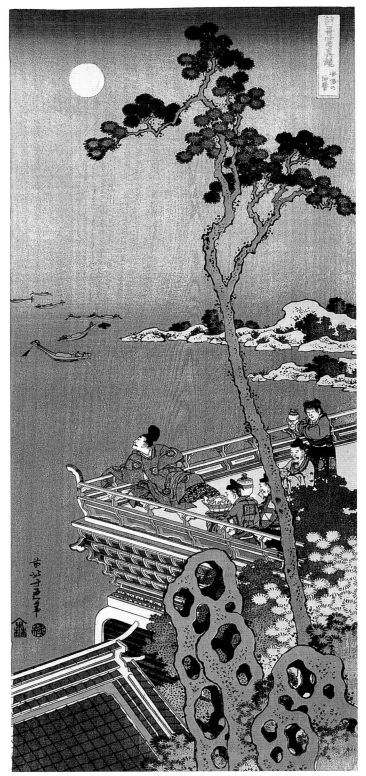

207
**Katsushika Hokusai,
*The Poet Abe no
Nakamora Gazing at the
Moon From a Terrace*,
1833–4.
Colour woodblock,
52·1 x 22·6 cm
(20$^1_2$ x 8$^7_8$ in)**

While attendants ply him with food the homesick poet muses:

*When I look over Heaven's Plain
I wonder
Is that the same moon that rose
Over Mount Mikasa in Kasuga?*

Shinto shrines fit into the landscape – the sacred plum and cherry blossom of spring, the azaleas and magnolias of summer and the maples of autumn. The most famous discussions of the art of gardening occur in Lady Murasaki Shikibu's classic Japanese novel *The Tale of Genji* written *c.*1001–15, reaching their apogee in the fictitious palace of the amorous Prince Genji, who gave all his lady friends a garden unit planted to suit their personal tastes. The author describes how in his own home Prince Genji effected:

*great improvement in the
appearance of the grounds by a
judicious handling of knoll and lake
… finding it necessary to cut away
here a slope, there to dam a stream,
so that each occupant of the various
quarters might look out of her
windows upon a prospect that
pleased her best.*

Several of the most basic principles in establishing a Japanese garden were first formulated during the Heian era (794–1185) in a gardener's treatise, the *Sakuteiki* (*Essay on Garden Making*) by the poet and courtier, Tachibana no Toshitasuna, a book still widely consulted today.

At that time the residences of noblemen and imperial palaces invariably included large gardens with a lake with islands, bridges and rocks. Discussions focused on the ever absorbing topic of how to use stones and water in their garden designs. By following these precepts, his designs developed into what are now known as stroll gardens and viewing gardens. Part of the garden at the Katsura Imperial Villa near Kyoto, completed in 1658, is a splendid example of the landscaped stroll garden (208).

The Way of Zen is a school of behaviour based upon an appreciation of the simplest acts of life, and involves the practice of seeking enlightenment through meditation, which could take the form, for example, of the simplest manual labour. This provided an ideal discipline for monks, whose labours with a rake we admire particularly in the Abbot's Garden at Ryoan-ji in Kyoto (209). Itinerant monks and poets were inspired by its teachings to practise beautiful calligraphy, the tea ceremony and garden design.

Some aspects of the art of Oriental gardening reached Europe from China in the eighteenth century, producing that strange Rococo amalgam, the Anglo-Chinese garden, of which Sir William Chambers' (1723–96) pagoda at Kew Gardens so engagingly reminds us. The Japanese garden was to be much more imitated than the Chinese in the West, particularly after the beginning of the Meiji era in 1868.

208
Garden and Tea Pavilion
at the Imperial Villa,
Katsura, Kyoto,
completed 1658

209
Saomi,
The Abbot's Garden at
Ryoan-ji, Kyoto,
1473

210
Sumiyoshi from *Meisho-e*
('Pictures of Famous
Places'),
*c.*1670–92.
Ink on paper,
21·5 x 32·2 cm
(8¹₂ x 12⁵₈ in).
British Library, London

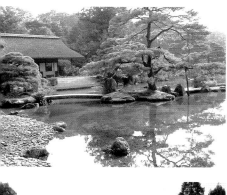

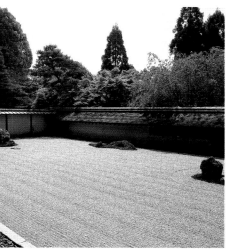

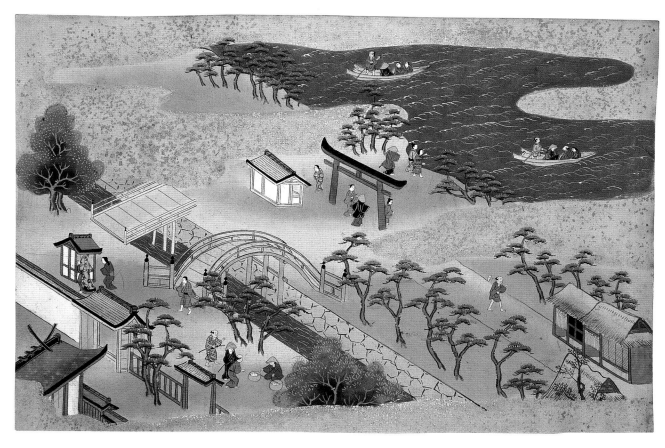

Knowledge of Japanese gardens spread via such albums as *Meisho-e* ('Pictures of Famous Places'; 210), brought back by Engelbert Kaempfer, a German physician who was in Nagasaki with the Dutch East India Company from 1690 to 1692. This painting shows a garden with pine trees and a bridge over water at Sumiyoshi, and it was probably the work of a town painter producing souvenirs for travellers. Kaempfer brought back extensive quantities of such pictures of famous landmarks and seasonal events, and their vibrant colours and lively images were to play a major part in shaping the West's view of Japan and its culture. Kaempfer hoped to publish his collection of personal notes and illustrations but died before utilizing this example, and much of his library passed to Sir Hans Sloane, the catalyst whose collections brought the British Museum into being. Sloane published Kaempfer's manuscript, *The History of Japan*, translated into English, in 1727.

It is a wonder that Deshima (see Chapter 1), not much bigger than a running track, should have housed all the great collections of new plants and botanical specimens formed by the physicians of the VOC, often at great risk to their lives.

Their amazing discoveries provided European eyes with their first glimpse of exotic plants from Japan. How did someone as acquisitive as Engelbert Kaempfer or Philip von Siebold manage to amass and bring back so much? Shipping plants was facilitated by long Japanese experience in the transportation of mature trees and shrubs by carefully wrapping their roots in sacking.

After Siebold's dramatic flight from Nagasaki in 1829, narrowly avoiding death for spying, he returned to Holland where he received a hero's welcome and was nominated for a knighthood. His huge ethnographical collection of 5,000 items was bought for the Dutch state for 60,000 guilders while his fauna of 200 mammals, 900 birds and 5,000 invertebrates were kept at the Museum of Natural History in Leiden. The 2,000 plants and 12,000 dried specimens he had collected were acquired by the Hortus Botanicus, a great garden originally founded in 1587 'to expedite the instruction of all … who study medicine'.

The Leiden garden today possesses a peaceful inner garden dating from 1990 dedicated to the memory of Siebold, who himself planted several of the trees still growing in the original outer garden, notably a Japanese chestnut and a Japanese walnut. Siebold also commemorated his beloved 'wife' Kusumoto Otaksa in a romantic fashion by naming one of the most beautiful flowers he had brought back from Japan after her, the *Hydrangea otaksa* (211), commemorating it with a plate in his important book, *Flora Japonica* (1835–41). The Japanese garden of 1990 also uses elements of Japanese landscaping. The gravel symbolizes water and the rock composition opposite the pavilion symbolizes the mountains from which the water gushes downwards 'into' the gravel. The hills in the gravel sea are islands, the island closest to the rocks being the isle of the turtle, symbol of a long life. The island behind it is the crane island, wishing the visitor not only a long life but also a happy one. Most of the plants are 'Siebold' plants which he helped to introduce into Europe.

Excited by Siebold's discoveries, European botanists salivated at the thought of more unknown species of plants still to be discovered in Japan, although a steady stream of plants had filtered out via Deshima.

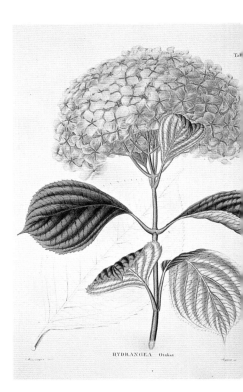

HYDRANGEA Otaksa

211

Hydrangea otaksa from
Philip von Siebold's
journal, *Flora Japonica*,
1835–41

212

Front cover of *Landscape
Gardening in Japan* by
Josiah Conder,
1893.
37 x 28 cm
(14¹₂ x 11 in)

Indeed the amazing influx of Japanese plants into European gardens began long before the 'official' opening-up of Japan. Trees introduced to Britain after the Meiji restoration of 1868 include the maples and magnolias, and most notably the Japanese cherries, especially the Sakura blossoms, the national flower beloved by the Japanese people and the very quintessence of Japanese spring – cherry blossom time. The name *Japonica*, which appears in numerous European novels and poems, is a plant which no one can seem to agree on exactly. Even the dictionary gives three possibilities: camellia, flowering quince and myrtle. It is amazing what a wide variety of plants in Western gardens have the species name *Japonica*, many of them recalling the plant explorers such as *kaempferii* (Kaempfer), *thunbergii* (Thunberg), *sieboldii* (Siebold) and *veitchii* (Veitch), whose lives and work would so alter the later appearance of gardens in the West.

A worthy successor to Siebold as a horticulturist was Josiah Conder (1852–1920), who worked for William Burges, the Gothic Revival architect, before settling in Japan in 1877. He was employed by the Ministry of Works to teach architecture at the Engineering College in Tokyo, and married a Japanese girl.

He designed the famous Deer Cry Pavilion, where throughout the 1880s fashionable dances were held with guests wearing Western style dress. In the early 1890s he wrote some important books, the first being *The Flowers of Japan, and the Art of Floral Arrangement* (1891), an early treatise in English on the subject of *ikebana* (also called *kado*), a traditional Japanese art of flower arrangement that has flourished since the sixteenth century. This art is said to have origins from the sixth century, when Buddhist priests offered up flowers before Buddha. The fundamental concept of Japanese flower arrangement is to express the three elements of heaven, earth and mankind in a balanced composition, using natural flowers. A wide-mouthed simple vase filled with water is used along with a metallic plate with thick needles pointing upwards on which the flowers are arranged. As a discipline *ikebana* has always appealed to British flower lovers, and *ikebana* societies continue to flourish. In 1893 Conder followed this work with a book, *Landscape Gardening in Japan* (212), which, along with a supplementary volume published the same year, greatly influenced landscape designers in Britain, Europe and America. In the supplement Conder proclaimed, 'a garden in Japan is a representation of the scenery of the country.'

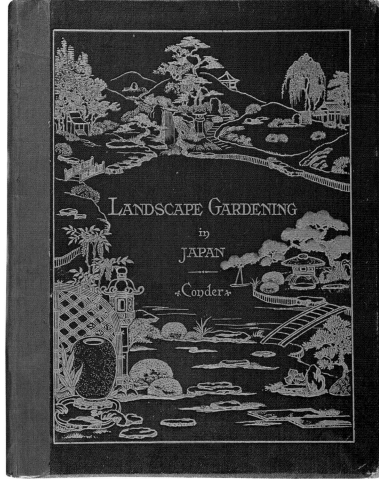

213
Utagawa Hiroshige,
*Wisteria Blooms Over
water at Kameido*
from *One Hundred Views
of Edo*,
c.1857.
Colour woodblock,
35·3 x 24 cm
(13⁷₈ x 9¹₂ in)

Conder detailed the rigid set of rules which gave each feature in a garden its own special significance, whether it was a small hill representing a religious principle, or the use of raked gravel and cones of sand. The book describes ten or more ways of arranging a waterfall and innumerable permutations in the placing of stones, trees, bridges and islands to allow the eye to wander from feature to feature, or to be caught by some harmonious yet unexpected objects, such as stepping stones of carefully chosen shapes, promontories, hump-backed 'drum' bridges and hills of varying sizes which carry the eye effortlessly to the tallest tree on the largest hill, the focal point of the whole effect. Quite apart from the numerous illustrations, the sheer practicality of Conder's lavish, beautifully bound books contributed to a European vogue for Japanese gardens.

These publications enabled those unable actually to visit Japan to enjoy vicariously its botanical pleasures, not just by leafing through a volume of views of Japanese gardens but by making a garden of their own and choosing the shrubs and plants. The first Japanese gardens in Europe on the whole tended to be 'stroll gardens' rather than *karesansui* – a dry garden made of raked gravel.

One of the basic components of a 'stroll garden' is surprise, the garden gradually imparting its beauties to visitors as they stroll around and encounter unexpected features, turning a corner to find yet another vista, and after a rest the pleasure of setting forth upon a new journey. Conder also discusses the whole question of ornamental water gardens:

In one or another of its many forms of lake, river, stream, torrent, or cascade, water is an almost indispensable feature of Japanese gardens. Even in localities where no natural supply can be obtained, the idea of watery scenery is expressed in the design by the arrangement of surrounding hills, stones and plants. A sudden stretch of bare beaten earth or well raked sand, with isolated boulders scattered here or there will often indicate a lake or jutting rocks. In other cases, a meandering bed, spread with pebbles and crossed by a small bridge or stepping stones, will serve to convey the impression of a stream, which is further sustained by distributing water plants, rushes and rounded river boulders on its banks ... It is essential that a garden should, above all things, look cool and refreshing in the summertime, and such a character is best maintained by the presence, or at least the idea of water.

Later chapters in Conder's book deal with the shape of garden lakes, garden cascades, garden rivers, garden islands ... and duck ponds. Such gardens were often a curious hybrid, and one can readily believe the remark, 'How beautiful – we have nothing like this in Japan!' made by a senior Japanese diplomat on visiting the Japanese garden created in 1906 by Sir Frank Crisp at Friar Park, Henley-on-Thames.

The Impressionists also shared the profound Japanese preoccupation with water, most notably Claude Monet who, when an old man in his eighties, recalled his first purchase of Japanese prints in his home town of Le Havre. He would continue to collect throughout his life, both landscapes such as Hokusai's *Red Fuji* (see 39), and works relating to his garden such as *Wisteria Blooms Over Water at Kameido* (213) from Hiroshige's *One Hundred Views of Edo*. Hokusai and Hiroshige both tackled similar themes, among them the depiction of the effects of water in waterfalls, rivers, ponds, rainstorms and seascapes.

In 1883 Monet settled in Giverny and as he began to prosper, enjoyed creating a garden. The original garden (a neglected orchard) was gradually transformed by planting long archways of climbing plants and vividly coloured flowers and shrubs, and the apple trees were replaced with Japanese cherries, apricots and wisteria. Nearby he created a dazzling complement to the flower garden by diverting a tributary of the River Epte to make a large pond with rafts of water lilies. Inevitably Monet modified his ideas as the scheme progressed, developing a keen interest in the new hybrid water lilies which were then being introduced into France. To encourage their growth he dug out a series of beds and paths. He also loved to use other flowers and plants from Japan. Writing to his gardener in February 1900 from Giverny, Monet discussed the layout of his garden with a real plantsman's expertise and enthusiastic curiosity about the way a new planting would turn out:

Sowing: around 300 pots Poppies – 60 Sweet Peas – around 60 pots white Agrimony – 30 yellow Agrimony – blue Water-lilies in beds (green houses) – Dahlias – Iris Kaempferi ... Don't forget the lily bulbs. Should the Japanese peonies arrive plant them immediately if weather permits.

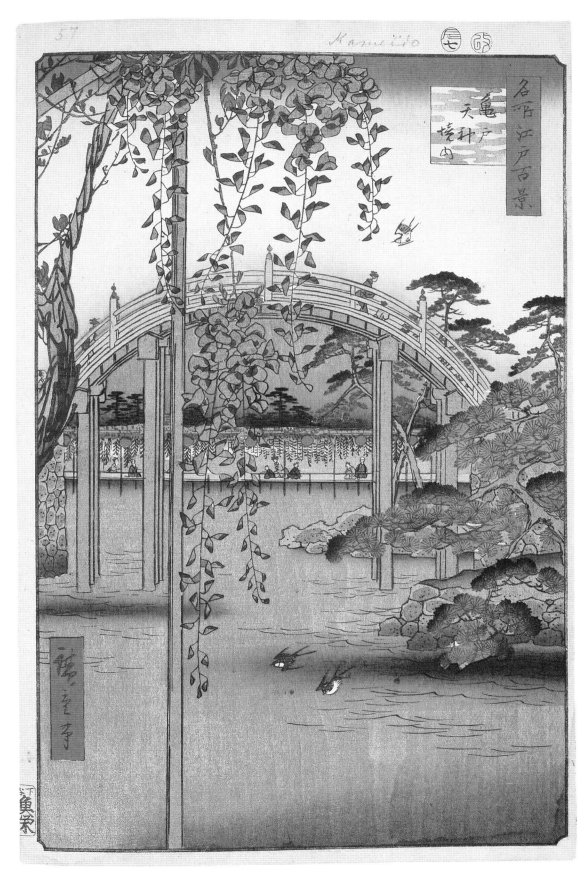

It would be interesting to know whether Monet was aware of the advice in the *Sakuteiki* (*Essay on Garden Making*) that 'water takes its shape from the container into which it flows, with both good and bad results. Therefore you should always exercise the greatest care with the design of your ponds.' The eleventh-century author also advises on the best method of beginning a garden 'by positioning a particularly well-shaped stone and letting it dictate the arrangement of all other stones'. Wise though this advice is, there are no major or minor stones in the garden at Giverny, which it must be stressed is not an authentic Japanese garden. The ornaments, stones and lanterns found in true Japanese gardens were missing, and even the bridge (214), built heavier and flatter than the traditional full moon shape, was painted green, unlike the red of the bridges within Shinto shrines in Japanese temples. Although not entirely in the Japanese tradition, Monet's garden has many Japanese influences.

214
Claude Monet
The Water -Lily Pond (Japanese Bridge),
1899.
Oil on canvas,
88·3 x 93·1 cm (34¹₄ x 36⁵₈ in).
National Gallery, London

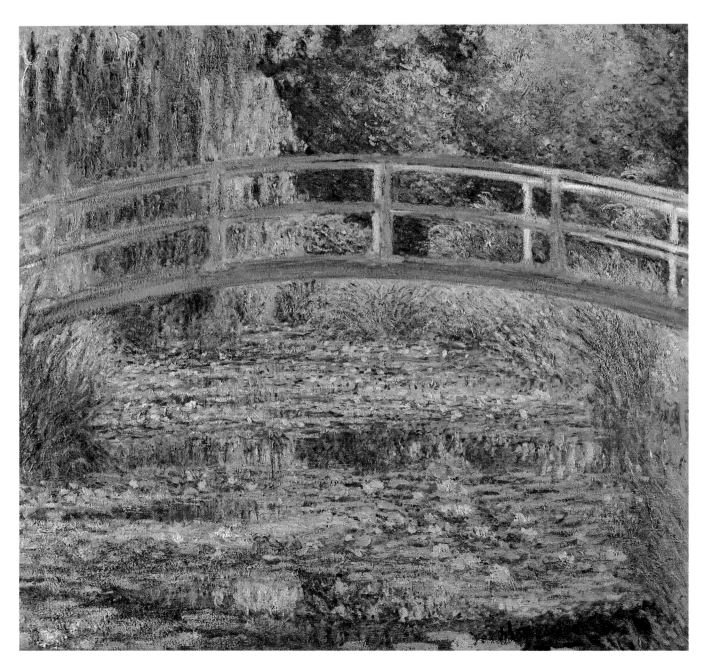

Utagawa Hiroshige,
Flowering Irises at Horikiri,
1857.
Colour woodblock,
37·2 x 24·8 cm
(14⁵⁄₈ x 9¾ in)

Its most important element was water, and also Japanese plants such as huge willows, wisteria, water lilies, azaleas, bamboo and iris. This species of iris (215) was introduced by Siebold into Europe shortly before Hiroshige made this print for the series *One Hundred Views in Edo*. The water lilies would not prove so malleable a subject as his other sequence paintings of Rouen Cathedral, haystacks, Waterloo Bridge or the Houses of Parliament, for they deliquesced, melted and demanded more space, the freedom of the far wider spectrum of a panorama. Monet began to experiment with more panoramic forms so that when the canvases were butted together they re-created the 360-degree illusionism of the early nineteenth-century panorama painters, producing the effect that you, the viewer, were virtually experiencing the same view that the artist saw, whichever way you turned. Monet may also have enjoyed looking at painted Japanese six-fold screens of landscape subjects imported by dealers. He may also have seen a full-scale reconstruction of the 'Room of Cranes' in the Nishi-Hongan-ji temple in Kyoto, which was shown in London, Paris and Lyon. The transoms were decorated with carvings of cranes, but the sliding screens depicted chrysanthemums, which may be profitably compared to Monet's water lilies, the subject which from 1899 began to dominate his work completely.

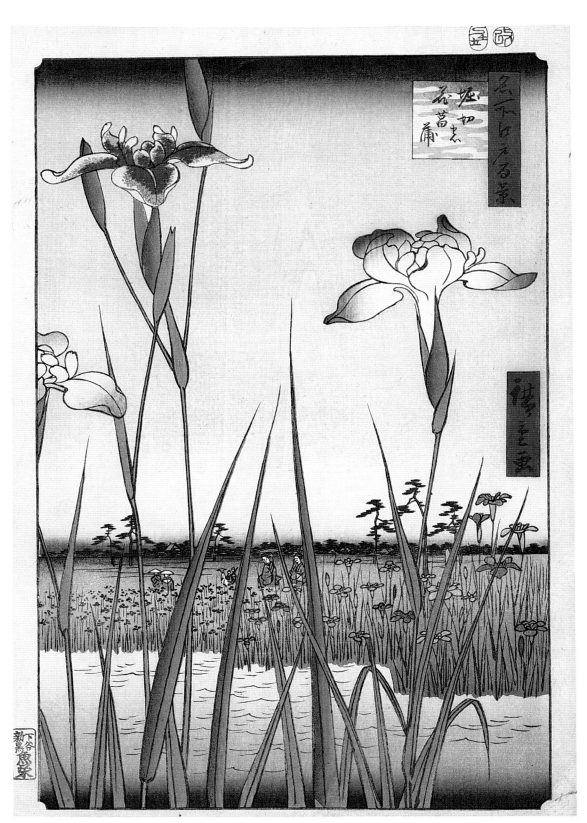

216
Monet in his studio
*c.*1923

217
**Advertisement for Carters
Japanese Lanterns,**
*c.*1920

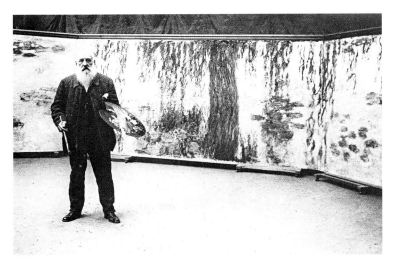

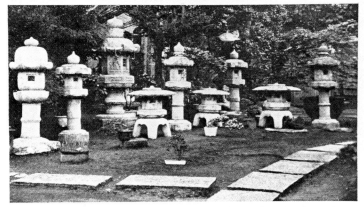

CARTERS JAPANESE LANTERNS

Direct from Japan, made of solid granite, and weighing from 5 cwt. to 1 ton.
Prices from 8 to 25 Guineas. Inspection invited.

As early as 1885 Judith Gautier translated a *haiku* by an unknown writer in a collection of Japanese poems which goes to the heart of Monet's vision:

On the pool's surface
Waterplants are intertwined
A green carpet, spreading
No gaze can descend
Into the depth of my thoughts.

These thoughts became his consuming passion and led him in 1914 to have a special studio built so he could work on the huge canvases of which he wrote:

These landscapes of water and
reflections have become an obsession
… quite beyond my powers at my
age, and yet I want to succeed in
expressing what I feel. I've destroyed
some … I start others … and I hope
that something will come out of so
much effort.

In the last twenty-five years of his life Monet continued to paint the surface of his water-lily pool and in the process came close to the precepts of Zen Buddhism, through his own long and contemplative communion with one aspect of nature. As the Belgian Symbolist poet, Émile Verhaeren, commented in 1901, when Monet painted nature, 'little by little he becomes alive in it … The poet becomes the universe that he translates.'

The abstract painters of a later generation would claim Monet's paintings as their precursors and justification. A photograph (*c.*1923; 216) shows him at work on the water lilies in the studio. Monet died at the age of eighty-six in 1926. An epitaph on his tomb might well have been that on the grave of the poet, John Keats, 'Here lies one whose name was writ in water.'

Although the introduction of Japanese plants to Europe and North America was taken seriously by botanists and horticulturists, seekers after novelty in garden design often had little understanding of the fundamental ideas in the creation of a Japanese garden, and the cultural issues which its Shinto and Zen roots raised. A B Freeman Mitford, later Lord Redesdale, in his book *Tales of Old Japan* (1871), dismissed Japanese gardens, finding them 'all spick and span – intensely artificial and a monument to wasted labour', while Reginald Farrer, a Tokyo-based plant collector and writer, commented that he thought the Japanese hated plants because they 'butchered' them, referring to the severe pruning which is such a feature of Japanese horticulture. Such austerity was very alien to Western eyes, which found it far easier to appreciate the unexpected pleasures of the stroll gardens. Between 1880 and 1910 a number of Japanese stroll gardens were established in Britain and America.

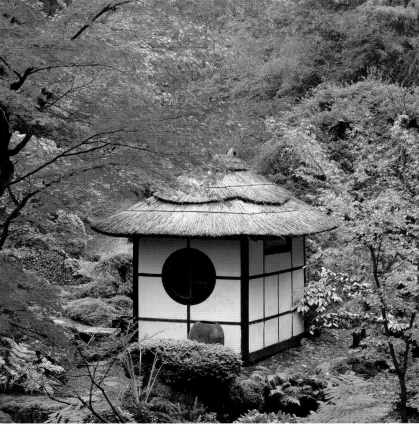

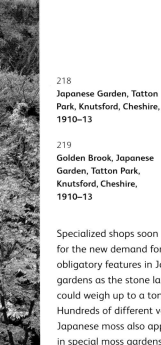

218
**Japanese Garden, Tatton
Park, Knutsford, Cheshire,
1910–13**

219
**Golden Brook, Japanese
Garden, Tatton Park,
Knutsford, Cheshire,
1910–13**

Specialized shops soon arose to cater for the new demand for such virtually obligatory features in Japanese gardens as the stone lanterns which could weigh up to a ton (217). Hundreds of different varieties of Japanese moss also appeared both in special moss gardens or on stone lanterns, which were rarely furnished with the candles that in former times gave many gardens a strangely ghostly appearance at night.

Smooth recumbent rocks formed the stepping-stone journey through the garden, twisting obliquely to reveal views both near and far. In forming Japanese gardens massive boulders are a very highly valued commodity. Tall standing stones can act as the support for a short poem which can vary from the trite to far more profound texts. Such gardens, whether made at home or abroad, needed maintenance, and to this end Japanese gardeners were employed. Just as in the eighteenth century no ambitious large-scale landscape garden was deemed quite complete without a resident hermit, so in the late nineteenth and early twentieth centuries a Japanese gardener was deemed a vital ingredient of the scene to create and maintain gardens on correct philosophical principles. One of the most successful gardens was established in 1906 by the first Lord Wavertree at Tully near Kildare in Ireland, across the road from the Irish National Stud.

Designed by the Japanese gardener, Tassa Eida, its teahouse, stone lanterns, bonsai and a model village were made of lava from Fujiyama, imported from Japan. The path though the garden was designed as a symbol of man's pilgrimage through life, taking the visitor from the Gate of Oblivion along the Path of Childhood, up the Hill of Learning, across the Bridge of Matrimony and finally through the Gates of Eternity.

A permanent aspect of the great temporary international exhibitions through which Japan became known to the outside world were the Japanese gardens which were left behind after the close of the exhibitions, and the Japanese gardeners who were left behind to tend them, or establish new gardens based upon those seen in the exhibitions. In England one of the more notable of those gardens is at Tatton Park, near Knutsford, Cheshire (218), which was inspired by a visit by its owner, Alan de Tatton, to the Anglo-Japanese exhibition of 1910 at the White City, London. One of its best features is the Golden Brook (219), an informal garden lake with a Shinto temple at one end overlooking the gardens. After years of neglect it was completely restored in 2001.

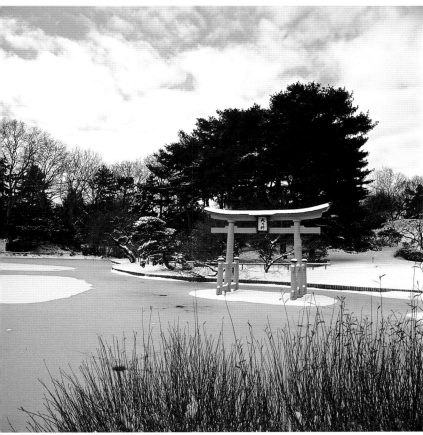

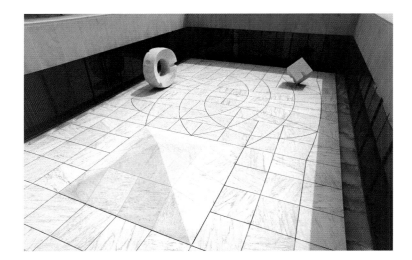

220
Isamu Noguchi,
Sunken Garden for
Beinecke Rare Book and
Manuscript Library, Yale
University, New Haven,
1960–4

Careful restoration is also planned at Gunnersbury Park, London, built by Leopold de Rothschild in 1906, which typically for its time merged both Chinese and Japanese features, with palms and bamboos mingled with stone lanterns and a red-painted hump-backed wooden bridge over the water lily pool. Hot water was piped into this outdoor pool 'to bring on the water lilies', a process of pampering the flower that would have surprised even Monet.

Another particularly charming garden can be seen at Fanhams Hall near Ware, Hertfordshire. It was created between 1905 and 1933 by Herbert Goode, using stone lanterns, rocks and a variety of rare trees and shrubs imported from Japan. Goode was a porcelain importer, whose ceramic shop in Mayfair remains a key monument of the Aesthetic Move-ment. Goode's garden is an early Edwardian interpretation of a Japanese theme with a charming teahouse, which would have provided an ideal setting for Gwendoline to pass Cecily a cucumber sandwich in Oscar Wilde's *The Importance of Being Earnest*. Today, with an irony Wilde would surely relish, it is used as a centre for the study of the Japanese tea ceremony.

One famous garden that sadly has disappeared only in recent years was created by a great Victorian woman traveller, Ella Christie, whose later years were devoted to its creation at Cowden, Perthshire, at the marshy foot of the Ochil Hills in Scotland. The gardens were laid out in 1907 by Taki Honda, a female Japanese garden designer from Nagoya. A ditch was turned into a lake, weeping willows, azaleas and primulas were planted and a Shinto shrine was constructed from Japanese cedars. Groups of stones were arranged to symbolize the five virtues – patriotism, obedience, faith, loyalty to family life and obedience to parents. The last two precepts were not without bitter irony for Ella, for her father had tried to disinherit her, thus starting her travels. The gardens were maintained for over ten years by a Japanese gardener, Matsuo, who arrived as Head Gardener in 1925 and is buried in the local churchyard. In the 1960s the gardens were systematically vandalized, and the pavilions, bridges and ornaments destroyed. Today little is left except for a few mature shrubs and pines.

A characteristic American success story can be found in the career of the Japanese gardener, Takeo Shiota, who came to America in 1907 and laid out a successful contemporary 'Tea House' garden in fashionable Tuxedo Park near New York. His masterpiece, still easily accessible and well maintained, was the Brooklyn Botanic Garden designed in 1915 around the existing feature of a tiny lake, which Shiota embellished with a *Torii*, an island near the artificial cascade, and a viewing pavilion built over the water. A shrine, several bridges, a covered resting bench, imported stone lanterns and realistic metal statues of cranes added an amusing illusion to a garden which today is considered one of the finest of its kind in America.

The Nitobe Memorial Garden at the University of British Columbia in Vancouver, Canada, is one of the best traditional gardens in North America. Nestled in 0.8 hectares (2 acres) of native British Columbian forest, this Shinto-style enclosure includes a stroll garden which uses symbolism. The garden may be interpreted as a symbolic journey through life from infancy to teenage years, marriage and adulthood, thus achieving spiritual growth. The stone lanterns symbolize light dispelling darkness, and when placed at the junction of paths indicate choices in life – appropriate questions for a garden in a university.

Waterfalls illustrate both male and female traits of nature in the Shinto religion, the strength and masculinity of the waterfall contrasting with the calm feminine stream.

In more recent years the American-Japanese designer Isamu Noguchi (1904–88) who worked in the studio of Constantin Brancusi (1876–57) has created a garden at the UNESCO building in Paris and a memorable Zen garden, completely without plants, for contemplation at the Beinecke Library at Yale University (1960–4; 220). In the following year he completed gardens at the Chase Manhattan Bank and also the IBM headquarters in New York.

The immensely successful Anglo-Japanese exhibition of 1910 saw the re-creation to scale of Japanese buildings including a four-fifth actual size ceremonial gateway of a famous Buddist temple gateway in Kyoto known as the Chokushi Mon (Gate of the Imperial Messenger) dating from the latter part of the sixteenth century. After the exhibition the replica was removed to Kew and erected near William Chambers' eighteenth-century Chinese pagoda. The gateway was restored in November 1995, and is now complemented by a Japanese garden completed in October 1996. In 1991 the Kyoto Garden in Holland Park, London, was opened by the Crown Prince of Japan and the Prince of Wales near the site of a garden planted in the 1930s, which had almost disappeared.

One of the most remarkable of all Japanese gardens ever erected outside Japan is in the process of being constructed today in Silicon Valley, California, where 'dot.com' millionaires grow weary of looking for unusual ways to spend their fortunes. An exception is the Oracle impresario, Larry Ellison, who has found an imaginative solution to the problem and is currently in the process of building the largest Japanese garden in America. In an interview in *Xpress Magazine* in May 2002 Ellison spoke of his first visit to Japan and love of Kyoto:

There were these wonderful gardens that were designed to promote intimacy between the viewer in the garden and the garden itself … when you spend time in a forest, and especially those wonderful, small reproductions of forests – those Japanese Zen gardens – it is a wonderfully reassuring and tranquil experience.

I always hear artists saying, 'I don't want to do that, it's been done before.' Well, the Japanese say 'I want to do exactly what has been done before, but just a little better.'

This motivation absorbed from Japan gives Ellison the determination to use as a model for the 9·3-hectare (23-acre) site, his favourite Japanese garden, Katsura Risky in Kyoto.

To achieve that result his gardener Shigeru Namba has restributed 81,000 cubic yards of earth dug out from the pond in the form of hills and islands. Over 500 trees have been added to about 700 existing natural trees, and 3,500 tons of boulders placed around the extensive pond. Stone lanterns and other hard-to-get Japanese materials have been brought from Japan.

The estate includes a large waterfall, a cascade, a pond and seven buildings, a round stone bridge and beautiful pathways with colourful trees and pink and yellow flowers leading to a serene courtyard where guests can see the main residence's north and south wings over the pond. The teahouse, which was reassembled in Woodside after being brought from Japan, stands peacefully in the deep forest. The moon pavilion, where a resident can enjoy watching the moon while soaking in the wooden bathtub, looks as though it is floating in the water. All the architectural structures are pavilions of varying dimensions, placed a few hundred metres apart around the five lakes which have been excavated, much to the concern of neighbours who were kept awake by the noise of lorries removing the smaller rocks and stones and returning with boulders (221).

When completed the garden complex will form a new chapter in the ongoing story of the West's fascinating variations on Japanese garden themes.

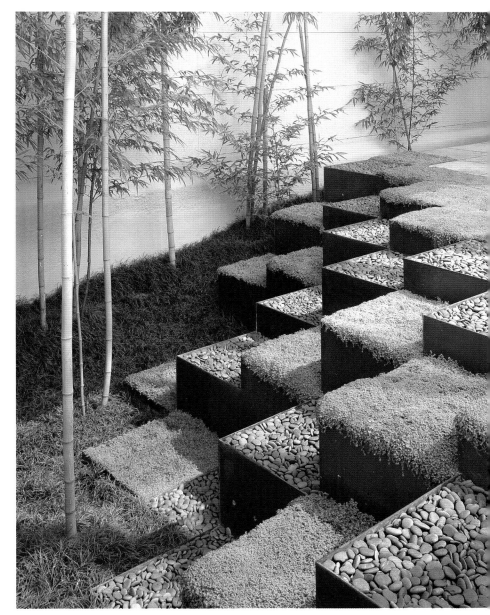

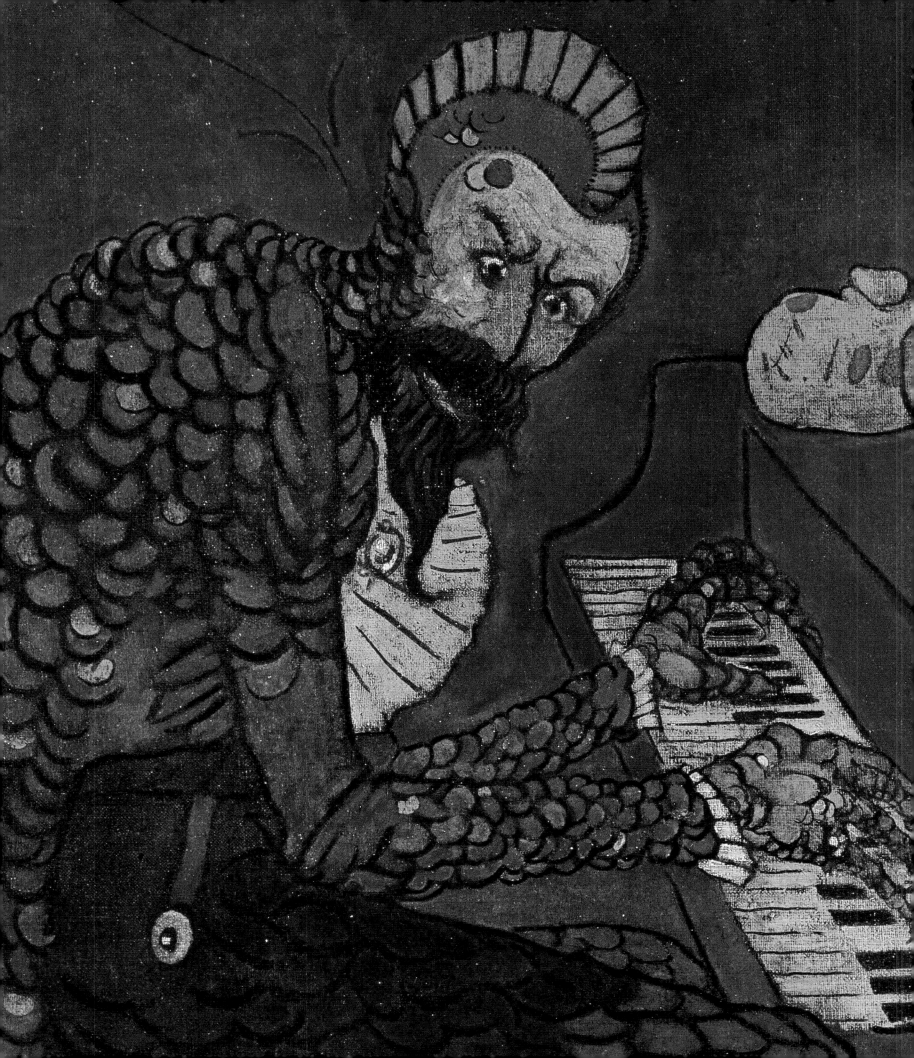

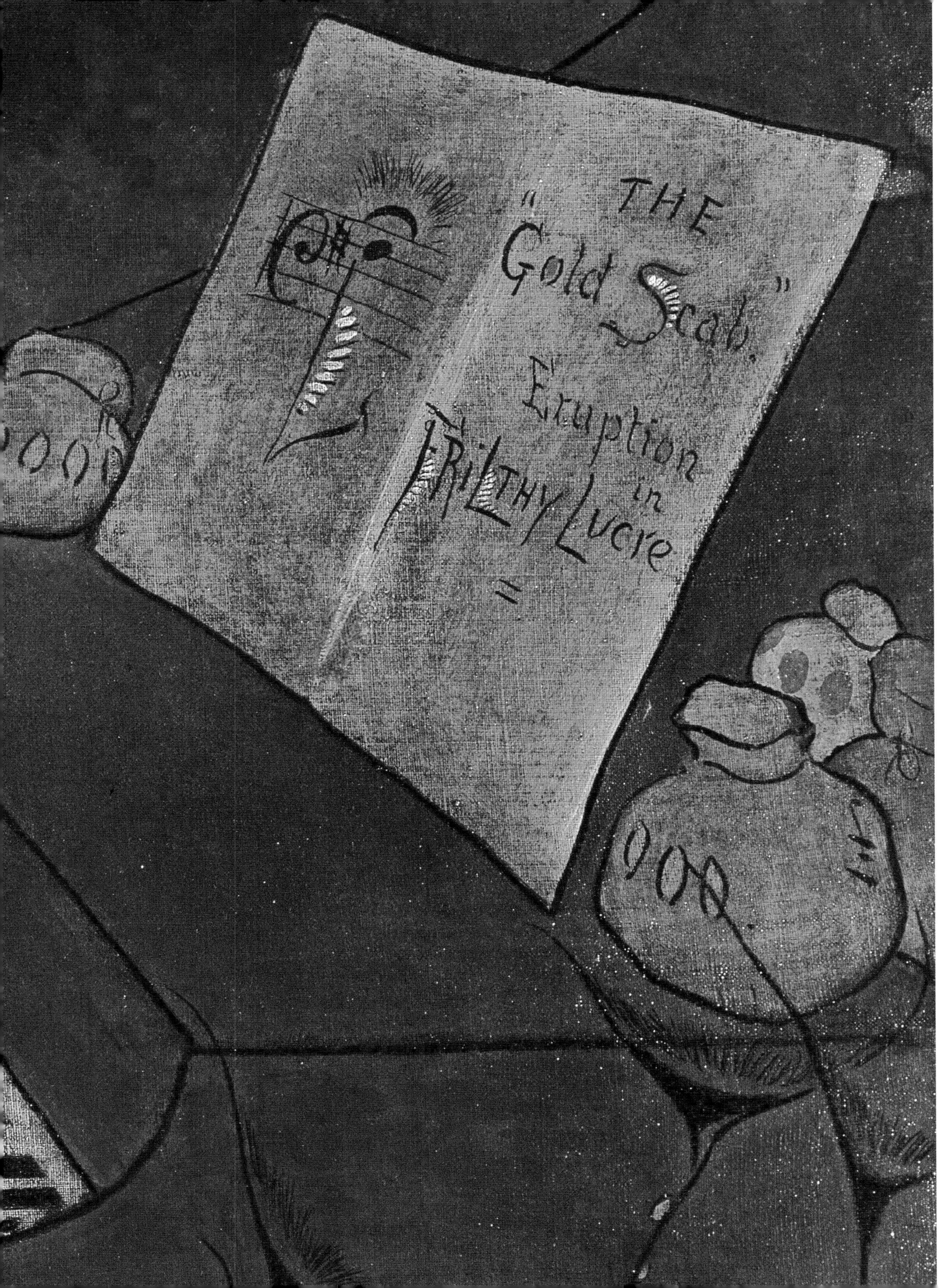
THE
"Gold Scab."
Eruption
in
FRiLTHY Lucre

Previous page
James Abbott McNeill Whistler,
The Gold Scab: Eruption in Frilthy Lucre
(detail of 224)

222
Katsushika Hokusai,
Self-Portrait,
1843.
Ink on paper,
26·9 x 16·9 cm
(10⁵⁸ x 6⁵⁸ in).
Museum of Ethnology,
Leiden

The King of Hell being very old is
retiring from business, so he has built
a pretty country house and asks me
to go and paint a kakemono for him.
I am thus obliged to leave, and when
I do so I shall carry my drawings with
me. I am going to take a room at the
corner of Hell Street and shall be
happy to see you whenever you pass
that way.
Reputed to be Hokusai's last letter,
1843, written with his last self-portrait,
aged 83 (222)

I have one aim – the grotesque.
If I am not grotesque, I am nothing.
Aubrey Beardsley, 1896

What exactly was the Symbolist
Movement and in what ways was
it influenced by Japonisme? Unlike
Impressionism, Symbolism was a
loosely organized artistic movement
which arose in the 1880s and 1890s,
a group of painters closely allied with
the Symbolist Movement in French
literature, which began rather earlier.
Proto-Symbolists included such names
as the founder of the movement,
Alfred de Vigny, author of a play on
the tragic suicide of the seventeen-
year-old poet Thomas Chatterton, and
Charles Baudelaire, creator of the
notorious cycle of poems *Les Fleurs du*
mal (*The Flowers of Evil*).

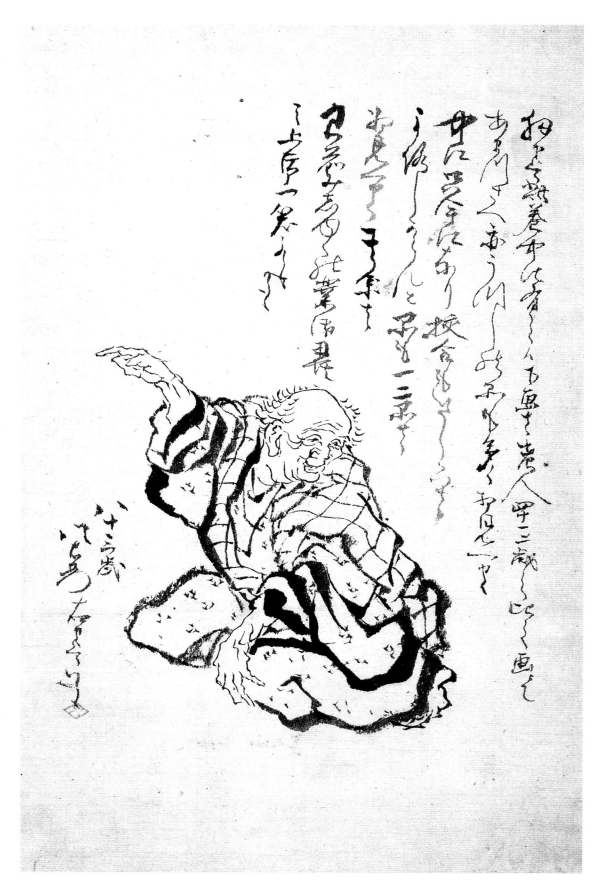

223
Katsushika Hokusai,
Yuten and the Ghost
from the *Manga* **vol. XII,**
1834.
Colour woodblock,
17·5 x 11·5 cm
(7 x 4¹₂ in)

Later Symbolists included the poets Paul Verlaine and Stéphane Mallarmé, who coined the famous dictum, 'paint not the thing, but the effect which it produces', and embraced a manifesto which asserted:

We are tired of the everyday, the near at hand and the contemporaneous; we wish to be able to place the development of the symbol in any period, even in dreams (dreams being indistinguishable from life). We want to substitute for the battle of individuals the battle of feelings and ideas ...

Nothing could be further from the principle of realism as formulated by Gustave Courbet (1819–77), who declared that painting should only deal with 'real and existing things'. Symbolism on the contrary strove to give visual expression to the mystical and occult. For both artists and writers the choice of subject was of major importance, and this helps to explain the enthusiasm generated by the arrival of the arts of Japan with their novel scenes and themes.

As with other aspects of the arts already discussed, Hokusai's *Manga* contains many pages dealing with stories and superstitions, an extraordinary bran-tub of stimulating ideas which got the creative process going for Western eyes.

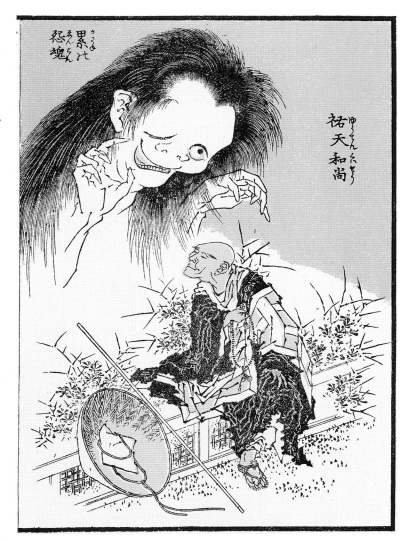

For the Symbolists the morbid themes of Japanese mythology and the grotesque element in its folk tales such as *Yuten and the Ghost* had an especial appeal (223). The woodcut tells the story of Kasane, a woman cursed with the legacy of both a hideously ugly face and a large tract of land. She married the land-hungry Yoemon, a peasant who promptly murdered her. For years she haunted the countryside driving Yoemon's subsequent wives to their death. In despair Yoemon begged the priest Yuten, shown here, to exorcise Kasane's apparition.

To this day the Japanese are fascinated by such ghost stories, either when performed on the *kabuki* stage, enacted in traditional processions and festivals, or in the oral tradition of the spoken word.

One of the major tenets of the Symbolist Movement was a belief in the interrelationships, parallels and analogies between the arts of painting, music, poetry and prose. The painter Whistler also subscribed to this view, giving his paintings musical titles such as *Arrangement*, *Symphony* or *Nocturne*.

**James Abbott McNeill
Whistler,**
*The Gold Scab: Eruption
in Frilthy Lucre*
(*The Creditor*),
1879.
Oil on canvas,
186·7 x 139·7 cm
(73½ x 55 in).
Fine Arts Museum of
San Francisco

Odilon Redon,
*The Siren Rising From the
Waves Clothed in Barbs,*
1888.
Lithograph,
27·5 x 17 cm
(10⅞ x 6¾ in)

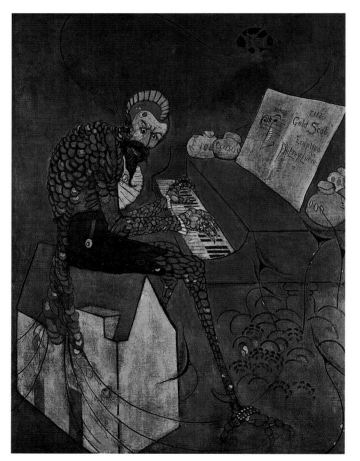

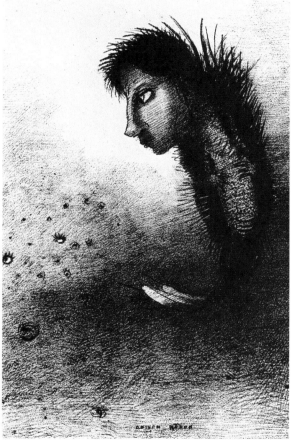

The story of Whistler's creation in
1876–7 of the *Harmony in Blue
and Gold: the Peacock Room* for the
shipping magnate F R Leyland and the
consequent quarrel with his patron,
symbolized in a mural by a pair of
fighting peacocks, has been recounted
above (see Chapter 5). It has become
recognized as a key work in the story
of both the Symbolist Movement and
Japonisme. Whistler believed that
Leyland subsequently drove him into
bankruptcy, and painted in oils a
caricature of Leyland entitled *The
Gold Scab: Eruption in Frilthy Lucre*
(224). It shows his victim with an
engorged peacock's head playing the
piano while perched on the gabled roof
of Whistler's home, the White House,
and erupting a shower of gold
sovereigns from his frilly shirt. This
horrifying creation is given a very
Japoniste effect by the depiction
of the peacock's erect crest and
the great claw feet, an exercise in
anthropomorphic comparison and
abuse, one of the oldest weapons in
the cartoonist's quiver. This theme
would also be used by Symbolist
artists, notably Odilon Redon
(1840–1916) in his memorable
*The Siren Rising From the Waves
Clothed in Barbs* (225).

Gustave Moreau,
Two **Kabuki** *actors*
in Female Roles,
1869.
Watercolour and pencil,
26 x 21·1 cm
(10¹₄ x 8¹₄ in).
Musée Gustave Moreau,
Paris

The Symbolist poetry of Mallarmé and Verlaine (and in England the work of Swinburne) was labelled 'decadent' and associated with two of the most important French Symbolist painters, Redon and Gustave Moreau (1826–98). In 1869 the latter made one of his rare excursions into the watercolour medium when he visited the Japanese Exhibition in the Palace of Industry, where a *kabuki* company performed a traditional play. In it two actors fought a mimic battle, brilliantly recorded by Moreau (226).

The work of Moreau and Redon together with that of the mural painter, Puvis de Chavannes (1824–98) provided a focus for the movement. By its nature, however, Symbolism recognized no national barriers. There were always significant contributions from abroad by artists who admired Symbolist aims, ranging from Edvard Munch (1863–1944) to Edward Burne-Jones, and most strikingly, the young British illustrator, Aubrey Beardsley.

On a visit to Paris in 1892, Beardsley showed his portfolio to a sympathetic Puvis de Chavannes. It contained many examples of what he called his 'Japonesque' style in which the dramatic use of black areas was arrived at by experimenting with blots of Indian ink. Beardsley also used the asymmetric composition and the narrow upright format of the *kakemono*, a space which he found particularly congenial.

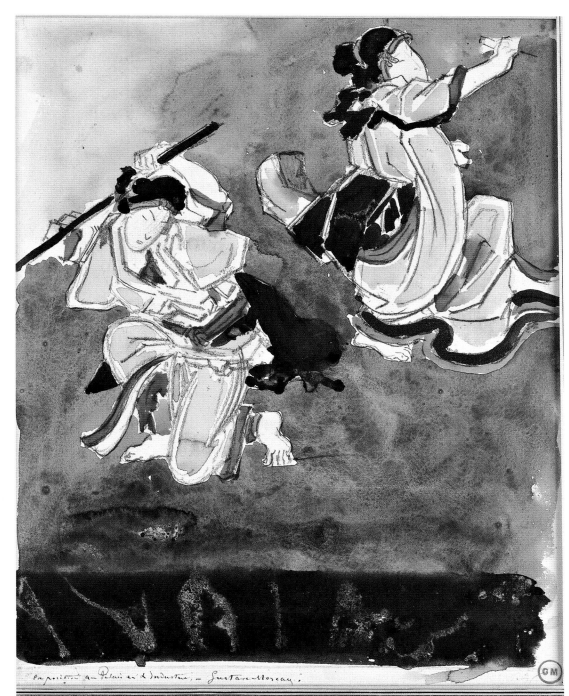

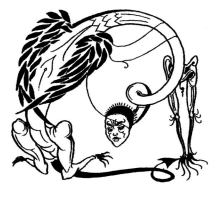

Japonisme

227
Aubrey Beardsley,
Vignette in *Bon-Mots*,
by Sydney Smith and
R Brindsley Sheridan,
1893.
5·1 x 5·7 cm
(2¹⁄₈ x 2¹⁄₄ in)

228
Katsushika Hokusai,
Monsters from the
Manga vol. XII,
1834.
Colour woodblock,
17·5 x 11·5 cm
(7 x 4¹⁄₂ in)

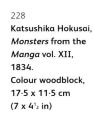

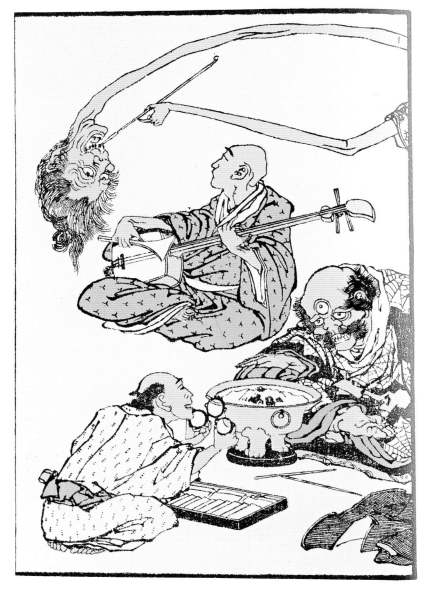

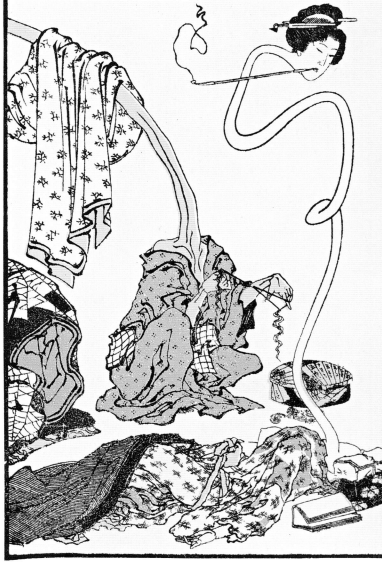

229
Aubrey Beardsley,
The Peacock Skirt from
Salomé by Oscar Wilde,
1894.
Ink drawing,
22·8 x 19·7 cm
(9 x 7³⁄₄ in).
Fogg Art Museum,
Harvard University,
Cambridge, MA

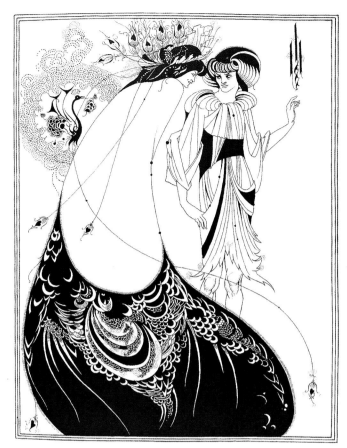

Beardsley made black the most
exciting colour on the palette, and in
his more straightforward drawings he
abraded the surface of the black areas
to obtain a richness of tone resembling
a mezzotint effect. These experiments
led him to become aware of the work
of Redon, whose lithographs record his
dreams by putting 'the logic of the
visible world at the service of the
invisible', and at the same time
dallying with the supernatural.

It is possible that Beardsley saw
examples of Redon's work either on
his visit to Paris in 1892 or at the
bookshop of Frederick Evans, from
whom came the great commission for
Beardsley of Malory's *Morte D'Arthur*
and also a project for illustrations for a
mini-anthology of aphorisms and wit
entitled *Bon-Mots* (227). In creating
over 200 drawings for *Bon-Mots*,
Beardsley, the most original
of artists, delved into the apparently
inexhaustible resources of the *Manga*
when seeking inspiration. Among the
grotesque drawings that he made for
this venture are several which have
Japanese prototypes in the *Manga*,
notably a creature with an immensely
long neck (228), a geisha and two
spiders with grotesque semi-human
faces and wide-open eyes.

230
Kitagawa Utamaro,
The Outer Robe,
*c.*1797.
Colour woodblock,
37·3 x 25 cm
(14⁵⁄₈ x 9⁷⁄₈ in)

Another important early experience for
Beardsley occurred in July 1891 when
he and his sister visited Whistler's
Peacock Room and illustrated a letter
describing the experience with a
watercolour sketch of *La Princesse du
pays de la porcelaine* (see Chapter 5),
the room's centrepiece, surrounded by
little peacocks all flourishing their
feathers. The experience much later
reappeared in his work in the guise of
The Peacock Skirt (229), an illustration
for Wilde's *Salomé*, published in 1894.
This was among the most famous and
most Japanese of all Beardsley's works,
and forms an intriguing comparison
with Kitagawa Utamaro's *The Outer
Robe* (230). Beardsley's *Salomé*
illustrations formed a watershed
both for the Aesthetic Movement
and Japonisme. *The Peacock Skirt*
was denounced by the critic of the
Saturday Review as 'a derisive parody
of Félicien Rops embroidered on to
Japanese themes'. Rops (1833–98)
was a brilliant but perverse artist who
shared with Beardsley a taste for the
erotic and macabre themes so beloved
by the masters of the Japanese print.

By their very nature the Symbolists
were a constantly fluctuating group
with links to several other movements
of the time, in particular the Nabis and
followers of Synthetism who formed
themselves around the compelling
personality of Paul Gauguin.

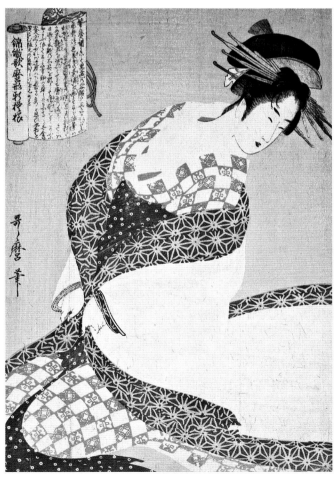

231
Paul Gauguin,
*Vision After the Sermon;
Jacob Wrestling With
the Angel*,
1888.
Oil on canvas,
73 x 92 cm (28³⁄₄ x 36¹⁄₄ in).
National Gallery of Scotland,
Edinburgh

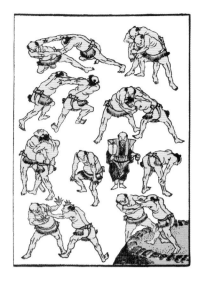

232
Katsushika Hokusai,
Sumo Wrestlers, from
the *Manga* vol. III,
1815.
Colour woodblock,
page: 17·5 x 11·5 cm
(7 x 4¹⁄₂ in)

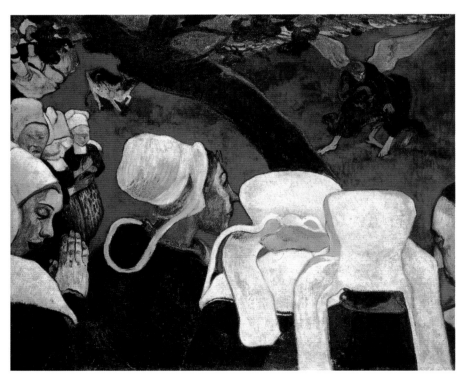

Gauguin was a keen collector of Japanese prints, which he used to decorate his rooms in Brittany, the Pacific and Paris, where his studio contained 'a sort of frieze made by prints by Utamaro and Hokusai'. Prints appear in the background of several of his paintings, notably in *Still Life With a Japanese Print* (1879).

In *The Vision After the Sermon – Jacob Wrestling With the Angel* (1888; 231), Gauguin used a composition showing sumo wrestlers lifted directly from the *Manga* (232), a crib which aroused the ire of the Impressionist Camille Pissarro, who in February 1891 wrote to his son Lucien in London, specifically singling out Gauguin's painting for criticism:

I do not criticize Gauguin for having painted a vermilion background nor do I object to the two struggling warriors and the Breton peasant woman in the foreground … What I do mind is that he swiped these ideas from the Japanese, the Byzantine painters and others.

The extent to which Gauguin 'swiped' from the Japanese is tellingly evident in several works, for he looked to Japan not only for inspiration on line and subject but also for bold colours.

Gauguin hoped in the South Seas to be able to live on ecstasy, calmness and art, and until the day he died, continued to value his Japanese collection, noting down in his intimate journal, *Before and After*, the contents of his home in the South Pacific:

In my hut there are all sorts of odds and ends that appear extraordinary because here they are unusual: Japanese prints, photographs of pictures by Manet, Puvis de Chavannes, Degas, Rembrandt, Raphael, Michel Angelo.

After his demise in 1903 the inventory of Gauguin's possessions included a Japanese book, a Japanese sword and forty-five prints tacked to the walls of his dwelling, many of which were undoubtedly Japanese.

The Nabis, a group of French painters active in the 1890s, derived their title from the Hebrew word meaning 'the prophets'. They were followers of Gauguin's expressive use of colour and, like him, admirers of the bold imagery and rich patterns and motifs of Japanese art. Paul Gauguin, in a letter to Émile Bernard (1868–1941) in December 1888, observed admiringly that the Japanese drew 'life outdoors and the sun without shadows', and resolved that he would do the same.

233
Émile Bernard,
Women Hanging Laundry,
from *Les Brettoneries*,
1889.
Zincograph with
hand-colouring,
24·7 x 31·7cm
(9³₄ x 12¹₂ in).
Indianapolis Museum of Art

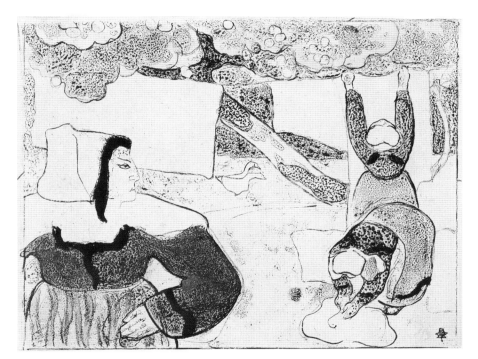

Although Bonnard, Vuillard and Maurice Denis, the main theorist of the Nabis, all went their separate ways after their successful exhibition of 1899, one figure of the group stands out for works which demonstrate particularly Japanese qualities: Émile Bernard, who was aged twenty when he first met Gauguin during the summer of 1888 at Pont Aven. Both artists shared enthusiasms for medieval art, stained glass and Breton culture. Together they enjoyed experimenting with the techniques made possible with the new medium of zincography, an easy method of producing lithographic images. That winter Bernard conceived a series of seven prints which would form an examination of the life of Breton peasants at work and play, one of which was *Women Hanging Laundry* (233). Like Gauguin, Bernard collected Japanese prints and it is fascinating to see in the dominant figure on the left, the static pose of a *kabuki* actor.

The provision of images of ghosts, such a feature of the *kabuki* theatre, provided an important part of Hokusai's income. Public demand for his grotesque pictured imaginings led him to produce some of the most terrifying of all the monsters and ghost stories which abound in Japanese mythology.

He was not alone in creating in this lucrative field, as we can see in a book of ghost stories, *Once Upon a Time, or Stories of Strange Demons*: *The Former Wife's Return*, by Shun'ei and Shunsho. The illustrations for such ghost stories inspired several Symbolist painters, notably Odilon Redon and the Belgian, Félicien Rops. The influence of Japanese artefacts other than prints had a particular appeal for novelists and writers looking for copy in describing interiors, figures such as Philippe Burty who wrote a novel, *Grave Imprudence* (1880). The book's hero Brissot was a composite of Manet and Monet, and an early collector of Japanese prints. A sensual moment in the novel portrays Brissot painting Pauline, a Parisian model who is naked except for a Japanese red-orange robe, a clear reference to Monet's *La Japonaise* (see 132).

A writer who also trailed the Symbolist banner was Joris-Karl Huysmans. In Huysmans's notorious novel *Against Nature* (1884), his hero des Esseintes tries:

to rejuvenate the stereotyped forms of poetry, the sonnet for example, which he turned upside down, like those Japanese fish in coloured earthenware that are stood gills-down on their pedestals.

234
Ashinaga With a Fish,
18th century.
Ivory,
height: 15·1 (6 in).
Linden-Museum,
Stuttgart

235
Katsushika Hokusai,
[The Ghost] of Oiwa, from
One Hundred [Ghost] Tales,
1831.
Colour woodblock,
26·3 x 18·9 cm
(10³⁄₈ x 7¹⁄₂ in)

236
Utagawa Kuniyoshi,
*Takiyashi the Witch and the
Skeleton Spectre* from
Somai dairi
(*The Palace of Soma*),
c.1845.
Colour woodblock,
each panel: 37·3 x 25 cm
(14¹⁄₂ x 9⁷⁄₈ in)

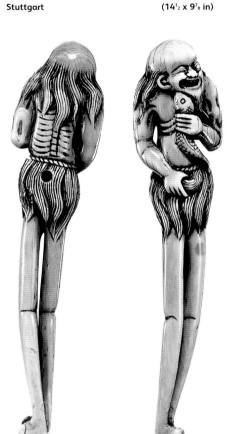

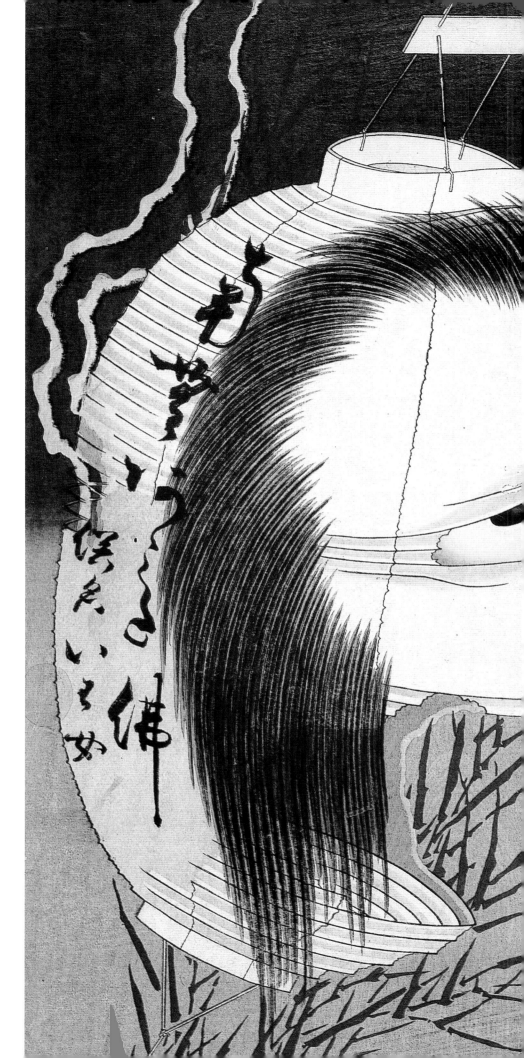

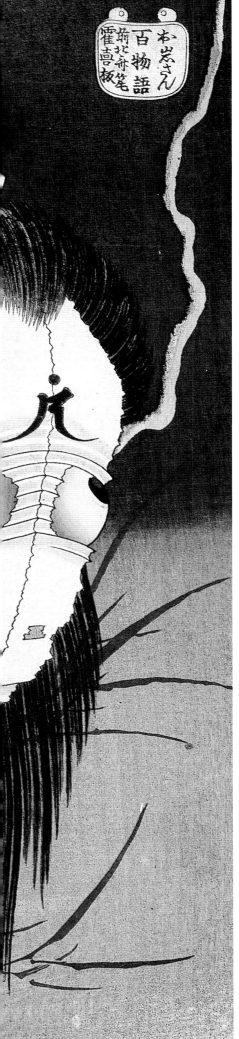

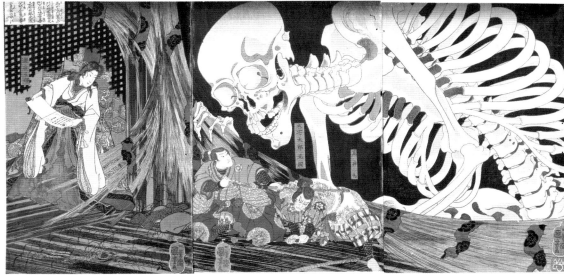

Elsewhere in the novel its hero des Esseintes 'enjoyed a perverted sense of pleasure in handling books whose covers, made of Japanese felt, were as white as curdled milk'. The extraordinary lifestyle of his hero is derived from 'those Japanese boxes that fit one inside the other', achieved by inserting a ship's cabin inside a real dining-room and setting off on imaginary voyages. In one of the most 'purple passages' in the novel, des Esseintes plans the decoration of the shell of a huge tortoise, so that as it moved it would set off the gleaming tints of his rich Oriental carpets:

From a collection of Japanese art he selected a drawing representing a huge bunch of flowers springing from a single slender stalk, took it to a jeweller's ... and informed the astonished lapidary that the leaves and petals of each and every flower were to be executed in precious stones and mounted on the actual shell of the tortoise.

Needless to say the poor creature dies:

unable to bear the dazzling luxury imposed upon it, the glittering cape in which it had been clad, the precious stones which had been used to decorate its shell like a jewelled ciborium.

Such exotic European fantasies combined with the Japanese love of the grotesque and bizarre provoked exciting artistic cross-pollination, recorded in both the pages of Hokusai's *Manga* and such works as *Japan: Its Architecture, Art and Art Manufactures* by Christopher Dresser. He describes in it an ivory carving of two men violently disagreeing:

The one has long legs and short arms; the other has long arms and short legs. The tale goes that fish can only be caught in deep water, where the man with short legs could not stand. The man with long legs can get into the deep water, but, owing to his short arms, he cannot reach to the bottom and fish. The difficulty is overcome by the long legged man carrying the man with the long arms on his back. The two together can thus catch fish, but neither can do so alone. Hence the absurdity of these men quarrelling.

Such grotesque juxtapositions provided *netsuke* carvers with apposite subjects (234). *Netsuke* are the small carvings used as toggles to secure cord hanging from the *obi* or sashes. Another popular theme in Japanese folklore goes into the advantages and disadvantages of having a long neck, a subject which Hokusai depicts in the *Manga* (see 228). The lady on the right demonstrates that it can prove very useful if you want to smoke in bed.

Next to her an old woman remains seated but nevertheless gets her head into a better position for listening to the monk play the *samisen* while having a third arm helps with her pipe-smoking too. An enterprising oculist in the bottom of the left-hand sheet is quite unphased by a customer with three, instead of the more usual two, eyes.

Another popular symbolic theme both in Japan and the West was the use of skulls and skeletons, not only to signify *memento mori* (emblems of mortality) but also when animated to symbolize ghosts and apparitions. One of the most horrifying of all ghosts by Hokusai grins at us with a leer carefully calculated to make the most doubtful sceptic believe all too vividly in 'things that go bump in the night' (235).

A fine example of a print inspired by a theatrical production is provided by Kuniyoshi and entitled *Takiyashi and the Skeleton Spectre*, a triptych dating from *c.*1845 (236). This dramatic print shows a sorceress holding a scroll and conjuring up a skeleton spectre. She is Takiyasha, daughter of Taira Masakado (d.940), who attempted to become Emperor. After he was killed his castle was believed to be haunted by the ghost of his daughter.

237
James Ensor,
Chinoiseries,
1907.
Oil on canvas,
62 x 75 cm
(24$^3_8$ x 29$^1_2$ in).
Museum Dhondt-
Dhaenens, Deurle

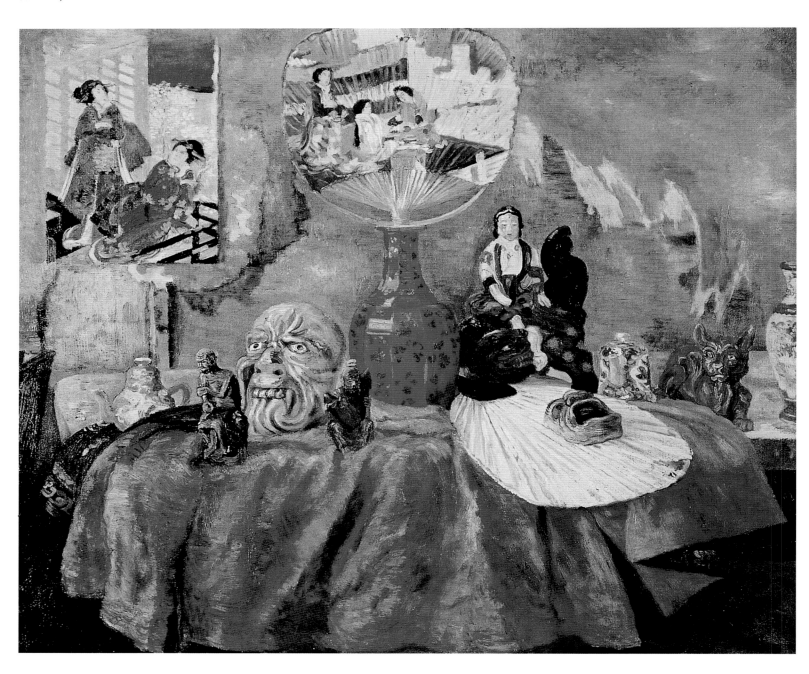

238
Félicien Rops,
Le Vice Suprême,
c.1884.
Etching and aquatint,
35·3 x 26·5 cm
(13⁷₈ x 10¹₂ in)

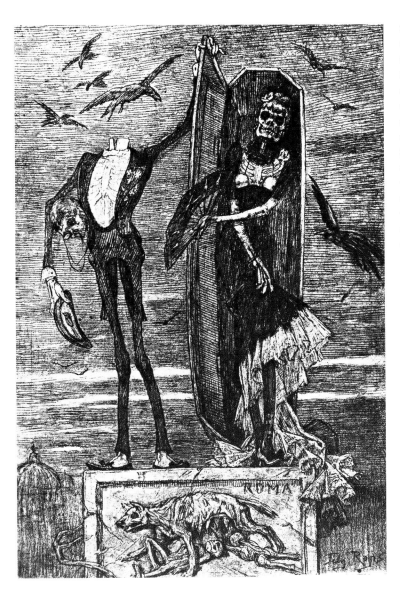

Such a theme has obvious parallels with the obsessive use of skeletons by the Belgian artists, James Ensor (1860–1949) and Félicien Rops (237 and 238). Death and the Devil are awesomely symbolized by piles of skulls and death's head moths, such as are seen in Hiroshige's *Taira Kiyomori Sees Strange Sights in his Garden* (239), which tells the story of the tyrant Kiyomori who, shortly before he died, was haunted by the spirits of all the people whose death he had caused. Hiroshige has brilliantly captured the delirium of the dying man as the snow-laden garden is revealed as being completely composed of a horrifying pile of skulls. This image strikingly parallels an illustration by the English artist, Sidney Sime (1867–1941), *The Gate of Knowledge* (240), which was published in the *Pall Mall Magazine* in June 1905. Sime lived a strange, lonely life, creating such skull-infested landscapes, which often accompanied the macabre short stories by his patron, the eccentric Irish peer Lord Dunsany. Today, sadly, their joint work is virtually forgotten, yet it embodies the very quintessence of the spookier side of Japonisme.

That most rigorous of dramatic disciplines, the *noh* play, intrigued one of the great poets of the twentieth century, William Butler Yeats. In 1916 he wrote an essay, *Certain Noble Plays of Japan*, which discussed the *noh* theatre.

He later wrote four *noh* plays, two being entitled *At the Hawk's Well* (1917) and *The Dreaming of the Bones* (1919). They formed a part of a series of 'four plays for dancers' using extreme simplicity of design and setting, the work of the illustrator Edmund Dulac (who also composed the music for the plays). In *The Dreaming of the Bones*, Yeats cleverly interwove the historic Irish symbols of nationalist struggle, seeking to convey his meaning by 'calling to the eye of the mind', deliberately stylizing his actors' movements and using masks.

The early twentieth century also produced artists whose work continued to show evidence of Japanese inspiration. One particularly interesting group of students became known as 'the Spooks' during their years at the Glasgow School of Art. Their 'spooky' works reveal a strange blend of Celtic romanticism filtered through Beardsley and Japan. The chief 'Spook' was Jessie M King (1875–1949). Her watercolour, '*I had never seen anyone so pale*' (241), illustrates Oscar Wilde's fairy story, *A Fisherman and his Soul* in *A House of Pomegranates*, and it succeeds in being both classically Japanese and thoroughly modern in its composition.

239
Utagawa Hiroshige,
*Taira Kiyomori Sees
Strange Sights in
his Garden*,
1843–5.
Colour woodblock,
36·8 x 76·2 cm,
(14½ x 30 in)

240
Sidney Sime,
*The Gate of
Knowledge* from
Pall Mall Magazine,
June 1905

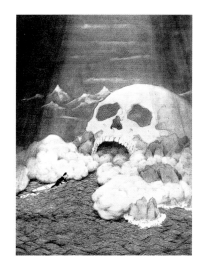

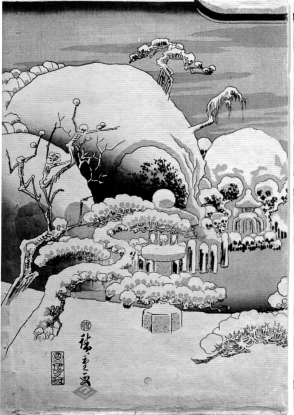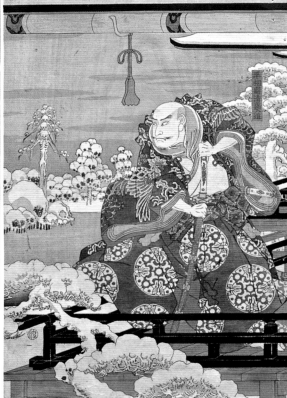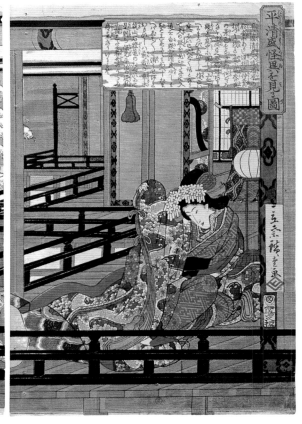

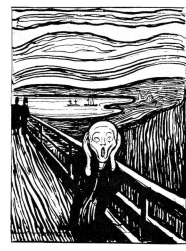

241
Jessie M. King
'*I had never seen anyone
so pale*', pen, ink and
watercolour illustration
for *A House of
Pomegranates* by Oscar
Wilde, 1915

242
Edvard Munch,
The Scream,
1895.
Lithograph

'Illness, madness and death were the black angels that kept watch over my cradle', wrote the Norwegian artist Edvard Munch, whose mother and sister died while he was young, and whose father was a religious maniac. Munch made his first visit to Paris in 1885 and, while there, became interested in the Symbolists, Gauguin, and also the Japanese print. He gained mastery of painting and the graphic techniques of etching, lithography and notably the woodcut, at which he excelled. Certain images, in particular *The Scream* (1895; 242), recur again and again in different media. *The Kiss*, a supreme example of the use of the grain of the plank as background, reveals his knowledge of Japanese woodcuts, and the anguished intensity of his art is also in evidence in the themes of *Melancholy* (1896), *Despair* (1892), and *The Girl and Death* (1896).

After the horrors of the First World War different concerns would take precedence over Japonisme, although as Roger Fry (1866–34), High Priest of Modernism, observed:

It is partly due to Japanese influence that our own impressionists have made an attempt to get back to ... ultra primitiveness of vision. Indeed they deliberately sought to de-conceptualize art.

In the 1900s a new interest in the art of Africa would overtake Japonisme. Yet, today Japanese aesthetics continue to affect the sensibilities of the West.

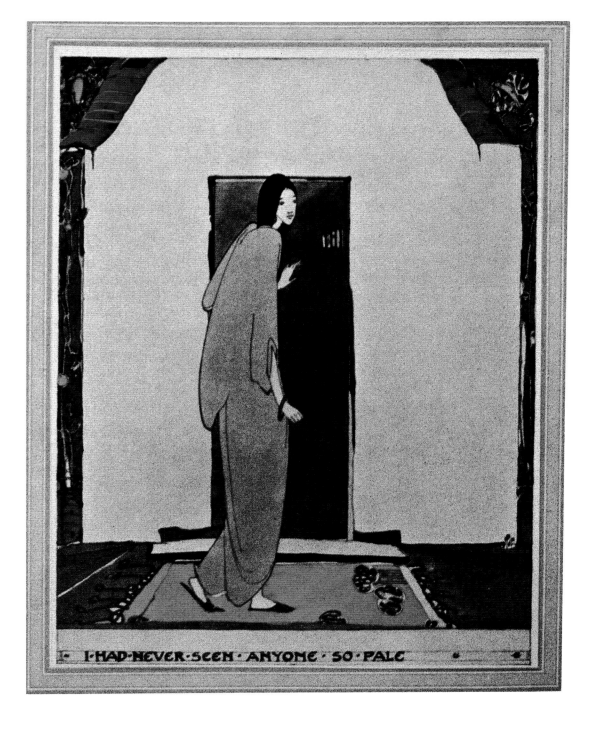

I·HAD·NEVER·SEEN·ANYONE·SO·PALE

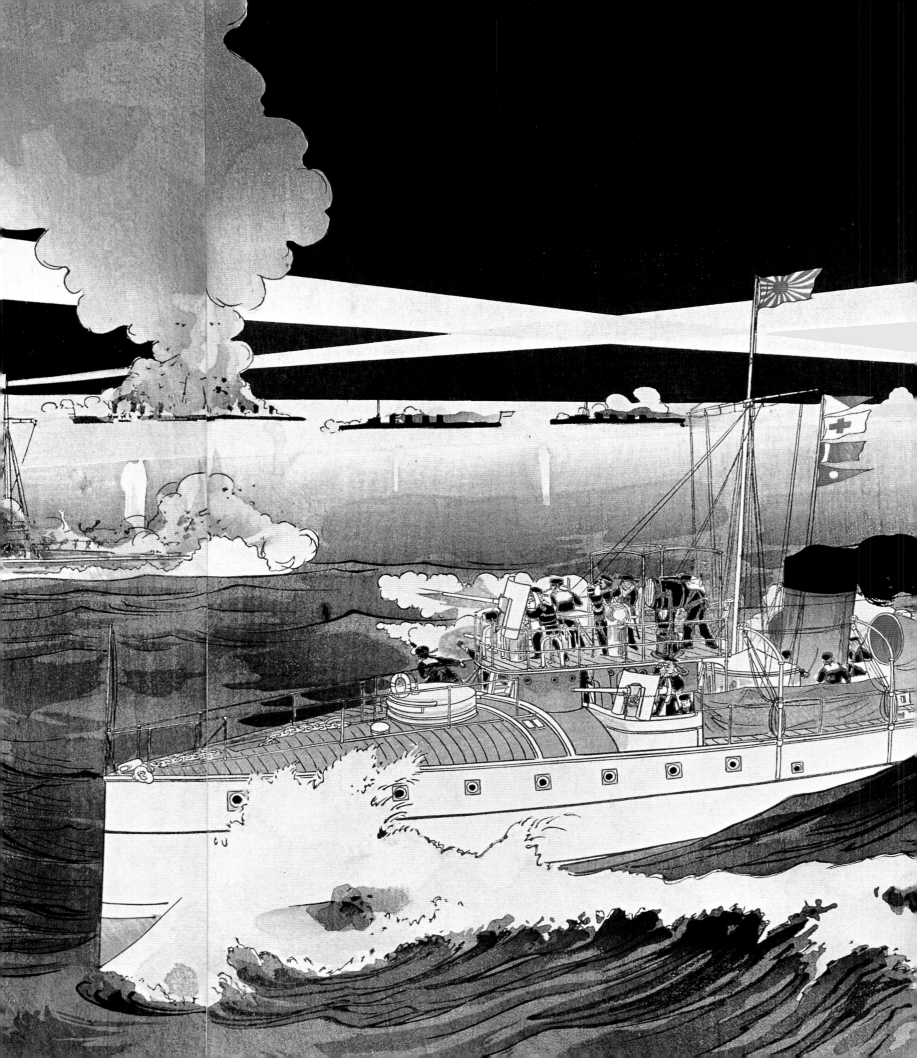

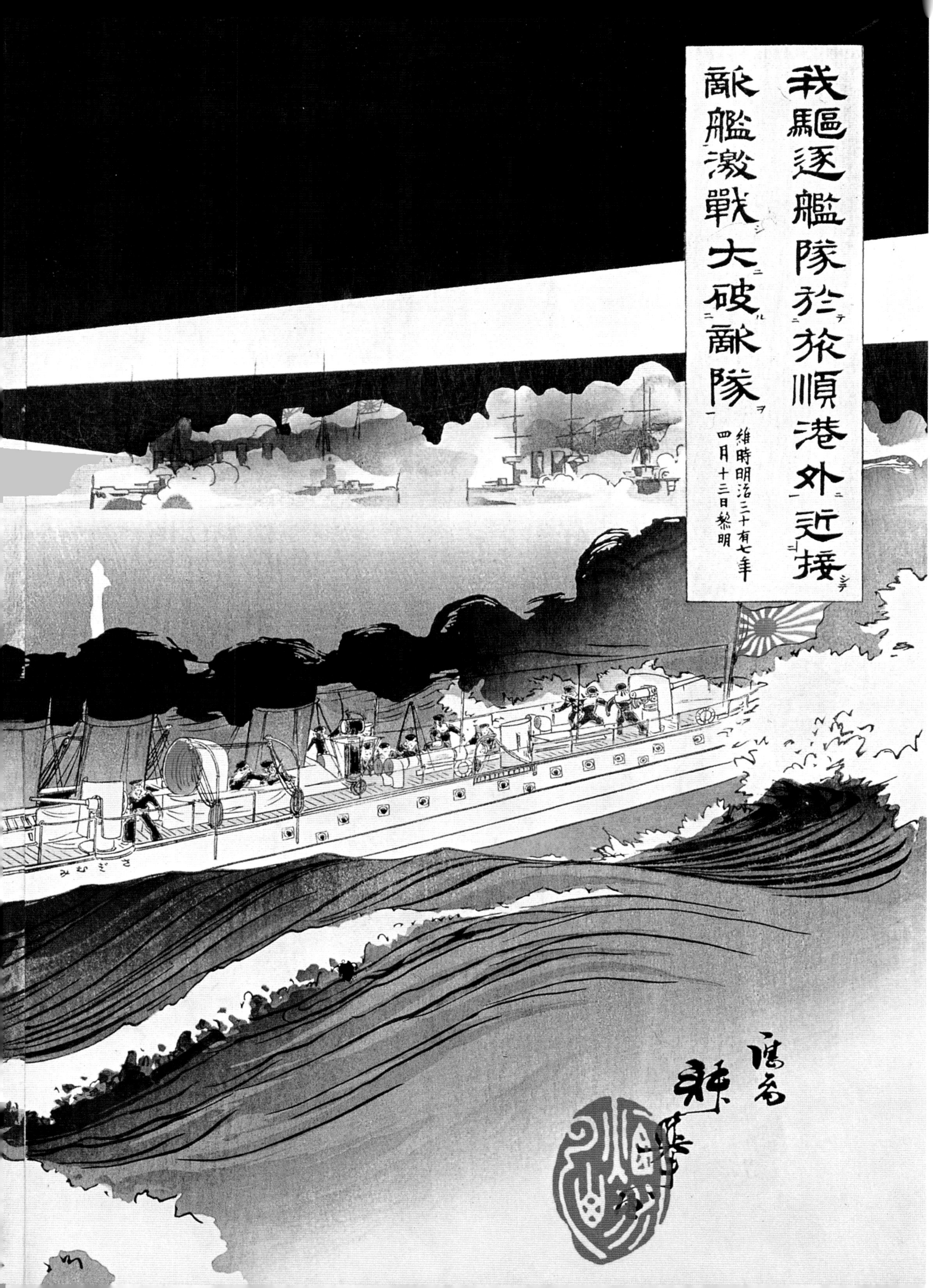

我驅逐艦隊於旅順港外近接敵艦激戰大破敵隊

敵艦激戰大破敵隊

維時明治三十有七年四月十三日黎明

Chapter twelve:
Coda: Floating World or Moving Image?

Previous page
Kokyo,
*Japanese Destroyer
Squadron Outside Port
Arthur* (detail of 246)

243
Henri Rivière,
The Painter in the Tower
from *The Thirty-Six Views
of the Eiffel Tower*,
1902.
Lithograph,
page: 17 x 20 cm
(6⅝ x 7⅞ in)

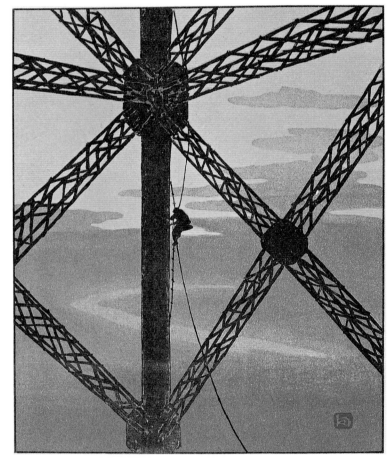

*Put Oriental Art entirely out of
your heads.*
John Ruskin, 1878

*Japan has been infected by the
western culture virus, and is losing
its fondness for admiring the moon,
picnics for flower viewing, and
meditations at tea ceremonies
in the industrial smog.*
Charlie Chaplin, 1935

As we have seen, the triumph of
Japonisme took place because it
was adopted more or less at the same
time by the most progressive artists
and designers in the closing years of
the nineteenth century. But, like all
fashionable vogues, its very popularity
soon led to it becoming distinctly
'outmoded'. Its influence still
continued, however, in the field
of book illustration, fashion and the
graphic arts. One of the minor marvels
of Japonisme is a series of prints by
Henri Rivière (1864–1951), entitled
The Thirty-Six Views of the Eiffel Tower,
compositions published in 1902 as
lithographs but first conceived as
woodcuts in the 1880s. Rivière first
encountered Japanese art through
seeing prints circulate at Rudolphe
Salis's famous cabaret, Le Chat Noir.
He became a habitué and joined the
staff working on the house journal and,
later, as stage director, ran the puppet
shadow theatre.

During his years at Le Chat Noir,
Rivière met the dealers in Japanese art,
Bing and Hayashi, and began to collect
prints himself. He also practised the
technique of cutting woodblocks,
mixing his own inks and using
Japanese paper on which to print. For
his act of homage to Hokusai's *Thirty-
Six Views of Mount Fuji* (*c*.1830–5),
however, Rivière used with great
sensitivity the medium of lithography
(243). Rivière's prints were published
not only as an explicit homage to
Hokusai's series but also as an ironic
comment on the permanence of the
controversial Eiffel Tower, built as a
'temporary' structure for the World
Exhibition of 1889, but which by 1902
had become a universally recognized
symbol of Paris. *The Eiffel Tower Under
Construction, Seen From the Trocadéro*
(244) reflects Rivière's special affinity
with the theme, while the shape of the
tower affectionately parodies the
flawless cone of the great volcano
and the Japanese woodcut technique
in the depiction of falling snow upon
the umbrellas of passers-by. All thirty-
six of Rivière's prints are not mere
pastiche but provide an informed
comment from a mid-point between
Eastern and Western art.

244
Henri Rivière,
*The Eiffel Tower Under
Construction, Seen From
the Trocadéro* from *The
Thirty-Six Views of the
Eiffel Tower*,
1902.
Lithograph,
page: 17 x 20 cm
(6⅝ x 7⅞ in)

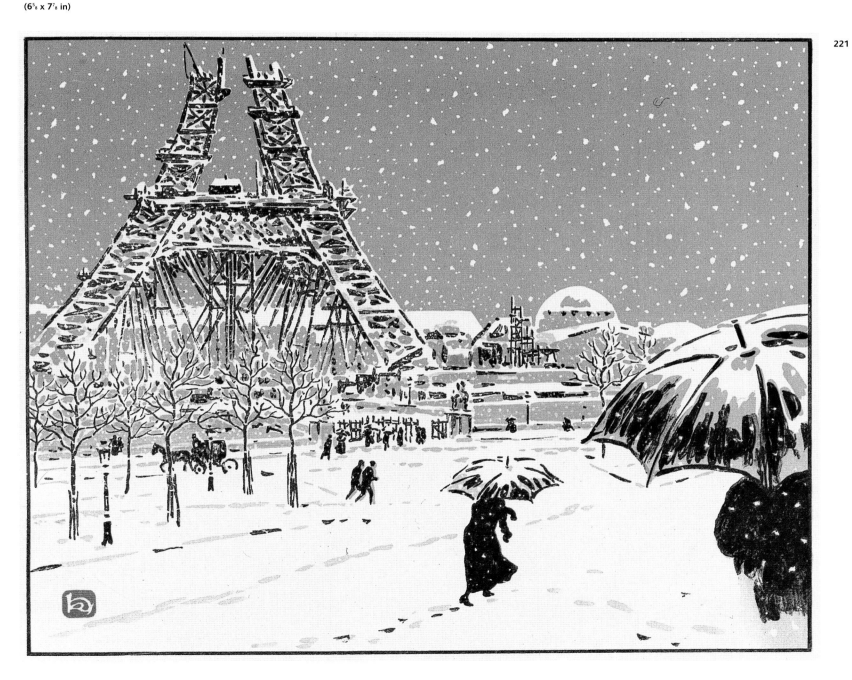

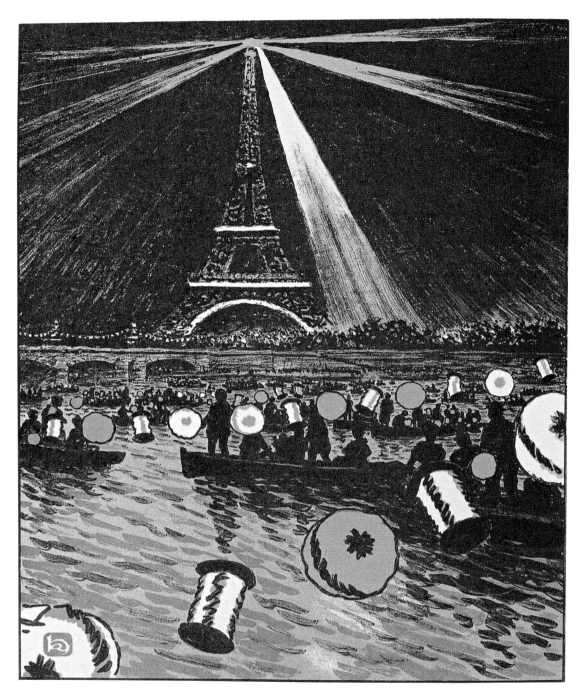

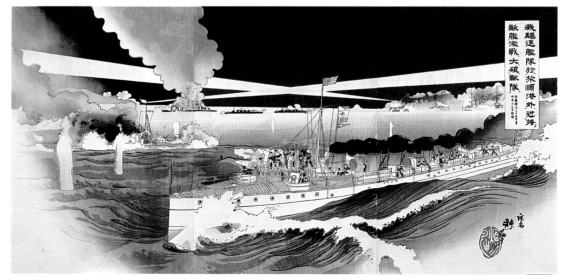

我驅逐艦隊於旅順港外迎撃
敵艦激戰大破敵隊

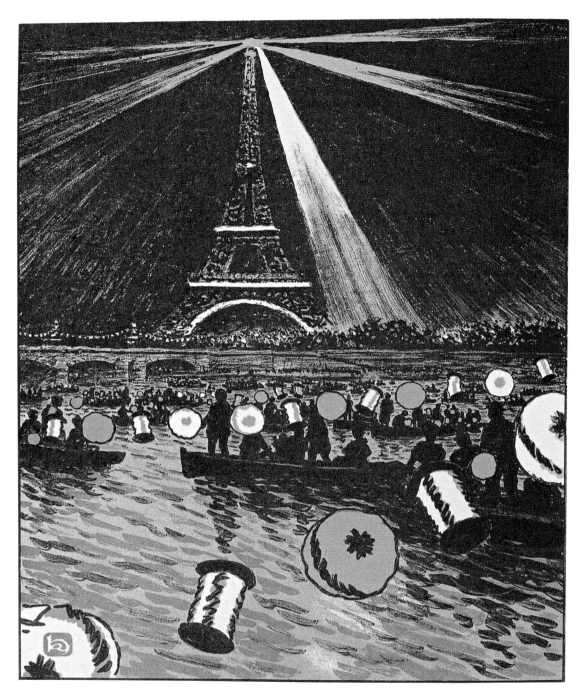

245
Henri Rivière,
*Celebrations on the
Seine, 14 July* from
*Thirty-Six Views of the
Eiffel Tower*,
1902.
Lithograph,
page: 17 x 20 cm
(6⅝ x 7⅞ in)

246
Kokyo,
*Japanese Destroyer
Squadron Outside
Port Arthur*,
1903.
Colour woodblock,
31·1 x 76·2 cm
(12¼ x 30 in)

Rivière shared with Hokusai a strong interest in the seasons, weather and the time of day and how these varying factors affect the human condition. These comparisons, or rather parallels, are strikingly conveyed in Rivière's depiction of the fireworks, Japanese lanterns and searchlights against the night sky in *Celebrations on the Seine, 14 July* (245). Rivière's lithograph showing the beams of intense light used in the celebratory display was published in 1902. Within a year searchlights would be depicted in military, not celebratory use, playing a part in one of the major events in the dreadnought race that involved the great powers at the turn of the century. Japan had become alarmed by the steady growth of the Russian presence in Manchuria, symbolized by the development of the Trans-Siberian Railway to Port Arthur, providing Russia with a supply route that could be used to take over Korea. This was seen as a territorial threat by Japan. Events escalated, a major incident taking place on 13 April 1903 when the Russian flagship was blown up by a Japanese destroyer. In Kokyo's print (246) the squadron ships are shown with their lights probing the night sky, revealing ships disabled by exploding torpedoes. Within a week of this event this triptych was for sale on the streets of Tokyo to a public avid for news. But the print marked the end of an era. New technology of mechanical photographic reproduction sounded the death knell of the popular woodblock print in both the East and the West.

Rivière's work, and the celebration in Paris of the Universal Exposition of 1900, marked the end of an era, but the old themes continued to work their magic. In 1905, Henri Matisse (1869–1954) painted a study of a woman beside water entitled *La Japonaise, Madame Matisse*. There is something reassuring, a sense of the continuity of artistic inspiration, that Matisse, the supreme decorative master of the twentieth century, should begin his career with a look back at the decorative art of the Japanese print.

In the world of high fashion, rather than that of avant-garde art, there was still inspiration to be gained from Japanese designs for fabrics. The old magical glamour continued to work when new fashionable dresses were worn by Sadayakko and reproduced in the pages of the fashion journal, *Femina* (see 168). Even the dislike of the young Picasso for Japanese subjects was overcome sufficiently for him to create four designs for a poster of her in a performance, although it does not seem to have been produced.

The needs of the fashion industry created a demand for Oriental themes far more wide-ranging in its borrowings than Japonisme. A list of the Oriental exhibitions held in Paris from 1900 to 1912 would take in every country in the East, creating vogue after vogue, crowned by a great Orientalist exhibition at the Grand Palais in 1909 which coincided with the triumphant arrival of the Ballets Russes. Although none of the new ballets had a Japanese subject, the great impresario Serge Diaghilev did start his career with a real appreciation of the subject. From 1899 to 1905 he ran a challenging magazine, *The World of Art*, published in St Petersburg in a large format and illustrated by black-and-white drawings. A large part of the February 1902 issue was devoted to the drawings of Hokusai and Hiroshige, somewhat incongruously accompanying long articles on Nietzsche, Dostoevsky and Tolstoy, followed by nine pages of drawings by Aubrey Beardsley, whom Diaghilev had met in Dieppe just before Beardsley died.

Although fashion was always changing, Japonisme would remain a constant factor to be reckoned with, whether on the catwalk, the potter's wheel or the cinema screen. In 1897, the Lumière brothers' representative, Gabriel Veyre, had made the first tentative short films in Japan of two or three minutes' duration.

Predictably, his first choice of subject for the new medium of film was *Geisha in a Jinrikisha* (247). Veyre also filmed such subjects as *Kendo Combat* (Japanese broad-stick fencing) and *Rain Dance of Spring*. Today in Kyoto, where many of the first Japanese films were made, the visitor can see a display in the city museum of a bank of videos showing excerpts from the period costume dramas which come so naturally to Japanese actors. The earliest clips date from the very turn of the nineteenth and twentieth centuries and they continue right up to present-day popular TV soap operas on period themes.

By 1925 the *kabuki*-orientated films of the early days of Japanese cinema had consciously changed into two genres that continue today, the *Jidai-geki* or period film set before 1868 (the year marking the beginning of the Meiji era), and the *gendai-geki* or film of contemporary life. The great success of Akira Kurosawa's films, such as *Rashomon* (1950) and *The Seven Samurai* (1954) owes much to these genres.

The Japanese cinema went through a much longer 'primitive' period than the cinemas of the West, for the perennial popularity of *kabuki* meant that the earliest Japanese films were versions of *kabuki* plays, of which there exist at least 350.

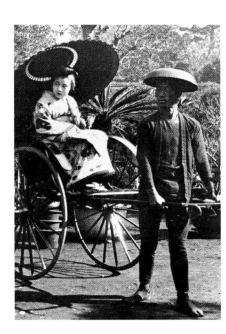

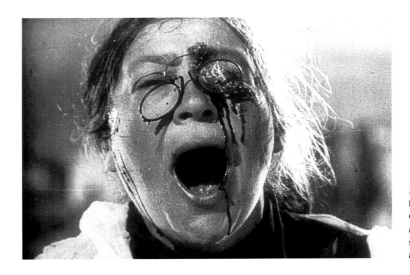

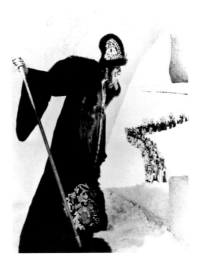

248
Eisenstein,
Old lady wearing *pince-nez*, broken by a bullet, still from *Battleship Potemkin*, 1925.

One *kabuki* convention – the use of *onnagata* professional female impersonators – was discarded in the 1920s, for it worked against any form of close-up photographic realism. However, another important convention was retained, that of the *benshi* – an actor-narrator who stands beside the stage (or screen) commentating on the action rather like the chorus in the Greek classical drama. As a result the introduction of sound in the 1930s was a much more gradual process in Japan than in the West.

The great Russian film director, Sergei Mikhailovich Eisenstein, first became interested in *kabuki* during the civil war when in 1920 he was sent back from active service at the front to study the Japanese language, the ideograms of which came to his mind later and played an important part in formulating his theories on montage and the swift flow of contrasting images. From this time Eisenstein began to collect Japanese prints, such as the close-up heads of *kabuki* actors by Sharaku (see 45). The convention of the frozen pose in an *otokodate* role had just the bold simplicity of outline which appealed to Eisenstein. In *Battleship Potemkin* in 1925 he elaborated his radically innovative theory of 'montage' (cutting) exemplified in one of the most famous film sequences ever made, the Odessa Steps.

In it Eisenstein combined close-ups of the action at decelerated camera speeds, and the frozen poses of such memorable subjects as the old lady wearing *pince-nez* which are broken by a bullet (248).

It was not, however, until August 1928, when the *kabuki* theatre visited Moscow, that Eisenstein enjoyed his first exciting experience of their acting, which he studied intently. His initial reaction was to compare the actors' performances with sportsmen:

The first association that occurs to us in our perception of the Kabuki is football, the most collective ensemble sport. Voice, rattle, mime, the narrator's cries, the folding sets, seem like innumerable backs, half-backs, goal-keepers forward passing the dramatic ball to one another and scoring a goal against the astonished audience.

The following year (1929) he published *Beyond the Shot (the Cinematographic Principle and Japanese Culture)*.

In 1941, nearing the end of his career, Eisenstein was commissioned to make a large-scale historical epic glorifying the sixteenth-century tyrant *Ivan the Terrible*. One of the most moving scenes in the film shows the grief-stricken Ivan retired to a provincial palace where he is petitioned to return to Moscow by his people. They form a long winding procession glimpsed by Ivan through slits in the castle wall (249).

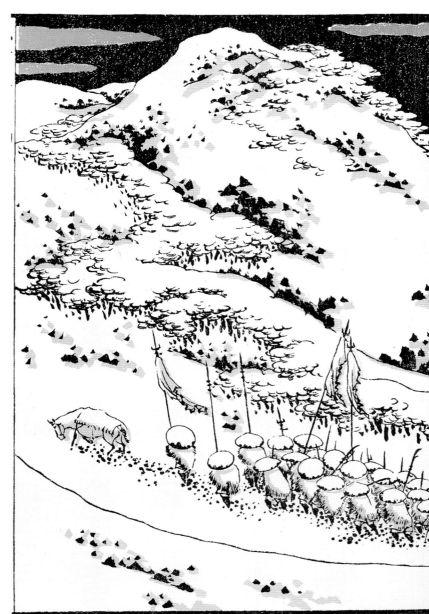

249
Eisenstein,
The masses arriving at
the mountain retreat of
Ivan, still from *Ivan the
Terrible Part I*, 1944.

250
Katsushika Hokusai,
*The Duke Huan Returning
His Army Home,
Following the Lead of an
Old Horse* from the
Manga,
1834.
Colour woodblock,
17·5 x 11·5 cm
(7 x 4½ in)

251
Akira Kurosawa,
still from *Rashomon*,
1950

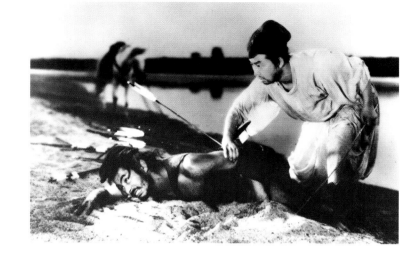

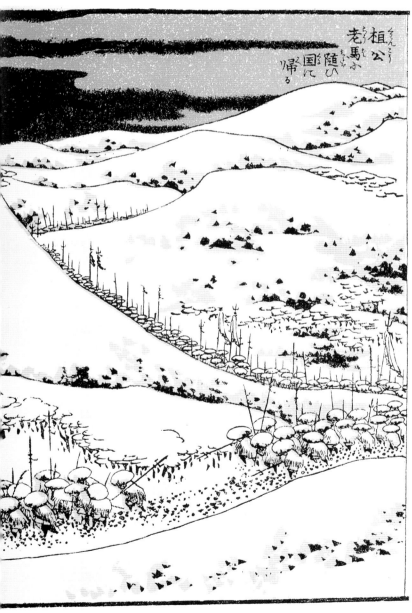

The sequence has an eerie resemblance to a double-page plate in the *Manga* depicting the Duke of Huan returning home with his army, following in the footsteps of an old riderless horse (250). The eagle-like profile of Ivan the Terrible recalls the bird of prey in Hiroshige's *Eagle over Fukugawa* (see 89). Yet again a print by Hiroshige and the magical bran-tub of Hokusai's sketches of things 'just as they come' had provided a major Western artist with direct inspiration.

The Japanese film director, Akira Kurosawa, started his career in the bellicose 1930s as a propaganda film-maker. In 1945, the last year of the war, he produced a film based on a *kabuki* drama and began to work on *Rashomon* (251). The worldwide fame of the film began with its success at the Venice Film Festival in 1951, where it won the Golden Lion of Venice award for best foreign film. It is difficult, half a century later, to realize how cut off from the outside world post-war Japan appeared. The country was still separated from the rest of the world by the events of World War II and the shadow of the atomic bomb's 'mushroom cloud'. Nothing of any artistic significance had emerged from Japan for some decades. The West, still fascinated by the Japanese legend, fell upon Kurosawa's epic with an enthusiasm that closely recalls the excitement with which their ancestors greeted the *Manga* a century earlier.

The film, set in medieval Japan, tells a story which, like Robert Browning's poem *The Ring and the Book*, deals with a murder and rape from the differing viewpoints of the principal characters in the drama. All the versions are different but which is the true one? One sequence in the film, in which the bandit kisses the victim while her eyes remain wide open, brought much criticism from Japanese audiences who accused Kurosawa of making films directed at Western audiences, a question to which he had replied, 'exoticism on its own isn't enough. I didn't think of being internationally famous: I just wanted to make good films.' This he went on to do with *The Seven Samurai* of 1958, with compelling characters who tell the story of an élite cadre of brave and heroic mercenaries who are hired by a village to protect them from bandits. The mercenaries' bravery is contrasted with the cowardly conduct of the civilians who pay them for their defence. For the concluding scene in the film, the battle between the samurai and bandits, Kurosawa created a montage sequence that rivals the massacre in *Battleship Potemkin*.

The American director, John Sturges, saw *The Seven Samurai* and realized that its story was as exciting as a good Western, and remade the film in Hollywood as *The Magnificent Seven* in 1960.

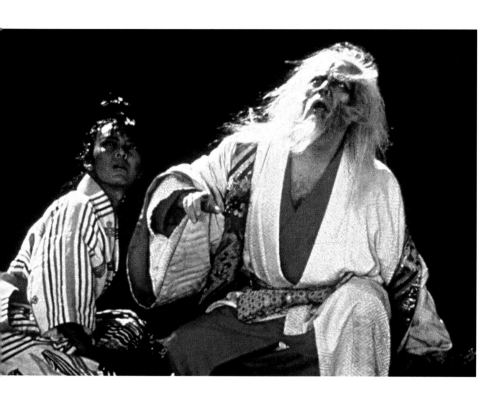

Such borrowings were by no means all one way and, in tracing the following chain of events, it is intriguing to discover that Shinobu Hashimoto, the scriptwriter of both *Rashomon* and *The Seven Samurai*, admitted that John Ford's *Stagecoach* (1939) was his favourite film.

The Magnificent Seven was just one of several Hollywood Westerns which reflect the influence of Japanese samurai films with their emphasis on violence, loyalty and heroic death. Their popular success when remade by Hollywood ultimately spawned the 'Spaghetti Western' – violent films of the American West, starring American actors and shot for economic reasons in Italy, Spain and Yugoslavia. A classic example of a film of this type was Sergio Leone's *A Fistful of Dollars*, a painstaking shot-by-shot copy of Kurosawa's *Yojimbo* of 1961. *Rashomon* also could not escape the copying process, being insensitively remade in a 1964 Hollywood Western, *The Outrage*, starring Paul Newman, and again as *Iron Maze* in 1991, a US/Japanese version set in Pittsburgh. Several other films that Kurosawa made as tributes to American genres were remade yet again in Hollywood with varying results.

Today when watching these plagiarisms we recall Pierre-Auguste Renoir's prophecy which he made of prints but is equally applicable to films:

Japanese prints are certainly very interesting as Japanese prints in other words as long as they stay in Japan … people should not appropriate what belongs to another race; in so doing they are apt to make stupid mistakes. There would be soon a kind of universal art, without any individual characteristics.

Two of Kurosawa's finest films have Shakespearean themes: *Throne of Blood* (1957), a version of *Macbeth*, and *Ran* (1985; 252), literally *Chaos*, a version of *King Lear*, transposed to medieval Japan and described by Kurosawa as 'Human deeds as viewed from heaven'. In *Ran*, Lear's daughters are replaced by three sons but the fool is retained. Chaos reigns in powerful stylized battle scenes as brother wages war upon brother. Kurosawa spent ten years raising the money for the film and was 75-years old when he made it. While admired in the West as a master, in Japan Kurosawa is still merely regarded as a commercial film-maker.

The continuing interrelationship between East and West in the field of the cinema, the great visual art form of today, could equally be found in other disciplines. In examining such exchanges we can put into proper perspective the questions raised by Japonisme of the late nineteenth century and the process of borrowing, plagiarism or reinterpretation which still continues today.

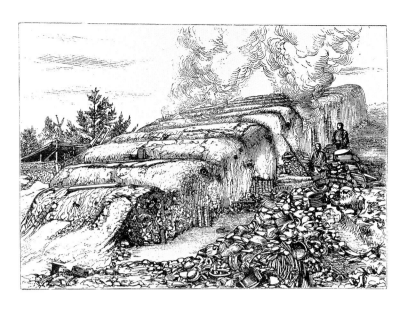

253
Christopher Dresser,
Climbing Kilns, from
*Traditional Arts and
Crafts of Japan*,
1882

254
Bernard Leach,
Vase decorated with
leaping fish,
c.1965.
Stoneware,
height: 36·1 cm (14⅛ in).
Private collection

Since Whistler's demise, butterflies had found a different resting place with an artist such as Redon adding his own delicate colours to their wings. They had lost none of the magical powers of inspiration for Redon, who only took up the use of colour in his late middle age. As a theme for poetry they appealed to the Imagist poets, on whom Japanese themes still continued to cast a spell. Poets such as Ezra Pound and Amy Lowell experimented with the Japanese verse forms, the *Tanka* and the *Haiku*, with powerful and prophetic effect:

*On a Temple Bell
A tiny butterfly is settled
Upon a massive temple bell
Asleep.*

*Perched upon the muzzle of a cannon
A yellow butterfly is slowly opening
and shutting its wings.*

'I think without doubt that the Japanese are the most pottery-minded people in the whole world,' wrote Bernard Leach in the introduction to an exhibition:

We were not folk potters, nor were we simple country folk, like those who had made the best English medieval pots (or their counterparts in the Far East) – we were artist potters and, as such, our horizons had begun to be all horizons.

Bernard Leach is here describing his years with the Japanese potter, Hamada, whose own terse précis of similar thoughts reads, 'beauty is not in the head or heart, but in the abdomen.' Together in England and Japan the two men did more than anyone else to prove that although Japonisme as a fashionable craze was over, the dual aesthetic disciplines of Britain and Japan had still much to contribute to each other.

Leach, like William Morris before him, was one of those protean figures who is almost more important for what he represents than for his actual productions. Born in China in 1887, Leach was educated in England, a circumstance which enabled him to write, 'having these two extremes of culture to draw upon caused me to return to Japan, where the synthesis of East and West has gone farthest.' Aged twenty-one, attracted by the writing of Lafcadio Hearn, he went out to Japan, and remained there and in Beijing for eleven years, studying stoneware and going through full-time training as a potter under Kenzan Ogata VI, before returning to England in 1920. With Hamada he set up some traditional Japanese climbing kilns (the first to be made in the Western hemisphere; 253) at St Ives in Cornwall, the famous artists' colony.

The Leach kiln consisted of several chambers. The heat from the fire passed through the first chamber and into the second where it ignited extra wood to boost its heat level. This happened in each chamber until the last, which contained ware for biscuit firing. In 1936 he built more kilns at Dartington Hall in Devon. Leach's practice was based on an attitude to the craftsman's role which echoed Morris's views, combined with a sensitivity to materials that came from the traditional Japanese potter's search for aesthetic purity of form. For some time he continued to produce stoneware in the Japanese manner (254) before turning his attention to the English slipware tradition. When he died in 1979 at the age of ninety-two he had done more to interest the public at large in pottery than any other man, by his work, teaching and books, in particular his guide to the practical and aesthetic experience of pottery, *A Potter's Book*. Leach had become, like Morris, a legend in his own lifetime. As he remarked in 1968:

all my life I have been a courier between East and West. I believe in the interplay and marriage of the two complementary branches of human culture as the prelude to the unity and maturity of man.

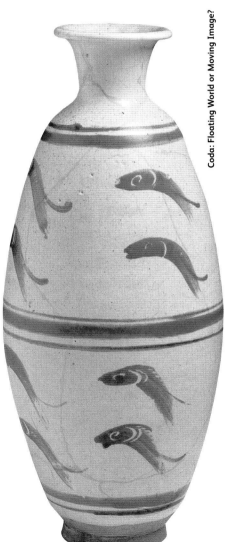

255
Cecil Beaton,
'Sandwich' men
advertising a samurai
film from *Japanese*,
published by Weidenfeld
& Nicolson, 1959

His views on what makes a good pot he once summarized as:

curves for beauty, angles for stability. A small foot for grace, a broad one for stability. Enduring forms are full of quiet assurance. Overstatement is worse than understatement. Technique is a means to an end. It is no end in itself.

In his last years Bernard Leach's failing eyesight shielded him from the electronic cybernetic age and such strange artistic phenomena as the arrival of 'Japan Animation' and 'Techno Orientalism'. In the eyes of the West, Japan became the new Cyburg, a theme closely identified with the name of Osamu Tezuka (1928–89), whose science fiction led to the glorification of the robot, now seen in many fields and perceived as an object of both fascination and fear. Robots now manifest themselves in the sinister science-fiction world of Pokemon, popular not only in Japan but globally.

A much more reassuring development of cultural affinities between the East and West was provided by the composer Benjamin Britten, who in 1957 made an extensive tour of the Far East to study the musical instru-ments of different lands and visited Japan, where he heard *samisen* recitals by geisha and a *gagaku* orchestra whose reverberating sounds led him to declare, 'Oh! To find some equivalent to those extraordinary noises the Japanese musicans made!'

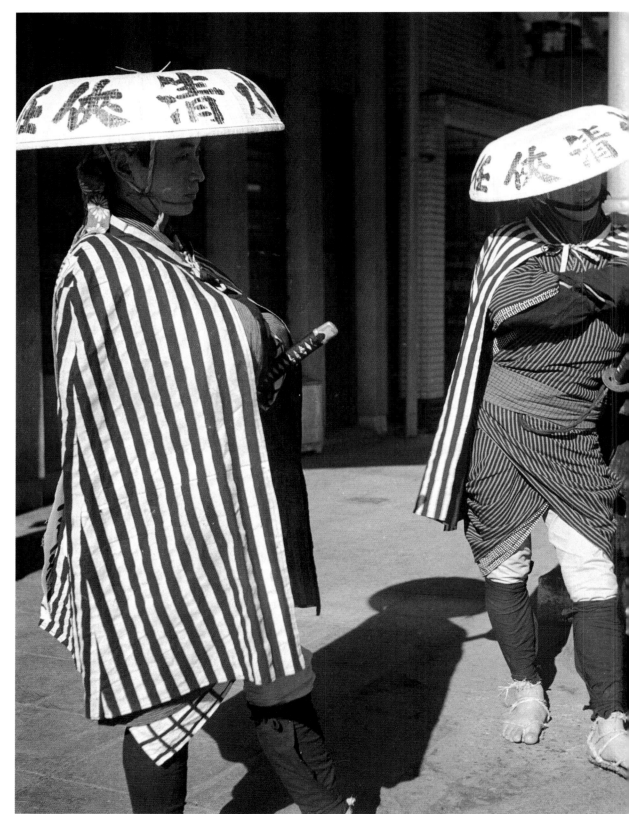

256
**Cecil Beaton,
Front cover design of
Japanese, published by
Weidenfeld & Nicolson,
1959**

On his return to England, acting on the advice of his librettist William Plomer, Britten used a Japanese libretto based upon a *noh* play he admired, entitled *Sumida Gawa* (*Sumida River*), in one of his three Church Parables. The result was a haunting work entitled *Curlew River*. Britten also used Japanese instruments and themes in his music for the choreographer John Cranko's ballet *The Prince of the Pagodas*, also written in 1957.

The name of Cecil Beaton (1904–80) has become virtually synonymous with glamour and high fashion, but he also had an amazing eye for the landscape, people and customs of foreign lands, which he put to good use when touring China, Egypt and India in the 1940s as a war correspondent. In 1959 just over a century after Wirgman's first European *ad vivum* studies of the daily life of Japan, Beaton followed his lead and visited Japan, commissioned by the American magazine, *Harper's Bazaar*. Both his camera and his pen created some of his finest landscapes and also captured the dramatic essence of *noh* and *kabuki* performances.

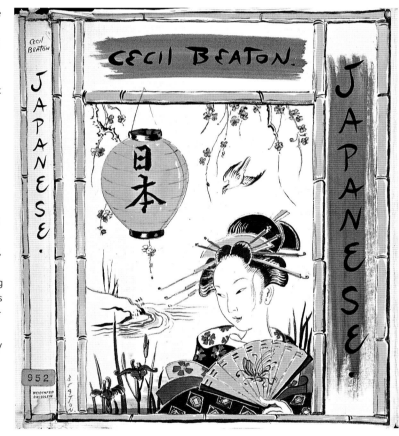

On the streets his eye noted 'sandwich' men lounging at a street corner, 'their salad-bowl hats and striped cloaks advertising the latest film' (255), and also shrines, tea ceremonies and contemporary writers, such as the dramatist and dandy, Mishima, whose ritual suicide shocked the nation in the 1960s. For Beaton:

Japan is in some respects like England. Both are island nations; both have a terrible climate. Both have traditions they are proud of, traditions that can be a glory but also an anachronistic curse in a world where time never stands still.

Whether using the camera lens or a brush, Beaton's genius resulted in a highly personal interpretation of the country. On the cover of his book *Japanese* he portrayed such pictorial clichés as trailing wisteria, irises, rocks and water, lanterns, a geisha – all subjects which when treated by less skillful hands teeter on the edge of kitsch, but which Beaton could make into unforgettable images (256).

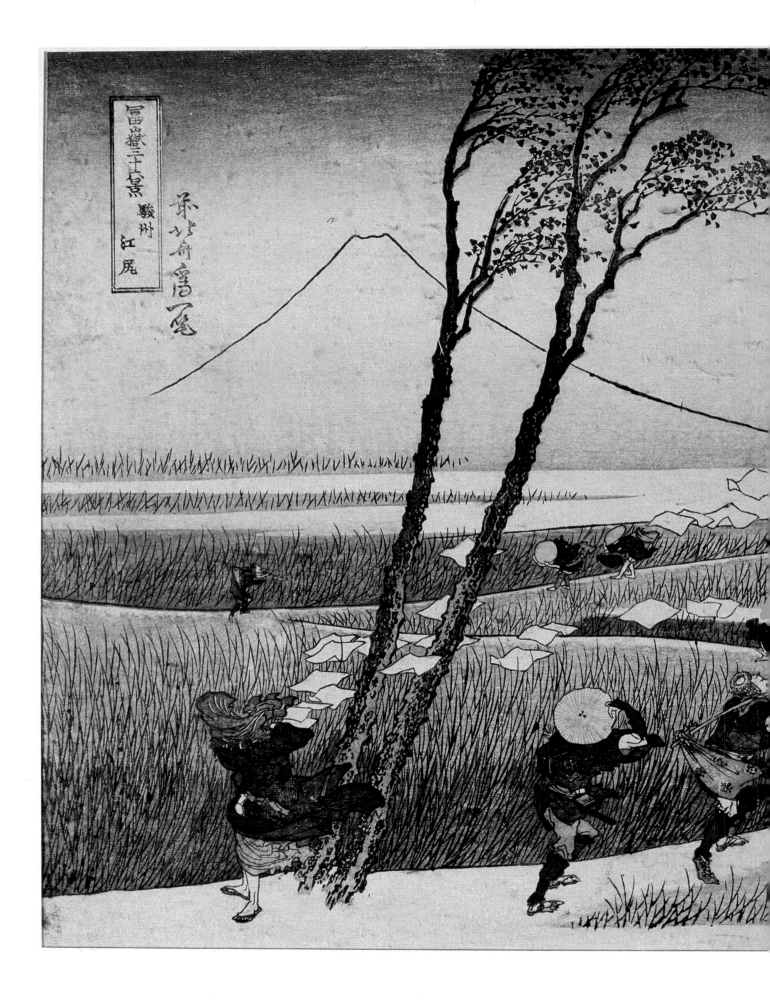

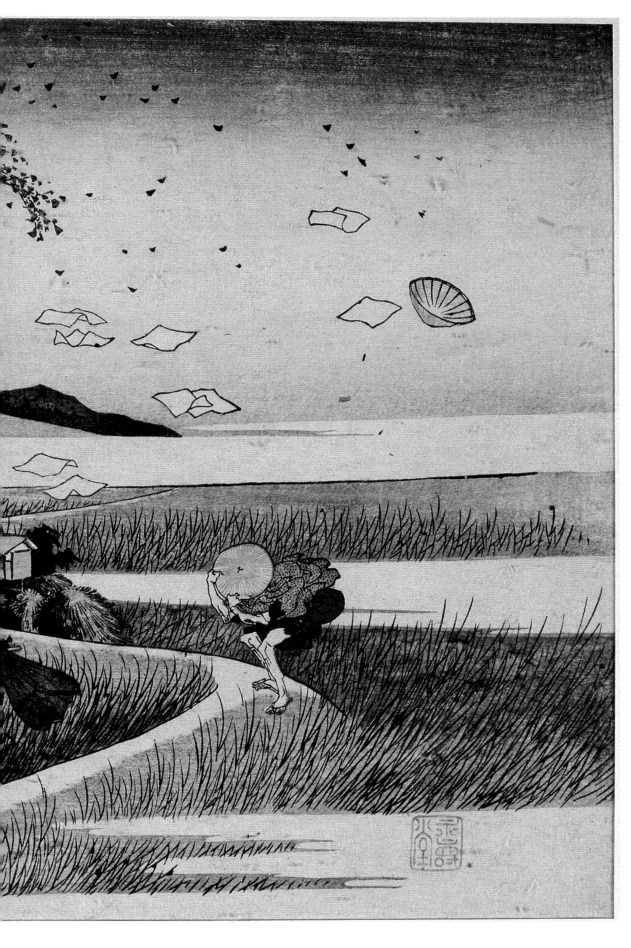

257
Katsushika Hokusai,
*A Sudden Gust of Wind
at Ejiri,* **from the series**
*Thirty-Six Views of
Mount Fuji,*
*c.*1830–2.
Colour woodblock,
25·7 x 38 cm
(10⅛ x 15 in)

Today it is just over 150 years since the arrival in Japan of Perry and the black ships in Edo (see Chapter 1). Although so long ago, the old magic continues to give inspiration, notably in the work of the Canadian artist, Jeff Wall (b.1946). Using the landscape just outside Vancouver in British Columbia, Wall creates a vibrant photographic collage based upon Hokusai's print *A Sudden Gust of Wind at Ejiri* from the series *Thirty-Six Views of Mount Fuji* (257, 258). In both pictures the wind playfully snatches at the paper handkerchiefs which have escaped from the kimono worn by the lady with a headscarf. Free as air they fly skywards to join the dancing leaves and an escaped hat.

A wind from the East still continues to blow …

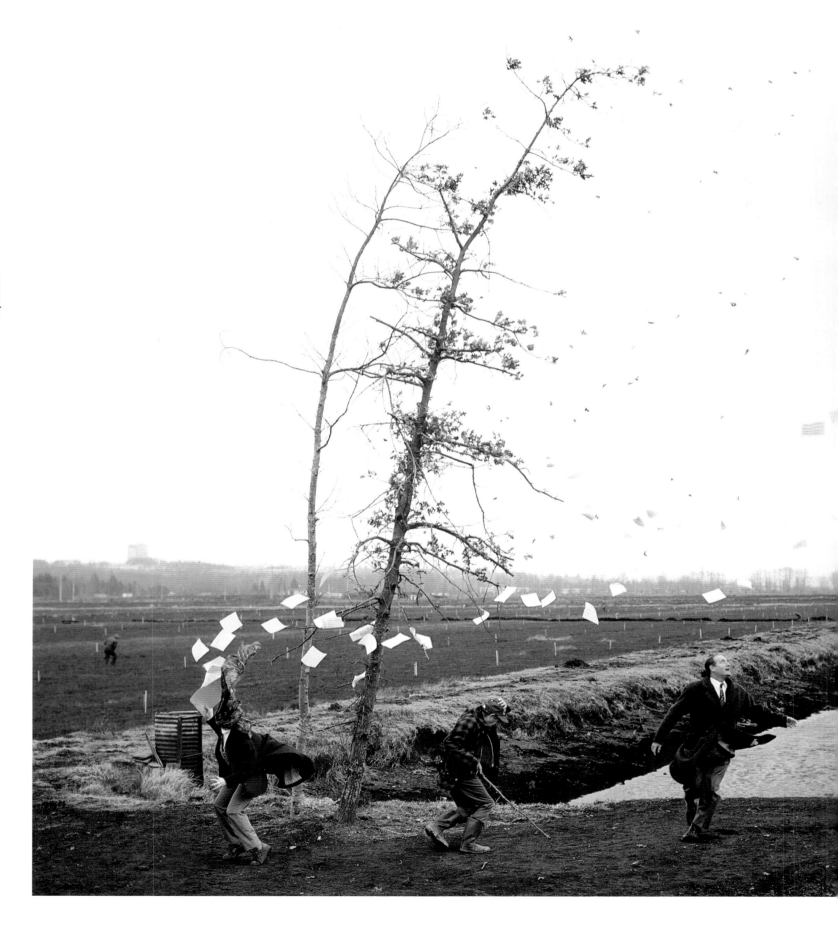

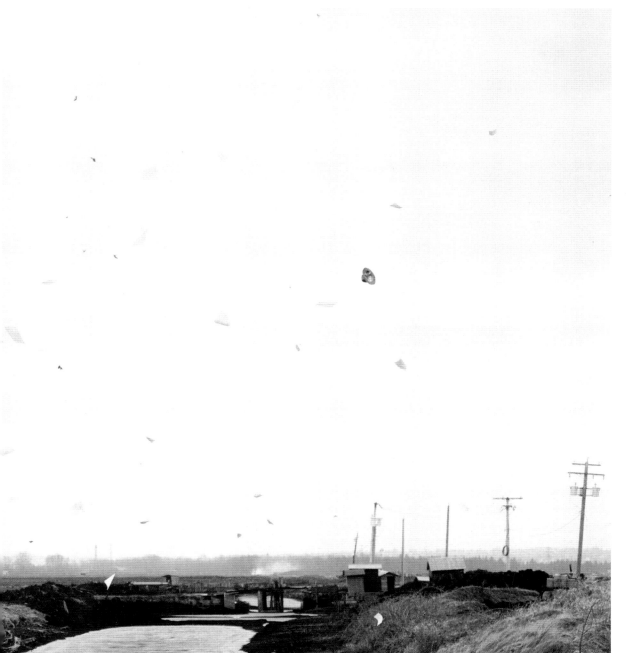

258
Jeff Wall,
A Sudden Gust of Wind
(after Hokusai),
1993.
Photographic
transparency and
illuminated display case,
250 x 397 x 34 cm
(98¹₂ x 156¹₄ x 13³₈ in).
Tate Collection, London

For Maureen

I would like to thank the following for their advice over the years: Stephen Calloway, Richard Dennis, Amanda Jane Doran, the late Albert Gallichan, Peter Rose and Peyton Skipwith. Catherine Haill of the Theatre Museum shared with me her knowledge of Gilbert and Sullivan, and Ann Leane her love of fans, while Tomoko Sato gave encouragement and the long-term loan of books. Joan Navarre pointed out the interesting literary phenomenon of earlier versions of the Madame Butterfly story by American writers. In Alsace, Beatrix and Michael Everett were admirable guides to the Théodore Deck Collection, Guebwiller. In Leiden, Chris and Nellie Smeenk introduced me to Matthi Forrer, who showed me the riches of the Ethnology Museum at a very busy time. At Phaidon Press, Bernard Dod faced the strain of editing yet another book by me with equanimity. His colleagues, Beulah Davies, Maya Gartner, Sophia Gibb and Susannah Stone also kindly coped with my aesthetic demands.

Bibliography

Adburgham, Alison. Liberty's: A Biography of a Shop. London, 1975
Alcock, Sir Rutherford. The Capital of the Tycoon. 2 vols. London, 1863
Applebaum, Stephen (ed.). The Complete Masters of the Poster. New York, 1990
Asleson, Robyn. Albert Moore. London, 2000
Aslin, Elizabeth. The Aesthetic Movement: Prelude to Art Nouveau. London, 1969
Aslin, Elizabeth. E W Godwin: Furniture and Interior Decoration. London, 1986
Baily, Leslie. The Gilbert and Sullivan Book. London, 1952
Baldry, A L. Albert Moore: His Life and Work. London, 1894
Beardsley, Aubrey. 'The Art of the Hoarding', in The New Review. July, 1894
Beardsley, Aubrey. The Letters of Aubrey Beardsley. Maas, Duncan and Good (eds). London, 1971
Beaton, Cecil. Japanese. London, 1959
Beckson, Karl E. Aesthetes and Decadents of the 1890s: An Anthology of British Poetry and Prose. New York, 1966
Beerbohm, Sir Max. Rossetti and His Circle. London, 1922
Blussé, Leonard, Willem Remmelink and Ivo Smits (eds). Bridging the Divide: 400 Years The Netherlands – Japan. Amsterdam, 2000
Budden, Julian. Puccini: His Life and Works. Oxford, 2002
Burty, Philippe. Japonisme. Paris, 1875
Calloway, Stephen. Charles Ricketts. London, 1979
Carner, M. Puccini: A Critical Biography. London, 1992
Carr, Mrs J. Comyns. Comyns Carr's Reminiscences. London, 1926
Chesneau, E. 'Le Japon a Paris', in Gazette des Beaux-Arts, 1879
Cook, Clarence. The House Beautiful: Essays on Beds and Tables, Stools and Candlesticks. New York, 1895
Cooper, Emmanuel. Bernard Leach: Life and Work. New Haven and London, 2003

Cooper, Nicholas. The Opulent Eye: Late Victorian and Edwardian Taste in Interior Design. London, 1976
Crane, Lucy. Art and the Formation of Taste. London, 1882
Crane, Walter. An Artist's Reminiscences. London, 1907
Crane, Walter. William Morris to Whistler. London, 1911
Crauzat, Ernest de. L'Oeuvre gravé et lithographié de Steinlen. Paris, 1913
Crawford, T S. A History of the Umbrella. London, 1970
Dalby, Liza Crihfield. Geisha. London, 2001
Dalby, Liza Crihfield. Kimono. London, 2000
Downer, Lesley. Madame Sadayakko: The Geisha who Seduced the West. London, 2003
Dresser, Dr Christopher. Japan, its Architecture, Art and Art Manufactures. London, 1882
Dresser, Dr Christopher. Traditional Arts and Crafts of Japan. London, 1882, reprinted London and New York, 1994
Eastlake, C L. Hints on Household Taste in Furniture, Upholstery and Other Details. London, 1867
Ellmann, Richard. Oscar Wilde. London, 1987
Ferriday, Peter. 'The Peacock Room', in Architectural Review, CXXV, 1959, pp 407–14
Fletcher, Ian. Romantic Mythologies. London, 1967
Fletcher, Ian. Walter Pater. London, 1959
Floyd, P. Seeking the Floating World: The Japanese Spirit in Turn of the Century France. Toyko, 1989
Franklin, Colin. The Private Presses. Aldershot, 1969
French, Calvin L. Shiba Kokan: Artist, Innovator, and Pioneer in the Westernization of Japan. New York, 1974
Fry, Roger. Vision and Design. London, 1920
Gaunt, William. The Aesthetic Adventure. London, 1945
Gillespie, John K. and Yoichi Sugiura. Traditional Japanese Culture and Modern Japan. Tokyo, 1993
Girouard, M. Sweetness and Light: The 'Queen Anne' Movement 1860–1900. Oxford, 1977
Golden, Arthur. Memoirs of a Geisha. London, 1997
de Goncourt, Edmond and Jules. The Goncourt Journals 1851–1896. A complete scholarly edition appeared between 1956–9 and various selections have since been published.
Goodman, Andrew. Gilbert and Sullivan's London. London, 2000
Grossmith, George and Weedon. The Diary of a Nobody. First published as a serial in Punch, 1888. First published as a book with Weedon's illustrations in London, 1892.
Haill, Catherine. Fun without Vulgarity. London, 1996
Halen, Widar. Christopher Dresser: A Pioneer of Modern Design. London, 1990
Hamilton, James. Arthur Rackham. London, 1990
Hamilton, Walter. The Aesthetic

Movement in England. London, 1882
Harbron, Dudley. The Conscious Stone: The Life of Edward William Godwin. London, 1949
Hardwick, Michael. Discovery of Japan. London, 1970
Hart-Davis, R (ed.). The Letters of Oscar Wilde. London, 1962
Hart-Davis, R (ed.). More Letters of Oscar Wilde. London, 1985
Haslam, Malcolm. The Martin Brothers: Potters. London, 1978
Haweis, Mrs H R. The Art of Beauty. London, 1878
Haweis, Mrs H R. The Art of Decoration. London, 1881
Haweis, Mrs H R. Beautiful Houses. London, 1882
Heneage, Simon and Henry Ford. Sidney Syme: Master of the Mysterious. London, 1980
Herries, Amanda. Japanese Gardens in Britain. Princes Risborough, 2001
Hiatt, Charles. Picture Posters. London, 1895
Hillier, Bevis. Posters. London, 1969
Hobbs, Richard. Odilon Redon. London, 1977
Holland, Merlin and Rupert Hart-Davis (eds). The Complete Letters of Oscar Wilde. London, 2000
Hornung, Clarence P (ed.). Will Bradley: His Graphic Art. New York, 1974
Hutt, Julia and Alexander, Hélene. Ogi: A History of the Japanese Fan. London, 1992
Huysmans, J-K. Against Nature. 1884. Robert Baldick (trans.), Harmondsworth, 1959
Jacquier, Phillippe and Marion Pranal. Gabriel Veyre, Opérateur Lumière. Arles, 1996
John, N (ed.). Madama Butterfly, English National Opera Guide, No. 26. London, 1984
Kouwenhoven, Arlette and Matthi Forrer. Siebold and Japan: His Life and Work. Leiden, 2000
Lambourne, Lionel. The Aesthetic Movement. London, 1996
Lane, Richard. Masters of the Japanese Print: Their World and their Work. London, 1962
Luckhurst, Kenneth W. The Story of Exhibitions. London, 1951
Meech, Julia. Frank Lloyd Wright and the Art of Japan: The Architect's Other Passion. New York and London, 2001
Meech, Julia. Rain and Snow: The Umbrella in Japanese Art. New York, 1993
Merrill, Linda. A Pot of Paint: Aesthetics on Trial in Whistler v. Ruskin. Washington, DC, and London, 1992
Merrill, Linda. The Peacock Room: A Cultural Biography. Washington, DC, and London, 1998
Michener, James A. The Floating World. London, 1955
Michener, James A. The Hokusai Sketch Books: Selections from the Manga. Tokyo and Rutland, VT, 1958
Milner, John. Symbolists and Decadents. London, 1971
Milner, John. The Studios of Paris: The Capital of Art in the Nineteenth Century. London and New Haven, 1988
Omoto, Keiko and Francis Macouin. Quand le Japon s'ouvrit au monde: Émile

Guimet et les arts d'Asie. Paris, 2001
Ono, Ayako. Japonisme in Britain. London, 2003
Page, Jesse. Japan: Its People and its Missions. London, 1896
Pennell, Elizabeth and Joseph. The Life of James McNeill Whistler. 2 vols. London and Philadelphia, 1908
Pevsner, Sir Nikolaus. Studies in Art, Architecture and Design: Vol II Victorian and After. London, 1968
Quennell, Peter (ed.). Marcel Proust, 1871–1922. A Centenary Volume. London, 1971
Rossetti, W M. 'Japanese Woodcuts', in The Reader. 31 October, 1863
Reade, Brian. Aubrey Beardsley. Woodbridge, 1987
Reade, Brian. Sexual Heretics: Male Homosexuality in English Literature from 1850–1900. London, 1970
Ricketts, Charles. Recollections of Oscar Wilde. London, 1932
Rothenstein, William. Men and Memories: Recollections of William Rothenstein. London, 1931
Salwey, Charlotte M. Fans of Japan. 1894
Sansom, William. Proust and His World. London, 1973
Screech, Timon. Sex and the Floating World: Erotic Images in Japan 1700–1820. London, 1999
Soros, Susan (ed.). E W Godwin: Aesthetic Movement Architect and Designer. New Haven and London, 1999
Spencer, Isobel. Walter Crane. London, 1975
Spencer, Robin. The Aesthetic Movement: Theory and Practice. London and New York, 1972
Sturgis, Matthew. Aubrey Beardsley: A Biography. London, 1999
Sutton, Denys. Nocturne: The Art of James McNeill Whistler. London, 1963
Swinburne, Algernon Charles. Poems and Ballads. London, 1866
Taylor, Hilary. James McNeill Whistler. London, 1978
Taylor, Ina. The Art of Kate Greenaway: A Nostalgic Portrait of Childhood. Exeter, 1991
Thiébaut, Philippe and Fumi Yosano. Les dessins de Gallé: Emile Gallé et ses ateliers. Tokyo, 1988
Watkins, Nicholas. Bonnard. London, 1994
Watson, Oliver. Studio Pottery. London, 1993
Whistler, J M. The Gentle Art of Making Enemies. London, 1890, reprinted New York, 1967
White, Colin. The Enchanted World of Jesse M King. Edinburgh, 1989
Wichmann, Siegfried. Japonisme: The Japanese Influence on Western Art Since 1858. London, 1981
Wordell, Charles B. Japan in American Fiction, 1880–1905. Bristol, 2001
Yamada, Chisaburoh F (ed.). Dialogue in Art: Japan and the West. London, 1976
Young, Andrew McLaren, Margaret F MacDonald, Robin Spencer and Hamish Miles. The Paintings of James McNeill Whistler. 2 vols. New Haven and London, 1980

Exhibition Catalogues

In recent years much of the most rewarding research into Japonisme has been published in the form of increasingly weighty exhibition catalogues.

Art Nouveau. Museum of Modern Art, New York, 1960
Becker, Vivienne. The Jewellery of Rene Lalique. Goldsmiths' Company, London, 1987
Burke, Doreen Bolger. In Pursuit of Beauty: Americans and the Aesthetic Movement. Metropolitan Museum of Art, New York, 1986
Bury, Shirley (ed.). Liberty's, 1875–1975. Victoria and Albert Museum, London, 1975
Catalogue of the Van Gogh Museum's Collection of Japanese Prints. Van Gogh Museum, Amsterdam, 1991
Ceramiques: Théodore Deck (1823–1891). Musée du Florival, Guebwiller. 1991
Chrighton, R A. The Floating World: Japanese Popular Prints, 1700–1900. Victoria and Albert Museum, London, 1973
Christie, Ian, and David Elliot (eds). Eisenstein at Ninety. Museum of Modern Art, Oxford, 1988
The Dawn of the Floating World 1650–1765: Early Ukiyo-e Treasures from the Museum of Fine Arts, Boston. Museum of Fine Arts, Boston, and Royal Academy of Arts, London, 2001
Dorment, Richard and Margaret F MacDonald. James McNeill Whistler. Tate Gallery, London, 1994
Druick, Douglas W and Peter Kort Zegers. Van Gogh and Gauguin: The Studio of the South. The Art Institute of Chicago and Van Gogh Museum, Amsterdam, 2002
Faulkner, Rupert. Hiroshige Fan Prints. Victoria and Albert Museum, London, 2001
Farrer, Anne (ed.). A Garden Bequest – Plants from Japan. The Japan Society, London, 2001
Farrington, Anthony. Trading Places; The East India Company and Asia 1600–1834. British Library, London, 2002
Forrer, Matthi. Hokusai: Prints and Drawings. Royal Academy of Arts, London, 1991
The Great Japan Exhibition: Art of the Edo Period 1600–1868. Royal Academy of Arts, London, 1981–2
Hamilton, Vivien. Joseph Crawhall 1861–1913. Glasgow Museums and Art Galleries and The Fine Art Society, London, 1990
Hayes Tucker, Paul. Monet in the '90s: The Series Paintings. Museum of Fine Arts, Boston, and Royal Academy of Arts, London, 1989
Ives, Colta Fella. The Great Wave: The Influence of Japanese Woodcuts on French Prints. Metropolitan Museum of Art, New York, 1974
Japan und Europa 1543–1929. Berliner Festspiele 1993
Japanese Amazement: Shiba Kokan 1747–1818. Artist under the Spell

of the West. Historisch Museum, Amsterdam
Le Japonisme. Grand Palais, Paris, and National Museum of Western Art, Tokyo, 1988
Japonisme Mode. Palais Galliera, Paris, 1996
Jervis, Simon. Art and Design in Europe and America 1800–1900. Victoria and Albert Museum, London, 1987
Komanecky, Michael and Virginia Fabbri Butera. The Folding Image: Screens by Western Artists. National Gallery of Art, Washington, DC, and Yale University Art Gallery, New Haven, 1984
Mackenzie, John M. The Victorian Vision. Victoria and Albert Museum, London, 2001
Matyjaszkiewicz, Krystyna (ed.). James Tissot. Barbican Art Gallery, London, 1984
Musée des Tissus de Lyons, Guide des Collections. Lyon, 1988
Monet and Japan. National Gallery of Australia, Canberra, and Art Gallery of Western Australia, Perth, 2001
The New Painting: Impressionism 1874–1886. Fine Arts Museums, San Francisco, and National Gallery of Art, Washington, DC, 1986
Reade, Brian Edmund. Art Nouveau and Alphonse Mucha. Victoria and Albert Museum, London, 1963
Reade, Brian Edmund. Aubrey Beardsley. Victoria and Albert Museum, London, 1966
Rivière Henri. Les trente-six vues de la tour Eiffel. New Otani Art Museum, Tokyo, 1989
Sato, Tomoko and Toshio Watanabe (eds). Japan and Britain: An Aesthetic Dialogue 1850–1930. Barbican Art Gallery, London, and Setagaya Art Museum, Tokyo, 1991
Smith, Lawrence (ed.). Ukiyoe: Images of Unknown Japan. British Museum, London, 1988
Soros, Susan (ed.) E W Godwin. Bard Graduate Center for Studies in the Decorative Arts, New York, 1999
Spencer, Robin. The Aesthetic Movement and the Cult of Japan. The Fine Art Society, London, 1972
Toulouse-Lautrec. Hayward Gallery, London, and Grand Palais, Paris, 1991–2
Wichmann, Siegfried (ed.). World Cultures and Modern Art: The Encounter of 19th and 20th century European Art and Music with Asia, Africa, Oceania, Afro- and Indo-America. Haus der Junst and Organisationskomitee für die Spiele der XX Olympiade, Munich, 1972
Yonemura, Ann. Yokohama: Prints from Nineteenth-Century Japan. Smithsonian Institution, Washington, DC, 1990

Picture Credits

akg-images: photo Susan Held: 208
Arcaid: photo Alan Weintraub: 201
Art Archive: British Museum, London: 187, Museo de Art Antoga, Lisbon: ch. op. 1, Museo Nacional de Soares dos Reis, Porto: 2
Artothek: 132
Ashmolean Museum, Oxford: 82, 134
Bridgeman Art Library, London: 10, 128, 146, 153, 182, 185, 190, 233
British Library, London: 210
British Museum, London: 5, 8, 230
Bröhan Museum, Berlin: photo Hans-Joachim Bartsch: 86
The Burrell Collection, Glasgow: 183
Calouste Gulbenkian Museum, Lisbon: 152
Chicago Historical Society, Chicago: 200
Christie's Images Ltd: 145
Courtauld Institute of Art Gallery, London: 195
Davison Art Center Collection: photo: R J Phil: 138
Richard Dennis: 74–9
Dixon Gallery and Gardens, Memphis, Tennessee: 133
Fine Arts Museums of San Francisco: ch. op. 11, 224
Freer Gallery of Art, Smithsonian Institution, Washington, DC: 21, Gift of Charles Lang Freer: 1
Glasgow Picture Library, Glasgow School of Art: 127
Hornby Library, Liverpool: 1, 137
Hunterian Art Gallery, University of Glasgow: 115, 116, ch. op. 8, 184
Isamu Noguchi Foundation, Inc., New York: 220
Kobe City Museum of Namban Art, Kobe: 3, 6, 7, 17
Kunstsammlung Nordrhein-Wesfalen, Düsseldorf: photo Walter Klein: 143
Kyoto Costume Institute, Kyoto: 147
Marianne North Gallery, Kew Gardens, Kew: 177
Metropolitan Museum of Art, New York: Bequest of Miss Louise Velton, 1937: 196, Gift of Alfred Corning Clark, 1904: 159, Gift of H. O. Havemayer, 1896: 192, Gift of Kenneth O. Smith, 1969: photo Schecter Lee: ch. op. 9, 189, Gift of Frank Lloyd Wright, 1921: 22, Lent by Charles Hosmer Morse Museum of American Art, Winter Park, Florida, in memory of Charles Hosmer Morse: 191, Rogers Fund, 1919: 122
Musée de Beaux-Arts de Dijon: ch. op. 2, 23
Musée de l'École de Nancy: 124
Musée de l'Impression sur Étoffes, Mulhouse: 93
Musée des Arts Décoratifs, Paris: photo Larent-Sully Jaulmes: 81
Musée des Tissus de Lyon: 95
Museum für Angewandte Kunst, Vienna: 150
Museum für Kunst und Gewerbe, Hamburg: 91
Museum of Art, Rhode Island School of Design: Gift of Mrs John D Rockefeller Jr., 109
Nagasaki City Museum, Nagasaki: 12
National Gallery, London: ch. op. 10, 214
National Gallery of Victoria,

Melbourne: 101
National Museum of Ethnology, Leiden: 13
Oberösterreichisches Landesmuseum, Linz: 149
RMN, Paris: photo Harry Bréjat: 59, 257, photo Christian Jean: 226, photo R-G Ojéda: 117, photo Jean Schormans: 123
Roland Grant Archive: 248, 249, 251, 252
Peter Rose and the Albert Gallichan Foundation: 72, 73, 179
The Royal Archives © H M Queen Elizabeth II: ch. op. 6
Potteries Musem and Art Gallery, Stoke-on-Trent: 110
Sterling and Francine Clark Art Institute, Williamstown: ch. op. 4, 80
Sotheby's Picture Library, London: 255
Suntory Museum, Osaka: 65
Tate Collection, London: 19, 258
Tokogawa Museum, Mito: 24
Van Gogh Museum, Amsterdam, Vincent van Gogh Foundation: 83
Victoria and Albert Museum, London: 9, ch. op. 3, 44, 49, 57, 71, 84, 97, 98, 118, 125, 126, 136, 154, 176, 206, 236, 239, 245
Werner Forman Archive, London: cover, 18
Yokohama Museum of Art, Yokohama: 174

Index

Figures in italics indicate illustrations.

Index